CHE

30119 027 848 06 0

ROBI..935. After training as a laboratory technician and developing an interest in forensic science, he turned to crime writing as a pastime. His first book, *Jack the Ripper in Fact & Fiction*, published in 1965, is still regarded as an important contribution to the subject. In a writing career spanning more than forty years, he has written or co-written eighteen books in the fields of true crime, forensic investigation and criminal history. He won an Edgar Award from the Mystery Writers of America in 1980 for *The Murderers' Who's Who* and again in 2007 for *Ripperology*. He also lectures extensively to clubs and societies on crime cases.

PAUL DONNELLEY was born in London, and raised in the tiny hamlet of Harold Hill in Essex. He has written more than twenty-five books including *Essex Murders*, *Assassins and Assassinations* and *501 Most Notorious Crimes*. He has worked for several magazines and newspapers including the *Times*, the *Sun*, the *Sunday Telegraph*, *Punch*, and, since 2008, *Master Detective* where he writes "Paul Donnelley's Murder Month", a column on criminal history.

D0307697

Recent Mammoth titles

The Mammoth Book of New Sherlock Holmes Adventures
The Mammoth Book of Historical Crime Fiction
The Mammoth Book of Best New SF 27
The Mammoth Book of Really Silly Jokes
The Mammoth Book of Best New Horror 25
The Mammoth Book of Special Forces Training
The Mammoth Book of New Tattoo Art
The Mammoth Book of Muhammad Ali
The Mammoth Book of Best British Crime 11
The Mammoth Book of Conspiracies
The Mammoth Book of Lost Symbols
The Mammoth Book of Body Horror
The Mammoth Book of Steampunk
The Mammoth Book of New CSI
The Mammoth Book of Gangs
The Mammoth Book of SF Wars
The Mammoth Book of One-Liners
The Mammoth Book of Ghost Romance
The Mammoth Book of Brain Games
The Mammoth Book of Jokes 2
The Mammoth Book of Horror 23
The Mammoth Book of Slasher Movies
The Mammoth Book of Street Art
The Mammoth Book of SF Stories by Women
The Mammoth Book of the Vietnam War

The Mammoth Book of
More
Bizarre Crimes

Robin Odell and Paul Donnelley

ROBINSON

RUNNING PRESS
PHILADELPHIA · LONDON

ROBINSON

First published in Great Britain in 2016 by Robinson

Copyright © Robin Odell and Paul Donnelley, 2016
1 3 5 7 9 8 6 4 2

The moral right of the authors has been asserted.

All rights reserved.
No part of this publication may be reproduced, stored in a retrieval system, or transmitted, in any form, or
by any means, without the prior permission in writing of the publisher, nor be otherwise circulated in any
form of binding or cover other than that in which it is published and without a similar condition including
this condition being imposed on the subsequent purchaser.

A CIP catalogue record for this book
is available from the British Library.

ISBN 978-1-47211-803-5 (paperback)
ISBN 978-1-47211-804-2 (ebook)

Robinson
An imprint of
Little, Brown Book Group
Carmelite House
50 Victoria Embankment
London EC4Y 0DZ

An Hachette UK Company
www.hachette.co.uk

www.littlebrown.co.uk

First published in the United States in 2016 by Running Press Book Publishers,
A Member of the Perseus Books Group

All rights reserved under the Pan-American and International Copyright Conventions

*This book may not be reproduced in whole or in part, in any form or by any means, electronic or mechanical,
including photocopy, recording, or by any information storage and retrieval system now known or hereafter
invented, without permission from the publishers.*

Books published by Running Press are available at special discounts for bulk
purchases in the United States by corporations, institutions and other organizations.
For more information, please contact the Special Markets Department at the
Perseus Books Group, 2300 Chestnut Street, Suite 200, Philadelphia, PA 19103,
or call (800) 810-4145, ext. 5000, or email special.markets@perseusbooks.com.

US ISBN: 978-0-7624-5983-4
US Library of Congress Control Number: 2015941157

9 8 7 6 5 4 3 2 1
Digit on the right indicates the number of this printing
Running Press Book Publishers
2300 Chestnut Street
Philadelphia, PA 19103-4371

Visit us on the web!
www.runningpress.com

Typeset in Plantin Light by Hewer Text UK Ltd, Edinburgh
Printed and bound in Great Britain by CPI Group (UK) Ltd, Croydon CR0 4YY

Papers used by Robinson are from well-managed forests and other responsible sources

MIX
Paper from
responsible sources
FSC
www.fsc.org   FSC® C104740

In loving memory of Jeremy Beadle, fellow traveller on
the criminal highway and much missed friend

LONDON BOROUGH OF SUTTON LIBRARY SERVICE	
30119 027 848 06 0	
Askews & Holts	Feb-2016
364.1523	

Contents

Introduction

More Bizarre Crimes is a title with a double thrust. On the one hand, it is a collection of weird and unimaginably horrid crimes, while on the other hand it also implies that the circumstances of crime are becoming ever more bizarre.

A perfect example of a crime that is in a realm almost beyond belief is that committed in 2013 by Nathan Robinson, twenty-seven. He owed his father £36,000, a debt which he wiped out by stabbing him to death and dismembering his body in the flat which they shared. He put the body parts into storage boxes stacked in the victim's bedroom and placed a television set on top of them. The severed head was also boxed up and stored in a filing cabinet. Along with the other remains, it was discovered a month later.

After the killing, Robinson cashed in his victim's savings to the tune of £8,000 and used some of the money to entertain his friends. He claimed that he had only limited memories of the killing and pleaded guilty to manslaughter on the grounds of diminished responsibility, a plea which the trial court rejected in favour of murder.

One of the phenomena of the twenty-first century is the ease with which individuals resort to crime in all its varied categories. There seems to be an unspoken consensus that crime is a tool to achieve particular objectives in life. It is the domain of weirdly conceived plots and unplanned outcomes – a world in which fiction becomes a kind of reality and, in its wake, fosters drama and entertainment. Somewhere in between lie the elements of detection and justice.

That crime makes news and commands big headlines was never more evident than in the reporting of the murder of Joanna Yeates in December 2010. (See *A Detached Crazy Person.*) The young woman went missing from her flat in Bristol just before Christmas and her body was found six days later on Christmas Day. During the police investigation, suspicion began to focus on Christopher Jefferies, a retired schoolteacher, who was also Joanna's landlord.

Once news reached the media that Mr Jefferies had been arrested as a murder suspect, he was subjected to a vile campaign of character assassination, which focused on his appearance and eccentricity. He was completely innocent of any crime and the press was obliged to retreat, which it did with few apologies, when Vincent Tabak, Joanna's neighbour, was found guilty of murdering her.

Mr Jefferies won damages from the newspapers and, four years later, in the spirit of redressing a wrong, a television drama was broadcast which poignantly depicted the ordeal he had suffered. Events had come full circle, with one branch of the media making up for the unfair treatment meted out by another. In a partially fictionalized programme entitled *The Lost Honour of Christopher Jefferies*, a man unfairly vilified because of his perceived eccentricity was restored to his rightful place. Justice was, thereby, eventually restored along with his honour.

Crime is usually about opportunity and gain, whether it is straightforward theft or serial killing. But it also involves exercising power and control. There are few better examples than that provided in 1993 by Colin Ash-Smith who brutally murdered sixteen-year-old Claire Tiltman. He stabbed her in a frenzied killing, which he got away with for twenty years, during which time he subjected other women to violent attacks. On returning home after these episodes, he bragged about them and rated his successes in his diary.

The 46-year-old former milkman described himself as an "animal" and admitted being obsessed with knives. He related at his trial in 2014 how he went out on late-night excursions looking for someone to attack. "I wanted to feel empowered," he said, "That I had control over someone." The murder of his teenage victim was described as "killing for the sake of killing", by a ruthless predator. Ash-Smith was given a life prison sentence.

So, what are the fundamental questions facing criminologists in the twenty-first century? In many respects they are no different to those confronted by their predecessors. In simple language, they may be summed up as Who?, What? and Why? The answers that have evolved are bedded in increasingly sophisticated science and an understanding of the human attributes which constitute criminality. Computer applications have added new dimensions to every sphere, from facial recognition to the virtual autopsy.

Attempts to understand the roots of criminality have a long history, going back to Cesare Lombroso who is regarded by some as the father of criminology. His concept of the "criminal man", aired in 1876, was based on observations of facial asymmetry, which he believed were the outward stigmata of the born criminal. In essence, his idea was that the criminal is a different physical type to the non-criminal. Although his theories were ultimately discredited, he opened up a new field of study which is that of forensic anthropology.

In the present century, the emphasis has switched from outward appearances to the inner sanctum of the human brain. These studies have developed into the new discipline of neurocriminology. Researchers have located significant reduction in the development of the pre-frontal cortex in scans made of murderers' brains. This is the part of the brain which controls what is called "executive function" and determines an individual's ability to deal with angry and violent impulses.

The idea that evidence of brain abnormality might be used as a defence by defendants in criminal trials was put to the test in the USA in 1982 when John Hinckley, who shot and wounded President Reagan, was put on trial. It was not denied that he had planned and carried out the crime but it was suggested he was acting under an irresistible impulse. A scan showed that Hinckley had areas in his brain which exhibited degeneration consistent with schizophrenia. After deliberating for four days, the jury found him not guilty on the grounds of insanity, a verdict which created an angry public debate.

Thus began a move away from the emphasis on social and environmental causes for criminal behaviour with a new emphasis placed on brain activity. This was set out by Adrian Raine in his book, *The Anatomy of Violence*, published in 2013. His researches were at the forefront of neuroscience and based on studies made over thirty years. In the USA, defence lawyers began to use brain scans indicating cerebral abnormalities as evidence of mental impairment and, hence, grounds for mitigation of sentences in criminal trials. This came to be called the "my brain made me do it" defence. Worries were voiced that a culture was developing to excuse criminals of violent actions by treating them as medical problems.

The new thinking embraced studies of epigenetics or the ways in which environmental factors exert an influence on an individual's genetic code. Researchers at Duke University in the USA developed genetic studies aimed at increasing the understanding of criminal behaviour. While agreeing that an individual's genetic make-up is subject to variation by nature and nurture, scientists have ruled out the idea of a "crime gene".

Meanwhile, "neurolaw" cases are on the increase, particularly in the USA. Thirty such cases were reported in 2005, increasing to a hundred in 2012. Brain scan evidence was used in court to demonstrate functional abnormalities resulting from causes such as head trauma and tumours. In 2010, a male defendant in Florida convicted of murdering his wife escaped the death penalty after neuroscience evidence was offered in his defence. This showed abnormality in the frontal lobe, and it was argued that this was responsible for his violent behaviour. Concerns were expressed about the ability of juries to understand the new wave of scientific evidence.

That physical manifestation of criminality may lie hidden in the recesses of the brain or be lurking in genetic changes prompted by external factors is, perhaps, an echo of Lombroso? A development of which the Italian criminologist would probably have approved is that of facial recognition technology

(FRT). This is now the most widely used form of biometrics, second only to fingerprints, used to check identities.

FRT depends on the geometric shape of the face and its chief features, the eyes, ears, nose and mouth. The development of a photometric variation of the system converts images into numerical values. Hence, where CCTV footage is available, images can be compared with databases to find matching identities. Systems are being constantly refined with the emergence of three-dimensional recognition, based on the bone structure of the head. Ears, in particular, have long been recognized for their identifying characteristics. In 2010, researchers at Southampton University developed a method of scanning and measuring ears which they believe could be used to check the identity of travellers at airports. Every ear is different, even the ears on the same head, as Arthur Conan Doyle, the creator of Sherlock Holmes, reminded us.

All of this, perhaps, brings closer the essential idea behind Lombroso's thinking. Might it be possible to distinguish a criminal type from a normal individual by studying their physiognomy? An independent researcher in the USA has made a study over two decades of the faces of convicted murderers and devised a system of classification. This is based on bone structure and the observation that one characteristic shared by all human beings is the asymmetry of their facial features. It has been noted, for example, that eye orbital structure and cheek bones appear to follow consistent asymmetrical patterns in individuals disposed to homicidal violence. There appears to be scope here for further study, perhaps using FRT, with a view to identifying and classifying criminal types.

From the living to the dead, new technology continues to explore ever wider frontiers. The claim that in future there will be no such thing as "the perfect murder" has been made about a new computer-assisted system for carrying out autopsies on dead bodies. Scientists at Zurich University have developed a three-dimensional method of examining corpses, which reveals every conceivable trace of pathological evidence.

The virtual autopsy, or virtopsy, as it has become known, combines inputs from magnetic resonance imaging (MRI), computed tomography and surface scans of bodies. Pathologists are, thereby, enabled to gain in-depth views of the darkest recesses of the body's interior without the need to carry out dissection. In this way, lesions, haemorrhages and subtle trauma, which might previously have been overlooked by conventional methods, are revealed.

The system is seen as complementing traditional autopsy methods but with the advantage that interpretation does not rely on the judgement of a pathologist working in isolation. The virtopsy allows a permanent record to be created of the examination of a dead body which can be stored and down-loaded for discussion with other experts.

While scientists continue to break new ground, criminals in many cases stick to the methods they know best. One such is the contract killing, once the prerogative of Chicago gangsters in the 1920s, and now a favoured disposal option for those with a lethal grudge and money to spend. The principle of hiring a hitman to carry out the task of elimination has not changed in nearly a century. Using a contract killer means that the instigator puts distance between himself and his victim. This was a modus operandi at which Albert Anastasia, chief executioner for Murder Inc in New York, excelled. Most of the hits he arranged, and there were hundreds, remain unsolved, including his own death at the hands of hired assassins in 1957.

The phenomenon of contract killing has been the subject of studies carried out at Birmingham City University. Researchers found that most contract hits in the UK were carried out in the open, close to the victim's home territory and at a time when the target was off guard. This requires surveillance and planning on the part of assassins, the most accomplished of whom are known in the criminal trade as "masters". Typically paid £15,000 to carry out a hit, the targets are usually victims of business or domestic disputes. The skilled operator has three objectives – take out his target, protect his paymaster and escape with his anonymity intact.

Kenneth Minor failed on the anonymity test and ended up in court on a murder charge in 2011. He claimed he had been hired to kill a man who asked for an assisted suicide. The arguments in court were that the victim wanted a mercy killing while the accomplice committed murder for money. The defendant claimed that he held the knife while the victim impaled himself upon it. A New York jury was asked to consider whether hiring an assassin in such circumstances amounted to murder or suicide. They opted for murder.

One of the phenomena of the twenty-first century crime scene is the flow of stories posted on social media by people either confessing to crimes or simply bragging about them. All types of criminals, from bank robbers to murderers, have a wish to share their exploits with others. Consider Joanna Dennehy, convicted of three killings in 2014, who took a "selfie", posing with a grin and tongue extruded as she went on the prowl for fresh victims. As Shakespeare observed in *The Merchant of Venice*, "Truth will come to light; murder cannot be hid long." Certainly, social media have proved a boon to law enforcement agencies worldwide.

To quote an American jurist's comment, "Millstones of justice turn exceedingly slow, but grind exceeding fine." The truth of this is borne out by many instances of justice being served in the long term by dogged investigators using time-honoured methods and aided by advances in forensic science. DNA has provided them with a long arm to reach out after many years to bring felons to justice.

DNA has the power both to convict the guilty and protect the innocent. The murder of a teenage girl in 1966 remained unsolved for forty-six years before the killer was finally brought to justice. Advances in DNA testing applied to bloodstains left by the murderer on the victim's clothing and kept in an evidence store, enabled a match to be made to David Burgess in 2012 (see *Triumph for DNA*). During the early stages of the murder investigation, a DNA screening programme was carried out to eliminate potential suspects from the enquiry.

Time also works advantageously for those who may have been wrongfully convicted or seemed to have suffered enough punishment. In 2014, Glenn Ford, who spent thirty years on death row in a Louisiana prison, was released, following a review showing that his original conviction was unsafe. In the same year, a Japanese man who had been on death row for forty-five years was also released after it was discovered the evidence against him had been fabricated. Less welcome news on the time front was that the idyllic Mediterranean island of Lipari experienced its first murder for fifty-six years.

That time is a great leveller was borne out by a remarkable piece of retrospective crime-solving in 2014. A hundred and five years previously, Joe Petrosino, a New York detective, had been sent to Italy on a mission to gather intelligence on Mafia operations. On 12 March 1909, he was shot dead in the street by a hitman. The crime remained unsolved for over a century until Italian authorities carried out a series of Mafia-related arrests in Palermo. In the course of this operation and subsequent questioning, a man volunteered the information that his great uncle had been the hitman who killed Petrosino all that time ago.

Sir Harold Scott, a former Metropolitan Police Commissioner, observed that crime "is a subject in which almost everyone feels some degree of interest . . ." That interest may amount to little more than natural human curiosity but it can also embrace the serious issues which confront society. Hence, understanding what makes criminals tick, their motivation, methods and exploitation of opportunities, remains as important as ever. The maxim, "opportunity makes the thief", remains a valid proposition.

Describing the scope of criminal activities in forensic detail and with a bias towards the often incredible background features is the focus of *More Bizarre Crimes*. These mostly fall into that category of "You couldn't make it up" and, for the curious reader, demonstrate the amazingly misplaced ingenuity, planning and resourcefulness which criminals employ.

Crime, of course, also provides a stimulus for those professionally involved in detection, which, in the modern world, means police forces backed by increasingly sophisticated forensic resources. These are provided by scientific research involving a wide spectrum of disciplines allied to crime prevention and crime scene investigation.

Part of the evolution of crime has been the emergence of the digital age. While this has added a degree of sophistication to criminal activities, it has also aided the forces of law and order. The compulsion that some criminals have to glorify in their exploits by recording their presence at a crime scene and storing the images can backfire. Such actions can place the perpetrator in a matrix of identification, time and place that is beyond denial. And the power of computer technology to search large databases has speeded up fingerprint and DNA recognition, as well as paving the way for technical advances in every branch of forensic science.

In his comprehensive survey, *Mysteries of Police and Crime*, published in 1898, Arthur Griffiths referred to crime as "the birthmark of humanity", a kind of fatal inheritance; he also spoke of "the hydra-headed varieties of crime". Gain, grievance, elimination and empowerment over others remain the touchstones of criminal activities. Meanwhile, motive, method and opportunity continue to exert their magnetism and are drawn together in circumstances that are frequently beyond comprehension and certainly belong to the realm of the truly bizarre.

Robin Odell and Paul Donnelley
www.pauldonnelley.com

CHAPTER 1

Justice Delayed

In some instances, it takes a long time for the wheels of justice to turn in favour of someone wrongly convicted. In the case of Glenn Ford, it took thirty years. That was the amount of time he spent on Death Row in Louisiana, USA, until his release in 2014.

He was convicted of murdering a jeweller in Shreveport in 1984 following an unsatisfactory trial in which everything was stacked against him. Ford was a black man convicted by an all-white jury, defended by an inexperienced, court-appointed attorney and facing questionable witness testimony.

In 2013, an informant provided the authorities with a statement, which exonerated Ford by showing that false testimony as to his involvement had been given at his trial. Released from his ordeal at the age of sixty-four, he appeared to harbour little bitterness; he said simply "It feels good." A spokesman for the Death Penalty Information Centre commented that the case showed "the fallibility of the death penalty and the risks we take with every death sentence".

Misguided verdicts are arrived at for a variety of reasons. False testimony is one, as shown in Glenn Ford's case, and false confession is another. Sean Hodgson made false admissions to murder in 1980 for which he forfeited twenty-seven years of his life in prison.

Once made, a false confession is easy to retract, but convincing the prosecuting authorities can be tricky. In Hodgson's case, the real murderer, suffering pangs of guilt, owned up. At the time of his release in 2009, it was reckoned that up to 20 per cent of convicted criminals make false admissions.

Another long-running miscarriage of justice involved Stephen Downing who, like Hodgson, spent twenty-seven years in prison for a crime he did not commit. As a seventeen-year-old suspect in a murder enquiry he made a confession after being subjected to remorseless questioning by the police and without legal representation.

There was considerable public disquiet over the teenager's fate and the editor of a local newspaper took up Downing's cause and helped to overturn his conviction. The part played by the media in re-examining questionable legal decisions and securing justice for wronged individuals is considerable. In this, the BBC programme Crimewatch *has been a leader, together with both local and national newspapers.*

The murder in 1978 of Lynn Siddons remained unsolved for eighteen years and was finally brought to a conclusion by the persistence of the dead girl's grandmother. A campaigning journalist, Paul Foot, and the Daily Mirror *helped her. Between them, they secured a landmark legal ruling, which resulted in the conviction of the murderer.*

Having unwittingly secured a place in The Guinness Book of Records *as Britain's worst serial killer, Bruce Lee was ultimately saved from his confessions by an investigation carried out by* The Sunday Times. *The fires and resultant deaths, which he claimed to have caused, were shown to be the result of an accident and not arson.*

Challenging expert testimony is a brave step for the ordinary person to take in contesting a criminal charge. Having been convicted of taking the life of his own child, Kevin Callan used his time in prison to study neuropathology and brain damage. Armed with his newly acquired knowledge, this self-taught expert successfully contested a miscarriage of justice. After four years swotting up medical textbooks in the prison library, Callan regained his freedom in 1995.

Placing too much reliance on circumstantial evidence, while it may lead to successful conviction in the short term, may also have long-term consequences. Such was the case with the identification in 1988 of Eddie Browning as the "M50 Killer". In law, circumstantial evidence is derived from facts not in dispute from which can be inferred a fact that is at issue.

Such was the case with Browning who was identified by comparison with a likeness drawn up from witnesses' recollections *of a man seen close to the spot where a woman was abducted and murdered. Added to this was a policeman's memory recall aided by hypnosis. The unsatisfactory nature of this evidence was exposed and justice was served.*

Forensic investigators justifiably earn praise when, against the odds, they use their knowledge and experience to pinpoint guilt. In the case of DNA, long-unsolved crime cases may be resolved following cold case review procedures. But the process sometimes works in the opposite direction when evidence, and the deductions that can be made from it, are overlooked. In the case of two murder suspects held by the police in 1927, this had irretrievably fatal consequences.

On 31 May 1928, Frederick Guy Browne and William Henry Kennedy were hanged for murdering PC George Gutteridge in a case that captured big headlines at the time. While both men were judged guilty, one of them was almost certainly innocent of the crime, as a re-examination of the evidence decades later showed.

The policeman had been gunned down in an execution-style killing on a rural road in Essex. In an act of utter callousness, he was also shot through both eyes. A stolen car was traced to Browne and Kennedy, men with criminal records for armed robbery, and they became the chief suspects. Kennedy admitted being at the crime scene but sought to absolve himself from any blame by pinning the shooting on Browne.

For his part, Browne denied being present, but his big mistake, and one for which he paid dearly, was to admit ownership of the revolver which would prove to be the murder weapon. Two identical revolvers were found in the suspect's car and, when questioned by police, Browne unhesitatingly accepted as his, the gun that had been passed to him by Kennedy. There was confusion over the two weapons, which lasted throughout the murder enquiry and subsequent trial.

Using their powers of deduction, the police had it in their grasp to resolve doubts over the two weapons but no resolution emerged. In all probability, Kennedy had carried out the shooting and shifted the blame and the murder weapon onto Browne who had not been present at the crime scene. So, while both were hanged, one was probably innocent, in which case, justice was ill served.

An ill-judged confession combined with possibly falsified evidence led to a conviction which placed Iwao Hakamada, a former professional boxer, on death row for forty-five years. On 11 September 1968, he was sentenced to hang, having been found guilty of murdering a family of four in Shizuoka Prefecture, Japan. He repudiated his confession when he faced trial and his appeal against conviction was rejected in 1980.

On 27 March 2014, a further appeal based on new DNA evidence brought Hakamada his freedom. The judges revoked the death sentence and ordered a retrial, allowing the world's longest-serving prisoner on death row, now aged seventy-eight, to walk free. One of the judges who had sat through the original trial expressed his belief in Hakamada's innocence.

The omens for the elderly former inmate were good. Records showed that five other death row prisoners had secured a retrial and all had been acquitted. Hakamada's case highlighted concerns about the way capital punishment is administered in Japan where, currently, more than a hundred people remain under sentence of death.

Justice at Last

On 18 May 1993, Andrew Adams, an aircraft engineer with a promising career, was found guilty of murdering retired school science teacher, Jack Royal, on the evening of 19 March 1990, at his modern, spacious home in Laburnum Grove, Sunniside, Newcastle. Thus began a tangled legal saga that deprived an innocent man of fifteen years of his life.

The case against Adams was that he had conspired with two others to carry out a revenge attack on Royal who was believed to have fatally injured David Thompson in a street fight on 10 January 1987. It was alleged that Adams and John Hands had been persuaded to commit this act at the instigation of the dead man's sister.

One of many twists in the story was that Mr Royal was posthumously cleared of the murder charge, having been judged to have acted in self-defence. The prosecution of another man accused of killing Royal was unsuccessful, which left Andrew Adams and John Hands to face the music. Hands was acquitted of the murder and the dead man's sister was absolved of the charge of soliciting murder.

The sequence of events left Adams as the sole defendant to face the murder charge in the Royal case. He steadfastly maintained his innocence and, in the trial that followed, was ill served by his legal team. The main prosecution witness had made a deal with the police whereby he avoided a likely prison sentence for robbery in return for testifying against Adams.

The prosecution case was largely uncontested by Adams's defence team and, in consequence, he was found guilty of murder and sentenced to life. After leave of appeal was rejected in 1997, his case was referred to the Criminal Cases Review Commission, which, in turn, referred the whole matter back to the Court of Appeal in 2007. The result was vindication for Adams and the original conviction against him was quashed on 12 January. The outcome was widely acclaimed and legal history was made by the Court's judgement, which declared that flawed legal representation had deprived Adams of a fair trial. Another unusual aspect of the proceedings was that jurors from the first trial gave evidence in the Appeal Court.

Many people had fought tirelessly to help Andrew Adams's cause, not least his solicitor, Ben Rose, who worked for years pro bono. Adams expressed his gratitude to all who had maintained faith in his innocence during the fifteen years he spent in prison. He expressed no bitterness and made the point that the murderer of Jack Royal was still at liberty.

Not the M50 Killer

There were scenes of jubilation at Shrewsbury Crown Court when 36-year-old Eddie Browning was convicted of murdering Marie Wilks in 1988. The "M50 Killer", as he was called, was sentenced to life imprisonment. Five years later, it was Browning's turn to cheer when the Court of Appeal cleared him of murder and quashed his conviction.

This turn of events resulted from irregularities in the evidence produced at the murder trial, which began on 3

October 1989. In June the previous year, 22-year-old Marie Wilks, who was seven months' pregnant, was driving home along the M50 motorway when her Morris Marina Coupé overheated. She pulled onto the hard shoulder 700 yards from emergency phone 2076B and telephoned for assistance. When the police arrived, they found the emergency call box telephone receiver dangling from its connection and no sign of Marie Wilks. Two days later, a search team found her body where it had been dumped in undergrowth three miles further along the motorway. She had been fatally stabbed.

An alert was put out for the M50 Killer and a likeness was circulated, drawn up from witnesses' descriptions of a man seen standing on the hard shoulder close to the spot where Marie was abducted. Enquiries led to Eddie Browning, a former soldier who worked at a nightclub in South Wales. He was charged with murder on 29 June 1988, and, seventeen months later on 10 November 1989, convicted of killing Marie Wilks.

Browning's first appeal against the sentence was rejected in May 1991 but he gained a hearing with his second appeal in April 1994. The outcome hinged on allegations that the police had withheld evidence from the defence at the Shrewsbury trial.

Several witnesses driving on the motorway on Saturday, 18 June 1988, claimed to have seen a silver-grey car on the hard shoulder near the spot where Marie Wilks had stopped. One of the witnesses was Peter Clarke, an off-duty West Mercia Police inspector who did not stop and later could not remember the make, model or registration of the car.

As enquiries were pursued, the inspector saw a psychiatrist who used hypnosis to help his memory recall. By this means, he came up with a car registration number and a brief description. This counselling session was recorded on video but was not disclosed at Browning's trial. When the inspector gave evidence, no mention was made of the hypnosis session.

When the Home Secretary was made aware of this development, the case was referred back to the Court of Appeal. It was shown that the police inspector had not described the car he saw as a hatchback, which was the type driven by Browning, and the registration number he recalled was totally different, with the exception of the letter "C".

Giving judgement, Lord Taylor said the original prosecution case depended entirely on circumstantial evidence. Neither Browning nor his car could be identified at the scene and there was no forensic evidence linking him to the victim. Withholding the police inspector's evidence obtained under hypnosis amounted to an irregularity, which the judge decided merited the quashing of the original murder conviction.

On 14 May 1994, Eddie Browning walked from the court a free man, saying, "Justice has been done here." He was later awarded damages, believed to be more than £600,000.

Who Killed Lynn Siddons?

On Monday, 3 April 1978, sixteen-year-old Lynn Siddons went missing from her home, a council house in Sinfin, a working-class suburb of Derby, which she shared with her grandmother, Florence. Lynn had gone shopping but when she had not returned by 10pm her grandmother called the police. After a perfunctory search, the police told Mrs Siddons that Lynn had run away and took no further action. The Siddons family mounted their own search and even persuaded Derby County to appeal to fans for information at their game against Wolverhampton Wanderers on the Saturday. The next day, Lynn's remains were found by the old Trent and Mersey canal about twenty minutes' walk away. The girl's body bore forty-three knife wounds and she had been unsuccessfully strangled before drowning in a puddle.

Mrs Siddons remembered that Lynn had said that she might visit fourteen-year-old Fitzroy "Roy" Brookes who lived nearby. Within forty-eight hours of the discovery of Lynn's body, Roy Brookes was arrested and charged with her murder. In a case in which many statements were made and then retracted, Roy said later that his stepfather Michael Brookes had put him up to accepting guilt. He said Michael was always talking about Jack the Ripper and about stabbing women and he said his stepfather had told him to get Lynn on her own down by the canal. He had followed them down there, grabbed Lynn from behind, stabbed her, then stuffed her mouth with mud and water to finish her off and threatened Roy that if he told anyone, he would kill Roy's mother, too.

After he had given evidence implicating his stepfather, Roy was discharged and acquitted in November 1978. With the police declining to make any move against Michael Brookes, official enquiries into Lynn Siddons's death ceased. But Lynn's grandmother determined another course by approaching Paul Foot, a columnist on the *Daily Mirror*.

Foot was asked to help find the truth and, to that end, the journalist, after exhaustive questioning, wrote a report for his newspaper asking the simple question, "Who Killed Lynn Siddons?" He believed that no one reading the article could believe that anyone other than Michael Brookes had murdered Lynne. The article was published across two pages on 8 April 1981, and the journalist awaited a reaction. There was none, no claim for libel and no response from the police.

Florence Siddons would not give up. With her two daughters, Cynthia and Gail (Lynn's mother), she determined to prove Michael Brookes had killed her granddaughter.

One Sunday afternoon, Dot, Brookes's wife, called on Florence Siddons and told her that her husband was at a caravan in Skegness with a sixteen-year-old girl. She had had enough of his behaviour and wanted to talk. That week Mrs Brookes spent four hours with the Siddons's lawyer. She revealed that the couple's sex life was punctuated by her husband's fantasies of stabbing women. She said that one night he had snapped and shouted, "If you must know, I did kill Lynn – and I fucking enjoyed it."

Florence and her daughters began stalking Michael Brookes, staring at him in the street, painting "murderer" across his front path. When he moved house, they tracked him down and the harassment began again. Florence wrote to politicians and newspapers telling them that Michael Brookes had killed her granddaughter.

Twice she persuaded the police to send a file to the Director of Public Prosecutions, but on both occasions the DPP failed to act. Cynthia saw Brookes and Dot in the street and drove her car at them. She was fined £100 for reckless driving.

In 1983, Brookes changed his name to Goodwood and moved to Peterborough. The Siddons women found him in no time and again began their campaign against him. In light of these developments, the police authorized a new enquiry in 1985 but the Director of Public Prosecutions quashed this. Then, in 1989, Jane Deighton, Mrs Siddons's legal advisor, suggested suing Michael Brookes for assault and battery in the civil court. This move was rejected in 1989 by Mr Justice Schiemann, but that decision was subsequently overturned on appeal and the case came before Mr Justice Rougier, the son of the romance novelist Georgette Heyer, in 1991. This proved to be a turning point. The judge ruled that the Siddons family were entitled to damages from Brookes because he had murdered Lynn. Florence was awarded £27.

Michael Brookes had made several conflicting statements. He confessed privately to his wife that he had killed Lynn and enjoyed it because she was a slut. When the police questioned him he denied murder and claimed his wife was motivated by jealousy because he had left her for another woman.

Finally, in 1996, Brookes was tried for murder and found guilty of the crime he had committed eighteen years previously. Thanks to the persistence of Florence Siddons and the campaigning zeal of Paul Foot and the *Daily Mirror*, justice was finally achieved.

The "Murder" of Helen Smith

The daughter of a former policeman, Helen Smith failed the exams needed to become a policewoman and so took to nursing instead. She found work at St George's Hospital in Tooting, south London, before moving to St James's Hospital – the Jimmy's of the television series of that name – in Leeds in 1977.

West Yorkshire did not hold enough allure for Helen so she applied and found a job in Jeddah, Saudi Arabia, and on 5 December 1978, she flew out to begin work at the new Bakhsh Hospital.

Five months later, on 19 May 1979, she went to a party held for diver Tim Hayter at the sixth-floor home of Bakhsh's senior surgeon Richard Arnot and his wife Penny Thornton, at which alcohol was illegally served. Helen Smith was one of eleven guests and she turned up at 9.45pm. At some point between then and early the next morning Helen and another guest, a tugboat captain called Johannes Otten, thirty-five, fell to their deaths. Captain Otten's corpse was impaled on railings outside the building while Helen's lay on the marble floor nearby.

The Saudi authorities said that they had fallen while drunk and possibly during sex. The pro-Arab Foreign Office agreed with the conclusion. That was the official story. When Helen's father, Ron, saw her body in the morgue, however, he was shocked to find there appeared to be no broken bones or anything to suggest that she had fallen any distance let alone from the sixth floor. There was a deep indent in the middle of her forehead, and her right side and inner thighs were badly bruised.

As he was leaving the Bakhsh Hospital the next day Mr Smith was approached by friends of his daughter who told him that she had been murdered. Penny and Richard Arnot were both arrested – she was charged with unlawful inter-course with Tim Hayter and, on 24 March 1980, was sentenced to eighty strokes of the cane. Her husband received a year in prison and thirty lashes.

In June 1980, Helen Smith's remains were flown back to England and a post-mortem examination was performed on 16 December. Home Office pathologist Dr Michael Green said, "If I was to say Helen Smith's death was an accident, I would be a liar."

A second post-mortem investigation found an injury to the left side of the scalp that would have knocked Helen uncon-scious if not killed her. It seemed that far from death resulting from falling from a great height, Helen Smith was beaten in the face several times, received a potentially fatal blow to the head and had been raped. Ron Smith campaigned for a full inquiry and won his case in 1982 when the Court of Appeal ruled inquests should be held into the deaths of Britons who died abroad in violent or unnatural circumstances once their bodies were returned to the UK. It was this legislation that allowed the inquest into the death of Diana, Princess of Wales.

An inquest into Helen's death opened in Leeds on 18 November 1982. At 6.47pm on 9 December, the jury returned a majority open verdict. Ron Smith refused to allow his daughter to be buried for thirty years and during that time her remains stayed in storage at Leeds General Infirmary. He was determined that the truth should come out before he died.

During discussions with Jeryl, his ex-wife and Helen's mother, however, he finally agreed to hold a funeral. Helen was cremated on 9 November 2009, and her ashes scattered on Ilkley Moor. Ron Smith died aged 83 in a Leeds hospital on 15 April 2011, his search for justice for his daughter incomplete.

So Close to Safety

On 21 November 1963 – the day before President John F. Kennedy was assassinated by Lee Harvey Oswald – Kathleen Heathcote, twenty-one, went to visit her fiancé at Selston, six miles from her home in Mansfield, Nottingham. Around 11pm, she was seen at a bus stop about four hundred yards from her front door in Princess Street. Somewhere between the bus stop and the front door she vanished. She was reported missing and the police began making enquiries in her area.

A number of her possessions were found on a piece of waste ground, where she had taken a short cut. A policeman reported having given a lift in his patrol car to a motorist whose own vehicle was stuck in the mud. The man was soon identified as Ronald Evans, a 22-year-old electrician working in a colliery and living in Shirebrook, four miles away. When the police searched his home, they found other items belonging to Kathleen including her house keys. Evans, who was married, confessed to being responsible for her death. He said that he had been drinking that night and saw Kathleen crossing the waste ground.

It was raining but he attacked her, knocking her unconscious, and then raped her. She came round and began moaning, whereupon he dragged her to his car intending, he said, to take her to the nearest hospital. But the car was stuck in the mud and Kathleen continued to moan so he placed her in the boot. He returned to the car the next day and found Kathleen was dead.

Then the policeman arrived and offered a lift to the nearest garage. A breakdown truck pulled the car out of the mud and Evans drove home with the body still in the boot. That evening, while his pregnant wife and mother were at the bingo, he drove to Ladybower Reservoir on High Peak, Derbyshire, where he stripped the body and threw it into the water. Evans was charged with murder on 27 November and the next day frogmen began searching for Kathleen's body.

It was found on 1 December, in the submerged village of Ashopton, which had been flooded in 1943 to build the reservoir. Evans went on trial at the Nottingham Assizes in March 1964. Found guilty, he was sent to prison for life.

He was released in 1975 and moved to Bristol where a number of sex attacks soon began. The local police knew that Evans was a murderer but not that he was a rapist so he was not a suspect. In 1978 a policewoman acting as a decoy was attacked in a dark alley. She fought back, and when help arrived the attacker nicknamed the "Beast of Bristol" was arrested. It was Ronald Evans.

In July 1979, he was tried at Bristol Crown Court and pleaded guilty to four charges of indecent assault against women. He was sentenced to nine years in prison and also ordered to serve out the life sentence imposed on him fifteen years earlier. Once again, he was let out of prison, but in May 2005, thanks to work by the cold case review team, Evans was sentenced to a further ten years for a rape in 1977 and an indecent assault in 1978.

"I'm Going to Get Away With Murder. I'm a Kennedy."

Michael Skakel's cousin was Robert F. Kennedy, Jr and, like other members of the family, Skakel lived a comfortable life. On 30 October 1975, Martha Moxley, a blonde fifteen-year-old, and some friends visited the home of Michael Skakel.

The following day, her body was found under some trees at her family home at Belle Haven, Connecticut. Her body was so bloody that Martha's long blonde hair appeared black. She had been beaten to death with a golf club and stabbed in the throat with the six-iron's shattered shaft.

Among the suspects were Michael, also fifteen, and his seventeen-year-old brother Thomas who, she wrote in her diary, had hit on her. Martha was popular with boys but her autopsy made clear, however, that she was a virgin. It was claimed the two boys were sent away to avoid the police investigation.

Michael Skakel was sent to a clinic that dealt with mental and alcohol problems. It was later alleged that during a session at the clinic he confessed that he had murdered Martha Moxley. No action was taken. Skakel continued with his life, married, fathered a son and became a professional skier.

In 1978, he was charged with drink driving near the family's New York ski lodge. Then, remarkably, in January 2000, the police charged Skakel, by now thirty-nine, with the murder of Martha Moxley. Skakel's lawyer claimed that since he was fifteen at the time of the crime he should be tried as a juvenile – a request that the court refused. At the trial, lawyers argued that there were no eyewitnesses to the crime and no forensic evidence that linked Skakel to Martha Moxley.

Some witnesses claimed that at the rehabilitation clinic Skakel had confessed to the murder on several occasions and that he once said, "I'm going to get away with murder. I'm a Kennedy." Despite the lack of forensic evidence, Skakel was convicted of murder on 7 June 2002, and sentenced to twenty years to life in prison.

The Connecticut Supreme Court dismissed appeals against the conviction and, on 13 November 2006, the United States Supreme Court declined to hear the case.

On 23 October 2013, Skakel was granted a new trial by Judge Thomas A. Bishop, who ruled that his lawyer, Michael

Sherman, had failed to adequately represent him when he was convicted in 2002.

On 21 November 2013, Skakel was released on a $1.2million bond to await the new trial.

Justice Restored

Kevin Callan left school in Manchester at the age of sixteen without qualifications and worked as a truck driver. Following a personal tragedy, he stunned the legal world with his grasp of the intricacies of neuropathology learned while serving a prison term.

Callan lived with Lesley Allman, his girlfriend, and her two children, of whom the youngest was Amanda Allman, aged four, in Hyde, Greater Manchester. Amanda suffered from cerebral palsy and was prone to falls in and around the home. On 15 April 1991, the little girl took a tumble which resulted in vomiting and loss of breathing. Callan's efforts to restore her breathing failed and Amanda died the day after her fourth birthday.

The shock of losing his stepdaughter was compounded when, following a post-mortem examination, he was questioned by the police and subsequently arrested. This stemmed from the pathologist's report that Amanda's brain injuries resulted not from a fall but from being severely shaken.

Callan was tried on the charge of killing Amanda. The key witness was the pathologist, Dr Geoffrey Garrett, who examined the child and determined that her injuries were not consistent with a fall. The prosecution angle was that Callan, out of frustration, had shaken the little girl severely enough to cause injury to her brain. He vigorously maintained his innocence and was dutifully supported by his girlfriend. In January 1992, the jury returned a guilty verdict and Callan was sentenced to life imprisonment.

Spurred on by a strong sense of injustice, he spent as much time as possible in the prison library reading medical books dealing with neuropathology. He later said, "I read the same books over and over again" and, in the process, acquired a depth of technical knowledge about the brain and its reaction to injury. Buoyed up by his research, he made contact with experts in the field to discuss what had happened to Amanda.

One of his correspondents was Philip Wrightson, the New Zealand author of one of the medical books Callan had been reading. Mr Wrightson found fault with the trial pathologist's conclusions and was supported in this by Helen Whitwell, another neuropathologist. As a result of these activities, Callan secured legal aid to mount an appeal against his conviction.

His appeal was heard in 1995, four years after he had been sentenced to life imprisonment. He was represented by Michael Mansfield QC, who argued that the doctors who had carried out the autopsy on Amanda had failed to consult either a neurosurgeon or a neuropathologist. Moreover, the examining doctors had failed to keep brain samples. Counsel for Callan said it reflected badly on the system that a miscarriage of justice was only recognized due to the persistence of the victim.

The appeal judges ruled that the new evidence substantiating the conclusion that Amanda had died as the result of a fall made the conviction of her stepfather unsafe. Kevin Callan, a self-taught medical specialist, left the court on 6 April 1995, with his reputation not only restored but enhanced. His relief was short-lived however. He died of liver failure on 5 August 2003, aged 45.

Shotgun Killer Who Liked a Bit of Bully

The 160-mile long Pembrokeshire Coastal Path takes walkers through some of the most scenic parts of Wales. Every summer, walkers make their way to the county and hike their favourite trails. Two such walkers and regular visitors to the region were Peter and Gwenda Dixon, both in their fifties, whose home was in Oxfordshire.

On 29 June 1989, the couple set up their tent on a farm near the village of Little Haven. They told fellow campers that they planned a six-mile cliff-top walk to St Brides. When they failed to return home from their holiday, there were concerns for their safety. The police made local enquiries and found the Dixons' car and tent intact. There was no indication of the whereabouts of the couple – they had just disappeared.

Extensive searches were made of the area, involving helicopter and marine rescue services. Six days later, police tracker dogs found two bodies hidden in undergrowth on a cliff-top less than a mile from the campsite at Little Haven. Peter and Gwenda Dixon had been found dead from gunshot wounds. Huge resources were devoted in attempts to solve the crimes but it would be another twenty years before justice was served.

Examination of the crime scene suggested that 52-year-old Gwenda had been subjected to a sexual attack, while 51-year-old Peter's hands had been tied behind his back. They had been killed by blasts from a shotgun. A key question was motive. Why would a middle-aged couple out walking be targeted for a virtual execution? People living in the local area were not without theories, one of which was that the Dixons had stumbled across a gang of smugglers. A later theory linked the killings to the discovery in Wales of an IRA arms cache.

A hundred police officers were involved in the hunt for clues. Efforts were made to contact dozens of families who had been in the area to see if they could recall anything significant. At the back of investigators' minds was another double murder in Pembrokeshire four years previously and the possibility that there might be a link.

A significant development was that Peter Dixon's credit card had been used to make a withdrawal at a bank in Haverfordwest. A passer-by recalled seeing a man standing by the cash machine on the morning the card was used. His description of this scruffy-looking individual, aged between thirty and forty-five, tall and sunburned, formed the basis of an artist's impression of a person the police wished to question.

The public interest in the murder was enormous, and when the case was featured on BBC *Crimewatch* there was a strong response, including further sightings of the wanted man. But the outcome was negative and, although the investigation remained open, there were no further developments, at least, not until 2006.

Seventeen years after the Dixons' bodies were found, the police carried out a cold case review, with startling results. They began to focus on John Cooper, a farm labourer who lived in Fishguard and had form as a serial burglar. He was jailed in 1998, having been convicted of thirty burglaries and served ten years in prison. Prior to this, in 1996, he had carried out a sex attack on two teenagers near his home.

A month before he murdered the Dixons, Cooper had appeared on the television game show *Bullseye*. A researcher unearthed the footage in February 2009, which showed Cooper admitting a deep knowledge of the area where he murdered the middle-aged couple.

Thanks to the footage, the investigators could match the artist's likeness of the prime suspect to actual pictures of what Cooper would have looked like at the time of the murders. The resemblance was uncanny.

As part of their cold case review, investigators re-examined clothing found in Cooper's home when he was arrested in 1998. Stains were revealed which showed a match with the DNA of Peter Dixon and the dead man's DNA was also found on a shotgun. The outcome was that Cooper was charged with the murders of Peter and Gwenda Dixon and of the earlier double murder of millionaire farmer Richard Thomas, fifty-eight, and his sister Helen, fifty-six, at their Scoveston Manor home near Milford Haven on 22 December 1985.

John Cooper appeared on trial at Swansea Crown Court in 2011. He was accused of forcing Peter Dixon to reveal his bank PIN so that he could use his card, and then killing him and his wife. He was also charged with shooting Richard and Helen Thomas in 1985 and of starting a fire to destroy evidence.

The court was told something about Cooper's character. He was a man obsessed with aggressive survival based on SAS practice. He went out at night dressed in dark clothing and carrying a shotgun. He told a psychiatrist that he took to a life of crime following the death of his wife in an accident.

Found guilty of four murders and condemned by the judge for his "evil wickedness", Cooper responded with a shout of "utter rubbish". He was given four life sentences in May 2011. The case was a triumph for Dyfed Powys Police who never gave up hope of solving the two double murders. That Cooper, the "Shotgun Killer", was captured and eventually brought to justice was also a measure of the increasingly vital role played by DNA technology in forensic investigation.

"That Negro Hire Doun Here"

At midday on 26 April 1913, a public holiday known as Confederate Memorial Day, fourteen-year-old Mary Phagan went to the National Pencil Factory in Atlanta, Georgia, where she worked, to collect her $1.20 wages before going to watch the parade. Also working that day was the manager Leo Frank, a 29-year-old married, Jewish university graduate.

At 3am the next day, Mary Phagan's body was found in the basement by the black night watchman, Newt Lee. She had been strangled and beaten but not sexually assaulted. Next to her body was a note that read in part, "That negro hire doun here".

Lee and Frank were both arrested and charged with her murder. The case against Frank was dependent on the testimony of a 29-year-old black factory janitor called James Conley. He accused Frank of sexually abusing the factory girls.

The trial, which began on 28 July 1913, was anti-Semitic and, for the first time in America, a white man was convicted on the word of a black man. According to Georgia law, Frank gave a statement in which he refuted all the allegations against him – cross-examination of the four-hour statement was not allowed. Such was the hostility surrounding the trial that the judge ruled that Frank and his lawyers not be present in court when the verdict was read in case he was found not guilty and the courtroom erupted.

The jury found him guilty and Frank was sentenced to death. Public opinion rallied to his aid and, on 20 June 1915, John M. Slaton, the governor of Georgia, commuted the sentence to life imprisonment.

On 17 August 1915, a gang calling itself the Knights of Mary Phagan broke into the jail and kidnapped Frank, taking him to Marietta, 240 miles away, where he was lynched. The mob featured several prominent citizens including Joseph Mackey Brown, the ex-governor of the state, Judge Newt Morris, a doctor, three lawyers, and the former sheriff of Cobb County.

Frank asked that he be allowed to write a note to his wife, that his wedding ring be returned to his wife, and that his lower body be covered before he was hanged since he was clad in only a nightshirt. On 11 March 1986, Leo Frank was pardoned for the crime he did not commit.

Murder Conviction Overturned

Wendy Sewell was a 32-year-old typist working for the Forestry Commission in Bakewell, Derbyshire. On 12 September 1973, she left her office at lunchtime to go for a short walk. She was seen in Bakewell cemetery by a passing schoolgirl who later said Wendy was embracing a man. A short while later, she was found dying in the graveyard by seventeen-year-old Stephen Downing, one of the gardeners, who raised the alarm.

Downing led police to the spot where the body lay. The young woman had been battered to death with a pickaxe handle, which lay nearby on the path. Downing, who was a familiar figure in Bakewell, had learning difficulties, with a reading age of eleven. Questioned by the police for seven hours without recourse to a solicitor, Downing admitted assaulting Wendy Sewell. This was now a murder case with consequences that would stretch over twenty years.

The teenager was put on trial in February 1974, having, by this time, retracted his confession. He was found guilty and sentenced to life imprisonment. Once in the system he was classed as a prisoner in denial of murder which meant that he could never be released. Downing continued to assert his innocence.

Evidence from local witnesses who had seen a man other than Downing with Wendy Sewell on the day she died was belittled by the authorities. The people of Bakewell began to feel that an injustice had been perpetrated and that an innocent youth was being punished. If he had been prepared to admit guilt, Downing would have qualified for parole, but by maintaining his innocence he ensured that he stayed in prison and the years spent behind bars mounted up.

In 1994, Don Hale, the editor of the *Matlock Mercury*, took up Downing's cause and uncovered some interesting, if not disturbing, background information. For example, it was evident that Wendy Sewell, although married, led a promiscuous life and may well have had an assignation in the churchyard on the day she was clubbed to death.

Inconsistencies in police procedure, including scant regard for the protocols of examining the crime scene, were alleged and the integrity of certain policemen was questioned. The circumstances in which Downing's confession was made also came under scrutiny. The teenager was questioned for hour after hour and denied access to a solicitor. Many people in Bakewell felt strongly enough about the case to sign a petition in 1997 calling for Stephen Downing to be released. There were whispers in a close community that the identity of the real killer was known.

After spending twenty-seven years in prison and now aged forty-five, Downing's conviction was quashed by the Court of Appeal. The chief grounds were the unreliability of the evidence surrounding his confession and also inconsistencies in the forensic procedures. So, after years of patient campaigning by his parents and aided by the investigations carried out by Don Hale, he became a free man entitled to compensation for his years of suffering. He reputedly received an interim payment of £250,000 but refused to confirm what the final figure was.

But controversy continued to dog this case. Don Hale, who had been awarded the OBE, wrote a book called *Town Without Pity* in which he named a person he believed had aided the murderer of Wendy Sewell. His intervention was criticized by the police who, in 2003, reiterated their belief that Downing remained the only suspect. Derbyshire Police Deputy Chief Constable Bob Wood said: "Despite the lengthy investigation, we have not been able to eliminate Stephen Downing from the inquiry." Others may take the view that the Appeal Court's decision established his innocence and that the murder of Wendy Sewell is an unsolved crime.

The Light of Death

As the Reverend George Hollest, the vicar of Frinley, and his wife, Caroline, lay in their Grove House, Surrey, bed at 3am on 27 September 1850, they heard an intruder in their bedroom. Curtains sheltered their four-poster bed but they were part open at the foot of the bed. Mrs Hollest later recalled, "I noticed an increase in light in the room, but could not perceive how it was occasioned."

Reverend Hollest told his wife not to worry, that it was probably their young sons playing a trick. Mrs Hollest was not reassured and put her hand through the curtains to reach for the bell to ring for a servant. As she did so, someone grabbed her wrist and, pulling back the curtain, she saw it was a man in a mask. Another man grabbed her husband and the Hollests were told to be silent on pain of death. Neither took notice and fought back.

A man with a squeaky voice forced Mrs Hollest onto the floor. As she was pushed down, she heard a gun discharge on her husband's side of the bed. Mrs Hollest struggled more and managed to reach the cord to summon help from the servants.

Three men ran out of the house and into the garden hotly pursued by Reverend Hollest who had managed to find his pistol. A fourth man, keeping watch under a tree, fled too. When Reverend Hollest returned to the house, he told his wife that he had been shot and pulled his hand away from his abdomen where blood was soaking his nightshirt. A surgeon and a policeman were summoned. At 1pm the next day the clergyman died. A reward of £150 was offered and four men were quickly arrested.

They were Levi Harwood and his brother Samuel, James Jones, and Richard Fowler who usually went by the name of Hiram Smith. The last turned Queen's Evidence. He revealed

that he, Jones and Levi Harwood went into the house while
Samuel waited under a tree. They ransacked the ground floor
before going upstairs where they attacked the Hollests. Jones
and the Harwood brothers went on trial in April 1851.

Samuel Harwood was acquitted but the other two were
sentenced to death and went to the gallows on 15 April 1851.
Just before his death, Levi Harwood confessed to shooting
George Hollest.

Death of an Intern

The disappearance of 24-year-old Chandra Levy in
Washington DC in 2001 created a mystery that remained
unsolved for nine years. The young woman, who worked as an
intern in the Federal Bureau of Prisons, was last seen in a gym
on 30 April, after which she was believed to have gone jogging
in a nearby park. She did not return to her apartment.

News reports focused on the life of interns in the capital –
bright young people drawn into the political and social
scene – and rumours abounded. There was speculation that
Chandra Levy was planning to meet someone in the park and
gossip that she was having an affair with Congressman Gary
Condit. Suspicion quickly centred on him. At first he denied
any involvement but then admitted there was a relationship.
This led to questioning by the police and considerable damage
to his reputation.

The media had a field day with endless speculation about
the missing intern, at least until the terrorist attack of 9/11
when the emphasis changed. Then, on 22 May 2002, Chandra
Levy was back in the headlines again with news that her body
had been discovered. A man out walking in Rock Creek Park,
a large area of parkland popular with walkers, joggers and
cyclists in Washington DC, came across the missing woman's
remains.

Her body had been reduced to a skeleton and there were
remnants of her jogging outfit. Identification was confirmed
by examination of the teeth and comparison with Levy's dental
records. There were suggestions that she might have been tied

up with her own clothing but there were no visible signs of violence. There was no murder weapon, no DNA and no verifiable cause of death. Homicide was suspected and one theory was that Levy had been killed elsewhere and her body dumped in a remote spot away from the regular jogging trails.

The circumstances of Levy's disappearance and discovery of her body led the police to look again at two incidents, which had occurred in Rock Creek Park in May and July 2001. Two women joggers were attacked by a man who attempted to drag them off into the woods. Both escaped, but their assailant was identified as Ingmar Guandique, who was jailed for the assaults. While serving his sentence, he admitted to a fellow inmate that he had killed Chandra Levy.

This admission completely exonerated Congressman Gary Condit and dispelled the cloud of suspicion which had hovered around him. Guandique, a man of Salvadorian origin, was put on trial for the murder of Chandra Levy in November 2010, nine years after she had died. There was virtually no evidence directly connecting him to her murder, apart from his own admission. On 22 November, a Washington DC jury found him guilty of murder, thereby bringing resolution to a crime which had attracted a great deal of public interest. On 11 February 2011, he was sentenced to sixty years in jail.

"Sinister and Deadly"

Hollywood is a town with a deserved reputation for ruthlessness. It chews and spits out people who don't match up to its ideals – some retreat with integrity intact, some never give up on their dreams and others end up in rehab or worse.

Lana Clarkson was one such casualty – tall, blonde and beautiful, she had never quite made it in Tinseltown although she appeared in a few films. By the time she turned forty she was reduced to working as a nightclub hostess.

It was at the House of Blues in West Hollywood, California, that she met the eccentric record producer Phil Spector. They left for his home in the early hours of 3 February 2003.

Spector's chauffeur waited in the car while the producer and Miss Clarkson went into the mansion.

An hour later, a shot rang out and Spector, carrying a gun, left the house by the back. He told the driver, "I think I just shot her." Miss Clarkson was sprawled on a chair, a gunshot wound to her mouth. A .36 revolver was on the floor nearby.

When the police arrived, Spector was rambling, and after he refused to co-operate, they tasered him. Spector was obsessed with weaponry and owned many guns. He told a magazine that Miss Clarkson "kissed the gun" and committed "accidental suicide". The diminutive and eccentric Spector came to trial for the murder of Miss Clarkson in 2007 and turned up for court in a series of outlandish wigs including a large afro covering his virtually bald head. His defence team pointed to his apparent lack of motive for killing the actress but the prosecution called him "sinister and deadly". They claimed he put a loaded revolver in Miss Clarkson's mouth and pulled the trigger.

On 26 September 2007, the judge declared a mistrial when the jury was unable to reach a unanimous verdict, opting ten to two for convicting. Spector was freed on $1million bail and ordered to stand retrial.

A second trial opened on 20 October 2008. The defence claimed that Miss Clarkson was depressed over her lack of career success and shot herself. Spector spent millions on lawyers but did not take the stand. Several women came forward to say that he had threatened them with guns.

On 13 April 2009, the jury found him guilty of second-degree murder and on 29 May the judge sentenced Spector to nineteen years to life, meaning he will be eighty-eight before he is eligible for parole.

The Perils of False Confession

Southern Gas Board clerk Teresa de Simone worked two nights a week as a barmaid in the Tom Tackle pub (now The Encore) in Commercial Road, Southampton, to help pay for her new Ford Escort.

On 4 December 1979, after her shift finished she went to a nearby disco with a friend, Jenni Savage. Although the disco wasn't far away, the two women decided to drive and went in Jenni's car, leaving Teresa's in the pub car park. After an hour or so in the club, they left and Jenni dropped her friend off at the car park between 12.30am and 1am. They chatted for a while before Teresa got out of the car and walked to her vehicle. Jenni reversed out and drove away.

The following morning, Anthony Pocock, the pub landlord, noted the car was still there and discovered the half-naked body of a young woman inside. Teresa de Simone had been raped and strangled. Her jewellery had also been stolen.

Two days later, the police interviewed 28-year-old former Borstal boy Sean Hodgson (also known as Robert Graham Hodgson) after he was arrested on an unrelated motoring offence. He claimed to have information about the murder and gave police a name.

No action was taken at the time, but several months later he ended up in prison having been convicted of car theft.

On 14 July 1980, he was sentenced to three years' imprisonment. While in custody, on 11 December, he asked to see a priest, Father Frank Moran, to whom he confessed that he had raped and strangled Teresa de Simone. He made the same confession to the police and included admissions about other crimes.

Hodgson was tried for the murder of Teresa de Simone at Winchester Crown Court in 1982. His barrister, Robin Grey QC, explained that his client was a compulsive liar.

The jury retired to consider their verdict at 11am on 5 February 1982, and their unanimous guilty verdict was returned at 2.15pm the same day.

The judge, Mr Justice Sheldon, told him: "It is a verdict with which I entirely agree. I have no doubt whatsoever that you were guilty of this appalling, horrible crime of killing that girl."

Thus began one of the longest-running miscarriages of justice in British legal history.

In September 1983, 21-year-old David Lace was arrested in Southampton in connection with a series of burglaries.

When questioned, he told the police he wanted to talk about a murder he had committed, saying he could not live with what he had done. The murder he was referring to was that of Teresa de Simone, but his confession was discounted because of inconsistencies in his story.

Meanwhile, Sean Hodgson was pressing his case for an appeal against sentence on the grounds that he had falsely confessed to a crime he had not committed. The ongoing saga took another turn when David Lace committed suicide on 9 December 1988; he was twenty-six and living at Brixham, Devon. He was buried at Kingston Cemetery in Portsmouth. After hiring and firing a succession of lawyers, Hodgson finally made his claim stick. In 2008, the police agreed to resubmit all their evidence relating to de Simone's murder to the Forensic Science Service for review. The result was that DNA found on the victim's body was shown not to be a match to Sean Hodgson.

In March 2009, having served twenty-seven years in prison, Hodgson was granted an appeal. The new DNA test results proved his innocence and the man who had made a false confession walked from the Royal Courts of Justice, a free man. The evidence which would have cleared him eleven years earlier was reported to have been destroyed in 1998 but, in fact, lay forgotten in a forensic store.

Several months after Hodgson's release, the remains of David Lace were exhumed – on 12 August 2009 – and subjected to DNA tests. The results proved that he had indeed murdered Teresa de Simone in 1979. The police said there was a one in a billion chance that he was not the killer.

In May 2011, Hodgson, then living in Willington, was given a community order with supervision at Durham Crown Court, after sexually assaulting a 22-year-old vulnerable woman. Sean Hodgson died of emphysema in late October 2012 at the age of sixty-one.

Sean Hodgson's case highlighted the phenomenon of false confessions and the need for greater awareness among police investigators.

Did a Double Murderer Get a Royal Pardon?

On 9 March 1950, Albert Pierrepoint hanged Timothy John Evans for the murder of Geraldine, his baby daughter. At a Merthyr Tydfil police station the previous 30 November, Evans had confessed to murdering his wife, Beryl Thorley. Evans and his family had been living in the top-floor flat at 10 Rillington Place in Notting Hill, west London. John Christie, a post office clerk and former Special Constable, and his wife, Ethel, occupied the bottom flat in the property.

The Evanses' marriage was not a happy one, even after the birth of Geraldine on 10 October 1948. When Beryl fell pregnant again, tensions became worse. The couple decided on an abortion and Christie offered to perform it.

On 8 November, Evans returned from work and Christie told him that the operation had gone wrong and Beryl had died at 3pm. The men decided to store the body in the middle flat, unoccupied because the tenant was in hospital. Christie took charge and told Evans that he would dispose of the body, arrange for the care of Geraldine and, in addition, that Evans should get out of London.

On 14 November, Evans left for Wales to stay with his aunt. On 2 December, the police discovered Beryl's body in the outside washhouse at Rillington Place. Geraldine's body was also found – both had been strangled. That night Evans again confessed to killing his wife but also this time murdering his daughter (on 10 November).

Evans went on trial for the murder of Geraldine on 11 January 1950; Beryl's murder lay on file. John Christie and his wife, Ethel, were key prosecution witnesses. The jury retired for only a short time before returning a verdict of guilty.

Three years later, Christie was revealed to be a serial killer and he, too, went to the same gallows on which Evans had died.

In 1961, Ludovic Kennedy, the author, published a book about the case claiming that Evans had been innocent and the wrong man had been executed. The campaign to clear Evans gained pace and was ultimately successful. On 18 October

1966, Evans received a royal pardon exonerating him of the murder of Geraldine but not Beryl.

Who killed Beryl and Geraldine? John Christie's modus operandi was to render his victim unconscious with carbon monoxide and then strangle them during sex. There were no signs of carbon monoxide or semen in Beryl's body. There was, however, significant bruising and evidence of rape that was a few days old.

Christie was not known to be physical whereas Evans was. If Christie had raped Beryl, why did she not go to the police or at the very least tell her husband? If Evans was the perpetrator then it is indicative of his violent nature.

On the night of the murder, the Christies had left for the cinema at 5.30pm and Evans returned to Rillington Place an hour later. If Christie was the killer, he must have left the body in the flat (Ethel was around so he could not carry it to the outhouse), so why didn't Evans go to the police then?

That night, while in bed, the Christies heard a loud bump from upstairs (Evans moving the body to the middle flat). There was no reason for Ethel to make up hearing the noise. Therefore, it is likely that Evans did murder his wife and daughter. If Christie had not killed Beryl, he had no reason to kill the baby. Thus Timothy Evans is the only killer to receive a royal pardon for a murder he committed.

Justice Deferred

Harry and Megan Tooze, a retired couple in their mid-sixties, were shot dead at their farmhouse in mid-Wales in July 1993. Their assailant, wielding a shotgun, killed Mr Tooze in the cowshed and his wife outside the farmhouse. He hid the bodies under bales of hay in the cowshed and disappeared.

The alarm was raised by the Toozes' daughter, Cheryl, when she failed to get a response to her regular call to her parents. She reported them missing and a police search at the farmhouse led to the discovery of the bodies. There had been no sightings of strangers in the area and no murder weapon was found. The only evidence that a visitor had called at the farmhouse was cups and saucers in which tea had been served. As this was the Toozes' best china, the supposition was made that the visitor was someone they knew.

Suspicion fell on 34-year-old Jonathan Jones who was engaged to Cheryl Tooze. The couple lived at Orpington in Kent. On the basis of little evidence and a great deal of speculation, Jones was arrested five months after the farmhouse tragedy and charged with double murder.

In the absence of any witness sightings or recovery of a murder weapon, the evidence was purely circumstantial. The only evidence of note was the recovery of Jones's fingerprints from one of the teacups in the farmhouse. While this indicated his presence at the farmhouse it was not necessarily related to the day of the murders. Jones was a regular visitor to his prospective parents-in-law, when the best china would have been used, and he was known to do the washing-up occasionally. The motive imputed to him was the desire to secure his fiancée's share of her parents' wealth.

Jonathan Jones was tried for double murder at Newport Crown Court in April 1995. The prosecution alleged that he had carried out "execution-style" killings and created a false alibi. Despite the weak nature of the evidence against him, Jones was found guilty on a majority verdict, over which the jury had deliberated for twelve hours. Mr Justice Rougier sentenced him to life imprisonment.

Then, four days after the trial concluded, the judge made a highly unusual move. He wrote privately to John Rees QC, who had defended Jonathan Jones, setting out his misgivings and doubts over the verdict. He had also logged these thoughts in a communication sent to the Home Secretary. In essence, Mr Justice Rougier was concerned that a miscarriage of justice had taken place.

This provided a considerable boost to Cheryl Tooze and her fight to establish Jones's innocence. The case went to the Court of Appeal in 1996 and three judges ruled that the original trial verdict was unsafe. On 25 April, Jonathan Jones regained his liberty and a savage double murder was returned to the realm of unsolved cases.

Words Do Come Easily

John Cleland worked for the East India Company in Bombay from August 1728 until 1740 when his father fell ill and he returned to London. He wrote one book that was prosecuted for obscenity and spent the rest of his life trying various genres of writing – mostly unsuccessfully. Cleland never married and was the subject of rumours that he was homosexual.

In the 1740s several businesses failed, and in February 1748, Cleland was arrested for non-payment of debts of £840 owed to two creditors, and spent more than a year in Fleet Prison. It is generally believed that he wrote his famous erotic novel, *Memoirs of a Woman of Pleasure*, published in two instalments, in November 1748 and February 1749, while incarcerated, although Cleland told James Boswell that he had written most of it in Bombay as a bet to prove that it was possible to write about a prostitute without using vulgar language.

Freed from jail in March 1749, Cleland was arrested in November of that year when he and his printer (Thomas Parker) and publishers (Ralph Griffiths and his brother Fenton) were accused of libel. Fenton Griffiths disappeared but the other three were found guilty. Cleland himself renounced the novel as "a Book I disdain to defend, and wish, from my Soul, buried and forgot".

Memoirs of a Woman of Pleasure was pulled from the shelves and remained officially unavailable until the 1970s. At the request of Ralph Griffiths, Cleland prepared a heavily expurgated version, *Memoirs of Fanny Hill*, which was published in March 1750. It, too, was prosecuted for obscenity but the case was dropped.

The Man Who Got Away With Murder and Killed Again

John Donald Merrett was born at Levin on New Zealand's North Island on 17 August 1908, and arrived in Britain in 1924 with his mother, Bertha. They moved to Scotland where

Merrett enrolled at Edinburgh University. Like many young men away from home, Merrett's interests lay more in the social rather than academic side of student life.

After blowing his money, he began forging his mother's name on cheques worth £450 13s 6d. Then on 17 March 1926, a gunshot was heard in their home, 31 Buckingham Terrace, Edinburgh, and Merrett told the servant, "My mother has shot herself." The wound was fatal but not immediately, and Mrs Merrett babbled incoherently until she died on 1 April, at the city's Royal Infirmary. The authorities put her death down to suicide.

However, when Merrett's forgeries came to light, the police took another look at the case and charged him with forgery and murder. He went on trial at Edinburgh on 1 February 1927. Expert witnesses disagreed on much of the evidence and the jury returned the peculiarly Scottish verdict of not proven after an absence of fifty-five minutes. He was, however, sentenced to a year in jail for the forgery.

When he was released after eight months, Merrett inherited £50,000 from his grandfather, changed his name to Ronald John Chesney and married, giving £8,400 to his wife, Veronica Bonnar. When he had spent all his money, he returned to fraud and began blackmailing. After serving in the Royal Navy Volunteer Reserve during the Second World War he moved to Germany where he dabbled in the black market.

In February 1954, he returned to England and went to stay with his wife and mother-in-law who were living at 22 Montpelier Road, Ealing, west London, where they were running an old people's home. On the eleventh of the month he got his wife drunk on gin before drowning her in the bath. He then strangled her mother, Mary Menzies, because she knew too much of his actions. Chesney fled to Germany where he shot himself in the mouth in a wood near Cologne on 16 February 1954.

"Prolific Killer" Redeemed

In January 1977, an entire wing of Wensley Lodge, an old people's home near Hull, was consumed by fire. In the blaze, eleven people died and eighteen suffered injuries. There had been a spate of fires in the region, all attributed to accidental causes.

The devastating fire at Wensley Lodge looked like another tragic accident. Investigators attributed the cause to plumbing work involving a blowlamp which had been carried out on the boiler situated on the floor beneath the residential wing.

There the matter rested, until 1980 when twenty-year-old Bruce Lee, the son of a prostitute, was arrested in Humberside for drunkenness. During questioning he was asked about a fire on 4 December 1979, in Selby Street, Hull, which had claimed the lives of fifteen-year-old Charles Hastie and his brothers Paul, twelve, and Peter, eight. He confessed at once and, while in custody, began confessing to starting other fires, including the one at Wensley Lodge three years earlier.

He claimed to have stolen a bicycle and ridden to Wensley Lodge carrying a can of paraffin. He climbed through a window and made his way to the first floor and bedroom number eleven which was situated above the boiler room. He said that he poured the paraffin onto the floor and set fire to it. Lee confessed, "I did it and I knew it was going to kill people in there".

Bruce Lee was put on trial at Leeds Crown Court on 20 January 1981. He pleaded not guilty to twenty-six counts of murder, but guilty to twenty-six counts of manslaughter on the grounds of diminished responsibility, and to eleven counts of arson. He was ordered to be detained in a psychiatric institution. His admissions won him a place in *The Guinness Book of Records* as Britain's most prolific killer.

The prosecution of Lee was based entirely on his confessions and without the benefit of fire assessors' views. There were doubts about the validity of Lee's admissions and the predicament he found himself in. He had an IQ of 68 and a disability affecting his right arm and leg. He had a drink problem and lived in a Salvation Army hostel.

The Sunday Times began an investigation into the circumstances of the fire at Wensley Lodge and published a case for retrying Bruce Lee in 1982. From his place of detention, Lee said he was not responsible for the fires and claimed that he felt under pressure and pleaded guilty to avoid a long trial.

Fire experts consulted by *The Sunday Times* examined the scene of the fire at Wensley Lodge and concluded that the source of the blaze was the plumber's blowlamp that had inadvertently ignited fibres beneath bedroom number eleven, which smouldered and developed into the resultant conflagration. The newspaper investigation also showed the discrepancies in Lee's confession. Not least was the fact that a man with a deformed arm and leg would have found it impossible to ride a bicycle while balancing a can of paraffin.

As a result of the doubts, Bruce Lee's case was heard at the Court of Appeal in November 1983. Independent fire assessors showed conclusively that the fire at Wensley Lodge was an accident and ruled out arson. Together with the circumstances in which it was given and the inconsistencies it contained, Lee's confession was viewed as implausible. Thus, the arson and manslaughter convictions against him were quashed.

The Obscene Comedian

Lenny Bruce was a controversial American stand-up comedian and satirist of the 1950s and 1960s. Leonard Alfred Schneider was born in Mineola, Long Island, New York, in 1926, the son of Sally Marr, a stage performer.

After spending time working on a farm, he joined the US Navy at the age of seventeen in 1942, and saw active duty in Europe until his discharge in 1946. In 1947, soon after changing his last name to Bruce, he earned $12 and a free spaghetti dinner for his first stand-up performance in Brooklyn.

In 1951, he was arrested in Miami, Florida, for impersonating a priest. He was soliciting donations for a leper colony in British Guiana after he legally chartered the Brother Mathias

Foundation (a name of his own invention) and, unknown to the police, stole several priests' clergy shirts and a clerical collar while posing as a laundry man. He was found not guilty due to the legality of the New York state-chartered foundation, the actual existence of the Guiana leper colony, and the inability of local clergy to expose him as an impostor.

Later in his semi-fictional autobiography, *How to Talk Dirty and Influence People*, he revealed that he had made approximately $8,000 in three weeks, sending $2,500 to the leper colony and keeping the rest.

On 4 October 1961, Bruce was arrested for obscenity at the Jazz Workshop in San Francisco; he had used the words "cocksucker" and "to come" (for orgasm). Although the jury acquitted him, other communities began monitoring his appearances, resulting in frequent arrests under charges of obscenity.

The increased scrutiny also led to an arrest in Philadelphia for drug possession in the same year, and again in Los Angeles, California, two years later. By the end of 1963, he had become a target of Frank Hogan, the Manhattan district attorney, who was working closely with Francis, Cardinal Spellman, the Archbishop of New York.

In April 1964, Bruce appeared twice at the Café Au Go Go in Greenwich Village, with undercover police detectives in the audience. On both occasions, he was arrested after leaving the stage, the complaints again resting on his use of various obscenities. The club owners Howard and Elly Solomon were also arrested.

A three-judge panel presided over his widely publicized six-month-long trial, with Bruce and Howard Solomon being found guilty of obscenity on 4 November 1964. The conviction was announced despite testimony and support from Jules Feiffer, Norman Mailer, William Styron and James Baldwin, as well as journalist and television personality Dorothy Kilgallen and sociologist Herbert Gans.

Bruce was sentenced on 21 December 1964, to four months in the workhouse; he was set free on bail during the appeals process and died before the appeal was decided.

Solomon's conviction was eventually overturned by New York's highest court, the New York Court of Appeals, in 1970.

Bruce was known for relating the details of his encounters with the police directly in his comedy routine; his criticism encouraged the police to put him under maximum scrutiny. These performances often included rants about his court battles over obscenity charges, tirades against fascism and complaints of his denial of his right to free speech. He was banned outright from several American cities, and in 1962 he was banned from performing in Sydney, Australia. At his first show there he got up on stage and declared "What a fucking wonderful audience" and was promptly arrested.

By 1966 he had been blacklisted by nearly every nightclub in the US, as owners feared prosecution for obscenity. His last performance was on 26 June 1966, at the Fillmore in San Francisco, on a bill with Frank Zappa and The Mothers of Invention.

On 3 August 1966, Bruce was found dead at the age of forty in the bathroom of his Hollywood Hills home at 8825 West Hollywood Boulevard, lying naked with a pair of trousers around his ankles. A syringe and burned bottle cap were found nearby, along with sundry other narcotic paraphernalia. The official cause of death was "acute morphine poisoning caused by an accidental overdose".

On 23 December 2003 – thirty-seven years after his death – Bruce was granted a pardon by New York's Republican governor George Pataki, for the obscenity conviction arising from his 1964 New York performances in the Café Au Go Go.

It was the first posthumous pardon in the state's history. Governor Pataki called his decision "a declaration of New York's commitment to upholding the First Amendment".

Escaping Devil's Island

Another criminal story that was made into a film was that of Henri Charrière, better known as Papillon (he had tattoos of butterflies on his chest). Some critics have suggested that

Charrière's story was embellished, although he insisted it was a true account. He was born at Ardeche, France, on 16 November 1906 (the same day that Enrico Caruso was having problems in the Monkey House in New York's Central Park Zoo, see page 348).

Aged sixteen, Charrière joined the French navy where he spent the two years of his military service. Demobbed, he wandered into a criminal life and, on 26 October 1931, he was sentenced to hard labour for life in the penal colony of French Guiana for the murder of pimp Roland le Petit, a crime he denied committing.

Charrière was sent to St Laurent-du-Maroni Prison, but just over two years later, on 29 November 1933, he escaped from the hospital with two fellow convicts, Joanes Clousiot and André Maturette. The trio of escapees was aided by the residents of a leper colony, a British family and others, and they made it to Colombia but poor weather stopped them leaving. Recaptured, they were sent back to French Guiana in 1934, where they were sentenced to two years' solitary confinement – nicknamed the "Devourer of Men" – as punishment. They were released from solitary on 26 June 1936, but Clousiot, broken by the ordeal, died a few days later.

Determined to escape again, Charrière's plan was foiled and he murdered the inmate who informed on him. He was sentenced to eight more years in solitary confinement but was released after nineteen months. Charrière next feigned madness, and when he "recovered" he asked to be transferred to the seemingly inescapable Devil's Island.

With much time on his hands, Charrière began to formulate his escape plan. Watching the tides, he spotted that the seventh wave was always stronger than the previous six and might be enough to push him away from Devil's Island.

In 1944, using a bag of coconuts as a raft, he threw himself into the sea alongside a prisoner called Sylvain. For four days and three nights the two men drifted on their rafts until they spotted land. Then Sylvain let go of his bag and was pulled under by quicksand, just 300 yards from shore. Charrière allowed the tide to take him to land.

Charrière travelled to Georgetown and then on to Venezuela where he was jailed near El Dorado. Finally, on 18 October 1945, he was granted his freedom. He stayed in the country and became a celebrity chef. He published his autobiography in 1969 and Steve McQueen took the lead role when it was filmed in 1973. Henri Charrière's book sold more than a million copies in France alone. He died of throat cancer in Madrid on 29 July 1973.

The Red Car Mystery

Hilda Marchbank, eighty-nine, was murdered in her home when she was suffocated with a pillow. Her death at Royton, Oldham, on 11 March 1992, raised many questions but immediate suspicion was focused on the dead woman's niece, Susan May, who the police believed had killed her aunt for gain.

Apart from rumours, the evidence against May, who held power of attorney over her aunt's affairs, was scanty. Nevertheless, she was tried for murder in 1993 and found guilty. A life sentence was handed down as her punishment for a crime that she was adamant she had not committed. She appealed against wrongful conviction in 2001 and again the following year. Despite refusals to review her case, Susan May fought on.

Released in 2005 after serving twelve years in prison, May set about clearing her name. Piece by piece, the case made against her began to unravel. Doubts were raised about the testing method used to examine crime scene fingerprints claimed to have been left by May. It was also discovered that the police failed to follow up a suspect whose name they had been given in an anonymous telephone call.

The person named was Michael Rawlinson, a known drug addict with convictions for burglary in which elderly people had been targeted. The possible link with the death of Hilda Marchbank was never pursued and Rawlinson died in 2001 following a drug-related incident.

In 2012, nearly seven years after Susan May was released from prison, *The Guardian* took up her story and set out the anomalies in the evidence which surrounded her conviction. Chief of these was the failure by investigators to pursue the link to Michael Rawlinson. On the day of the murder at Royton, witnesses reported seeing a red Ford Fiesta car outside the house. It was noted that it was left without an occupant and with the engine running for fifteen minutes. The car was later seen driving away with three men in it. Michael Rawlinson had access to a red car, which was sold soon after the crime.

A worrying aspect of a re-examination of the events of 1992 was the suggestion that the police were so fixated on accusing Susan May that they failed to pursue other lines of enquiry. Added to which was the belief that officers had tried to persuade a witness to lie, in order to achieve this outcome.

The questions raised by a review of the evidence have been passed to the Criminal Cases Review Commission (CCRC) with the expectation that Susan May's conviction will be over-turned and justice served.

The Murder That Never Was

Following an encounter with the forces of law and order, Paddy Nicholls harboured a distrust of the police. It was an attitude that, eventually, led him into serious trouble.

In April 1975, he met a friend for a drink and a chat at the Clifton Arms public house in Worthing, West Sussex. His friend, seventy-four-year-old Gladys Heath, wanted to sell her house but could not afford the advertising fees. Nicholls had agreed to buy a few household ornaments and jewellery from her for cash. They completed their transaction and Gladys prepared to leave. It was noted that she looked unwell as she made her way home. Nicholls said he would call in on her later.

After he left the pub, as promised, he called at Gladys's house. There was no response to his knock, so he peered through the letterbox. To his consternation, he saw his friend lying on the floor, apparently unconscious. He gained entry through the back door and comforted Gladys while she died in his arms. For Nicholls, this was a case of déjà vu for, several weeks earlier, he had helped another distressed woman who collapsed and died outside his house. He had called the police on that occasion, and was mortified when they treated him as a murder suspect.

Although he was later cleared of any suspicion, the experience had coloured Nicholls's attitude to the police. Consequently, when he found Gladys Heath in her death throes, he did not call an ambulance or alert the police. He walked away from the house carrying a plastic bag containing the items he had bought. He had, though, been seen by a neighbour, and in due course the police came knocking at his door.

It was at that point he made a fatal mistake by lying about his presence at the house. He said afterwards that finding two dead women in a short space of time was too much to bear. Nicholls later admitted being at the house, but by then the damage had been done. When officers found the plastic bag containing some of Gladys Heath's jewellery, they took the view that he had attacked and robbed her.

The pathologist who carried out the post-mortem examination on Gladys believed she had died of natural causes, while another expert ruled that out, saying she had been killed. Nicholls was arrested, and while he was held in custody at Lewes Prison, he was alleged to have made a confession to the murder to a fellow inmate. When he stood trial in 1975, Paddy Nicholls was found guilty and sentenced to life imprisonment.

While, to a great extent, the victim of his own misfortunes, Nicholls nevertheless felt wronged and set out to clear his name. The prisoner who claimed he had made a confession retracted his statement. But despite reviews in the press highlighting the flaws in the case against Nicholls, his request for an appeal was dismissed in 1977.

Nicholls continued to press for a review and his case was taken up by the Criminal Cases Review Commission in 1997 which recommended that it went to appeal. Fresh expert evidence was brought forward which reinforced the doubts concerning the original post-mortem findings. The weight of new evidence was that Gladys Heath had died of natural causes.

In June 1998, after spending twenty-three years in prison, Paddy Nicholls was released as a free and guiltless man. At least he could share the story of "The Murder That Never Was" with his friends in the pub.

Attempted Rape Leads to Murder – Or Does It?

On 23 April 1911, the Proudlock family – husband William, thirty-one, wife Ethel Mabel, twenty-three, and their three-year-old daughter Dorothy – went to Evensong and then back to the bungalow in the grounds of the Victoria Institution, Kuala Lumpur's leading school where William Proudlock was acting headmaster.

Back home, they both changed – he for dinner with a colleague and she to relax writing letters to family and friends. William Proudlock left and his wife sat on the veranda. As she was onto her second letter, she was to later say, a family friend, William Steward, thirty-four, a mine manager, arrived and she told him that her husband was away.

After making small talk for a while, he lunged at her, saying, "You do look bonny. I love you. Let me have you. I must have you." He tried to kiss her but she fought him off. He grabbed her and lifted her dress to grope her. Mr Steward began to force himself on her but, luckily for her, Mr Proudlock had bought his wife a Webley revolver for her birthday five days earlier.

It was on a table on the veranda and the next thing she remembered William Steward was dead – having had six bullets pumped into him. On 11 June 1911, Ethel Proudlock went on trial accused of murder at the Supreme Court in Kuala Lumpur.

At this time, jury trials had been abolished in Malaya so Proudlock was tried before Mr Justice Sercombe Smith and two members of the public known as assessors. The prosecutor decried Proudlock's claim that Mr Steward had been attempting to rape her and stated in court that the mine manager's trousers were done up and his underwear was undisturbed.

The counsel claimed that Proudlock had been sleeping with Mr Steward and shot him when he told her that the affair was at an end because he was now seeing a Chinese woman. Mr Justice Sercombe Smith and the assessors found Proudlock guilty and sentenced her to death.

The Sultan of Selangor commuted her sentence, citing her youth and motherhood. Most reports say that Proudlock returned to England and was put in an asylum where she died hopelessly insane. In fact, she moved to Manitoba, Canada, in 1913, and then three years later went to New York. She died, aged eighty-six, on 22 September 1974, at her daughter's home in Florida – sixty-three years after she escaped the gallows.

Alphabet Murders

Roxene Roggasch, Carmen Colon, Pamela Parsons and Tracy Tefoya shared a number of common features. They were all prostitutes living in the San Francisco area and they all ended up being raped and strangled. Another feature which bonded them was that their first and second names had the same initial letter. Thus they became victims of the Alphabet Murderer, with echoes of Agatha Christie's novel, *The ABC Murders*.

The San Francisco killings, beginning on 11 January 1977 and ending in 1994, followed three Alphabet Murders, which occurred in Rochester, New York, beginning on 16 November 1971 and ending on 26 November 1973. In an extraordinary example of ironic synchronicity, one of the Rochester victims was also called Carmen Colon. Investigation into the "Double Digit" murders led to speculation that the murderer might have been Kenneth Bianchi, later to achieve notoriety as the "Hillside Strangler", convicted of five serial killings in Los Angeles. Two suspects in the Rochester murder enquiry committed suicide. Nothing was proved against either of them, nor against Bianchi.

Consequently, the Alphabet Murders in both Rochester and San Francisco remained unsolved, at least until 2010. In

April of that year, a 77-year-old man named Joseph Naso, who lived in Reno, Nevada, came to the attention of the police. A suspected violation of the terms of his probation, following a conviction for theft, led to a search of his home. This turned up some revealing information about his interests and major preoccupation.

There was a collection of female clothing, which was odd, bearing in mind that he lived alone. Then, a trove of photographs featuring partly clothed or naked women including several scenes of bondage. A collection of notebooks describing acts of torture also came to light, but the most valuable find was what investigators came to call Naso's "Rape Diary". Entries dated from the 1950s were quite explicit, logging sex attacks he had made while living in New York. He used expressions such as, "I raped her in an alley" and "I raped her in the front seat of the car". Four entries seemed to tally with the Alphabet Murders committed in California in the late 1970s and 1990s. The diary was an extraordinary litany of sex crimes committed over fifty years.

When questioned by the police, Naso accused them of misunderstanding his references to "rape" which he preferred to think of as "romancing". Among his notebooks were three devoted to his intention to torture and murder a woman who lived in the apartment above his in San Francisco. She escaped his predations and told investigators she referred to her neighbour as "Crazy Joe".

In 2012, Joseph Naso was charged with the four San Francisco murders. He defended the "Rape Diary" and the references made to it by investigators as an invasion of privacy. He was tried for murder in the following year and found guilty on 20 August. The California Alphabet Murders were thereby resolved, leaving the investigation of their New York counterpart killings still to be concluded.

The story of the Alphabet Murders or Double Initial Murders was turned into a film in 2008, followed by a book in 2010. On 22 November 2013, the perpetrator of at least one of the sets of serial killings, Joseph Naso, was sentenced to death.

"Tango Priorities"

Disaster struck twice at St Leonards, East Sussex, with two unrelated murders little more than a year apart. In 1999, John Smith, occasional organist at Christ Church, was kidnapped and murdered, followed by Ronald Glazebrook, a preacher at the same church, who went missing in 2001. Local people began to wonder if their town was jinxed.

Mr Glazebrook, though eighty-one and retired, remained active in the church and was highly regarded by the congregation. He disappeared on 20 April 2001, and, after finding blood traces in his car and also in his dinghy at Newhaven, police concluded that he had been murdered.

Nothing appeared to have been stolen from his flat and the motive behind his disappearance remained elusive. Witnesses reported seeing the preacher's car carrying two occupants and also observed two people manhandling a boat at moorings in Newhaven. This led to the theory that Glazebrook had been murdered, with his body being transferred by car to Newhaven where it was taken out to sea and dumped. This proved not to be the case when a few weeks later the dismembered remains of the preacher were discovered in Hastings and Eastbourne.

Suspicion focused on two seventeen-year-old youths, one of whom, Christopher Hunnisett, had been befriended by Glazebrook who allowed him to live in his flat. The teenager was charged with murder and put on trial in 2002. His defence was that he woke up one morning to find the preacher dead in the bath. He did not report his discovery to the police but panicked and enlisted the help of a friend to dismember the body and dispose of it. Hunnisett was found guilty of murder and given a minimum sentence of five and a half years.

When he appealed against the verdict in 2003, the judge doubled the prison term on the grounds that the earlier sentence had been too lenient. Then in 2010, he achieved a retrial at which he offered a new defence. Where, previously, he had denied there was any sexual aspect to his relationship with Glazebrook, he now claimed there was. On the evening in question, he said the older man had made sexual advances to which he responded by hitting him, causing him to fall into the bath and drown. Having served nine years in prison, Hunnisett was now cleared of murder and had his conviction quashed.

What was not known was that he had used his time in prison to work up a hate campaign against sexual predators and paedophiles. He had compiled a hit list, which he called "Tango Priorities", recording the names and addresses of potential victims.

Four months after his release from prison, Hunnisett put his plan into action when he attacked a gay man with a hammer and killed him. Police found that he travelled about carrying a bag containing a knife, passport, map and hit list. At his trial in April 2011 for murdering Peter Bick, he denied the charge and pleaded guilty of manslaughter on the grounds of diminished responsibility. He told the court that he wanted to rid the world of paedophiles. His list contained nine hundred names.

The former altar boy who had suffered abuse as a child was found guilty of murder and sentenced to life imprisonment.

CHAPTER 2

Simply Horrible

The "Great Beast" was a title espoused by Aleister Crowley, the occultist and practitioner of black magic who died in 1947. Its origins lie in the Book of Revelation which describes a creature rising up from the sea, displaying seven heads adorned with countless horns. The Beast, which carried the cryptic reference, "666", was the epitome of all the world's evils.

The attribution of beast-like characteristics to perpetrators of violent crimes has a long tradition. Some titles were conferred by public consent and on other occasions it was by self-appointment. In 2000, John Sweeney styled himself as "666", a coded reference to the Great Beast. More accurately, he described himself as a "manimal", implying that he was half human and half animal.

Sweeney's modus operandi was to commit murder and dismember the bodies for disposal. Remains were placed in bags or holdalls and then thrown into a watercourse, such as a canal, to provide "food for the fish". He kept a murder bag, which contained the tools of his dismembering trade. Applying some self-appreciation, he described himself as "twisted, confused and very dysfunctional".

The advent of the popular press in the nineteenth century gave a boost to the monsterization of the worst murderers. Thus, Earle Nelson, a Bible-loving sexual predator, who committed twenty-two murders in US and Canadian cities in the 1920s, came to be called the "Gorilla Murderer". His speciality was to prey on women who offered rooms for rent, whom he raped and strangled. As his crimes progressed in number and savagery, his original appellation of the "Dark Strangler" hardly seemed to reflect public abhorrence, so an enterprising newspaper coined the term "Gorilla Murderer". L. C. Douthwaite, writing in 1928, referred to Nelson as a "human wolf with a lust for blood". Truly, then, a "manimal".

Murderers are frequently named in recognition of their preferred modus operandi, such as the fifteenth-century Vlad the Impaler and the equally notorious, although anonymous, Jack the Ripper, four centuries later. Such titles owe much to the influence of myth-makers, storytellers and headline writers. The "Brides in the Bath Murderer" and the "Acid Bath Murderer" were creations of enter-prising journalists homing in on a commonplace reference.

In another dimension, trunk crimes became quite fashionable in an age when the portmanteau was an essential accoutrement of travel, especially by rail. And, for murderers adopting the trunk as a useful device for hiding and transporting the remains of their victims, left-lug-gage offices at railway stations held a particular fascination.

When Winnie Ruth Judd embarked on a train journey from Phoenix, Arizona to Los Angeles, she took two trunks with her. On arrival at her destination, station staff became aware of an evil-smelling liquid seeping from one of them and asked Mrs Judd to open it. She did so and then made a hasty exit. Her luggage contained the remains of two women she had murdered in her apartment on 16 October 1931, two days earlier. The "Tiger Woman", as the newspapers dubbed her, no doubt due to her blood lust, gave herself up and, following outbursts of hysteria, was judged to be insane.

The trouble with trunks as a means of transporting dismem-bered murder victims was that they usually leaked, leaving tell-tale residues and offensive smells. John Robinson discovered this draw-back when he deposited a large black trunk at the left-luggage office at Charing Cross Station in May 1927. After five days, station staff became aware of an all-pervading stench and decided to open the trunk, revealing several parcels containing portions of a dismembered female body. John Robinson's disposal plan had not taken account of the powers of decomposition. The "Charing Cross Murderer", as he was inevitably called, suffered death by judicial process three months later.

Disposal of the victim's body has always been a problem for murderers and one to which they seem to give scant regard.

Modern practitioners have resorted to the use of wheelie bins and freezers with varying degrees of success. Peter Wallner killed his wife in 2006 and pursued both options. He kept her body in the freezer for three years, successfully maintaining the pretence that she had died and been cremated. It was only when he decided to move house that his plan came unstuck. As part of the process of clearing the house contents, he moved the body from the freezer and placed it in the wheelie bin on the street. When a dustman discovered the corpse, Wallner's game was up and he became the "Wheelie Bin Killer".

The annals of crime are infested with the names of murdering monsters, some commonplace, others inventive. There is probably scope in this for a learned thesis on crime tags, and where better to start than with the exploits of "Doctor Death", a Russian physician more properly known as Dr Maxim Petrov?

He practised as an emergency doctor in St Petersburg where he preyed on elderly people whom he visited in their homes to administer advice and treatment. This tended to involve anaesthetics to induce unconsciousness, frequently followed by death. Once his victims had been despatched to never-never land, Petrov simply collected up articles of value and went on his way. Over three years in the 1970s, he committed dozens of robberies, leaving a trail of seventeen dead. The Russian media lost no time in finding an appropriate name for this particular monster. Petrov was so incensed at being called "Doctor Death" that he threatened to sue the newspapers for defamation.

More prosaically, murderers are frequently named after either the crime scene location or, more specifically, the town in which they operated. Thus, Kenneth Bianchi became the "Hillside Strangler", following his series of murders in Los Angeles in the late 1970s. His habit was to expose his victims' corpses on high ground as a demonstration of his achievement.

The discovery of a man's body dumped in a Surrey chalk pit in 1946 led inevitably to press reports of the "Chalk Pit Murder" and, as it turned out, to a most unusually qualified perpetrator. Two men were charged with murder, one of whom was Thomas Ley, a former Minister of Justice in New South Wales, Australia. Ley had orchestrated the killing of a man he believed to be undermining his amorous intentions to a middle-aged widow.

When more ingenious titles escaped the headline writers, specific place names defining the murder location come into play, such as the "Monster of Düsseldorf". This was a reference to Peter Kürten, whose reign of terror in that city in 1929–30 claimed nine victims and earned him comparison with Jack the Ripper. The "Axe Man of New Orleans" and the "Boston Strangler" were so named after the method chosen to eliminate their victims.

An intriguing category of monster naming is one based on a physical characteristic or personality trait of the perpetrator. Hence, the "Cleft Chin Murderer", which focused on American GI Gustav Hulton in 1944 by virtue of his deeply dimpled chin. The "Hooded Man", otherwise known as John Williams, attempted to disguise his identity from witnesses at the crime scene location in Eastbourne in 1912. And "Bible John", the anonymous slayer of three women in Glasgow in the 1960s, was known not by name but for his Bible-spouting propensity at the dance hall where he picked up his victims.

One of the most publicized monsters in America was identified only by the name given to his victim, the Black Dahlia. When the mutilated body of a woman was found in Los Angeles in 1947, it was noted that the letters BD had been carved into the flesh of her thighs. She was identified as Elizabeth Short, an aspiring film actress known as the Black Dahlia on account of her preference for wearing black clothes. Despite much subsequent publicity and a rash of confessions, her murderer was never identified.

Criminals like to taunt the world they seek to terrorize, and one such was the "Zodiac Killer". He killed five times in California in 1969 and teased the San Francisco newspapers with a letter enigmatically signed with a Zodiacal cross and circle. The authenticity of his letter was verified by the details he gave about the murders, but he was never caught.

In a moment of self-realization, Jessica Davies confessed to killing her sexual partner in her Paris flat in 2007, following a drink and drugs session. She told paramedics called to the incident, "I just wanted to cut him a bit", adding "I am a monster". Another young woman, Joanna Dennehy, glorified in her murderous exploits in 2013 by posting images of herself on the internet, pictured with tongue extruded and holding a dagger. Killer of three men, she confided in her accomplices, "Oops! I've done it again". Thus was her transition to the ranks of monsterdom completed.

Smiling Assassin

It was perhaps ironic that Carl Williams, known to the Australian criminal underworld as the "Smiling Assassin", should suffer a violent end to his life. In April 2010, he was clubbed to death by fellow inmates in the exercise yard of Barwon Prison in Melbourne.

For more than ten years, 39-year-old Williams had ruled the roost as "Mr Big" in Melbourne's crime world, dealing in drugs and death. From small beginnings on the fringe of the drug scene, he emerged as the leader of a multi-million-dollar crime syndicate using a mixture of guile and ruthlessness. Starting as a small player in the enterprise controlled by the Moran family, he went on to become a leadership threat and, following bitter gangland feuds which claimed more than thirty lives, assumed the role of supremo.

In 2004, Williams was arrested after the murders of three members of the Moran family and Mark Malia, a major drug dealer. Answering charges at Victoria's Supreme Court, he sat, smiling, behind a bulletproof glass screen. Found guilty, he was sentenced to a jail term of thirty-five years on 7 May 2007.

The man of whom it was said he never ate at the same restaurant twice for fear of being assassinated, spent most of his time in prison in solitary confinement and revelling in a television series called *Underbelly*, which was based on Melbourne's crime world. Williams featured in the series in a less than flattering profile. He was due to give evidence in a number of court cases related to underworld activities but circumstances conspired against him.

On 19 April 2010, while in Barwon Prison's exercise yard, Williams was attacked by two fellow prisoners. They felled him using part of an exercise bike and battered him into unconsciousness. By the time help arrived he had suffered a cardiac arrest and died. The "Smiling Assassin" was no more.

Questions were asked about how a prisoner in a maximum security unit under constant CCTV surveillance could be killed in this manner. One thing was sure, though, which was that Williams died as he had lived. The Victoria state legislation banned the showing of the television series inspired by Williams's life of crime on the grounds that it might unduly influence jurors in any future legal proceedings.

Manimal

When Dutch police carried out a cold case review in 2008 using their new missing persons DNA database, they uncovered a grisly story of serial violence and murder. The headless body of a woman, found in an army surplus bag floating in the Westersingel canal in Amsterdam on 3 May 1990, was identified as Melissa Halstead, a 33-year-old freelance photographer from Ohio. The body had been sawn through the spine, folded in half and bound with rope.

Dutch police linked this case to reports in London of another "Canal Murder" on 19 February 2001, when the remains of 31-year-old Paula Fields, a crack-addicted prostitute and mother of three, were cut into ten pieces and found in six holdalls retrieved from Regent's Canal in Camden, north London. Her head, hands and feet were missing.

Paula had moved in with 54-year-old John Sweeney, a Liverpool carpenter, who was using an alias, but he accused her of stealing his tobacco and using his mobile. On the night of 13 December 2000, a neighbour was woken by a male voice screaming and shouting, "No, no, no." Detectives thought that this may have been Sweeney's reaction when Paula discovered his true identity, and he murdered her two days later.

Sweeney, already convicted for the attempted murder of a former girlfriend in December 1994, was charged as the killer of both Halstead and Fields.

When he was arrested, a search of Sweeney's house produced an armoury of weapons including sawn-off shotguns and knives together with a "murder bag" containing a saw, knife, rubber gloves and rolls of tape. His personal effects included 300 drawings depicting violent attacks on women and handwritten notes. He referred to himself as "666" (the Great Beast) and as a "manimal – twisted, confused and very dysfunctional". There was also a reference to "Poor old Melissa" whom he described as "chopped up in bits, food for the fish".

He had a relationship with Melissa when she was living in London. He attacked her on at least three occasions and, when she moved away, he stalked her to Vienna and attacked her again. Melissa confided in her sister, living in America, that, if she ever went missing, it would be because John Sweeney had killed her.

The Dutch police were anxious to trace two German men, acquaintances of Melissa, who had disappeared, while their British counterparts wanted to track down three women named by Sweeney as former girlfriends. There were fears that they may have become victims of a man described by the police as hateful and controlling and "prone to outbursts of rage and murderous violence". The jury heard that while on the run Sweeney had told his best friend that he found Melissa in bed with the two German men and had killed them all.

Found guilty at the Old Bailey of killing Melissa Halstead and Paula Fields, Sweeney was given a full-life sentence on 4 April 2011, by Mr Justice Saunders, meaning that he would stay in prison for the rest of his days. Sweeney refused to leave his cell at Belmarsh Prison to hear his sentence. "Scouse Joe", as he had been called by his building site workmates, had a great deal more that he could tell the police to help in their enquiries about missing persons.

The Stary-Eyed Killer Who Never Was

A former model and barmaid, Tracie Marguerite Andrews blamed her boyfriend's murder on a road rage attack by a "porky man with big staring eyes". According to Andrews, she and boyfriend, Lee Harvey, had been at the Marlbrook public house in Bromsgrove, Worcestershire, and were on the way back to their ground-floor maisonette in Alvechurch, Worcester, on Friday, 1 December 1996.

On the A38, a shabby F-registration Ford Sierra containing "two or three men" overtook their white G-registered Escort RS2000 turbo and there followed a chase between Burcot and Alvechurch. Andrews said that Harvey, an unemployed bus driver, stopped in Coopers Hill, a few hundred yards from their home.

The Sierra pulled up in front of them and the driver got out. A fight ensued and the driver, described as a teenager of below medium height, got back into his car. The passenger then got out and stabbed Lee Harvey thirty-five times, leaving him to die in the road. That was Tracie Andrews's story – it was also a pack of lies. Two days later, Andrews appeared at a press conference in Redditch holding hands with Lee Harvey's mother to tell her fairy story.

The following day, she took a drugs overdose of paracetamol, aspirin and tranquillizers and was taken to the Alexandra Hospital in Redditch. It was while she was recuperating that she was arrested shortly after 11am on Saturday, 7 December. At 10pm on Thursday, 19 December, she was charged with Harvey's murder. Still protesting her innocence, her trial began at Birmingham Crown Court on Monday, 30 June 1997.

The prosecution revealed that when Andrews was taken to hospital after the "attack", she hid the murder weapon she had used to stab Lee Harvey inside one of her stiletto boots, and then disposed of it in a waste bin when she washed her fiancé's blood from her face and hands. She was found guilty of murder by a unanimous verdict on Tuesday, 29 July 1997, and sentenced to life imprisonment; Mr Justice Buckley recommended that she serve a minimum of fourteen years behind bars.

In April 1999, she confessed to Lee Harvey's murder but claimed that she had acted in self-defence after he pulled a knife on her. In 2009, Andrews underwent plastic surgery to change her appearance. She was released on parole on Friday, 12 August 2011, from Ashkam Grange Prison, near York after serving fourteen years. She began using the name Tia Carter.

The Sanitation Poisoner

A man entered the Imperial Bank in north Tokyo, Japan, just before closing time at 3.30pm on 26 January 1948 – and poisoned the staff.

The man, wearing a white coat with an armband bearing the word "Sanitation", announced that he was Dr Jiro Yamaguchi from the city's health department and told the staff that there had been an outbreak of amoebic dysentery in the area and for their own health they had to drink a solution he gave them.

Unbeknown to them, rather than being good for them the solution was one of potassium chloride. As the staff collapsed in agony, the man raided the tills, taking ¥164,000. By the time medical help arrived, only four staff members were still alive.

On 21 August 1948, police arrested Sadamichi Hirasawa, a 56-year-old artist, for the murders. His neighbours had noticed that he had suddenly become comparatively wealthy after years of penury. He confessed to the murders but then changed his mind and denied having anything to do with them. He said that he had only confessed because he had been questioned for thirty-seven consecutive days and felt pressurized.

Nevertheless, he was found guilty and sentenced to death in 1950. For five years the situation stayed the same, and then in 1955 the death sentence was confirmed, but it was never carried out or commuted and Hirasawa sat on death row.

Interestingly, while no reason was ever given for the lengthy stays, there was some doubt as to his guilt. Of the four surviving bank staff, three said that he only looked a bit like the killer and the fourth added that he looked completely different.

In addition, several members of the Japanese police believed him to be innocent. In 1963 the policeman in charge of the investigation, Hideo Noruchi, retired and said that he believed that the real culprit had been a member of the 731st Regiment of the Imperial Japanese Army. The regiment had been known to use poison in experiments on Chinese prisoners, but Douglas MacArthur's occupying army had overlooked this breach of human rights and, rather than expose that, forced the Japanese police to frame an innocent man.

A plea for clemency for Hirasawa, then ninety-two and blind and bedridden in Sendai Prison, was refused, as was a demand that he be released in May 1985. Hirasawa died aged ninety-five from pneumonia on 10 May 1987, his supporters still protesting his innocence.

End of a Feckless Wife

An exasperated husband murdered his feckless wife on 28 March 1867, near Romford, Essex. Four years earlier, Sarah Ann Hopes, then twenty, had married James Bacon, a year older, at St Edward's in Romford's market place. He landed a job earning the high wage of £1 a week while she stayed at home, Aldborough Cottages, Ilford High Road.

Two children followed, Emma in July 1864 and Alice in November 1865, but soon after things changed at home. Whether Sarah was suffering from post-natal depression can now never be known, but in 1866 her behaviour altered. She lost interest in her children and her own appearance. Bacon gave his wife a generous housekeeping allowance but she frittered it away.

At the start of March 1867, Bacon came home to find that all his clothes were gone – Sarah admitted pawning them. On the morning of 23 March, a bailiff arrived demanding 25 shillings owed in rent and giving them four days' notice to leave the house. Sarah also admitted owing a local shopkeeper, Caroline Dowsett, even more money, which resulted in a violent argument. She told a friend that she thought that her husband was going to kill her.

That afternoon they travelled to the home of Sarah's cousin, Caroline Johnson and her husband William, in nearby Collier Row. Mr Johnson agreed to put a roof over their heads during their troubles and they agreed to move on 27 March.

On that morning as they were preparing to flit, a bailiff appeared demanding the rent and threatening to take the furniture in lieu. He agreed to take 5/6d. Then Mrs Dowsett presented her bill – £6 – but agreed to let Sarah have time to pay.

The move was delayed by a day, unknown to Bacon, who was working away. When he went to the new home in Collier Row and found no sign of his wife he became angry and set off to meet her, stopping at a few pubs on the way. Sometime later, Bacon met an old friend in Old Marks Fate pub and confessed that he had murdered Sarah, but he was not believed until Walter Fitch who had been driving his cart and horse along the road chanced upon the wounded Sarah and rushed to the pub for help.

Sarah died as the landlady arrived at the scene. A post-mortem revealed that she had bled to death after her throat was cut. At his trial Bacon was found guilty of murder with a recommendation to mercy. The sentence was commuted to ten years' penal servitude. Released in March 1875, he remarried and worked as a grocer. In April 1887, James Bacon, forty-five, hanged himself.

Child Killer and Nice Guy

To most people in his neighbourhood of Rochester, New York, Vietnam veteran Arthur Shawcross was a nice guy who helped the poor and the elderly. Little did they know that he was on parole after fourteen and a half years in prison for killing an eight-year-old girl he had also raped.

In May 1972, Shawcross sexually assaulted and murdered ten-year-old Jack Owen Blake before killing eight-year-old Karen Ann Hill. Although he confessed to both killings, the charges regarding Jack were dropped and Shawcross was found guilty and sentenced to twenty-five years' imprisonment for the manslaughter of Karen Ann.

When he was paroled, he was forced out of several places before relocating to Rochester. He landed a job in a factory that made pre-prepared salads. He also, unbeknown to his girl-friend, began visiting prostitutes. He was a popular punter because he paid over the odds and often gave them vegetables he had stolen from work.

On 18 March 1988, less than a year after his parole, Shawcross took his interest in prostitutes a step further and began killing them. His first victim was Dotsie Blackburn, twenty-seven. He would bludgeon or strangle the women, although on 23 October 1989, with thirty-year-old June Stotts, he slit her open from neck to pelvis and covered her body with carpet to hide it. His plan worked, as she lay undiscovered for a month.

It was pure luck that brought Shawcross's two-year reign of terror to an end. Three state troopers were in a helicopter looking for a missing prostitute when they spotted a man eating a salad sitting on a car that was parked on a bridge over Salmon Creek. As they looked more closely, the troopers saw a body in the water. It was that of his last victim Felicia Stephens – aged just twenty – who had been killed on 28 December 1989. The police followed the car to a nursing home where Shawcross's girlfriend worked.

Taken in for questioning, he was released until the next day when another body was found not far from the bridge. Shawcross was arrested and confessed to the killings and also said that he ate parts of two of his victims. In November 1990, Shawcross was found guilty of ten counts of second-degree murder and was sentenced to 250 years in prison. He died on 10 November 2008.

The First Identikit Murder

Elise May Batten was fifty-nine years old and the wife of a former president of the Royal Society of British Sculptors. She enjoyed meeting and talking to people and worked in Louis Meier's shop at 23 Cecil Court, off Charing Cross Road in central London, because it allowed her to be sociable. The shop sold antique curios such as shrunken heads, voodoo paraphernalia, exotic vases and swords.

On 2 March 1961, a young Eurasian man came into the shop with his blonde girlfriend while Mrs Batten was on her lunch break and enquired after a sword but left without buying anything. At 9.15am the next day Mrs Batten opened the shop. At noon Louis Meier discovered her corpse. Lying in an alcove at the back, she had an antique dagger in her neck and another in her heart. They were both items of stock and the price tags hung down pathetically from the handles. A third dagger was discovered in her back and pathologist Dr Keith Simpson revealed that she had also been hit over the head with a heavy object.

Mr Meier told police about the young man who had been in the shop the day before. At a nearby gunsmith's, police interviewed Paul Roberts, nineteen, the son of the owner, who recalled that a Eurasian youth had come into his shop at around 10am and tried to sell him a dress sword for £10. He asked the vendor to return at 11.15am when his father would be back.

The sword was left on the premises but the young man did not return to complete the transaction. Sergeant Ray Dagg had just completed a course on a new American crime solving procedure and used it to produce an identikit photograph of the suspect from descriptions by Louis Meier and Paul Roberts.

So accurate was it that on 8 March, PC John Cole arrested Edwin Albert Bush in nearby Old Compton Street. At his trial Bush claimed that he had lost his temper after Mrs Batten abused him racially: "I started haggling over the price. She let off about my colour and said, 'You niggers are all the same. You come in and never buy anything.' I lost my head and hit her with my fist . . . I lost my nerve and then I hit her with a stone jar." The jury did not believe Bush and he was hanged at Pentonville on 6 July 1961.

The Poking Death

When the creators of Facebook came up with a way to show your affection, admiration or even just lust for a fellow member – poking – they never envisaged it could lead to manslaughter.

Scott Humphrey, twenty-seven, was travelling with his friend Richard Rovetto in the back of a taxi after both had been out on a stag do in Mansfield, Nottinghamshire. The two men fell into an argument caused by the latter's attention to Humphrey's girlfriend on Facebook.

Nottingham Crown Court heard that Humphrey angrily demanded of Mr Rovetto, "If you're such a good friend why did you poke my missus?"

As the cab pulled up on Bestwood Park Road in Top Valley, Nottingham, the argument escalated and Humphrey punched Mr Rovetto in the face, giving him a nosebleed. He then hit him again and again, causing him to fall to the ground and bang his head on the kerb.

The blow caused head injuries and Mr Rovetto died at Queen's Medical Centre in the early hours of 27 July 2014. Humphrey fled the scene but later handed himself in to police.

Prosecutor Gareth Gimson told the court that: "The taxi driver recalls Scott Humphrey was accusing Richard Rovetto of contacting his girlfriend in the past and doing so via Facebook.

"The expression used is a 'poke'. Scott Humphrey said to Richard Rovetto, 'If you're such a good friend then why did you poke my missus?'

"Richard Rovetto said he didn't know it was his girlfriend. The exchange became more heated."

Humphrey admitted manslaughter on 18 August 2014, and was jailed for four years and four months on 3 October.

Judge Gregory Dickinson QC, sentencing, told him: "When you and him went out that evening, violence and death were the furthest things from your mind.

"You didn't intend to kill him. Part of the tragedy is that it's left to chance what happens. There will be a fight like this somewhere tonight and the person will get up and go home and the police will never hear about it."

Anger and Jealousy Causes Death of Pub Landlady

John William Leigh was a hard-drinking thug who also had a fondness for guns. Born illegitimately in 1840, he was nicknamed "Mad Leigh" and violence soon became a way of life.

As a teenager, he took delight in skipping school and shooting birds near his Brighton home. He joined the Royal Navy and took part in the Crimean War, although he quickly jumped ship and turned to piracy. He returned to Brighton in 1863.

Jane Stringer fell for his dubious charms and they married despite opposition from her friends. A brief spell running a pub in Brighton ended when he failed to make a profit, and he was refused a licence for another hostelry in Middlesex when the magistrates learned of his record. He was sentenced to three months' hard labour for criminal damage, leaving his wife destitute.

She moved in with her sister, Harriet Harton, at The Jolly Fisherman pub at 35 Market Street, Brighton. When Leigh was released from jail, he asked his wife to move to London to be with him, but, having put up with his violence and threats to kill her, she refused.

On 30 January 1866, he asked to meet her at the Bedford Tap pub and surprisingly she went. Leigh was carrying three loaded pistols that day. He believed that the reason that his wife refused to live with him was because her sister, Harriet, had turned her mind. The next day he tried to break into The Jolly Fisherman but couldn't manage it.

On 1 February, after sharing a drink with his wife, Leigh went to the pub alone. Leigh walked up to the bar, produced a pistol and shot Mrs Harton in the head before firing again as she attempted to flee, crying, "He has killed me. He has killed me." She fell down the cellar steps.

The doctor carrying out an autopsy found four bullet wounds in her corpse. Leigh appeared before Lord Chief Justice Erle at Lewes Assizes on 22 March 1866. The trial was a foregone conclusion and the judge donned the black cap. Between two thousand and three thousand people watched as Leigh was hanged on 10 April 1866.

Boy Killer

Paedophile Victor Miller killed a day after he had tried to kidnap another boy. Miller was born in 1956 but grew up a confused youth after his mother deserted the family and his father beat him.

After recovering from a mental breakdown at fifteen, he became a vicious bully. In 1976, he sexually assaulted a young man at knifepoint and was jailed for four years. Released after thirty months, he was soon sexually molesting more young men and was sent down for seven years.

Segregated on the nonces' wing, Miller met and began an affair with another paedophile, Trevor Peacher. When they were released they bought a maisonette together in Pennfields, Wolverhampton, and Miller found a job as a van driver. In early 1985, Miller grabbed a paperboy and bundled him into the back of his van, drove to a remote area and sexually assaulted the boy. Miller let him go when the boy promised he would not say anything.

On 15 January 1988, Miller went to Hereford in search of another victim and spotted eighteen-year-old Richard Holden on his bicycle. Miller stopped his van to ask for directions of the youth and then grabbed him and chloroformed him. Miller drove to a field into which he dragged the unconscious Richard and tore off his shirt. As he began to undo his flies, Richard came round and kicked out at Miller. Miller fell back and Richard took the opportunity to run and hide.

The next day Miller tried to abduct fourteen-year-old Anthony Dingley in Broome, but the boy became suspicious and ran away. Around 8am on 17 January, he kidnapped another paperboy, fourteen-year-old Stuart Gough, in Hagley. Miller drove the terrified boy forty miles to a country lane known as Cuckoo Pen in Bromsberrow, Herefordshire, where he raped him and murdered him. When he was unable to strangle him, he hit him over the head with a 7 lb rock, bludgeoning the boy so badly that he later had to be identified from fingerprints on his school desk. After he had finished his work, Miller drove eighty miles to Staffordshire where he buried

Stuart's clothing, asthma inhaler and newspaper sack as well as the murder weapon.

Miller was soon the prime suspect and his alibi collapsed when his boyfriend admitted lying to the police. Miller took them to Stuart's grave and later admitted sexually assaulting twenty-nine boys. He was jailed for life at Birmingham Crown Court on 3 November 1988. Trevor Peacher received three years for attempting to pervert the course of justice.

Teen Murdered Mother and Brother after Grounding

Brenda Wiley was born in January 1975, a pleasant young New Jersey girl who got on well with her parents and younger brother. However, as her body developed so did a wilful streak.

At the age of fifteen, she had the body of a much older woman and a slightly older boyfriend, eighteen-year-old Keith Santana. They were soon sleeping together, and when her parents found out they banned her from seeing him.

Wiley left her bedroom window open so that her young beau could climb in for late-night loving sessions. The young couple let their passions run away with them and her parents heard her bed banging and caught their daughter *in flagrante* with her older lover. This time they removed Wiley's bedroom door and absolutely forbade her from seeing him.

Wiley ignored her parents and met Keith in secret. Secrets will out and Mr and Mrs Wiley discovered their daughter's disobedience and grounded her.

On 8 November 1990, the last day of her punishment, Wiley was at home with mum Bonnie, forty-four, and brother, also Keith, fourteen. Bonnie was outside while her children were inside. Her brother began teasing Wiley and she snapped, hitting him over the head with a Pepsi bottle.

The boy was stunned but still alive – at least he was until Wiley began stabbing him with a ten-inch carving knife. He mumbled, "I won't tell, I won't tell" as she plunged the blade into him twenty times, piercing his heart, liver, neck and stomach.

Wiley began to mop up her brother's blood and locked the door to stop mum disturbing her. Bonnie heard the commotion and began banging on the door demanding to be let in. When Wiley opened the door, her mother was met by a rain of blows and stabs.

There were thirty stab wounds and Bonnie's skull was crushed. Her boyfriend arrived with some friends as Wiley drove off in her mother's car. She was arrested after her friends called the police.

Found guilty of murder, Wiley was sentenced to life on 24 January 1992 and must serve a minimum of thirty years. An appeal in 1994, others in 1997, 2005, 2006, 2011 and 2012, were all dismissed. Amazingly, her father stood by her, "Brenda is amazed . . . but I love her as much as I loved my wife and son."

Police Surgeon Guilty of Murder

In 1905, Bennett Clarke Hyde was appointed surgeon to the Kansas City Police Department (KCPD) but was sacked two years later for supposedly maltreating a patient. The same year he got a job with KCPD he married Frances Swope in a secret ceremony on 21 June. She had a very rich uncle, Colonel Thomas Hunton Swope, a childless bachelor who doted on his many nieces and nephews, some of whom lived in his mansion.

In September 1909 the colonel fell ill and Hyde arrived to take care of him. On 2 October he prescribed a pill for the eighty-year-old man. The next day, he died of "apoplexy" according to Hyde. A nurse who normally looked after Colonel Swope was suspicious, but Hyde insisted on moving into Colonel Swope's mansion.

However, several residents also became sick and one, Chrisman Swope, died. Nine further people were treated by Hyde and died of typhoid fever. To cope with the sickness there were five nurses working in the mansion and they reported Hyde to the police who authorized an autopsy on Colonel and Chrisman Swope. When both were found to have died of strychnine and cyanide poisoning, Hyde was taken into custody.

On 15 February 1910, he was charged with murder. Mrs Hyde believed in her husband and used her own money to hire the best lawyers money could buy. His trial opened at Kansas City on 16 April 1910, before Judge Ralph S. Latshaw. The evidence against Hyde appeared compelling and convincing, and he was found guilty of murder on 16 May.

The Ulster King of Arms Murdered by the IRA

Sir Arthur Vicars was appointed to the office of Ulster King of Arms on 2 February 1893, and his duties included guarding the regalia of the Order of St Patrick, otherwise known as the Irish Crown Jewels. On his staff were the Athlone Pursuivant (Francis Bennett-Goldney), the Dublin Herald (Francis Richard Shackleton, the younger brother of the explorer) and the Cork Herald (Pierce Gun Mahony).

On 10 July 1907, King Edward VII, Queen Alexandra and Princess Victoria paid a state visit to Dublin, Unfortunately, four days earlier, the jewels, which were valued at £33,000, had been stolen from the library of the Bedford Tower in Dublin Castle. When Irish police were unable to solve the case they called in Detective Chief Inspector John Kane of Scotland Yard.

A reward of £1,000 was offered for information leading to the recovery of the jewels and the capture of the thief or thieves. More than one hundred years later, no one has ever been convicted. Although Detective Chief Inspector Kane named a suspect, the Chief Commissioner of the Dublin Metropolitan Police refused to act on the information. On 23 October, Vicars was suspended as Ulster King of Arms and Bennett-Goldney and Shackleton were removed from their posts.

Tragedy befell the Office of Arms. Pierce Gun Mahony, thirty-six, was shot through the heart on 26 July 1914 in "a very peculiar shooting accident" near his home in Wicklow. The cause was given as his own shotgun discharging while climbing a fence, but was it more than an accident that blasted both barrels into his heart?

Francis Bennett-Goldney became Tory MP for Canterbury and was fifty-three and serving in the Royal Army Service Corps in France when he was involved in a motoring accident and died from his injuries on 27 July 1918, in an American hospital in Brest. He was the Assistant Military Attaché to the British Embassy in Paris.

Frank Shackleton went bankrupt, owing £84,441 12s 6d. He was convicted of fraud – for misappropriating a widow's savings – in 1913 and following his release from prison in 1921 he took the name Mellor and died in 1941, aged sixty-five.

In May 1920, 100 men attacked Vicars in his home, Kilmorna House, near Listowel, County Kerry. Eleven months later, on 14 April 1921, he was taken in his dressing gown from his bed by thirty men and murdered. His house was burned to the ground. A sign was placed around his neck: "Spy. Informers beware. IRA never forgets."

Christmas Nightmare

Eighteen-year-old Louise Smith went missing on Christmas Day 1995. The beautiful redheaded clerical worker went out to celebrate the festive season by going to Spirals nightclub at Yate, near Bristol, with friends. Louise left the club around 2am on Christmas Day to walk home after a visit to a burger bar – but she never made it.

When her parents became worried they called the police. A search for Louise was fruitless and it was to be seven weeks before her body was found in Barnhill quarry on 17 February 1996, by two thirteen-year-old boys. The corpse was hidden in scrub near a seventy-foot drop. Louise's body was partly decomposed but it could be ascertained that she was naked apart from her shoes.

An autopsy revealed that she had been sexually assaulted before death. Fortunately the temperature between Christmas and mid-February had not risen much above freezing so the DNA left by her killer was preserved in her body. More than 4,500 men were asked by police to provide a sample for analysis (at a cost of £37.50 each), and local residents were also asked if any men had stayed with them over Christmas.

The Frost family revealed that their 22-year-old son David had been home then from the University of Surrey where he was studying civil engineering. When approached by Avon and Somerset Police, Frost agreed to provide a sample, but a fortnight went by and he did not come forward. The police visited his home and were told that he had left for South Africa as part of his degree, an arrangement that he had forgotten to mention.

The police called their counterparts in South Africa and asked them to get a DNA sample from Frost. After much prevarication he acquiesced in March 1997 and the result was a perfect match. English detectives flew to South Africa to interview Frost, and when confronted with the evidence of his guilt, he broke down.

Back in England, over the course of seven interviews, he claimed that he had met Louise and she agreed to have sex with him in the quarry and he left her alive afterwards. However, the teen was a virgin and unlikely to surrender her innocence in a freezing quarry with someone she had just met. Frost was due to appear at Bristol Crown Court on 9 February 1998 but at the last minute he changed his plea to guilty, and he was jailed for life with a recommendation that he serve at least fourteen years. All the DNA swabs were reported destroyed.

In the Blink of an Eye

Anuj Bidve, an Indian postgraduate student, arrived in Britain in September 2011 to study at Lancaster University. The 23-year-old was regarded as an outstanding student with a promising career ahead of him. His life was snuffed out, as his father later described it, "in the blink of an eye", on 26 December.

He was walking through Salford with friends in the early hours of Boxing Day when two men approached. One asked what the time was. The reply given was 1.30 am. At that moment, one of the men produced a gun and shot Mr Bidve in the head at point blank range. The pair ran off, the gunman smirking as he did so.

He was identified as 21-year old Kiaran Stapleton who, two days after the shooting, turned up with friends at a tattoo parlour in Manchester to have a teardrop inked onto his face. This was to tell the world that he had taken a life.

Stapleton was on bail at the time of the murder, awaiting sentencing for a road rage assault he committed in the summer of 2010.

When he appeared before magistrates and was asked his name, he replied, "Psycho, Psycho Stapleton". At a subsequent hearing, he pleaded guilty to manslaughter and cited diminished responsibility. This was rejected and he was put on trial for murder at Manchester Crown Court in July 2012.

Stapleton worked at a local factory in Old Trafford and was recognized as a petty criminal with a fiery temperament. He had been a disruptive influence at school, frequently abusing teachers, to the point where he was permanently excluded. He had, so it was reported, become angry following the break-up with his girlfriend, Chelsea Holden, and was in an aggressive mood only hours before he encountered Mr Bidve and shot him.

He had been interviewed by psychologists while in custody and his personality gave cause for concern. One specialist said he showed depressive, anti-social and impulsive traits while experiencing difficulty controlling his aggressive impulses. Another psychologist concluded that he had "an anti-social personality disorder with psychopathic and sadistic features".

During his trial, Stapleton, in reply to a question raised by the prosecution, said, "I love prison. Lock me up for sixty-five years!" The jury took ninety minutes to return a guilty verdict. Passing sentence, the judge described his crime as a "truly wicked act". Stapleton was given a life sentence with a minimum term of thirty years.

The Man Who Liked Hurting People

Eric Edgar Cooke was born on 25 February 1931, in Victoria Park, a suburb of Perth, Western Australia, with a cleft palate that was made worse by an operation. He took against society and as a youth was jailed for burning down a church after he was rejected for the choir.

At twenty-one he joined the army but was discharged when they learned of his juvenile delinquency. Despite marrying and fathering seven children, he spent much of the time between 1955 and 1960 in prison for various offences.

He began a murder spree on 27 January 1963. He shot a couple enjoying an illicit fling but they escaped with no more than severe blood loss. George Walmsley was woken at 4am by someone ringing his front door bell. When he opened the door, Cooke shot him in the head. Cooke saw nineteen-year-old John Sturkey asleep on the balcony of the rooming house, it being a hot summer night. He shot the student where he lay. Accountant Brian Weir was shot the same night but did not die, suffering irreparable brain damage to which he succumbed three years later.

The local media demanded that something must be done to stop the night maniac and a large reward was offered for his capture. On 16 February, Cooke swooped on his next victim, raping and murdering Constance Madrill, a 24-year-old social worker.

The MO was different to the other cases so the police did not link it to the earlier killings and indeed announced that an aborigine was their prime suspect. On 10 August, after a break of almost six months, Cooke struck again, shooting eighteen-year-old Shirley McLeod as she babysat.

Now panicked into action, Perth police fingerprinted every male over the age of twelve to find the killer. As with many killers, it was a stroke of luck that led to Cooke's capture. A couple picking flowers came across a gun in Mount Pleasant and it was linked to the killings. Police believed that the killer would return for the weapon and set up a surveillance operation.

A fortnight later, Eric Cooke was arrested when he came to collect his gun. He confessed to more than 250 crimes including burglary, necrophilia and car theft as well as murder. He pleaded not guilty by reason of insanity, but the defence was rejected, and on 28 November 1963, Cooke was convicted of wilful murder after a three-day trial in the Supreme Court of Western Australia before Justice Virtue.

He was sentenced to death, and, despite having grounds to appeal, he ordered his lawyers not to apply, claiming that he had killed and deserved to pay for what he had done. On 26 October 1964 at Fremantle Prison he became the last man to be hanged in Western Australia.

"This is for You, You Damn Bitch"

In December 1825, not six months after they married, cobbler William Burt was in trouble for attacking his new wife, Harriet, with a poker at his mother-in-law Ann Young's Brighton home.

Mrs Burt, pregnant at the time, dropped the charges before the case could come to court but decided for her own safety not to live with her husband. Their son, Isaac, was born on 31 May 1826. A little under three months later, on 20 August, Ann Young sent an invitation to her daughter and grandson to visit. She had a lodger, William Harfield, who kept an eye over Mrs Burt and Isaac.

Two days later, both Mrs Young and Mr Harfield had gone to work, leaving Harriet and Isaac alone. At 3.30pm, Mr Harfield returned home to fetch a shovel and was surprised to see a crowd had gathered at the front door. Around the same time, Mrs Young was summoned from work and told to go home immediately. When she arrived she found the house locked and was told her daughter was with a neighbour, Mrs Isted. She went there and saw Harriet and Isaac covered in blood; the baby was dead.

Harriet explained that she had gone to visit her friend Ann Loveridge for a chat and to show off the baby. She had been followed and Burt forced himself into the house. Mrs Loveridge called to her friend to lock herself in while she fetched a beadle.

When she returned she saw that the baby was bloodied and screamed at her friend to run, which she did, to Mrs Isted's. Burt was taken into custody.

The coroner's jury visited Mrs Burt in her sick bed to depose her. She testified, "He took from his coat a shoemaker's knife, saying 'This is for you, you damn bitch. I have had it for a long time, now you shall have it.' He then violently plunged the knife into various parts of the body of the child, and likewise into me . . . He continued to kick and abuse me until assistance arrived."

Burt appeared before the Winter Assizes at Lewes in January 1827. His trial lasted three hours and the jury took barely a few minutes to find him guilty. Mr Justice Bayley's voice caught as he pronounced sentence and many women in court wept. Burt was hanged on 8 January 1827, before a crowd of around a thousand mostly female spectators "chiefly of the lowest class".

The Last Man Publicly Guillotined in France

Eugen Weidmann was born in Germany, and by the age of fourteen was leading a gang of teenage thieves before moving to Paris and progressing to more serious crimes including six murders. He was taken into custody on 8 December 1937, after a shoot-out at his home in St Cloud.

When asked if he had any remorse for his victims, he replied, "Remorse, what for? I didn't even know them." He confessed to police that he and his confederates had planned to kidnap wealthy people and demand high ransoms.

Two of his accomplices were acquitted but Weidmann and Roger Million were convicted and sentenced to death. Million's sentence was later commuted, but at 4.50am on 17 June 1939, Weidmann was beheaded in Rue Georges Clemenceau (in front of the Palais de Justice), Versailles.

The day before, every vantage point overlooking the guillotine site was rented out at fantastic prices. From his cell Weidmann could hear the hammering of his guillotine being erected and the laughter of the revellers in cafés waiting for the entertainment to begin. Even the morning drizzle didn't dampen the enthusiasm.

The executioner, Henri Desfourneaux, known for being very slow at the job, entered the record books as having officiated at the last public execution in France. It was also his only performance in front of a public audience. He was very nervous. Dressed in black, he set up the guillotine at 3am.

Due to delays and miscalculations the decapitation took place in daylight rather than at the break of dawn, which allowed photographers to take clear pictures. Weidmann was allowed a few puffs on a cigar and a mouthful of rum in his cell. The seesaw plank to which the victim was strapped then tipped horizontally and loaded under the blade had been badly adjusted, and it took Desfourneaux three attempts to get Weidmann's neck into the crescent-shaped head-holder (*lunette*) correctly.

Ultimately the assistant executioner (called *le photographe*) had to pull him forward by his hair and ears. As the blade finally dropped it was accompanied by the eerie whistling sound that is heard at beheadings. The photographs so shocked the public that a week later a statute was passed that all executions henceforth would be carried out in private.

Woman Raped and Killed on Boat Journey

In June 1839, Robert Collins sent his 37-year-old wife, Christina, some money so that she could join him in London from their Cheshire home. He was an actor at Covent Garden Theatre. She boarded a barge, the *Staffordshire Knot*, at Peston Brook for the journey south. Pickfords, who still move furniture around today, owned the boat.

The vessel was captained by 39-year-old James Owen and his crew consisted of 28-year-old William Ellis (aka Lambert), George Thomas and twelve-year-old William Musson, the cabin boy.

On the journey Owen took a shine to Mrs Collins, much to her discomfort. At one stop, she complained to a Pickfords' employee and asked if she could be transferred to the

London-bound stagecoach. Unfortunately, there was no space available. When the *Staffordshire Knot* reached Stone on a Sunday evening, Mrs Collins again complained to a local porter about the captain but was told to take her dissatisfaction direct to Pickfords; he was loath to intervene because Owen had a reputation for violence.

At 5am the next morning, 17 June 1839, young William was told to lead the horse while the three men negotiated the locks, a mile from Rugeley where the poisoner William Palmer carried out his nefarious trade (see page 278). When he returned to the barge, the boy noticed that Mrs Collins was not on board, and, fearing for his own safety, he fled as soon as he was able.

Not long after, the body of Christina Collins was found face down in the canal at Brindley Bank. There was some bruising on her elbows but no other marks on the corpse. The barge was discovered abandoned and a hunt for the three men began.

It was some months before any arrests were made. Ellis was the first to be taken into custody, followed by Owen. Owen told the authorities that Mrs Collins had been suicidal and that he had once saved her when she jumped overboard. Thomas and Ellis stated that they had never seen Mrs Collins in the water.

The three men went on trial in April 1840. One witness who had shared a cell with Owen while the latter was awaiting trial told the court that the captain had said that Ellis and Thomas had raped Mrs Collins before suffocating her. The three men were found guilty and sentenced to death, but for unknown reasons Ellis was reprieved. The other two were hanged on 11 April 1840.

Blaming the Immigrants

The Siege of Sidney Street began on 3 January 1911, at 100 Sidney Street in east London. The early twentieth century saw an untrammelled influx of immigrants from Russia and the Balkans and they headed to the East End of London to settle. The government encouraged the Eastern Europeans to come, much to the consternation of the indigenous population.

Crime levels began to rise among the immigrants, and a group of Latvian anarchists under the leadership of Peter Piatkow – known as Peter the Painter – attempted a wages snatch at Schnurmann's rubber factory on Chestnut Road on 23 January 1909, an incident that became known as the Tottenham Outrage.

On 16 December 1910, they killed three policemen – Sergeant Robert Bentley, forty, PC Walter Choate, thirty-two, and Sergeant Charles Tucker, forty-six – in a jewellery robbery at 119 Houndsditch, east London.

A large manhunt resulted in several of the gang being arrested, and an informant told police on New Year's Day 1911 that other members of the gang were hiding at 100 Sidney Street. By 2am on 3 January, 200 police surrounded the house and cordoned off the street. The gang had more and better materiel than the police and a contingent of Scots Guards was called from the Tower of London, the first time armed soldiers had been seen on the streets of the capital since Bloody Sunday in 1887.

When Home Secretary Winston Churchill heard that the military had been summoned, he was in the bath. He quickly dressed and hastened to Sidney Street where he was met by chants from the crowd of "Who let 'em in?" He did not take control but suggested that the house should be bombarded and then stormed by police and the Army – a suggestion that was not acted upon as smoke began billowing from the top floor.

Churchill refused to let the fire brigade in to extinguish the flames. In a few minutes the upper floors collapsed. When the police entered the building they found the charred remains of Fritz Svaars and William Sokolow. Of Peter the Painter, there was no sign. Churchill found himself heavily criticized for his role in the siege. The police later captured five more members of the gang but their prosecution was bungled and they were acquitted.

The Blonde and the Gangster

Glamorous film star Lana Turner really was discovered at Schwab's drug store and went on to appear in films and also became a mainstay of the gossip columns for her colourful life off-screen; she married seven times and had one child, a daughter called Cheryl Crane.

Lana's choice of men was not always sensible, and in the late 1950s she took up with a small-time hoodlum named Johnny Stompanato. Little of what he told Lana after they met in April 1957, during the making of *The Lady Takes a Flyer* (1958), was true. She preferred older men so Stompanato lied about his age – he was actually four years younger than her. He told her that his name was John Steele. They began an affair, by which time she had found out his real name. Still, she was enamoured of him and ignored all the warning signs.

On 18 September 1957, she flew to England to make the film *Another Time, Another Place* (1958) but it was not a happy time. She was lonely and the weather depressed her. To assuage her loneliness, she paid for Stompanato to visit her but he overstepped the mark and came to the set where he warned Lana's co-star Sean Connery to "stay away from the kid".

No one told former milkman Connery what to do and he punched Stompanato. Humiliated, the American thug could not punch the burly Scotsman so instead he attacked Lana. Quickly getting over her loneliness, she arranged for him to be deported soon afterwards.

Back in America, Stompanato often hit his girlfriend with the result that she was in fear for her life. Cheryl told her mother to leave the thug but Lana replied, "I'm deathly afraid of him."

Things came to a head on the rainy Good Friday (4 April) 1958, when Stompanato and Turner had a furious row in the bedroom of her Beverly Hills mansion at 730 North Bedford Drive. Fearing her mother's life was in danger, Cheryl picked up an eight-inch kitchen knife and when Stompanato opened the bedroom door either her hand went up and she accidentally stabbed him or he walked onto the weapon.

When the police arrived (after two hours) they arrested fourteen-year-old Cheryl. Stories have long persisted that it was, in fact, Lana herself who plunged the knife into her lover's stomach.

Two of the participants from that rainy day are now dead, and in her autobiography (written while her mother was still alive) Cheryl sticks to the story that she was the killer. Stompanato's family believed that Lana had killed him and sued her for $1million but accepted $20,000.

An inquest on 11 April 1958 found Cheryl Crane guilty of justifiable homicide. She appeared before a closed juvenile hearing on 24 April, and was made a ward of court. On 11 March 1960, she was sent to El Retiro, a reformatory for problematic girls. On 11 June 1961, Cheryl was arrested with two other girls during a "wild drinking party" and the police noted that one of the girls (Cheryl) was dressed in "mannish clothes".

In April 1970, police found three half-grown cannabis plants in the back seat of her car but charges were dropped through lack of evidence. In 1988, Cheryl published her story, the first public mention by her of the killing. She lives in Palm Springs, California, with her lesbian lover and works as an estate agent. Lana Turner died a little after 10pm on 29 June 1995 at her Californian home.

Years later, in 2008, Cheryl Crane said, "Do you think that I, as an adult, with my mother and father gone, that I would continue to perpetrate a lie if I didn't do it?"

Little Girl Murdered and Mutilated

On 10 April 1969, Camellia Jo Hand was eight years old and on her way to school at Ocoee, Florida, when she disappeared between 7am and 8.30am. Her parents went to the police to report that their daughter was missing. The family pet, a dog, had also disappeared.

When questioned, several neighbours reported seeing a blue car in the locality and in the car were a little girl and a dog. None of the witnesses could give the complete number plate but most suggested that it contained the numerals 1 and 9.

On 12 April, the corpse of the dog was discovered in woods near Ocoee, and close to the pet was the body of Camellia Jo Hand, face down, clad only in shoes and socks. She had been sexually assaulted and her remains mutilated with razor blades. The blades were found in the locale. The cause of the death was a brain haemorrhage from blows to the head with a blunt instrument.

An All-Points Bulletin was immediately issued for all blue cars that had the numerals 1 and 9 in the registration plate. On 16 April, in a car park in the centre of Ocoee, a deputy sheriff spotted a blue Pontiac that had 1 and 9 on its number plate. Cautiously, the policeman waited for the owner to return. He then approached the car and questioned the driver who identified himself as Kenneth Ray Wright, a painter, who had been born at Siloam Spring, Arkansas, on 31 May 1940. He said that he had been to a tip near where the bodies had been discovered. Further examination revealed that he had a long record for petty thievery, breaking and entering, and indecent assault, and had spent a considerable part of his life behind bars.

In a bid to escape his background, he had moved to Ocoee in 1968. When his fingerprints were found to match those on the razor blades used to mutilate Camellia Jo he was arrested and charged with her murder.

At Lee County, Florida, on 20 September 1969, Wright was convicted of first-degree murder. He has consistently proclaimed his innocence and has regularly lobbied the Florida Department of Corrections for parole, citing his model prison record and successful therapy in overcoming his sexual aberrations.

On 8 November 1996, Wright was transferred to the Kansas Department of Corrections under the Interstate Corrections Compact. He remains behind bars.

Murdered While Asleep

Laundress Sarah Malcolm murdered eighty-year-old Lydia Dunscombe as she slept on 3 February 1733. Mrs Dunscombe lived in Tanfield Court, London, with her two servants, Elizabeth Harrison, a cook in her sixties, and housemaid Ann Price who was seventeen.

Sarah Malcolm, twenty-two, was the daughter of a wealthy property owner from Durham, but his financial circumstances changed and she was obliged to go into service. Fate had not finished with her and far from living and working for reputable families, Malcolm found herself in the employ of the landlord of the Black Horse, a rough pub in Boswell Court, near Temple Bar.

It was there she fell in with bad company. Mary Tracy was in the argot of the day a "light character" and she associated with the Alexander brothers, Thomas and James, villains all. Malcolm fell in love with one of the brothers and assumed that he would not be interested in her unless she had some money behind her.

Around this time she was offered a job as a laundress, which she willingly took. One of the people whose laundry she would do was Mrs Dunscombe, and rumour had it that she was very wealthy. With her confederates, Tracy and the Alexander brothers, Malcolm decided to rob the old lady. On the night they planned to carry out the felony, a storm broke.

Around 7pm Malcolm went to visit Mrs Harrison who was ill and sat with her awhile, all the time remembering the layout of the house. She then left, but only for a short time, and returned with her partners in crime. As they climbed the stairs, they encountered Ann Price who was on her way out to fetch some milk for her mistress. She had left the door open because Mrs Harrison was too ill to get up to open it. James Alexander crept into Mrs Dunscombe's room and hid under her bed while the others remained hidden in the darkness of the staircase.

At midnight, another tenant, a Mr Knight, returned and went to his quarters. Two hours later, another gentleman returned and a few minutes later James Alexander slid out from under the bed and opened the door to let the others into the room. The next morning Mrs Dunscombe and Mrs Harrison were found strangled, while Ann Price's throat was slit open from ear to ear.

Malcolm was arrested when a bloodstained tankard and linen were discovered at another of her employer's rooms, a place only she had access to. Despite admitting that she had intended to rob Mrs Dunscombe but had no part in her murder, Sarah Malcolm went to the gallows on 7 March 1733.

The Modern-Day Leopold and Loeb . . .

On 14 January 1994, Egyptian father-of-two Mohamed El-Sayed halted his car at a give way sign in Bayswater, west London. As he waited for the road to clear, the passenger door opened and a youth got into the car, pulling a knife on Mr El-Sayed as he did so.

The youth ordered him to drive for a short distance and then told him to stop. As soon as he braked, Mr El-Sayed was stabbed by the youth who left him to die.

The police had little to go on until a lucky break led them to Jamie Petrolini, a student at Modes Study Centre in Oxford, who had confessed to murder. He was taken to Paddington Green where he confessed and mentioned his friend Richard Elsey in connection with the murder.

Petrolini and Elsey came from a similar background – both had been educated at public school (Petrolini went to Gordonstoun) and had met at Modes Study Centre. Their teachers regarded the pair as immature and having a malign friendship; Petrolini especially was thought to be impressionable and liable to want to prove himself.

Elsey told his friend about the exploits of soldiers in Iraq and imagined himself to have been in the Parachute Regiment and SAS. In an Oxford pub one night, they became blood brothers. Their childish boasts became more serious as they began testing each other's mettle. They decided to go to London and kill a pimp or drug dealer at King's Cross.

When that plan failed, Petrolini said he and Elsey waited for a single, male motorist. This was how 44-year-old Mr El-Sayed became their unfortunate random victim – Elsey held him while Petrolini slashed his neck and stabbed him in the chest fourteen times.

The pair went on trial at the Old Bailey in October 1994 and each blamed the other for the murder. Petrolini claimed diminished responsibility and manslaughter while Elsey said that he was shocked when Petrolini stabbed Mr El-Sayed.

At the trial it was revealed that Petrolini, whose nineteenth birthday had been on the same day as the murder, had taken to roaming the streets of Oxford with camouflage make-up on his face while Elsey had his hair cut short and told friends that he was going on a special mission with the Paras. The jury took five hours to deliberate at the end of a seventeen-day trial before finding them guilty on 8 November. Mr Justice Denison passed life sentences for murder on both of them.

On 14 June 2012, Petrolini's conviction for murder was quashed, and one for manslaughter on grounds of diminished responsibility was put in its place as he was supposedly suffering from schizophrenia at the time of the killing. A hospital order without limit of time was substituted for the life term. Elsey has already been released.

A Daily Punishment

Lam Luong, thirty-eight, a jobless shrimper, had been in a relationship with Kieu Phan, twenty-three, and had fathered three of her children – Hannah Luong, two; Lindsey Luong, one; and Danny Luong, four months – while Ryan Phan, three, was from a previous relationship.

On 7 January 2008, Luong, a Vietnamese refugee, argued with his wife and drove to the Dauphin Island Bridge on mainland Mobile County, Alabama, which links the Alabama State Route 193 to Dauphin Island in the Gulf of Mexico. In the back of the car were the four terrified children. Taking them one by one, he tossed them over the side of the bridge into the water far below.

When he was arrested, Luong claimed that two Asian women had kidnapped the children. The bodies of three of his victims were found within days of their deaths, while the body of Hannah was found a fortnight later 144 miles from the bridge. Post-mortem examinations found the children were all alive when they were thrown off the bridge.

Luong, who lived in Irvington, Alabama, finally confessed to the four murders but later retracted his confession. At his trial Luong did not testify in his own defence but apologized to Miss Phan.

In court, she said that he had another girlfriend and had not bothered to find another job after the family returned from Georgia where they had gone in the aftermath of Hurricane Katrina. Luong's lawyers told the court that he was addicted to drugs and depressed and asked Judge Charles Graddick to sentence him to life without the possibility of parole. However, His Honour said that the aggravating circumstances were too great. He said the children must have felt "sheer terror" during their fall from the bridge and were still alive when they hit the water.

In March 2009, the jury returned a guilty verdict after just forty minutes spent deliberating and also recommended the death sentence. On 30 April, Luong was sentenced to death by lethal injection. Judge Graddick also imposed an additional punishment – he ordered prison guards to show Luong a picture of the four dead children every day until the death sentence was carried out as a reminder of what he had done.

In February 2013, the Alabama Court of Criminal Appeals threw out the conviction and death sentence saying that the publicity had made it impossible to hold a fair trial in Mobile. A new trial was ordered for Luong.

The court said that the trial judge should have allowed Luong's legal team to question individual jurors about their knowledge of the case. The appeals judges said that, of 156 potential jurors, 139 said they had heard about the case – and thirty-eight of those said they had heard that Luong confessed or tried to plead guilty.

In March 2014, the Alabama Supreme Court ruled five to three that the appeal court decision was wrong and the quashing of the verdict was overturned.

Doctor Death

Maxim Petrov, an emergency doctor working in Vasilievski, St Petersburg, earned himself the name "Doctor Death", on account of his off-duty practices. He began his criminal career in 1997 when he embarked on a string of robberies. He targeted vulnerable, elderly people, making unscheduled visits to their homes.

He introduced himself as a doctor from a local surgery calling to check out the patient's blood pressure. His modus operandi was to inject a drug, causing anaesthesia, and while his victim was senseless, he would steal whatever was accessible, money and jewellery, and then disappear. Over a three-year period, he committed forty-seven robberies.

Things started to go wrong when some of his anaesthetized victims regained consciousness and found him in the act of theft. On 2 February 1999, while committing his seventeenth robbery, he was interrupted when the victim's daughter called at the house and took him by surprise. His response was to stab her with a screwdriver and then strangle her mother.

These were his first murders, and from then on his plans started to unravel. He selected potential victims from a list he had obtained of elderly patients being treated for lung complaints. His skill at administering anaesthesia was questionable and, as more of his victims came round before he had completed his pilfering, he simply murdered them. It was believed that he killed seventeen times.

Petrov's activities become more erratic and he began to resort to fire-raising. One of his victims who survived later described how he called at her flat one afternoon to check her blood pressure. He said the reading was high and he would administer an injection. He had difficulty finding a vein which the lady thought was curious, to say the least. Having successfully injected an anaesthetic drug, he stole some of her jewellery and made off after setting the place on fire. Fortunately, the victim came out of anaesthesia in time to raise the alarm.

Another survivor later explained how she was saved by her husband who returned in time to turn off the gas supply, after Petrov had closed all the windows and turned the oven on. By now there was sufficient evidence available to arrest the murdering doctor, and in 2000 the St Petersburg police questioned him.

When news of his activities reached the press, bold headlines appeared above reports of Dr Death's activities. Petrov took exception to the publicity, denying all accusations of criminality and threatening to sue for libel. He particularly challenged the notion that he was enjoying his moment of fame. At one stage, he admitted the murders but then retracted saying he had made the confession while subjected to psychological pressure.

Petrov was put on trial in 2002, charged with seventeen counts of murder. The court found him guilty of twelve and he was sentenced to life imprisonment.

The Big Yellow Storage Murder

A special needs teacher went missing on 14 March 2003, after a chance telephone call. Jane Longhurst, thirty-one, lived with her boyfriend, Malcolm Sentance, and often socialized with fellow teacher Lisa Stephens, who was pregnant, and her boyfriend Graham Coutts, a guitarist and part-time salesman, whom they had known for around five years.

Miss Stephens often took time off work because of morning sickness and at 10.05am on 14 March Miss Longhurst rang her but Coutts answered. He persuaded her to go swimming with him at the local baths and collected her from her home on Shaftesbury Road, Brighton.

Rather than going swimming, he took her to his home at 6 Waterloo Street, Hove. As he prepared tea, he pounced and wrapped a pair of Lisa's tights twice around Miss Longhurst's neck, pulling them so tight he could hold with one hand while he masturbated with the other. The death throes exacerbated Coutts's excitement and he tightened the ligature until, deprived of oxygen, she died.

It is believed that Coutts, who had an interest in necks, sexually abused her further after death. He put the body into a cardboard box and for eleven days kept it in his garden shed. He finally moved it when police came to question him and his girlfriend.

For the next twenty-four days, Jane's remains were stored in the cardboard box in unit C50 at the Big Yellow storage warehouse in Brighton. He visited the warehouse several times but only stayed short periods. Detectives found a used condom there and suspected necrophilia.

On 18 April, he returned to the storage unit and put the box containing the corpse into the boot of his car, left it overnight and then the next day drove to Wiggonholt Common near Pulborough, West Sussex, where he set alight the body, which was naked apart from the tights.

When Coutts was arrested, he claimed that she died after a "consensual asphyxial sex session". The jury did not believe him and Coutts was convicted of murder on 3 February 2004, and sentenced to life with a recommendation that he serve at least thirty years (reduced to twenty-six years on appeal on 26 January 2005).

The agony for Jane's family was not over and the Court of Appeal overturned the verdict on 19 July 2006, because the jury were not offered the chance of a manslaughter conviction. At his new trial Coutts was convicted by an eleven to one majority verdict on 4 July.

Totally Out of Control

"Mad Mel", as Melanie Myers would be called, was one of a family of four and regularly in trouble from her early teenage years. At the age of thirteen, she was expelled from school for attacking fellow pupils and went on to acquire a long list of convictions for assault, wounding and causing affray.

In 1991, Myers attacked a waitress in a restaurant, jabbing a broken glass into her face and causing the young woman to lose an eye. This resulted in a custodial sentence, which did little to curb her enthusiasm for violence. On 12 April 1994, and in need of money, Myers and her eighteen-year-old accomplice, Clifton Quartey, hit on a moneymaking scheme.

Their idea was to target taxi drivers in the area of northwest London where they lived. They reasoned that cab drivers always had cash on them and they especially picked out Asian drivers who they believed would put up the least resistance. They hired a cab driven by 39-year-old Mazhar Hussein, a father of three children, and asked him to drive to a secluded area in Dollis Hill.

Pulling out a knife, Quartey threatened the driver and demanded money. When he responded by saying he did not have much money on him, Myers flew into a rage, grabbed the knife and stabbed the driver in the neck and chest. Mortally wounded, Mr Hussein was left in a pool of blood while Myers ran off laughing. At 9.45pm the driver was found by a couple who lived on the Howarden Hill estate. Myers and Quartey then watched the unfolding scene from a safe distance as paramedics arrived to aid the stricken driver.

House-to-house searches turned up bloodstains on the door of the flat which Myers had used as a safe haven. She and Quartey were arrested and charged with murder. While awaiting trial in Holloway Prison, Myers managed to escape with two other women, although she injured herself in the process. She was re-arrested three days later.

Tried at the Old Bailey in 1995, she was given to frequent outbursts of screaming and several times was taken back to the cells. When the jury delivered their guilty verdict on 17 February, she ranted at them, calling them "bastards". She was given a sentence of life imprisonment.

It appeared that Myers was addicted to violence, keeping a collection of books about murder in her room. One of the detectives involved in the murder enquiry said she was one of the most violent women he had ever dealt with, adding "she is totally out of control".

"Financial Promiscuity, Sexual Promiscuity, Emotional Shallowness"

On 23 October 1943, Patricia Burton, a 22-year-old socialite and brewery heiress to a $6million fortune, was found naked and dead in her apartment after going to a party. She had been struck with a candlestick and strangled.

At the time of her death she was estranged from her husband Wayne Lonergan, a handsome, six-foot tall, crop-headed Royal Canadian Air Force aircraftman, three years her senior.

The police contacted his commanding officer and discovered that Lonergan had been on leave in New York during the weekend of his wife's death. He was discovered in Toronto and returned to New York voluntarily.

He was interrogated for eighty-four hours and supposedly confessed to killing his wife during a quarrel. He also spoke of their sex life or lack of one, leading to speculation that Lonergan was homosexual. Unfortunately, much of the interview was leaked to the press, resulting in him being labelled a murderer before a court had had the chance to try him.

At his trial in March 1944, doubt was cast on his confession, and although the police could prove that he was indeed in New York at the time of the killing, they could not prove he had been at the murder scene.

Assistant District Attorney Jacob Grumet said that Lonergan confessed (the unsigned confession was repudiated by the defendant and his lawyers) to homosexual relations, both before and after his marriage. One of the men involved was said to have been William Burton, Lonergan's wife's father, who had set up the younger man in his own apartment and given him money to live.

When Mr Burton died in October 1940, Lonergan moved on to his daughter and they were married on 30 July 1941. ADA Grumet also quoted Lonergan as saying that he derived "a certain amount" of satisfaction from his married life but that his separation from his wife was the result of "mutual boredom". One Manhattan psychiatrist spoke of Lonergan's "financial promiscuity, sexual promiscuity, emotional shallowness". Oddly, given the early press leaks, Judge James Garrett Wallace barred all spectators from the court except newspapermen. Lonergan was convicted of second-degree murder on 17 April 1944, and sentenced to thirty years to life in jail. After spending twenty-two years in Sing Sing, Lonergan was released on 2 December 1965, and deported to Canada.

Mad Father Kills Daughter

Like many families in nineteenth century Lancashire and indeed nationwide, James Leaver and his wife Melinda could not afford their own home and rented rooms from her cousin Nanny Smith and husband John at 92 Water Street, Accrington. James and Melinda, both worked as weavers at the Park Shed. They had two children – Henrietta, six, and Albert, two.

It was James Leaver's habit to go home for lunch, prepared for him by Nanny Smith, but on 25 January 1881, he stayed at work and was observed by his workmates sharpening a knife on a whetstone.

When the day's work was finished, Leaver and his wife went home and had tea and put the children to bed. Then she and Mrs Smith went shopping, leaving Leaver home alone with his two children. When they left he was sitting by the fire, his clogs at his side. Not long after, he got up and locked the front door.

Taking some old clothes, he went upstairs to where his children slept. Taking hold of Henrietta, he stabbed his daughter in the neck before using the clothes to staunch the blood. Albert was woken by the commotion and looked on crying. Leaver went back downstairs.

At 7.40pm John Smith returned and found the door locked. He made to leave when the door was opened briefly and closed again but not locked. Entering, he saw Leaver sitting by the fire. The lodger told Mr Smith that he had killed his daughter and held up the bloodied knife. Mr Smith rushed upstairs and saw the little girl's bloodied body. When he saw that she was still breathing he ran for a doctor.

However, when the doctor arrived, Henrietta was already dead. Taken into custody, Leaver, five foot three and bearded, went on trial at Liverpool Assizes on 8 February 1881, before Mr Justice Stephens. The defence's case was that Leaver was suffering from an uncontrolled mania to kill, whereas the prosecution claimed that the locked door was evidence that he knew exactly what he was doing when he killed Henrietta.

The jury returned a verdict of not guilty by reason of insanity and he was sent to Broadmoor Lunatic Asylum where he died on 10 July 1927. Melinda was pregnant at the time of the murder and gave birth to her third child, Ernest, in August 1881. She never remarried.

Viagra Man

The criminal career of Viagra Man came to an end on 10 February 2005, when he was convicted of rape and murder. Paul Culshaw lived at Ryelands, Lancaster, and allowed junkies to use his rented flat to take drugs. However, once the female addicts passed out he would use their bodies to satisfy his lust.

Stories began to circulate among the junkies that Culshaw was dangerous and they should not visit alone. However, on 20 June 2004, 23-year-old Clare Benson-Jewry did just that. Three weeks later, neighbours complained of a terrible smell emanating from the premises and called police.

On 15 July, they found Clare's rotting body in Culshaw's bedroom. She was half-naked and had been sexually assaulted and then garrotted with a shoelace. Of Culshaw there was no sign, but police soon discovered that he had a reputation for violence against women.

In 1985, aged eighteen, he had broken into the home of a 43-year-old woman and raped her. Jailed for three and a half years, he reoffended within weeks of being released in 1988, attempting to murder his victim after sexually assaulting her, for which he received a ten-year sentence.

In February 2005, Culshaw went on trial for Clare's murder but denied there was a sexual element to the killing. He told the court that he had "panicked" when he saw "one of my best friends" dead in his home and, fearing the police would "fit me up" because of his previous form, fled the scene.

Culshaw said that Clare would often come round to smoke heroin and although he fancied her, he did nothing about the attraction. On the night of her death he claimed that she had come over to smoke heroin and he left her to get some tobacco from a local newsagent and when he came back she was dead.

He left for Penrith in the Lake District where he lived rough for several days, only being caught when he tried to steal bread from a baker's. The jury found him guilty of murder after deliberating for less than an hour. The judge sentenced Culshaw to a whole of life tariff.

Shopping Trip Led to Murder

Blonde and beautiful heiress Janie Shepherd, a 24-year-old Australian, seemed to have it all. At 8.40pm on 4 February 1977, she hurriedly left 103 Clifton Hill, St John's Wood, north London, the luxury home that she shared with her cousin, Camilla Sampson, and Camilla's husband, Alastair, eager to start the weekend with boyfriend Roddy Kinkead-Weekes, a cricketer with the MCC, at his flat in Lennox Gardens, Knightsbridge.

Janie stopped off at the Europa supermarket on Queensway to buy trout, chicory, tomatoes and yoghurt for their dinner. Then she disappeared. The next day at 3.15am she was reported missing and on 8 February her dark blue Mini was found in Elgin Crescent, Notting Hill, covered in mud, with two parking tickets and the interior slashed with a knife.

There were, however, few clues to be had from it. Police waited for a ransom demand but none came. Janie's mother and stepfather arrived from Australia two days later to conduct their own search but no clues surfaced and weeks went by. Police interviewed all known sex offenders in the locale.

Janie's parents returned to Australia on 12 April, and six days later two schoolboys found Janie's body in an area called Devil's Dyke on Nomansland Common south of Harpenden in Hertfordshire. It was ten weeks and six days after her disappearance. An autopsy showed that Janie had died from compression of the neck but the pathologist was unable to say whether it was manual or the result of a firm object pressed against it. Oddly, when her body was found it was clad in slightly different clothes from the ones she was wearing when she disappeared.

Decomposition of the body made it difficult to ascertain whether she had been raped or sexually assaulted. The police took 825 statements but seemed no nearer to catching her killer when the coroner's jury returned a verdict of murder by person or persons unknown.

The prime suspect in the case was a former boxer called David Lashley, a fifty-year-old West Indian with a psychopathic hatred of white women, who worked as a driver, and on 13 December 1977, he was jailed for eighteen years for a number of crimes including attempted murder and two rapes (one of a young blonde woman).

Shortly before Lashley was due to be released he told fellow inmate Daniel Reece how he had waylaid Janie on Queensway before abducting, raping and murdering her. At 7am on 17 February 1989, Lashley was released from Frankland Prison and immediately arrested for the murder of Janie Shepherd. On 19 March 1990, after two and a quarter hours' deliberation, the jury found Lashley guilty of murder and he was jailed for life.

Evil Sorcerer

Kristy Bamu lived with his parents and two of his sisters in France, and a family visit was planned to spend Christmas with his sister Magalie and her boyfriend, Eric Bikubi, at their flat in Forest Gate. The fifteen-year-old arrived in London with his sisters on 16 December 2010. Perhaps out of excitement, the boy wet himself on arrival, an event that was to have tragic consequences.

Bikubi, whom the boy called Uncle Eric, reacted angrily to Kristy's wetting episode, accusing him of witchcraft. What followed was a sustained and brutal attack on a defenceless boy and two of his sisters. Aided by Magalie, Bikubi battered Kristy with an iron bar and beat him, knocking out some of his teeth in the process.

On Christmas Day, Bikubi forced Kristy and his two sisters into a bath, intent on washing away the evil spirits. The boy was forced under the water and drowned. His sisters were ordered to clean up the mess. Magalie Bamu called 999, saying that her brother had drowned himself in the bath. Attempts by

Magalie to revive her brother failed and when paramedics arrived, they found the boy lying dead on the bathroom floor. There was blood splattered across the floor, walls and furniture in the flat and the dead boy's three sisters were soaking wet and hysterical.

It was later revealed that during Kristy's ordeal, lengthy telephone calls were made to his parents in Paris. In one of these Bikubi said he would kill the boy if he was not collected. Kristy himself told his parents, "Uncle Eric will kill me".

The trial of Bikubi and Bamu for murder provoked a great deal of discussion about witchcraft and sorcery practised by some followers of African religions. The two defendants, both aged twenty-eight, were born in the Democratic Republic of the Congo. Bikubi, in particular, believed he had a special gift to sense other people's spirits. Witch branding was part of this.

The full extent of the savage treatment meted out to Kristy and his sisters was detailed in court. Bikubi denied murder but pleaded guilty to manslaughter on the grounds of diminished responsibility. Magalie also denied murder. A key witness was Kelly Bamu who, along with her younger sister, was accused of being a witch. She demonstrated her anger at what had taken place at the hands of Bikubi and Magalie and said they should undergo the same fate.

Descriptions such as "a prolonged attack of unspeakable savagery and brutality" using "an armoury of weapons" and "a staggering act of depravity and cruelty" were used in court. The judge, Mr Justice Paget, exempted the jury from jury service for the rest of their lives because of the stress they had endured. Eric Bikubi and Magalie Bamu were sentenced to life imprisonment for torturing and drowning Kristy.

As She Lay Dying, He Calmly Stood and Smoked

On 9 January 1912, Tom West took his wife, Bertha Richards, for a drink at the Cooper's Arms at 2 High Road in Chadwell Heath, near Romford in Essex. They married in December 1883 and had three daughters before moving to 15 Station Road, Ilford. Theirs was not a happy union – she drank too much and liked to spend her time in local pubs without her husband in tow.

The year before, Bertha became friendly with Alfred Faulkner and on 23 December spent the night at his house but denied any impropriety in the relationship. It did nothing to mend her marriage.

On 6 January 1912, the landlady arrived at Station Road to ask for the rent but West told her that he had given it to his wife to pay. He set off to look for Bertha who was believed to have gone shopping. In fact, she was drinking in the General Havelock at 229 Ilford High Road with Alfred Faulkner. They returned to Mr Faulkner's home where he began to serenade Bertha with his accordion and woo her with more drink. They had not been alone long when West burst in and beat up Mr Faulkner while Bertha looked on aghast.

They stayed at their elder daughter's home for three days, not talking to each other. Finally, West confronted Bertha who again denied there was any to-do with Mr Faulkner. On 9 January, they went to the Cooper's Arms where he had a pint of beer and she "a glass of ale with a dash [of gin]". They had another round then she got up to go.

West suggested that they eat there but Bertha said that she had brought her own lunch. As she rose, West stabbed her behind her ear and blood began gushing out of the three-inch wound.

As she lay dying, West calmly stood by and smoked. Put on trial at Essex Assizes, his daughter said that he was a good father, and in his testimony Mr Faulkner reiterated that his relationship with Bertha was entirely platonic and that he had no idea that it was West who had attacked him three days earlier and had not reported the assault to the police.

West was sentenced to fifteen years' penal servitude and was released in April 1922, having served ten years.

"I Am a Monster"

A telephone call at 2.35am to emergency services brought paramedics to a one-bedroom flat in the chic St Germain-en-Laye district in Paris. When they arrived they found a woman – naked apart from a green and white bathrobe – kneeling beside a man's body and attempting to stem the flow of blood from a deep knife wound in his neck. Efforts to save him failed and he died an hour later.

Jessica Davies, a former model and the niece of the Conservative-turned-Labour MP and Minister for Defence Equipment and Support, Quentin Davies, was living in Paris. She had been born in London in February 1979, and educated in France but began to exhibit odd behaviour – but then strangeness ran in the family. Her maternal grandmother made repeated attempts to kill herself ("She threw herself from a bridge as we were leaving on holiday," Davies said. "You have to be a moron to miss yourself like that, she should have jumped head first") and her uncle Julian was a schizophrenic who tried to kill his mother over the alleged non-payment of a debt.

Her parents divorced and her father paid for her flat, encouraging her to find a proper job. She got an average degree in literature at Toulouse and was briefly a model for the French mail order firm La Redoute but her modelling career did not take off. She worked occasionally in bars and offices ("I was very competent when I turned up," she said) but her major preoccupations were alcohol, drugs (ecstasy, cocaine and various kinds of antidepressant) and promiscuous sex. She said that she had slept with more than 100 men.

In 2005, she began a relationship with Laurent Couturier, thirty-seven, that was to last two years before he broke it off in August 2007 unable to handle her drinking. They remained in contact and on 1 November 2007 had sex.

On 11 November 2007, she ventured into O'Sullivan's, a bar five minutes from her home, where she met 24-year-old Olivier Mugnier, a local jobless man nicknamed "Funtime". They had several drinks (she downed shots and pints and had taken four different types of antidepressants) and then she invited him back to her flat. Did he have condoms, she asked. He followed her home, wearing his rollerskates. She had sex on her mind but his inability to get an erection led to a violent reaction.

She later said: "He was too drunk to go through with it, he went too fast and I reassured him," said Davies. "I told him 'Calm down'. I think he took off the condom. Then I completely blanked out, I don't remember."

What did happen was that, fuelled by the alcohol and drugs, Davies produced a knife and stabbed her would-be lover in the neck. She was reported as telling paramedics, "It's me who did it . . . I am a monster. I just wanted to cut him a bit and it went right in." When her blood was tested, Davies was found to be four times over the limit allowed by French authorities for driving.

She said she could not recall any details of the incident nor could she explain why she had taken up a knife. Among the speculation inspired by the attack was that Davies had tried to intensify her sexual experience by cutting her lover and drawing blood. There was also a suggestion that she had been stimulated by the circumstances of the murder, reported a few days earlier, of Meredith Kercher in Italy and tales of extreme sex.

Jessica Davies was charged with voluntary homicide without premeditation and sent for trial at Versailles Criminal Court in January 2010. In mitigation of her actions, the court heard that she had a troubled background as a teenager and, despite gaining academic qualifications, had difficulty securing a job. She was reported to use men as sex objects in order to relieve her distress and, twice, had attempted to commit suicide. The first time was in 2004 and the second was in August 2007 after the split from Laurent Couturier when she used the knife she would use to kill Olivier Mugnier on herself. She slashed her wrists in the bath, slicing right down to the tendons before attacking her thighs and legs, inflicting wounds requiring twenty-seven stitches.

The black-handled kitchen knife with a blade six inches long had been bought for food preparation by Laurent Couturier, and Davies would often use it as a bookmark.

Prosecutors characterized her as "a psychologically disturbed seductress", and a lawyer for her victim's family said that she was "a sulphurous seductress, with the devil's beauty".

The court found her guilty of murder and sentenced her to fifteen years' imprisonment. She remained impassive during the two-day trial, but minutes after the verdict was read she was laughing and joking with policemen guarding her. As well as fifteen years in prison, she was sentenced to ten years' probation and psychological monitoring. In addition, her family was ordered to pay €105,000 in damages to Olivier Mugnier's parents and twin brother, Benjamin.

"Oops! I've Done it Again"

Images of a young woman with her tongue extruded, and holding an ornamental dagger, dominated press reports about Joanna Dennehy and her murderous exploits. During a ten-day killing spree in March 2013, she stabbed to death three men who had the misfortune to know her.

The first was Lukasz Slaboszewski who turned up at her maisonette in Peterborough, possibly in expectation of a sexual encounter, and was stabbed through the heart on either 19 or 20 March. She stored his body in a wheelie bin outside the house for a couple of days. On 29 March, Dennehy also killed her housemate, John Chapman, and Kevin Lee, her landlord and lover. Aided and abetted by two willing accomplices who were completely under her spell, the bodies were dumped in ditches outside the town. She later told her helpers, Gary Stretch and Leslie Layton, "Oops! I've done it again".

But her blood lust was not yet sated. She told one of her associates, "I've killed three people . . . I want to do some more. I want my fun." Accompanied by Stretch, she drove 140 miles to Hereford where she targeted two men walking their dogs. She attacked both of them with a knife.

John Rogers was walking his dog along a cycle path in the Golden Post area of Hereford when Dennehy stabbed him forty times in the back and chest. He spent ten days in hospital and underwent surgery to both of his lungs, which were punctured in the attack. He died of his injuries in November 2014.

Retired fireman Robin Bereza, fifty-seven, was walking his Labrador, Samson, and had celebrated his thirty-sixth wedding anniversary the day before he was stabbed.

Dennehy and Stretch were quickly arrested and the bodies of her three murder victims were also discovered.

She was tried at the Old Bailey in November 2013, when she took her defence lawyer by surprise by admitting to three murders and pleading guilty to two attempted murders. When her legal team asked for time to discuss her plea, she responded, "I've pleaded guilty, and that's that". Appearing with her was Gary Stretch who denied charges of assisting Dennehy to dispose of victims' bodies and two counts of attempted murder.

Joanna Dennehy was regarded as a bright pupil at school; she had two children while in her teens and became estranged from her family. She lapsed into drugs and alcohol abuse and drifted into prostitution. Following time served in prison for theft and drug offences, she was treated for mental health problems. At the time of her arrest in 2012, doctors believed she was suffering from a kind of sadomasochism. She derived pleasure through inflicting pain and humiliation and she said that she killed "for fun". Dennehy had an intensely strong personality which enabled her to manipulate others and get them to do her bidding. She likened herself and Gary Stretch to Bonnie and Clyde, America's infamous murdering duo of the 1930s.

On 28 February 2014, Dennehy was sentenced to life imprisonment. The judge ruled that her crimes were so serious that she should serve a whole life sentence and die in prison. She thereby made criminal history by being only the third woman to be considered so dangerous that she be condemned to die in confinement.

CHAPTER 3

Unsolved and Unresolved

One of the strongest threads in the commission of crime is the concept of the perfect murder. Why else would a perpetrator commit the act if he didn't think he would get away with it? The idea is that careful planning and a meticulous cover-up will defeat the best efforts of detection. But this has to be balanced against the concept that "murder will out" and, over time, the most careful planning and execution may be undone.

Murderers sometimes get carried away with their own cleverness and they exalt in the idea that they have humiliated the forces of law and order. In this, they can become careless, leaving behind clues that will eventually trap them. Time is the great crime solver and it generally works more to the advantage of the investigator than the perpetrator, as Malcolm Webster discovered. He thought he had committed the perfect murder in Scotland in 1994 when his wife died in a faked car crash. But he had reckoned without the tenacity of his victim's family and retrospective toxicological evidence which, thirteen years after the event, showed he had rendered his wife unconscious before killing her.

Crimes are often solved by a chance discovery, such as the murder committed by Frederick Boyle. He shot his wife, Edwina, and hid her body in a metal drum at his house in Melbourne, Australia. To all intents and purposes, she had disappeared without trace and her widower was free to ask his newly acquired girlfriend to move in with him. But, over twenty years after she disappeared, Boyle's son-in-law, while cleaning out the house in 2006, came across the drum containing Edwina's remains.

Boyle's explanation was that he had found his wife shot dead when he returned to the house. He decided not to report his discovery because he did not think he would be believed, so he concealed her body. He was found guilty of murder at his trial in Melbourne.

Sometimes, the process works the other way when doubt is voiced about what appeared at the time to be a valid conviction with a perpetrator brought to justice. This appeared to be the case in the conviction of Andrew George in 2005 for the murder of Hilda Murrell. This was a high-profile case with many twists and turns which in all likelihood ended with an innocent man sentenced to life imprisonment.

It also happens that a perpetrator, having committed the perfect crime, and having got away with it for many years, has the urge to confess when he is contemplating his own demise. Such was the case with Billy Fisher who shot dead a cinema manager in Bristol in 1946. His confession forty-three years after the killing enabled an unsolved murder to be re-classified.

Time was also the crime solver in a murder case that defeated Liverpool's detectives for thirty-eight years and, again, resolution depended on confession. When bin men discovered the body of a teenage girl in an alleyway in 1970, it was the prelude to the city police force's longest unsolved case. Time and chance played their part when decorators moved in to renovate the house of Harry Richardson who had recently died.

Painters came across a satchel on top of a wardrobe in one of the rooms which contained a collection of press cuttings reporting the murder of Lorraine Jacob. Included among the papers were nine handwritten sheets which amounted to a murder confession. Although the note was unsigned and undated, it contained details of the crime not known to the public. The forensic evidence convinced the police of the authenticity of the self-confessed murderer's claims. In 2009, they decided to close what had, for so long, been an unsolved crime. In an interesting coincidence, just a few weeks before the discovery of the confession, the police had decided to conduct a cold case review. Chance had played a significant part in bringing resolution.

Another cold case review in 2009 brought answers to a murder that had remained unsolved for eighty-three years. In

1926, sixteen-year-old Emma Alice Smith, a domestic servant working in the Sussex village of Waldron, disappeared. No trace of her was ever found, but the mystery of what happened was discovered by chance when a local researcher came across an old, undated school photograph depicting the girls' rounders team.

A local man who saw the photograph pointed to one of the girls in the group and remarked that she had gone missing in 1926. This aroused local curiosity in an almost forgotten incident and prompted a relative to come forward with the information that the girl's murderer had made a death bed confession in 1953 in which he said he had dumped the body in a nearby pond. For reasons of their own, those privy to this admission of guilt decided to keep quiet about it. Nevertheless, the police were minded to reopen their investigation in the hope of locating Emma Smith's body.

A crime that was described as "A Midsomer Murder" involved the death by shooting of a retired army officer at his home in 2004. The crime led to a great deal of speculation, but no resolution, for eight years. Then, a man already serving a prison sentence for murder decided to brag to a cellmate about his role as a hitman. This resulted in him being identified as a double killer: a good example of the principle that "murder must advertise".

A bizarre example of this concept was provided by Thomas Quick, who falsely claimed to have killed thirty people in Sweden. He relished the idea of being a serial killer and followed stories in the media about unsolved crimes so that he could claim responsibility. It is well established that serial killers relish the notoriety their activities attract. Quick just wanted to be one of them.

For all those crimes which circumstances contrive to solve, there remain many that defy resolution. Caroline Hogg's last recorded words in 1906 were, "I'm murdered". Indeed she was, and her killer has remained undetected for more than a century. Equally frustrating for the police efforts to solve the case, was the murder of Joan Woodhouse in 1948. Their failure preyed on the mind of Inspector Narborough whose frustration was reflected in his book of memoirs. Perhaps they may be judged as perfect murders, as least for the present time?

Who Was D. B. Cooper?

On the day before 1971's Thanksgiving, a man calling himself Dan Cooper boarded a Boeing 727-100 at Portland International Airport in Oregon, bound for Seattle, Washington, on Northwest Orient (now Northwest Airlines) Flight 305. Later descriptions put him at mid-forties, about six foot tall, and sporting a black raincoat, loafers, a dark suit, a white shirt, a black tie, black sunglasses and a mother-of-pearl tie pin. He paid $18.52 and sat in seat 18C.

Not long after take-off, he passed a note to air hostess Florence Schaffner. Thinking that he was passing her his telephone number, she put it into her pocket without looking at it. He said, "Miss, you'd better look at that note. I have a bomb." Hands trembling, she unfurled the note and read, "I have a bomb in my briefcase. I will use it if necessary. I want you to sit next to me. You are being hijacked."

The note demanded $200,000 in used $20 notes and four parachutes. The FBI began to accede to Cooper's demands but scanned all the notes before passing them on. While the authorities were busy on the ground, Cooper relaxed and drank bourbon and soda. Another hostess on the flight, Tina Mucklow, later commented that the hijacker "seemed rather nice".

At 5.24pm, Cooper's demands were met and the plane landed at Seattle-Tacoma International Airport, Washington. The four parachutes and the money were delivered to Cooper who released all thirty-six passengers and Florence Schaffner as he had promised. The plane was refuelled and, having checked the parachutes and money, Cooper told the crew to take off at 7.40pm and head for Mexico City before the destination was altered to Reno, Nevada. At 8.13pm, during a heavy rainstorm, Cooper lowered the aft stairs and jumped from the plane over southwestern Washington. He would never be seen again.

At 10.15pm, the Boeing landed at Reno and the FBI recovered two of the four parachutes. More than forty years after the event, the authorities are no closer to identifying the hijacker or explaining what happened to the bulk of the money.

The FBI interviewed a man named D. B. Cooper who had no link with the crime but due to a mistake that name was transferred to the hijacker. The FBI, which has codenamed the case Norjak, believes that Cooper did not survive the parachute jump. On 10 February 1980, Brian Ingram, eight, found $5,880 in decaying $20 notes on the banks of the Columbia River, five miles northwest of Vancouver, Washington. It was part of Cooper's hoard and fifteen of the notes were auctioned in Dallas on 13 June 2008, raising $37,000.

The case remains the only unsolved air piracy in American aviation history.

"Murder on My Mind"

Joan Woodhouse, a 27-year-old librarian who worked in London, decided to spend the August Bank Holiday weekend in Arundel, Sussex. The weather was particularly warm that year and, being a sun-worshipper, she decided to make the most of the opportunity.

When she failed to turn up for work after the weekend, she was reported missing. A week later, on 10 August 1948, a man walking through a secluded part of Arundel Park discovered her body. Stripped to her underclothes, she lay on her back under beech trees. Some thirty feet away, her outer clothing lay in a neatly folded pile. She had been raped and strangled.

Enquiries into her background showed that she had recently broken up with her fiancé and her friends noticed that she had changed from her usual lively self to being a person who was plainly unhappy. Earlier in the year, she had overdosed on sleeping tablets. Her fiancé was interviewed by the police and quickly eliminated from enquiries.

Suspicion began to fall on the local man who had discovered her body, but he too was eliminated from further questioning. The job of the police was complicated by having to deal with a number of false confessions and an intervention on the part of the dead woman's parents. Dissatisfied with the rate of progress being made in solving the murder, her father hired a private detective to make enquiries.

None of this produced a solution and even Scotland Yard's Chief Inspector Fred Narborough made little headway. He and Dr Keith Simpson, the Home Office pathologist, attempted to reconstruct the crime scene. The secluded wooded location had perhaps been chosen by Joan Woodhouse with the intention of indulging in a sun-bathing session. She stripped down to her underclothes, placing her other garments in a neat pile close by. Perhaps she went to sleep, only to be surprised by a man walking off the beaten track who saw an opportunity for a lustful adventure.

The fact that the young woman's body was found some distance from her clothes suggested to investigators that she was attacked where she lay but managed to break free and attempt to escape. Her attacker pursued her and killed her at the spot thirty feet away where her body was discovered.

Despite the best efforts of Narborough and, later, Detective Superintendent Reginald Spooner, the murder of Joan Woodhouse remained unsolved and has done so for the last sixty-five years. Narborough was haunted by the case and later wrote "All the time, there is that murder on my mind."

Death in Dagenham

On 28 June 1846, twenty-year-old George Clark, a rookie policeman, stood in for the preacher at his local Methodist Chapel in Bull Street, Dagenham, Essex. He wore his police uniform as he took the service.

PC Clark had joined the Metropolitan Police Force on 2 June 1845, his nineteenth birthday, and a year later was transferred to Dagenham police station (also in Bull Street) with a colleague after three local PCs had been sacked for brutality.

His beat was Eastbrookend and included some lonely country roads. He was on duty between 9pm and 6.30am and carried a rattle, truncheon and cutlass for protection. On 29 June 1846, he began his usual patrol and at 10.30pm a labourer saw him, singing a hymn to himself to keep his spirits up. He never returned to the station at the end of his shift.

His colleagues searched for him but to no avail. His body was finally discovered on 3 July, near a pond close to Thorntons Farm, Rush Green. He was lying on his back, a sheaf of corn in his right hand, his throat cut, a knife wound to the back of his neck and another under his left ear.

His rattle, money and silver watch were in his pocket. His watch had stopped at 3 o'clock. An inquest opened on 4 July, and PC Abia Butfoy told the coroner that a Romford man named William Walker had threatened him. He suggested that perhaps Mr Walker had killed PC Clark mistaking him in the dark for PC Butfoy.

A £100 reward was announced for information leading to the apprehension of the murderer. The inquest returned a verdict of murder by person or persons unknown. In 1858, twelve years after the murder, Inspector Jonathan Whicher arrested a farm labourer called George Blewitt for the murder of PC Clark. The arrest was based on the testimony of the wife of a farm worker who claimed that her husband and three other men (including Blewitt) were going to carry out a robbery and if PC Clark intervened they would "stab the bastard down to the ground".

The case was thrown out before it could proceed to trial and no one was ever brought to justice for the killing of PC George Clark.

Seeing Red

On the evening of 2 June 1957, a police patrol came across a parked station wagon on a road under construction in Baltimore County, Maryland, USA. The occupant of the car was Robert J. Van Horn. He was holding a .32 pistol in one hand and a glass of whisky in the other, while threatening to kill himself. It took officers an hour to talk him into a reasonable frame of mind before disarming him.

While sitting in his car contemplating suicide, he had written a letter to his wife whom he had just murdered. It amounted to a confession in which he sought forgiveness but put the blame on her; "You have contributed to my becoming a murderer", he wrote. The badly beaten body of his wife, Bernice, was discovered nearby – she had suffered crushed ribs, a broken spine and head injuries. Van Horn admitted attacking her.

The 53-year-old executive of a local lumber company told police that he and his wife had attended a cocktail party and then drove to their farmhouse. On arrival, he said his wife made a sharp remark and struck him in the face. This provoked a violent reaction; "I actually saw red", he said. As a result he set about beating up Bernice.

Realizing he had killed her, Van Horn put her body in the station wagon and drove around for a while, disposing of his bloodstained clothes in the process. Next, he called at his office where he left letters for the attention of the police. Then he drove to the spot where he had dumped her body and sat in his car, pistol in hand.

Charged with murder, Van Horn pleaded guilty to manslaughter by reason of insanity. He was sentenced to ten years' imprisonment which he served in Maryland State Penitentiary. On release in 1960, he returned to his previous employment and married a widow, Evelyn Monte. The couple moved to Heritage Village in Connecticut in 1981 and, to all intents and purposes, lived a quiet life.

But there were sinister undertones to Van Horn's second marriage, for in November 1987, both he and his wife, Evelyn, were found dead in their home by the cleaning lady. They had died – a murder and a suicide – from gunshot wounds. A note from Van Horn was found in the house but its content was not divulged.

The man – whose neighbours saw him as a quiet, polite and gentlemanly individual – suffered from a neuropathic disease which may have given rise to his violent outbursts. In the note that Van Horn wrote to his first wife after he killed her, he described flying off the handle and said there would never be another such incident. This, as it turned out, proved to be tragically mistaken.

The Missing MP

Firebrand orator Albert Victor Grayson was elected Independent Labour Party MP for Colne Valley in July 1907, by 153 votes. Despite his electoral success he was not popular with the party hierarchy.

In the House of Commons, he attacked the Liberal Government and said, "I look forward to the day when the government bench will be occupied by socialists sent there by an indignant people." He also supported the Irish nationalists.

In 1908, he easily won a poll to find the most popular Yorkshire MP. In November that year, the Serjeant-at-Arms threw him out of the House after Grayson refused to obey James Lowther, the Speaker. In 1910, Grayson lost his seat and took to the bottle. On 7 November 1912, he married the actress Ruth Nightingale, but the following year he suffered a nervous breakdown.

Unlike most Left-wingers, Grayson spoke out in favour of the First World War. He was declared bankrupt on 26 August 1914, with debts of £496 3s (almost £50,000 in today's money). He later enlisted in the New Zealand Army and was wounded on 12 October 1917. His wife died in childbirth on 4 December 1918.

The next year, Grayson launched a bitter attack on Lloyd George and the selling of political honours. He also threatened to publicly name the middleman Maundy Gregory (see page 349) who he knew was spying on him.

In September 1920, Grayson was attacked on the Strand, central London, and left with a broken arm and needing stitches in his head. He was treated at Charing Cross Hospital. On 28 September, Grayson was drinking with friends at the Georgian Restaurant in Chandos Place when he received a message from the receptionist that his luggage had been sent to the Queen's Hotel in Leicester Square by mistake.

Grayson said, "Don't let anyone drink my whisky. I shall be back in a few minutes." He was never seen again. It was not until 1927 that the public even became aware that Grayson had disappeared. His family made an appeal via the BBC in 1934 but with no response. His sister Annie made another appeal in September 1942, again with no response.

Rumours abounded that Grayson had been murdered on the orders of Maundy Gregory, but nothing has been proved.

"A Classic Whodunnit"?

On 13 December 1988, tragedy struck at Broats Farm in Ryedale, Yorkshire, when the farmer's wife was shot dead. Jayne and William Smith had married six months previously and she had just returned home from her nursing job in Salton when she was ambushed and killed. The murderer had despatched her with a single shot to the head using a .22 rifle. Her body was dragged to a location where it would be found easily and the clothing was disarranged to simulate a sexual motive.

William Smith found his wife's body when he returned to the farm around 11.20pm. The starting point for the police inquiry was Smith's ex-girlfriends, and 36-year-old Yvonne Sleightholme in particular. She had been engaged to Smith and plans to marry were twice called off. Then Jayne moved in with him, leaving Yvonne out in the cold. A few days after the murder, Sleightholme was arrested.

Forensic evidence included bloodstains in her car, which matched the victim's, and a .22 rifle which had gone missing from her parents' farm turned up the day after the fatal shooting. Also, tyre tracks at the crime scene were consistent with the type of car driven by Sleightholme. She maintained that she was innocent of the charge. In a remarkable turn of events, traumatized by the accusations swirling around her, Yvonne began to lose her sight in February 1989, and within three months was blind.

She testified at her trial in April 1991, and admitted being at the farm on the night Jayne Smith died. She said that she had continued to see William Smith and they had arranged to meet that evening in Pickering, some five miles away. But Smith changed his mind and asked her to meet him at the farm.

When she arrived, he was very cold towards her and there were three other men present, one of whom was carrying what might have been a weapon. At some point she lost consciousness and, on coming round, was threatened to keep her silence or suffer the consequences.

There were anomalies in the crime scene evidence that worked in Sleightholme's favour. For instance, although bloodstains were found in her car, a thorough examination of her clothing revealed no such traces. Crucial to the whole case was the nature of the gunshot wound that killed Jayne Smith. The gun had been fired at the back of the head with the bullet traversing to the front of the brain. The forensic pathologist suggested it was the mark of a professional killer.

Despite the circumstantial nature of much of the evidence, Yvonne Sleightholme was found guilty of murder by a ten to two majority verdict. In his summing-up, conceivably reflecting doubts about the outcome, the judge referred to the case as "a classic whodunnit". Her appeal against sentence was heard at the Old Bailey in January 1993, and dismissed. *The Guardian* published a review of the evidence in February and asked the question, "is the wrong person in jail?"

In January 2002, Sleightholme gave her first media interview to the *Evening Press* from Styal Prison in Cheshire. She said that she would never admit to killing Jayne Smith – even though this might mean she would never be freed.

"I value the truth more than anything," she claimed. "I didn't do it, and nothing – not even the chance of freedom – will make me lie and say I did it . . . I was not responsible for that terrible murder."

Sleightholme was finally freed from prison just before Christmas 2005. She was driven to North Yorkshire to spend the festive season with members of her family, although her father, Bob, had died four months before her release.

The Serial Killer Who Never Was

Thomas Quick, believed to be Sweden's Hannibal Lecter, having confessed to killing thirty people, spent twenty-two years in a psychiatric hospital. He claimed to have murdered, raped and dismembered many of his young victims. On the basis of his admissions, the courts punished him on eight murder convictions.

But it was all make believe. Quick, whose real name was Sture Bergwall, made it all up and convinced the authorities that he was a serial killer. He hungered for attention and concocted confessions based on his intense studies of real criminal cases. Those whose responsibility it was to solve crimes were only too eager to listen to his admissions, while he wallowed in his notoriety.

He began his confessional spree in 1991 following a robbery that resulted in his admission to a psychiatric institution. Over the next nine years, while undergoing drug therapy, he confessed to twenty-five murders. Needless to say, some of these revelations had a traumatic effect on the victims' families.

In 2008, the documentary film-maker, Hannes Råstam, was given access to Quick who, by this time, had reverted to his real name. Råstam's conclusions, published in his book, *Thomas Quick: The Making of a Serial Killer* (2012), exposed for the first time the extent of the deception that he had practised.

Quick made a habit of gleaning information from the doctors, lawyers and officials who interviewed him at various times, which he drew into his own narrative and then regurgitated later as confessions. He also spent time researching crime reports in the newspapers. By this process, he acquired what investigators interpreted as inside knowledge. But the striking aspect of this charade, as uncovered by Råstam, was the lack of supporting evidence for Quick's claims. There was no DNA, no murder weapons, and no witness corroboration. Råstam's conclusions revealed one of the greatest miscarriages of justice in modern times, which had resulted from shortcomings in Sweden's criminal investigation procedures and judicial system.

The father of an eleven-year-old boy whom Quick claimed to have killed in 1980, commenting on the revelations, said, "The real killers are roaming free in our society because of the travelling circus surrounding Quick".

What followed was an unstitching of the fabric that Quick, now Bergwall, had woven with his confessions resulting in murder convictions, which were now quashed. His status as a free man was restored in 2012, by which time he had been off medication for ten years and his two decades of confinement in a psychiatric hospital came to an end. At the age of sixty-three, he made a new start in life, leaving behind serious questions about the judgement of those who, perhaps unwittingly, had encouraged him to indulge his fantasies.

Good-Time Girl and Her Older Married Lover

On 4 June 1904, Nan Patterson, a divorced nineteen-year-old dancer and actress, was riding with her much older, married New York-based bookmaker lover Caesar Young in a carriage down Broadway – he was on his way to the docks to meet his wife and go on a long overseas holiday with her. At some point in that journey, Mr Young was shot dead with a gun that belonged to Patterson. He had long promised to leave his wife for her and in fact paid for her divorce, after which time she lived "on Young's bounty".

Police arrested Patterson and she was charged with the murder of Caesar Young. Her first trial ended in a hung jury and she was tried again in the spring of 1905. The state alleged that Patterson killed Mr Young because she was furious he would not leave his wife and because he resisted her attempts at blackmail. The defence argued that the evidence showed that the bookie had committed suicide.

On 2 May 1905, the prosecution took five hours to deliver its closing arguments: "Mr Young would not have held the weapon upside down when he fired the shot . . . The murder in her heart flamed into action, and she shot and killed. A little crack, a puff of smoke, and a dead man lay prostrate on this woman's lap. False to her husband, false to her lover, and false to her oath, the defendant would have you believe by her story told at the previous trial that Young shot himself rather than be separated from her. A silly story – a lie she does not now dare attempt to support."

When the jury left for lunch they were "jostled by the crowd that packed the streets. All the way to the restaurant the jurymen heard yells of 'Free Nan Patterson! Set her free! Nan's all right! She's done nothing.'"

The jury foreman announced that they had not reached a decision and said, "I am convinced that there is no hope of an agreement." On 13 May, Patterson was finally freed – District Attorney Jerome said that it was a "miscarriage of justice of the most serious kind [attributable] to the attitude of the press of this city toward the accused woman." As soon as she was freed, Patterson and her sister went shopping on Sixth Avenue and posed for photographers.

The Enigmatic Theft

Leonardo da Vinci created the most famous painting in the world in the early sixteenth century. The *Mona Lisa*, or *La Gioconda*, measures just thirty inches by twenty-one inches, is owned by the French government, and is displayed at the Louvre in Paris.

Millions of people had viewed the painting, and then, in the summer of 1911, on a day when the museum was closed, it was stolen. The next day, Louis Béroud, an artist who copied works of art for tourists, arrived to paint the *Mona Lisa* but found an empty space where it had been. A guard thought that the painting was being photographed or having its frame fixed. It was not until 11am that the alarm was raised.

The *Mona Lisa* was painted on wood rather than canvas so could not be rolled up, and the police believed that the thief had waited in the museum overnight and then escaped during renovations and cleaning on the Monday. The police found a left thumbprint but unfortunately in those days only the prints on the right hand were kept so it was a dead end. The Louvre offered a reward of FF25,000, and the newspaper *Le Matin* put up FF5,000, but both were topped by the magazine *L'Illustration*, which offered FF40,000.

Rumours circulated that an American millionaire had commissioned the theft, or perhaps it was a German plot to discredit France. On 10 December 1913, a moustachioed young man calling himself Vincenzo Leonard went to the offices of Alfredo Geri, an antique dealer on the Via Borgognissanti, Florence. The visitor said that he had the *Mona Lisa* and would be willing to hand it over for 500,000 lire and a promise that it would stay in Italy.

Geri and a friend, Giovanne Poggi, the director of the Uffizi Gallery, went to the Hotel Tripoli where the young man was staying, to view the painting. Geri later recalled, "The man opened a trunk full of wretched belongings. Then he took out an object wrapped in red cloth, and to our astonished eyes the divine *Gioconda* appeared, intact and wonderfully preserved."

Leonard agreed to let the two men take the painting to the Uffizi to check its authenticity. Meantime, the head of Florence's police went to arrest the young man whose real name was Vincenzo Perugia. The painting was exhibited in Italy before its return to France.

On 4 January 1914 it was unveiled at the Louvre. In June that year, Perugia went on trial in Florence. He said that he had stolen the painting out of patriotic duty, a defence that endeared the public to him, and he was sentenced to just one year and fifteen days. The only person arrested by French police in connection with the theft was the poet and art critic Guillaume Apollinaire on 7 September 1911. He implicated Pablo Picasso, who was then also questioned. Both men were freed without charge.

The Atlanta Murders

The black teenage killings in Atlanta, Georgia, ended on 27 February 1982, when Wayne Williams was jailed for life. The murders had begun three years earlier on 21 July 1979, when black teenagers Edward Smith and Alfred Evans were killed.

On 4 September, Milton Harvey, a third teen, disappeared, and he was followed on 21 October by nine-year-old Yusuf, the son of civil rights leader Camille Bell. In March 1980, Angel

Laner, twelve, became the first female victim when she was raped and murdered, and, two months later, Eric Middlebrooks was also murdered.

On 9 June, Christopher Richardson became the latest victim – all of them young and black. A rumour went round that a racist was killing black children but this was soon discounted for two very sound reasons. The area in which the children were taken was a heavily black one where any unusual face would stand out and psychologists believe that serial killers tend to remain within their racial group.

By May 1981, the death toll had reached twenty-one, with another child on the missing list. The investigation was costing $250,000 a month and it took President Ronald Reagan's authorization of a government grant of $1,500,000 to prevent Atlanta going bankrupt. On 22 May, a young black local DJ named Wayne Bertram Williams was questioned after he was seen acting suspiciously near the Chattahoochee River where some of the victims had been dumped. With no evidence to connect him to any of the crimes, he was freed but put under police surveillance.

Two days later, the nude body of 27-year-old Nathaniel Cater was found in the river. A forensic test matched dog hairs found on Nathaniel to those in the back of Wayne Williams's car. When others came forward to claim that Williams had molested them, he was arrested on 21 June.

Williams went on trial on 6 January 1982, on two counts of murder. The evidence was mostly circumstantial, but it was also noted that while Williams was in custody the Atlanta child killings ended. Doubts exist as to the safety of Williams's conviction, especially when Charles T. Saunders of the Ku Klux Klan told the Georgia Bureau of Investigation that the killer "had wiped out a generation of niggers for good".

The parents of some victims do not believe that Williams was the murderer. Williams has continued to protest his innocence and his lawyers have demanded a new trial. As of this writing, the killings have stopped and the police refuse to reopen the case.

Who Killed the Countess?

She survived two German concentration camps but could not survive the London Underground.

Countess Teresa Łubienska, seventy-three, lost her husband in the Bolshevik uprising in 1918, and her son was killed on 19 September 1939, at the start of the Second World War. She joined the Polish Resistance but was arrested on 11 November 1942, and sent to Auschwitz where the number 44747 was tattooed on her arm.

In August 1944, she was moved to Ravensbrück where her efforts at comforting the inmates gave her almost legendary status. After the war, she moved to England where she lived in a flat in Cornwall Gardens, Kensington, west London.

On the evening of Friday, 24 May 1957, the countess visited some Polish friends for a birthday party at their home in Ealing. On the way back, a priest accompanied her as far as Earls Court and she continued on the Piccadilly Line to the next stop, Gloucester Road, where she got off at 10.19pm. Three minutes later, she collapsed in the lift at the station, crying out, "Bandits! Bandits!" Her last words were, "I was on the platform and I was stabbed." She died before reaching hospital.

When an autopsy was carried out, it showed that she had been stabbed three times in the chest (two piercing her heart) once in the stomach and once in the back with a two-inch blade.

The motive for her murder was unclear – it was not robbery as a valuable silver brooch was still pinned to her clothes and her handbag had not been taken. Was it revenge by some Nazi over her anti-Hitler remarks during the war? Or was it closer to home? She was vociferous in her criticism of the Polish government led by Władysław Gomułka.

The killer escaped by using the emergency stairs. It took forty-eight seconds for the lift to ascend or descend, while a reasonably fit person could run up the stairs in forty-five seconds. The police searched the station, adjacent tunnels and all 214 Piccadilly Line trains but could not find the murder weapon.

By the time the inquest came around, on 19 August 1957, police had interviewed an incredible 18,000 people including many who lived abroad. However, no one was brought to justice and the jury returned a verdict of murder by a person or persons unknown. The killer of Countess Teresa Łubienska remains unidentified to this day.

Murder or Accident?

Sam Whitehouse and his brother-in-law Joe Downing went shooting on 3 April 1822, in Halesowen, having met at 8am at the cottage of blacksmith Thomas Fox. Downing asked Fox to repair the barrel of a gun for him and, while he worked on it, Mr Fox loaned him a fowling piece.

Mr Whitehouse and Mr Downing disappeared into the woods for five hours. At 6pm, all three retired to the nearest pub, the Beech Tree Tavern, where they bought drinks before returning to Mr Fox's cottage. They drank heavily, downing twelve quarts of ale (about twenty-four pints). They began bragging and betting, and Mr Whitehouse pulled a wad of notes from his trousers and offered a £10 wager, but his companions demurred. They continued drinking until 9pm when they decided to go home.

Mr Downing lived in Rowley and Mr Whitehouse in West Bromwich, so after being helped onto their horses by Mr Fox they set off together. Mr Downing returned to ask for the gun barrel he had brought for repair and Mr Fox gave it to him. Mr Whitehouse didn't wait for his friend.

About an hour later, Richard Aston who lived at the pub came across a horse wandering aimlessly. Mr Aston mounted the horse and began to ride to Mr Fox's cottage. En route he saw an unconscious Mr Whitehouse lying by the side of the road. Mr Aston's horse galloped to the Fox cottage but Mr Fox was too drunk to wake so Mrs Fox went with Mr Aston to where Mr Whitehouse lay. They helped him to the pub, where it was discovered that he had a large head wound and his money was gone.

He succumbed to his injuries two days later. The next day, the inquest was held into the death, and the jury foreman announced that they believed that Mr Downing had murdered his brother-in-law using the gun barrel he had asked the black-smith to repair.

Mr Downing was arrested and sent for trial at the Salop Summer Sessions. He pleaded not guilty. The first two witnesses stated that only a gun barrel could have caused the injury, while a third said that he believed it had been caused by a horse's hoof, and another the fall from the horse.

Another witness testified to the temperamental nature of the horse and mentioned two men he had seen walking towards where Mr Whitehouse had been found. The jury declared Mr Downing innocent of murder and he broke down in tears. The killer or killers – or was it an accident? – were never found.

"Darling Dottie, I Want to Kiss Your Pretty Pink Toes"

Blonde, blue-eyed, sexy and petite Dorothy Keenan left home (a slum in Harlem, New York) in 1915 when she was nineteen. Like many attractive teenagers she became a model and worked for a dress shop on Fifth Avenue.

She married a chauffeur but they divorced after he caught her cheating. Her family believed that she was working as a model and an aspiring Broadway actress but instead she was living off rich men. Described in the press of the day as "a lady with more charm than virtue", using the name Dot King, she was soon noticed by New York's playboys and began to be spotted regularly on the arms of some of Manhattan's most eligible men at the hottest nightspots.

When the Volstead Act introduced Prohibition in January 1920, she became the hostess of a speakeasy and soon saw her name in the press – usually accompanied by the nickname the "Broadway Butterfly".

Sugar daddies paid for her outfits, and one – Dot claimed that she only knew him as "Mr Marshall" – paid for her apart-ment on the fourth floor at 144 West 57th Street, near Carnegie Hall and Central Park. "Mr Marshall" always visited with his lawyer John H. Jackson, who was referred to as "Mr Wilson".

"Mr Wilson" would enter first to make sure the coast was clear, then "Mr Marshall" would arrive. The three would have drinks, then "Mr Wilson" would make his excuses, leaving Dot alone with "Mr Marshall".

Alberto Santos Guimares, a Puerto Rican steel magnate, who would eventually loot his company and resort to stock fraud, befriended Dot and then moved in with her. Twice a week, "Mr Marshall" spent the night with Dot and on those occasions Guimares found an alternative berth. Dot paid for the gigolo's clothes and sent some of the money given to her by "Mr Marshall" to her mother, Anna Keenan.

However, unbeknown to Dot, Guimares was also romancing rich socialite Aurelia Dreyfus. In 1922, he beat up Dot for the first time and then made a regular habit of it. Her friends begged her to leave him, but she replied, "Someday Alberto will marry me." It was not to be.

On 14 March 1923, "Mr Marshall" came to pay a visit and gave Dot a bunch of orchids bound with a diamond and jade bracelet. He left around 2.30am the next day.

That day, Thursday, 15 March 1923, at around 11am, her maid Billie Bradford found Dot, clad only in a silky blue negligee, dead in bed. Her face was scratched and her mouth burned by chloroform. The intern who answered the call put the death down to suicide, but Dr Charles Norris, the Chief Medical Examiner, announced that it was a case of murder. He declared that the way Dot's right arm was twisted behind her back showed signs of a struggle.

He posited that the killer had used too much chloroform to subdue her during a robbery and Dot had died as a result. The time of death was estimated at somewhere after 6am based on body temperature and rigor mortis.

When police searched the apartment they discovered that a considerable amount of jewellery was missing – including a $15,000 ruby necklace, two diamond bracelets, a diamond-and emerald-studded wristwatch and other trinkets, adding up to about $30,000.

They also discovered love letters from "Mr Marshall", one of which read in part, "Darling Dottie, Only two days before I will be with you. I want to see you, O so much! And to kiss your pretty pink toes."

"Mr Marshall" turned out to be John Kearsley Mitchell, the married son-in-law of multi-millionaire Edward T. Stotesbury, celebrated in his time as the sole arbiter of Philadelphia's Four Hundred. He was arrested but later released without charge, although he was ruined in society. Guimares was questioned, but he told police that he was with Aurelia Dreyfus and Edmund McBrien and was released.

In the course of the police investigation, they discovered his fraud. Eventually, Guimares pleaded guilty to fraud and served three years in a federal prison.

In October 1929, Mrs Dreyfus mysteriously fell to her death from the Potomac Boat Club in Washington DC, after a party there the night before which she had attended with Edmund McBrien. He said that she had got drunk so he had taken her onto a balcony to get some fresh air. It was nippy so he went inside to get their coats. While he was gone, she either fell or was pushed off the balcony. In her effects was an affidavit swearing that Guimares had not been with her the night of Dot's death and that she had committed perjury. However, Guimares was not charged, and he died in 1953 aged sixty-three.

Death of Another Manhattan Good-Time Girl

Louise Lawson, unlike Dot King (see above), was not a native New Yorker. She was born at Alvarado and raised at Walnut Springs, Texas, where she sang in the church choir and played the piano. She was regarded as one of the best players of her generation.

Like many, she left her hometown for fame and fortune when she hit eighteen and headed for the bright lights of Broadway.

Six years later, fame was still a distant dream, although nurtured by $20 for work as an extra in the D. W. Griffith film *Way Down East* (1920) with Lillian Gish, and appearances in Florenz Ziegfeld's *Follies* in early 1921 which earned her $75 per week.

It was estimated that in her legitimate career she earned only $245, so in the era of speakeasies Lou found a way to earn a living by providing private shows for discerning, not to mention wealthy, gentlemen – men who could show a girl a good time for a price.

She was soon putting $500 a week into her savings account, and although it went against her Texan Christian morals, it was better than starving.

She also had stocks worth $12,000 for shares in the Brooklyn–Manhattan Transit Company, one of the three private subway and train companies serving New York City at the time.

Her sugar daddy was Gerhardt H. Dahl, the chairman of the executive committee of the Brooklyn–Manhattan Transit Company.

She lived in a luxurious apartment at 22 West 77th Street, around the corner from the Museum of Natural History. It was chock-full of the finest furniture and oriental rugs, a baby grand piano, original paintings and expensive vases. Police never found any evidence that she had bought any of these items herself. Her only companion was a pure-bred Cairn terrier named Texie.

On 8 February 1924, Lou Lawson was murdered in her apartment. Dahl, nicknamed "Jerry Doll" by Lou, came forward and said that there was no impropriety in his relationship with the young girl, although he did not totally rule out intimacy.

"Miss Lawson was an accomplished pianist, and I was interested in her talent," the married mogul told the press. "So as far as any other inferences are concerned they are cruel defamations of the dead."

Dahl said that he was not giving Lou $500 weekly and that he had no idea where the money came from.

On the morning of her death, two "serious-looking men" went to her apartment building, called The Monastery, and were overheard by lift operator Thomas Kane talking about a bootleg delivery for her.

It was not the first time that a delivery had been made to Lou's home. Kane remembered an occasion when she refused to let them in. "We brought gin and she wanted rye," one of the men told Kane. "You know how women are."

A mutual friend of Dot King and Lou, Charlotte Wakefield, told police about the earlier visit and how much it upset Lou. "She wasn't expecting any deliveries like that and shouted through the door that she wouldn't accept it," she remembered.

Lou was tied up with "silken hose and torn slips of filmy underwear," gagged with a piece of cloth and her mouth sealed with surgical tape. She suffocated to death.

Texie was tied up in another room and around $20,000 in jewellery was missing.

The case was never solved and the trail ran cold. However, one friend of Lou and Dot suggested a sinister explanation for Lou's murder.

"Dot and Lou were always together a lot before Dot was murdered," said Hilda Ferguson. "I always thought that Lou knew much more about Dot's death than she dared tell, and that she could have implicated certain people."

Louise Lawson was buried in the cemetery in her birthplace of Alvarado, Texas.

The Truth Will Out – Or Will It?

Hilda Murrell was an exceptional individual endowed both with green fingers and high intellect. The former was evident in her expertise as an acclaimed rose grower and the latter in her support for science-based opposition to what she regarded as dangerous developments in the use of nuclear power. In this context, she was a committed anti-nuclear campaigner.

Nearly thirty years after she was murdered, the death of the elderly rose grower continues to stir controversy. Hilda Murrell lived in a large house called Ravenscroft, near Shrewsbury. It was from here that she was forcibly abducted on 21 March 1984, with her body found three days later in a copse six miles away. She had been stabbed repeatedly and her clothing bore traces of semen.

When police entered Ravenscroft, they found signs of disorder, suggesting that the house had been searched and that a struggle had taken place. The telephone connection had also been tampered with. The initial assessment was that 78-year-old Hilda Murrell had surprised a burglar and grappled with him. He responded by killing her, putting the body into her car and driving to the spot where he dumped it, later abandoning the car. As more information came to light about Miss Murrell's background, so conspiracy theories developed regarding her death as alternatives to the idea that she had simply fallen foul of a burglar. For a start, she was due to testify before an inquiry into the problems involved in disposing of radioactive waste and she was in touch with several eminent scientists.

It was also learned that her nephew, Robert Green, a former Royal Navy officer, had worked in intelligence during the Falklands War. There was a suggestion that Hilda Murrell might have been targeted by agents looking for documents relating to the sinking of the Argentine battleship, *General Belgrano*. But, while conspiracy theories were rife, the coroner's inquest into her death, held in December 1984, returned a verdict of unlawful killing. The official view remained that the lady was the victim of a random burglary that went wrong. There, the matter rested for eighteen years until new developments in DNA technology stimulated a cold case review. Crime scene evidence was re-examined, leading police to arrest 37-year-old Andrew George on the basis that semen traces found on the murder victim's clothing matched his DNA profile. George was tried for the murder in April 2005. The prosecution contended that he broke into Ravenscroft while Miss Murrell was away but was taken by surprise when she returned. He produced a knife, stabbed her and then drove her body away in her car and dumped it. The DNA evidence connecting him to the crime convinced the jury and he was found guilty and given a life sentence, loudly protesting his innocence.

No doubt to the satisfaction of the police, the conviction of Andrew George was upheld in 2006, when his appeal was dismissed. But this official conclusion to the murder enquiry did not convince Robert Green, a man with an inquisitive mind and a strong desire to find the truth of what happened to his aunt. He was aided by an instinct for forensic investigation, which led him to challenge the accepted findings. In 2011, he published *A Thorn in Their Side*, a book that contained his detailed analysis of the evidence used to convict Andrew George. Green showed, in particular, that the DNA evidence was flawed, added to which was the fact that George could not drive. Hence he would not have been able to use Hilda Murrell's car to dump her body.

Green also made clear that witnesses' statements showing a pattern of strangers seen in the vicinity of Ravenscroft and suspicious vehicle movements were never investigated. The involvement of unidentified individuals in the events of March 1984 might suggest a search for documents held by Miss Murrell that were damaging to the Government.

In addition, there were anomalies in the interpretation of forensic evidence regarding the victim's clothing.

Michael Mansfield QC supported Robert Green in his quest for the truth, and in an interview with TV New Zealand's *Close Up* programme said, unequivocally, "This was not a murder carried out by a young man aged at that time sixteen, on his own – absolutely not." All of which leaves open the essential question of who really did kill Hilda Murrell? Meanwhile, a man who is, in all likelihood, innocent, remains in prison.

"We Only Kill Each Other"

Bugsy Siegel was not the romantic figure portrayed by Warren Beatty in the Oscar-winning 1991 film *Bugsy*. You would have to have been an idiot to call him Bugsy to his face, such was his violent reaction to what he perceived as an insult.

Benjamin Siegel began his first protection racket before he was a teenager, charging local stallholders in Brooklyn $1 or he would burn their goods. He met and befriended Meyer Lansky and the pair formed a gang of car thieves and ran illegal gambling dens.

Siegel began a semi-legitimate career as a taxi driver but used his position to work out rich pickings for burglary or robbery. With Meyer Lansky, "Lucky" Luciano and Frank Costello, Siegel began bootlegging in New York, New Jersey and Philadelphia.

On 22 November 1939, Thanksgiving Day, Siegel, his brother-in-law Whitey Krakower, Frank Carbo and Harry Segal killed gangster Harry "Big Greenie" Greenberg who, short of money, had written a letter asking for cash but couched in such terms that it appeared a threat to go to the police if he did not receive $5,000. Greenberg was shot as he sat in the front seat of his new yellow Ford convertible reading a newspaper.

When four gangsters turned evidence, Siegel was arrested. To protect himself, Siegel murdered his brother-in-law as Krakower sat on his stoop on Delancey Street on the lower East side on 31 July 1940.

In 1941, Siegel fell for the good-time girl Virginia "Sugar" Hill. In 1945, he began work on what would become the Flamingo casino and hotel in Las Vegas. At a cost of $6million the 105-room Pink Flamingo Hotel & Casino finally opened on Boxing Day 1946. The night was a disaster and the Flamingo promptly suffered huge losses. It was discovered that Siegel had been less than honest with the building costs of the Flamingo.

Flamingo was his nickname for Virginia Hill. Contractors ripped off Siegel, who had no experience in the construction business. Some would supply materials, steal them at night and then resell them to Siegel the next day. Costs mounted and Siegel became more and more angry. An honest building tycoon, Del Webb, became worried when Siegel arrived on the site and discovered more materials had gone missing. Siegel reassured him, "Don't worry, we only kill each other."

On 20 June 1947, after a night out, he returned to Virginia Hill's home, 810 North Linden Drive in Beverly Hills, and sat in the living room reading the previous day's *Los Angeles Times*. At 10.45pm, a mob hitman (reportedly Eddie Cannizzaro) opened up with an M1 Carbine. Seven rounds were fired and one of the .30-calibre bullets hit the bridge of Siegel's nose, blowing his left eyeball out of its socket and fourteen feet across the room, where it was found intact. No one was ever charged with the murder.

Dead Men Cleared of Murder

Four men intent on robbing the High Town Post Office in Luton hatched a plan whereby they would ambush the sub-postmaster and forcibly take his keys. On 10 September 1969, they drove in two cars to the station car park where they stole a van and then drove to the car park at Barclays Bank where the sub-postmaster, Reginald Stevens, 56, habitually left his car.

At around 6.10pm, they attacked Mr Stevens and, when he resisted their attempts to make him give up his keys, they shot him dead. The gang then made their getaway in the stolen van, returning to the car park where they had left their two vehicles. The toing and froing of the four bungling robbers was noticed by various bystanders who later gave descriptions of the men and their cars. Having sorted out their transport, the would-be robbers headed off towards the M1 motorway.

In the 1960s, post offices were frequently targeted by criminal gangs and, in the wake of the murder at Luton, the police began intensive enquiries which included questioning the usual suspects. One of the vehicles was traced to Alfred Mathews, a man with a criminal record, and the murder weapon, a shotgun which had been thrown onto a railway embankment, was traced to Michael Good, another member of the criminal fraternity.

In their round-up of likely suspects, the police questioned Michael Graham McMahon and David Cooper (whose real name was John Disher), who were already under investigation on charges of theft. Detectives also spoke to a third man, Patrick Murphy, and suspicions began to harden around them and Michael Good who made up the quartet. Leading the investigation was Detective Superintendent Kenneth Drury who enlisted Mathews and Good as informers, with the effect that McMahon, Murphy and Cooper were left to face the music.

The three were charged with the Luton Post Office murder and tried at the Old Bailey in March 1970. Mathews testified against them, giving incriminating evidence which sealed their fate. Addressing the possibility that Mathews had made up his story, Mr Justice Cusack suggested it was inconceivable because it would have been "wicked beyond belief". It was a phrase that would come back to haunt him. Meanwhile, McMahon, Murphy and Cooper were found guilty on 19 March, and sentenced to life imprisonment.

There followed many twists and turns, not least of which was that Detective Superintendent Drury, who had led the murder enquiry, was jailed for corruption on 7 July 1977. It was also shown that evidence which would have helped the defence case had been withheld. The strong impression was that the three men who had strongly protested their innocence throughout had been, to use underworld jargon, "fitted up".

A first appeal against conviction was heard on 26 February 1971, and was turned down. Then, on 13 November 1973, Murphy's conviction was quashed, but further appeals on 12 February 1975, 26 July 1976 and 11 April 1978 were dismissed. But a turning point had been reached, for in 1980, Sir Ludovic Kennedy took up the case. He had been shown accounts written in prison by McMahon and Cooper which set out their side of the story. He had no doubts that a miscarriage of justice had taken place and, for his book published on 26 June 1980, he chose a title which echoed the phrase used by Mr Justice Cusack at the murder trial, *Wicked Beyond Belief*.

Shortly after publication, the Home Secretary exercised his prerogative of mercy and ordered the release from prison of McMahon and Cooper on 18 July 1980, but he stopped short of issuing a pardon. The two men found it difficult to rehabilitate on their return to normal society, feeling that they continued to be victims of injustice. David Cooper died in September 1993, aged fifty-one, followed six years later by Michael McMahon, in Essex on 25 June 1999 – his fifty-fifth birthday.

A record sixth appeal, in what was regarded as Britain's most controversial miscarriage of justice, was heard at the

Court of Appeal in 2003. Counsel representing McMahon and Cooper's families said there could be no doubt that the convictions should be regarded as unsafe. The three appeal judges agreed and, on 31 July, *The Guardian* reported the verdict in a simple headline, "Dead Men Finally Cleared of Murder".

The Forty-Year Mystery

When her eleven-year-old daughter Brenda Sue Brown did not come home after being asked to walk her five years younger sister Patricia to school at Shelby, North Carolina, Gladys Brown began a door-to-door search on 27 July 1966.

The Brown sisters – there were three – had argued that morning over a powder-puff compact. After an hour of frantic but fruitless searching, Mrs Brown called Shelby Rescue Squad and they began to look for the pre-teen at 11.15am.

That evening, at 6.45, Brenda Sue's naked body was found in woods 150 feet from South Lafayette Street, not far from the family home. Atop her body were bits of tree and leaves, and her red and white dress had been folded with care and placed on the ground. A nearby rock was stained with blood.

A post-mortem examination revealed that the rock had been the murder weapon and her skull was fractured in a dozen places. Despite being naked, the little girl had not been raped or sexually assaulted.

Police assumed that the killer had been on foot and had two suspects – a black, mentally retarded thirteen-year-old called Robert Roseboro and a white bald flasher who had exposed himself to Brenda Sue's sister a few days earlier.

Local police believed that Roseboro had killed Brenda Sue, but they were unable to make any progress on the case and some believed that he was protected by a local crime syndicate. Two years later, on 22 June 1968, two customers arrived at 11.30am at Mary's Cannon Towel Outlet but the shop had a closed sign. They looked through the window and saw a naked and bloodied woman lying on the floor. Police were called and from the shop walked, hands in the air, Robert Roseboro.

The woman was the owner Mary Helen Williams and she had been beaten and stabbed with scissors. Like Brenda Sue, she had not been raped. Roseboro denied all knowledge of Mrs Williams's killing but after a two-day trial was found guilty and sentenced to death, later reduced to life. In 2006, after *The Shelby Star* ran a thirteen-part feature on the Brown case, Lori Lail told police that before his death on 26 June 2002, her grandfather Earl Mickey Parker told her that he and his friend Thurman Price had killed Brenda Sue Brown.

Both men had form for rape of a minor. On 12 February 2007, police arrested Price, now seventy-nine, on a murder charge. He continued to maintain his innocence until his death on 4 August 2012, while awaiting trial.

Murder in Mayfair

Mayfair's club scene attracted unwelcome publicity in 2008 when 23-year-old Martine Vik Magnussen was raped and strangled. The identity of her killer has never been confirmed.

Martine left her home in Norway the previous year to come to London to study Business Relations at Regents Business School. There, she met fellow student, Farouk Abdulhak, the son of a wealthy Yemeni businessman. The couple frequented Maddox nightclub in Mayfair and they spent their last evening together on 14 March 2008.

They were seen leaving together between 2 and 3am in a taxi. Two days later Martine's body was found by police, dumped in the basement of a block of flats in Portland Street, close to where Farouk had been living. Enquiries as to his whereabouts suggested that he had returned to Yemen by private jet on 15 March.

The police appealed to him to come forward with any information that might help with their enquiries. There was no response, but friends said he had been called home on urgent family business. While the investigation into Martine's murder proceeded, Farouk remained untouchable. In July 2009, the Crown Prosecution Service decided there was sufficient evidence to prosecute Farouk for the murder and his name was placed on Scotland Yard's Most Wanted List.

A European arrest warrant was issued but there were diplomatic difficulties as Britain did not have an extradition treaty with Yemen. A further complication was that if Farouk was prosecuted in his own country, he might face the death penalty. An unnamed friend in Yemen said that Farouk had panicked when he heard Martine was missing and believed that a third person was involved. His father had, apparently, hired investigators to pursue the matter.

Farouk was educated and brought up in Britain and was intent on continuing his studies. He and Martine were part of a group of friends who liked to socialize in London's fashionable clubs. Maddox nightclub had a wealthy clientele, including foreign business tycoons, who could afford to book a table for an evening costing £1,000.

Martine's father used every conceivable diplomatic channel to achieve justice for his daughter but his efforts have been defeated by Farouk's disappearance. Her murder remains unsolved and Farouk is the sole suspect.

Ladies' Man Murdered by Unknown Killer

Joseph Bowne Elwell was a regular member of New York society. Handsome, or so it appeared, much of 47-year-old Elwell's looks were due to outside help including plastic surgery.

When his Swedish housekeeper Marie Larsen arrived at 8.35am on 11 June 1920, at his home, 244 West 70th Street, Manhattan, New York, she was shocked to find that rather than being luxuriously coiffed he was bald, and upstairs in his dressing room were forty or so wigs. Also in his bedroom were his false teeth. She was also surprised to find him with a .45-calibre bullet wound in his forehead – a wound from which he died soon after at Flower Hospital on East 64th Street.

As well as being a ladies' man, Elwell was a bridge expert, his book on the subject, *Elwell on Bridge*, being the definitive work.

The night before his death, Elwell went to the Ritz Hotel to eat dinner with friends, and then his party went to watch the Midnight Frolic show at the New Amsterdam Roof Theatre. By 2.30am the next day Elwell was on his way home in a taxi, alone. He stopped to buy the *Morning Telegraph* and when he got home, made several phone calls, the last at 6.09am.

In Elwell's three-storey brownstone mansion was found a collection of lingerie, and a detailed list of more than fifty women dubbed by the press the "Love List". The senior detectives in the New York Police Department took charge of the case and interviewed Ewell's entire harem of women but no further action was taken against any of them.

No fingerprints were found in the house apart from Elwell's and Mrs Larsen's. Money and jewellery were still in Elwell's house ruling out robbery as a motive for the murder. Police believed that the killer was probably a man, it being thought the .45 too heavy a gun for a woman to handle. The murder weapon and the killer were never found. Edward Swann, the District Attorney, said, "The evidence is entirely devoid of any fact that would justify accusing any man or woman."

The case led the art critic Willard Wright, under the pseudonym of S. S. Van Dine, to create the detective Philo Vance in *The Benson Murder Case*, the first of a dozen books featuring the foppish sleuth.

The Iron Curtain Mystery . . .

Former nurse Stanislaw Sykut took his cob to be shod at the local blacksmiths at Cefn Hendre near Llandeilo, Wales, on 14 December 1953. With his partner, Michail Onufreczyk, a former sergeant-major in the Polish army, he owned a 120-acre farm in the valley. The business was not a success and Sykut claimed that Onufreczyk, known locally as Mr Whiskers because of his bushy beard (and probable inability of anyone to pronounce his name), bullied him.

He had complained to the police and had a solicitor draw up a document to dissolve the partnership. On 30 December, the local bobby made a routine visit to the farm and was told that Sykut had gone to London for a fortnight.

When mid-January came around, there was no sign of Sykut. This time Onufreczyk claimed that on 18 December, Sykut had left with three Poles after receiving a down payment of £450 for the farm with the balance due in May.

When Sykut's post remained uncollected Onufreczyk said that he thought his ex-partner had gone behind the Iron Curtain to be with his wife. Dissatisfied with Onufreczyk's explanation, the police searched the farm. They found 2,000 tiny blood specks on the walls and ceilings and a large blood-stain on the Welsh dresser. There was no body to be found. Despite this, Onufreczyk was arrested on 19 August 1954, and charged with the murder of his partner.

In November the trial began in Swansea; it led to the first conviction in modern times of a murder on land in which there was no body. Onufreczyk was sentenced to death on 1 December. Lord Goddard, the Lord Chief Justice, explained, "The fact of death can be proved, by circumstantial evidence, that is to say by evidence of facts which lead to one conclusion, provided that the jury are satisfied and are warned that the evidence must lead into one conclusion only."

Despite the evidence, Onufreczyk was reprieved and sentenced to life imprisonment on 24 January 1955. The Home Secretary Gwilym Lloyd George said that he was afraid if the death penalty was carried out someone might come forward from behind the Iron Curtain and claim to be Sykut. Onufreczyk, who spoke almost no English, spent his time in prison playing chess and was released on 26 May 1966. The following year, on Good Friday, he was killed in a hit and run in Bradford as he was leaving Mass.

Regicide in Siam – Or Was It Suicide?

On the evening of 8 June 1946, King Rama VIII Ananda Mahidol, the twenty-year-old monarch of Siam, informed the court doctor that he was feeling unwell. He had spent most of his life in Switzerland and found the heat and humidity oppressing.

The doctor prescribed sleeping pills and castor oil to be taken in the morning. At 6am, Princess Mahidol, his mother, woke the king and brought him water, milk and brandy to wash down the castor oil. He felt much better and at 8.30am a page, But Pathamasarin, gave the monarch a newspaper and some orange juice. His other page, Chit Singhaseni, was off duty.

The king returned to bed. At 9am, the king's brother Prince Bhoomipol visited but reported that he was dozing. At 9.20am, a shot was heard and the king's mother, brother, nanny and doctor rushed to his bedroom to find him lying dead in bed, a bullet hole over his right eyebrow.

The king's Colt .45 was near his left hand. The first thought of those in the palace was suicide. Prime Minister Pridi announced that the death had been an accident. He also announced an enquiry into the king's death but many believed that he had had a hand in the fatality.

On 7 November 1947, Pridi was deposed in a coup and fled to Singapore. The new regime named Pridi and Lieutenant Vacharachai as the prime suspects in what was now called a murder. Senator Chaleo Patoomros, the king's secretary, and pages But Pathamasarin and Chit Singhaseni were arrested and charged with conspiracy to murder the king. Their trial opened on 28 September 1948, with all three pleading not guilty. The trial lasted until 9 May 1951. On 27 September, the court delivered its verdict: the king had been assassinated.

Chaleo Patoomros and But Pathamasarin were acquitted but Chit Singhaseni was found guilty of aiding the unknown assassin and sentenced to death. Chit appealed his sentence and the prosecution appealed the acquittals. The appeal court confirmed Chit's sentence but also instituted guilty verdicts against the other two. At 4am on 17 February 1955, all three were strapped to crosses and machine-gunned to death. Was the king murdered or did he commit suicide? The truth is still not known.

"Dey've Kilt Massa! Dey've Kilt Massa!"

One of Hollywood's earliest murder mysteries began on 2 February 1922, when the body of Irish-born director William Desmond Taylor was discovered by his butler. Taylor had escorted numerous film stars, including Mabel Normand and Mary Miles Minter, but had not avoided gossip that he was bisexual.

By the time of his death, Taylor was head director at Famous Players-Lasky, a Paramount subsidiary. On the evening of 1 February 1922, Mabel Normand visited Taylor. His butler, Henry Peavey, a black man who spoke for some reason in a falsetto, gave Taylor and Normand drinks and left them at 6.30pm. One hour and fifteen minutes later, Normand was driven away by her chauffeur. At approximately 8.15pm a sound like a car backfiring was heard.

At 7.30 next morning Peavey arrived and found Taylor lying on the floor, a dried streak of blood at a corner of his mouth (and two .38-calibre slugs in his body). He ran into the street shouting, according to the *Los Angeles Examiner*, "Dey've kilt Massa! Dey've kilt Massa!" Mabel Normand alerted the studio who sent executives over to carry out a damage limitation exercise. Eventually the police were called when neighbours tired of Peavey's hysterics.

Mary Miles Minter was a beautiful blonde ingénue being groomed to replace Mary Pickford. Her mother, Charlotte Shelby, disapproved so much of her daughter's relationship with Taylor that she threatened him. Discovered in Taylor's bedroom was a love note with a letterhead in the shape of a butterfly. On the wings and body of the butterfly was written MMM. The note read: "Dearest – I love you – I love you – I love you – – –" Then followed a sequence of ten kisses in the shape of Xs. The note was signed "Yours always! Mary".

She admitted, "I did love William Desmond Taylor. I loved him deeply and tenderly, with all the admiration a young girl gives a man like Mr Taylor." Her mother confessed to owning a .38-calibre pistol, but insisted she obtained it for protection against burglars, not to use against Taylor.

In fact, Mrs Shelby insisted, she had no objection to her daughter's infatuation for the director. The murder ended Taylor's life and Mary Miles Minter's career. The public tarred her with guilt by association.

King Vidor, the film director, took a close interest in the murder in 1966 and spent a year investigating the crime. He concluded that the murder was committed in a fit of jealousy by Charlotte Shelby.

Private Eye Axed

Daniel Morgan and John Rees ran a private detective agency in London. They dealt mainly with routine cases including, for example, divorce and repossession of vehicles. On 10 March 1987, disaster struck when Morgan was found dead, lying in a pool of blood in the car park of the Golden Lion public house at Sydenham. He had been subjected to a brutal attack and the axe used to kill him was left embedded in his head. While the dead man's Rolex watch was missing, his cash and credit card remained untouched in his pocket. Police suspicions were aroused following close examination of the murder weapon.

While the axe was a commonplace tool readily available from most hardware stores, it had been adapted for its purpose. The handle had been bound with adhesive tape, leading investigators to believe the attacker had been intent on ensuring he had the best possible grip to deliver murderous blows to his victim's head.

Investigators started to think they were looking for a professional hitman. Scotland Yard spent a million pounds on their investigation into Danny Morgan's death and, in the process, unravelled a murky backdrop of malpractices possibly with the connivance of police. At the coroner's inquest it was suggested that Morgan's business partner wanted to get rid of him and discussed ways and means of achieving this with assistance from corrupt policemen.

One idea put forward was to get Morgan convicted on trumped-up drink-driving charges so that his private investigator's licence would be revoked. Another, more drastic, suggestion was to have him murdered in a plot involving officers who would be paid £1,000 for organizing a hit. Three policemen working out of Catford Police Station in south London were arrested as a result of these allegations but there was insufficient evidence to proceed against any of them. The eight-day inquest heard further allegations concerning threats to "fit up" a police inspector and carry out a faked robbery.

More than a thousand statements had been taken during the course of the police investigation and one of the three detectives whose integrity had been challenged said the idea of a plot against Morgan was "laughable". Another officer, asked who he thought might have killed Morgan, offered no suggestions beyond saying that the dead private investigator had been "messing about with lots of women".

On 25 April 1988, the inquest jury took a mere five minutes to reach its verdict that Morgan's death was an unlawful killing. The coroner emphasized that many questions remained unanswered and there was no evidence to link anyone with the private investigator's death. It was also stressed that there was no forensic evidence, no fingerprints and nothing to substantiate claims made about the police. More than twenty years later, following the fifth enquiry into the circumstance of Danny Morgan's death, six men were arrested, three of whom were due to stand trial in April 2009.

In the event, after lengthy delays, all charges were dropped on 2011. An independent panel was then set up by the Home Secretary to review the case. Meanwhile, the brutal murder of a man axed to death and left in a public place remains unsolved.

New York's "Most Famous Mystery Murder"

Benjamin Nathan was fifty-seven years old and a prominent Jewish businessman in New York when he met his death. He owned a summer home in Morristown, New Jersey, but on 28 July 1870, he and two of his four sons, Frederick, twenty-five, and Washington, twenty-three, returned to the family home at 12 West 23rd Street in New York.

The next day was the anniversary of his mother's death and he wanted to visit the 19th Street synagogue in commemoration. However, his house was full of decorators and so the Nathan housekeeper, Anne Kelly, made up a room for the master in the front parlour on the second floor and for the sons on the third floor of the Victorian mansion.

Just before 6am the next day the neighbourhood was woken by the shouts of Frederick and Washington Nathan. Washington's socks and nightgown were covered in blood after he had gone into his father's room to waken him and found the old man beaten to death. Patrolman John Mangam of the 29th Street Precinct was on his beat when he saw the two distraught sons. The police found the bedroom awash with blood and an eighteen-inch-long iron bar nearby which had been used to smash in Benjamin Nathan's head. There were twelve separate blows to the body.

It seemed initially that robbery was the motive for the crime as a safe and a small cash box in the room were both open. Abraham Oakey Hall, the mayor of New York, offered a large reward for information leading to the capture of the perpetrator or perpetrators.

Others came forward to add to the fund, which together with contributions from the Nathan family finally reached a total of $47,000. The New York Stock Exchange where Nathan worked also offered a reward, of $10,000. The media, especially the Jewish press, ran many stories on the case, hoping it would lead to an arrest.

The sons, Frederick and Washington Nathan, were investigated and cleared of any involvement in their father's death. Some imprisoned members of the underworld gave names of suspects they believed were involved, but when the police checked out the tales they turned out to be a waste of time.

Benjamin Nathan was buried at Beth Olom Cemetery in Queens on 1 August 1870, the day the inquest into his death opened. The case described by Chief Byrnes of the New York Police Department as the city's "most famous mystery murder" was never solved.

Man Overboard

"The Belvedere Garden Tragedy", as it would be called, was a big news story in Kent in 1931. The village of Belvedere, near Erith, became the centre of a great murder mystery. Charles Lewis was assistant education officer working for Erith Education Authority. While out shopping one morning in July, he called in at his local pharmacy and asked for a supply of potassium cyanide granules. He explained that he wanted the chemical to kill flies in his garden.

A few days later, Lewis telephoned his boss at the education authority, obviously in a distressed state and saying that he would not be able to come into work. The reason he gave was that his wife and daughter were dead. When friends called at the Lewis's house, there was no reply, not even the barking of the dog.

The police were alerted and a search of the house revealed nothing untoward. Attention then switched to the garden and officers noted there had been some recent reconstruction work done around the pond. Spades were fetched and a cement layer was broken up, underneath which was a metal plate. When this was prised off, the bodies were discovered of Maud Lewis and her nineteen-year-old adopted daughter, Freda. They had been clad in their nightdresses when buried and the family's dog lay beside them.

Enquiries as to Charles Lewis's whereabouts revealed that he had booked a passage on a steamer and was heading northbound, to Scotland. This proved to be an eventful journey, the details of which emerged later. It seems that an alert officer on the bridge of the steamer heard a splash, which he feared might indicate that a passenger had fallen overboard. Scanning the surrounding sea, he noted a body floating motionless on the surface. It was now dark and the ship was turned around in an attempt to retrieve the body. By this time, the body had disappeared from view, although some clothing was salvaged which was later identified as belonging to Charles Lewis. The evidence pointed to Lewis poisoning his wife and daughter, burying their bodies and then drowning at sea. The question arises as to whether he fell, jumped or was pushed: a conundrum that will remain unsolved. Those who knew him described Charles Lewis as a retiring individual, well liked and respected although keeping himself to himself. While his method for killing his wife and daughter was clear, the abiding mystery was why? What was his motive?

Dead On Arrival

Debbie Linsley had been visiting her parents in Bromley, Kent, and took her leave on 24 March 1988, before she boarded the 2.16pm train at Orpington and headed for Victoria Station in London. The 26-year-old management trainee was on the first leg of her return trip to Edinburgh where she was working at a hotel. She never completed the journey.

The compartment Debbie sat in was located in a non-corridor carriage of a type being phased out. It meant that once the train was under way, she was confined to that compartment in the company of whoever else might also be a passenger. The sixteen-mile journey included numerous stops and passage through a long tunnel at Penge East.

At some point she was attacked and, when the train reached Victoria, a railway employee discovered her lifeless body. She had been stabbed with what was judged to be a long-bladed knife, and the blood spattered throughout the compartment indicated that she had put up a fierce struggle. With no means of escape she was at the mercy of her attacker.

The story of the young woman's brutal death captured big headlines in the newspapers of the day. *The Sun* carried the news on its front page under the heading "The Death Trap". This was a reference to the type of non-corridor train on which Debbie Linsley had been a passenger and the dangers that might lie in wait for a woman travelling on her own.

All of this had uncanny echoes of the first murder of a woman on a British train in 1897. Elizabeth Camp boarded a train at Hounslow bound for Waterloo where, on arrival, her battered body was found by a train cleaner. Her murder was never solved and prompted Major Arthur Griffiths, the author of *Mysteries of Police and Crime*, to comment on "the isolation of a passenger in an old-fashioned railway carriage".

In their hunt for the "Railway Ripper", as the newspapers referred to Debbie Linsley's murderer, the police took statements from fellow passengers who had seen a man leaving the train at Penge East and running down the platform to board another train. He was described as a stockily built man in his thirties, of "scruffy" appearance and wearing a shabby jacket and jeans. From witnesses' descriptions, the police drew up an artist's impression that was widely circulated.

The victim suffered five knife wounds and police conducted a detailed search of the railway track in the hope of recovering the murder weapon. The possibility of a breakthrough in the investigation came with the discovery of bloodstains at the crime scene believed to have been left by the killer. The hope was that a match might be found by comparing it with samples from known sex offenders.

Meanwhile, the arguments about the rail company's use of non-corridor trains and the threat this posed to women passengers continued unabated. A much-needed breakthrough in police enquiries did not happen and the murder was unsolved. Scotland Yard reopened the case in 2002 and a reconstruction of the incident was screened by ITV in the same year. In 2013, a reward of £20,000 was offered by the police for information leading to an arrest. To date, there has been no resolution and the "scruffy man" seen running away from the train remains unidentified.

Who Was Jack the Stripper?

A series of six unsolved murders occurred between Sunday, 2 February 1964, and Tuesday, 16 February 1965, attributed to "Jack the Stripper" and known as the "Hammersmith Nudes Murders". Jack the Stripper's victims were all prostitutes from the Notting Hill-Bayswater area; they were all between five foot and five foot three tall; they had all suffered from some form of venereal disease; they all disappeared between 11pm and 1am and their bodies were thought to have been dumped between 5 and 6am.

On Sunday, 2 February 1964, thirty-year-old Hannah Tailford's naked body was found under a pontoon next to Hammersmith Bridge by two brothers preparing for a weekend's sailing. She had drowned. Her knickers were in her mouth and her stockings around her ankles. She had last been seen alive on Friday, 24 January 1964, at her home in Pembridge Villas, Notting Hill, which she shared with her boyfriend Alan Lynch and her three-year-old daughter, Linda. At first it was believed that she had been killed because of her reputation for hosting kinky parties and the fear that she may have been blackmailing someone. This was later discounted. At the autopsy it was discovered she was pregnant.

The second victim's naked body was found at 8.30am on Wednesday, 8 April 1964, at Duke's Meadow, about 300 yards from where Tailford's had been. The location was known both as a spot for courting couples and a place where prostitutes took their clients. Twenty-six-year-old Irene Charlotte Lockwood's speciality was stealing a client's wallet as he removed his trousers. She had also appeared in porn films and, like Hannah Tailford, five-foot Lockwood, of Denby Road, Ealing, was pregnant when she was murdered. On 27 April, Kenneth Archibald, a 54-year-old bachelor caretaker, walked into Notting Hill police station and confessed to the murder. After a six-day trial beginning on Friday, 19 June 1964, he was found not guilty. He had retracted his confession claiming to have made it while drunk, and he was scared he was going to be accused of theft at Holland Park Tennis Club, Addison Road, Notting Hill, where he was the caretaker.

On Friday, 24 April 1964, the body of convent-educated Helene Catherine Barthelemey, twenty-two, from Ormiston, East Lothian, was discovered in a driveway near Swincombe Avenue in Brentford, Middlesex. She was naked and four of her front teeth were missing. There were traces of spray paint on her body and sperm in her throat.

On Tuesday, 14 July 1964, the Stripper's fourth victim, Mary Fleming, thirty, was found naked outside a garage in

Berrymede Road, a cul-de-sac in Chiswick. She was sitting and at first she was mistaken for a shop dummy. Her false teeth were missing; she had paint on her body and sperm in her mouth. She had last been seen alive at 1am on Saturday, 11 July. She lived in one room in Lancaster Gardens, London, with her two children. Not long before the discovery of Fleming's body there had almost been an accident in Acton Lane, which adjoins Berrymede Road, when a van pulled out sharply nearly causing a collision with another motorist.

Victim number five, Margaret McGowan, a 21-year-old Glaswegian, was found naked in a car in Hornton Street car park opposite High Street Kensington Tube station in west London on Wednesday, 25 November 1964. Again there were traces of paint on her body and sperm in her mouth. A front tooth had been forcibly removed. The tattooed mother of three illegitimate children, she used a number of aliases including Frances Brown, which was the one she used when giving evidence at the trial of Stephen Ward, a friend of Christine Keeler of Profumo Affair notoriety (see page 246), the previous year. She disappeared on 23 October 1964.

The final victim, 27-year-old Dublin-born Bridie O'Hara, had last been seen alive on Monday, 11 January 1965, in the Shepherd's Bush Hotel. From the post-mortem examination, it appeared that her corpse had been kept for some time before being dumped in undergrowth in Acton where it was discovered by Ernest Beauchamp on Tuesday, 16 February 1965, behind a store-shed on Westpoint Trading Estate, Westfield Road. Again there was sperm in her mouth and some of her teeth were missing. Police discovered that paint flecks on the women's bodies matched those of a paint spraying shop on the Heron Factory Estate. It was likely that this was where the women had been kept prior to their corpses being dumped. It seemed that the women had all choked to death while performing fellatio on their killer. The removal of the teeth led some to believe that further oral relief was performed post-mortem. John du Rose, in charge of the case, waged a war of nerves with the killer. He announced that twenty suspects had been whittled down to three. One of them, a married security guard from Putney, committed suicide in June 1965 saying that he could not "stand the strain any longer". However, despite intensive searches of the man's home police found nothing to link him to any of the murders. Two unlikely suspects were the boxer Freddie Mills, and Tommy Butler, the detective who investigated the Great Train Robbery. Butler was a small, bald, unmarried man who lived with his mother near Hammersmith Bridge. Born in Shepherd's Bush, he knew the area well and as a senior policeman would have been aware of the detection methods. However, there is no real evidence linking either Mills or Butler to the murders, which remain unsolved. Butler died on 20 April 1970.

Boxing Day Babysitting Horror

Catherine Wynter, nineteen, known as Katie, met Tony Bushby, a nineteen-year-old karate instructor, when they were both studying at a college in Watford. They began a "secretive" relationship and it progressed on Facebook where he created four fictitious profiles – Dan Tress, Cyn Darwin, Shane Pleuon and Krystal Stanguard. They all wrote flattering things about him.

Katie was taken in by the deceit and the couple met in secluded parks and woodland. She never introduced Bushby to her family. On 26 December 2011, she agreed to babysit her sister Sabrina's two children, aged three and four, at her sister's home in Borehamwood, Hertfordshire, while Sabrina went away with her boyfriend.

At some point that night Bushby came to visit. The next morning, Katie was found by her mother Joy Davis in a pool of blood slumped against the fridge. She had been stabbed twenty-three times including thirteen described as "significant". Katie died from a severe wound to the neck and one to her stomach that penetrated her vital organs.

The police visited Bushby's home after finding mentions of him on her mobile and laptop and surmising that he was her boyfriend. They found blood on the front door. Seeking to cover his tracks, Bushby explained the blood as coming from a pair of gloves given to him by Dan Tress, his fictional friend. Bushby destroyed his mobile and contacted Facebook about deleting a profile. He was arrested and charged. At his trial, prosecutor Michael Speak said: "He tried to suppress evidence that might incriminate him. We will probably never know precisely why he murdered Katie. We will probably never know how far in advance he intended to kill her."

The murder weapon was never found. He denied murder, but on 25 July 2012, St Albans Crown Court Judge Andrew Bright sentenced Bushby to life with a recommendation that he serve twenty-five years. "You derived sexual excitement from the infliction of knife wounds on her," he said. "You inflicted stab wounds to the top of each of her thighs. I am currently of the view that you pose a very real danger to women."

Death of the Ice Cream Blonde, or Who Killed Hot Toddy?

Blonde Thelma Todd won the Miss Massachusetts beauty contest in 1925, which led to a call from Hollywood, and Thelma made her film debut in *Fascinating Youth* (1926). That led to a highly successful movie career working as a foil for virtually every film comedian.

By 1934, divorced from her husband, she opened Thelma Todd's Sidewalk Café at 17575 Pacific Coast Highway, north of Santa Monica, with producer and director Roland West. That year she began an affair with gangster "Lucky" Luciano who "arranged" for her to become hooked on diet pills. Luciano began pressing Thelma to let him use a room at the Sidewalk Café for a gambling den, but she refused.

On 14 December 1935, Thelma attended a party at the Café Trocadero in Hollywood. Before she left at 2.45am, a waiter told Thelma that a man was waiting to see her. He was an acolyte of Lucky Luciano but Thelma refused his "invitation".

Thelma was taken to the Sidewalk Café by her chauffeur Ernest Peters, arriving at 3.30am. Another car pulled up and Thelma got in, next to Luciano. At 10.30am on 16 December,

Thelma's body was found by her maid, May Whitehead, slumped on the front seat of her Packard convertible in her garage at 17531 Posetano Road, Pacific Palisades, the sliding doors slightly ajar.

According to Dr A. F. Wagner, Los Angeles County's autopsy surgeon, Thelma Todd died of carbon monoxide poisoning. The coroner's jury returned a verdict of suicide, but this was overturned and a Grand Jury hearing ordered. The jury foreman, George Rochester, said: "I and other members of the jury believe a plot is afoot to show that Thelma Todd had a suicide complex, even though she had youth, health, wealth, fame, admiration, love, and happy prospects. It looks as if they are trying to build up this case as a suicide, but in the actual evidence, I have found nothing to support this theory definitely. I suggest the possibility strongly exists this was a monoxide murder."

On 21 December 1935, the Los Angeles Police Department formally dropped their investigation into Thelma's death. They agreed with the county autopsy surgeon's report and coroner's jury verdict that the actress died "apparently accidentally". It seems likely that after Luciano dropped her off at the Café, two men grabbed Thelma and put her in her car, switched on the ignition and closed the garage door.

Triumph for DNA

The bodies of two nine-year-old girls, Jeanette Wigmore and Jacqueline Williams, were found in Blake's Pit, a disused gravel pit off Webbs Lane, Beenham, Berkshire, on 19 April 1967. David Burgess, who had been a suspect in a murder case the previous year, was convicted of the two killings and given a life sentence.

The murder of Yolande Washington in the same area on 28 October 1966 had continued to vex the police.

The seventeen-year-old had gone to the Six Bells public house just before last orders to buy a packet of cigarettes. She was never seen alive again after leaving the pub, where her killer had also been drinking.

Yolande was stabbed and strangled before being dumped in a ditch. She was found two days later, on 30 October 1966.

Burgess was known to have been in the vicinity. In a nearby barn with a reputation for use by courting couples, police found bloodstained clothing belonging to Yolande, and a large-scale murder investigation was launched.

In their efforts to get an identity on the blood, the police took blood samples from all 200 male villagers between the ages of fifteen and fifty. The mass screening included nineteen-year-old Burgess but the results were inconclusive and the murder case remained open. Then came the double murder for which he was convicted in July 1967, and while in Durham Prison he confessed to Yolande's murder to prison warders. When detectives quizzed him in jail, however, and said they thought he was guilty he replied: "Oh do you? You will have to prove it."

Having served thirty years of his sentence, Burgess was allowed out of an open prison in Bristol on licence in September 1996. He promptly absconded and it was two years before he was recaptured after an armed bank robbery in Havant, Hampshire, in February 1998.

While in prison, he was also convicted of wounding with intent in 1978 and making false statements to receive benefits in 1995.

During that period a number of other unsolved murders involving women victims became subjects of investigation.

Finally, thanks to advances in DNA testing, the murder of Yolande Washington was resolved. The bloodstains on the victim's clothing were re-examined and a match was found with Burgess's DNA. He had used a penknife to cut the young woman's throat and, in the process, cut his finger and left behind the trace that eventually trapped him.

He was tried for the murder of Yolande at Reading Crown Court in 2012, and convicted. A further twenty-seven years were added to his prison tariff on 23 July. Thus a long-unsolved murder was brought to a conclusion forty-six years after its commission, due to forensic advances in DNA testing. There remained several other unsolved murders that the police were keen to question Burgess about.

The Miscarriage of Justice That Wasn't

At 9.30pm on Tuesday, 22 August 1961, married Michael Gregsten, thirty-six, was in his parked Morris Minor in a Buckinghamshire cornfield with his 22-year-old lover Valerie Storie when a man approached with a gun. He told Gregsten to drive, and thirty miles later they pulled to a halt in a layby on the A6 in Bedfordshire known as Deadman's Hill, in the early hours of Wednesday, 23 August.

At 3am, the man shot Gregsten and then raped Storie before shooting her five times and driving away in the stolen car, eventually dumping it in Ilford, Essex, where it was found at 6.30am. Storie survived her appalling injuries to describe her assailant and an identikit was issued.

Two cartridge cases belonging to the gun were found in a room in the Vienna Hotel in Maida Vale and the occupant the night before the murder was petty crook James Hanratty. The following night, a man called Peter Alphon used it.

On 9 October 1961, Hanratty was arrested in Blackpool and identified as the A6 killer. At first Hanratty claimed he was in Liverpool on the night of the murder, then changed his story and said that he was in Rhyl. Changing his alibi probably cost him his life as he was convicted and hanged at Bedford at 8am on 4 April 1962.

There was little confidence in the soundness of Hanratty's conviction and a public campaign began to clear his name involving, among others, the pop star John Lennon, his wife Yoko Ono and Paul Foot, the campaigning journalist. On 12 May 1967, Peter Alphon confessed to the crime, saying he had been paid £5,000 to end the relationship between Gregsten and Storie.

The Hanratty family continued to campaign for a pardon, and their hopes were raised with the advent of DNA testing. On 22 March 2001, Hanratty's body was exhumed, a sample of his DNA taken and compared to that from the crime scene. The results were not what the Hanratty family and supporters were hoping for. The results showed there was a 2.5 million to one chance that the samples came from someone other than Hanratty.

On 10 May 2002, Lord Woolf, the Lord Chief Justice, said: "In our judgement . . . the DNA evidence establishes beyond doubt that James Hanratty was the murderer."

Justice Delayed

Rachel Manning and her boyfriend, Barri White, parted company after they had words during an evening out at a nightclub in Milton Keynes. She walked away alone, intending to take a taxi home. At 2.43am she phoned White to say she was lost. He arranged, with his friend, Keith Hyatt, to pick her up at 3.13am outside the Blockbuster video store. Rachel did not turn up.

Her body was found two days later, on 11 December 2002, hidden in some undergrowth at Woburn Golf Club. She had been strangled and beaten about the face with a car steering-wheel lock. White was charged with murder and Hyatt with conspiring to pervert the course of justice. Both were convicted and sentenced to terms of imprisonment.

Unease about the convictions led to an inquiry by the BBC television programme *Crimewatch*. Investigators found flaws in the prosecution case which were supported by a re-examination of the forensic evidence. Barri White's conviction was quashed in 2007 and, at a retrial in 2008, he was acquitted. Keith Hyatt also had his conviction set aside. Two innocent men were thereby cleared of wrongdoing, which meant that the murder of nineteen-year-old Rachel Manning returned to the unsolved category.

There matters rested until chance intervened in 2010, when a student was sexually assaulted by a man she thought to be a taxi driver. She fought him off and was assisted by a passer-by who took note of the vehicle registration number.

Enquiries led to 41-year-old Shahidul Ahmed who lived in Bletchley. He was questioned and his DNA was taken as a matter of course. When this was entered into the national DNA database, a match was found with traces left on the steering-wheel lock used to kill Rachel Manning eight years previously.

Ahmed was sent for trial in February 2013, but the jury failed to reach a verdict. There was a different outcome when he was retried seven months later. It was shown that he attacked Rachel Manning when she rejected his sexual advances, strangling her and bludgeoning her with the steering-wheel lock. Then, on his way back to Bletchley, he hid her body on the golf course. Found guilty, Ahmed was jailed for life.

Thus, eleven years after the murder was committed, justice triumphed, thanks to the efforts of *Crimewatch* and DNA technology.

South Africa's First Serial Killer

Born at Seven Fountains near Grahamstown, South Africa, 22-year-old nurse Daisy Hancorn-Smith married William Cowle, a 36-year-old plumber, in March 1909. She soon fell pregnant. Four of the five children they went on to have died early, but their deaths were put down to poor luck. Only the youngest son, Rhodes Cecil Cowle, lived. Then on 11 January 1923, Mr Cowle suddenly fell ill and died of what was described as a cerebral haemorrhage, although one doctor suspected strychnine poisoning. His widow inherited an insurance policy worth £1,795.

Four years to the day of her first husband's death, she married Robert Sproat, another plumber, and ten years her senior. In October 1927, he began feeling ill and suffered the same symptoms as William Cowle. He perked up before dying on 6 November 1927, also of a cerebral haemorrhage and arteriosclerosis. On this occasion the widow inherited more than £4,000, plus an additional £560 from Sproat's pension fund.

On 21 January 1931, Daisy Sproat married for the third time. Her third husband was Sydney Clarence de Melker, a widower, and, like the two previous incumbents, he was a plumber. Towards the end of February 1932, Daisy de Melker, using the name Sproat, bought some arsenic to kill, so she claimed, a sick cat.

On 2 March 1932, Rhodes Cowle became ill at work after drinking coffee from his flask. The coffee had been prepared that morning by his mother. Rhodes's malady worsened and he died on 5 March 1932. Cause of death was ascribed to cerebral malaria. His mother received £100 from his life insurance policy.

William Sproat became suspicious of his former sister-in-law, and on 15 April, the police were given permission to exhume the corpses of Rhodes Cowle, Robert Sproat and William Cowle. Rhodes's body contained arsenic while the other two had traces of strychnine. The police arrested Daisy de Melker and charged her with three murders.

However, at her trial, which began on 17 October, at Johannesburg High Court, Mr Justice Greenberg (who tried the case with two senior magistrates, Mr J. M. Graham and Mr A. A. Stanford, and no jury) said that the Crown had not been able to prove conclusively that the two husbands had died of strychnine poisoning. "It does not convince me, nor does it convict the accused," he said. He did convict de Melker of the murder of her son and sentenced her to death.

At Pretoria Central Prison Daisy de Melker was hanged on 30 December 1932. Although the reason for murdering her two husbands was undoubtedly financial, why she killed her son remains a mystery.

"You Will Never Get Me"

The unsolved murder of teenage trainee hairdresser, Colette Aram, in 1983 achieved the distinction of being the first case to be featured on BBC's *Crimewatch* programme on 7 June 1984. The young woman's murder remained unsolved for twenty-five years when chance and new technology combined to identify her killer.

Colette's naked body was found in a field about a mile and a half from where she had been abducted in Keyworth, Nottinghamshire, at 9am on 31 October 1983. She had been on her way to see her boyfriend when she was raped and strangled. Intensive police enquiries established that the likely murderer had called in at a local pub for a meal. The landlady noticed blood on his hand and offered him a paper towel to wipe it off. Crucially, she kept the soiled towel and handed it over to the police. It proved to have sixteen-year-old Colette's DNA on it and also unidentified traces.

A month after the murder, the police received a taunting letter which contained details of the crime known only to detectives. Clearly written by the murderer, it mocked them with the message, "You will never get me". Extensive DNA profiling was carried out in the local area but no match was found on the database.

Then, in a chance occurrence in June 2008, a man arrested by police over a traffic infringement was asked to give a DNA sample. This was submitted to new familial DNA profiling and the database found a match. The car driver was Jean-Paul Hutchinson who was twenty and thus not born at the time of the murder. His father was Paul Hutchinson, a man with no previous convictions, and he now had some questions to answer.

Hutchinson, fifty-one and a former railway worker, was arrested and charged with the murder in April 2009. It was proved that he had lain in wait for Colette and dragged her into a car he had stolen. He raped her at knifepoint, strangled her, dumped the body and abandoned the car.

To all intents and purposes, Hutchinson led a normal life. Twice married and with four sons, he lived at West Bridgford, Nottinghamshire. Hutchinson entered a plea of not guilty on 5 October, but, faced with the incontrovertible DNA evidence, changed his plea to guilty at a pre-trial hearing on 21 December 2009. Thus, justice was done when a murder which had remained an open case for twenty-six years was finally resolved.

Thanks to the quick thinking of a pub landlady, advanced DNA profiling techniques and police cold case review procedures, the "*Crimewatch* Killer", as he was dubbed by the press, was captured and jailed for life at Nottingham Crown Court on 25 January 2010.

Hutchinson refused to explain why he had murdered Colette and her family were never to know, as on 11 October 2010, Hutchinson was found unconscious in his cell at Nottingham Prison. He died in an ambulance on the way to hospital. A post-mortem examination was inconclusive.

"I'm Murdered!"

The Hogg sisters, Anne and Caroline, both spinsters, lived in a villa in Camberley, Surrey. They were known for their eccentric ways and local residents referred to their dress style as "shabby untidiness". Apart from a home help and the weekly services of a gardener, there were few visitors to the house.

On the afternoon of 11 June 1906, Caroline, the younger of the two, ran towards a neighbouring house, blood streaming from her head and throat and shouting, "I'm murdered! I'm murdered!" Police were called to the scene and in the house they found Anne Hogg's body lying in a pool of blood with her throat cut. The savage wound had nearly severed her head and, in addition, there were blunt force injuries to her skull. Her body was still warm and clasped loosely in her hand was a hammer.

In an age with very little in the way of forensic science, police struggled to understand what had happened. Caroline's explanation was that, after taking an afternoon walk, she and her sister returned to the house. As was her custom, Caroline retired for a nap and was awakened when she heard her sister screaming downstairs. She rushed down and saw a strange man who clubbed her unconscious. When she came round, she rushed out into the road. The time was between 4 and 4.30pm.

A curious feature was the hammer, the handle of which was broken, that lay in the hand of the dead woman as if someone else had placed it there. A search of the house and surrounding area failed to turn up the knife which had been used in the attack. The hammer was later identified as the property of a builder working nearby who reported that some of his tools had been stolen.

There were inconsistencies in Caroline's account of events including three witnesses who claimed to have seen the sisters in and around the house at the time she said they were out walking. There were, of course, plenty of theories voiced locally about what had taken place. One was that Caroline had killed

Anne and made a cut in her own throat to make it look as if a third party was involved.

At the inquest, dressed in black and heavily veiled, Caroline gave evidence. She described the man she claimed to have seen as a "sort of bricklayer" and said that he had demanded money. Professor Augustus Pepper, who gave expert testimony, stated his belief that Caroline's evidence was "not at all reliable". The jury returned a verdict of wilful murder by a person or persons unknown.

Caroline Hogg went back to live in the house where her sister had died. In a case that shocked the whole country, no one was ever charged with the murder of Anne Hogg. More than a century has passed and the case remains unsolved.

Who Was the Axeman of New Orleans?

During a sixteen-month period the residents of New Orleans lived in fear of attack from a maniac with an axe.

On the night of 23 May 1918, someone broke into the grocery store home of Joseph and Catherine Maggio on the corner of Upperline Street and Magnolia Street and attacked the sleeping couple with an axe before slitting their throats with a razor. Joseph Maggio's brother Andrew was arrested but released a few days later.

In 1911, three Italian grocers had been murdered with an axe and the police believed that the same fiend was at work again. On 28 June, grocer Louis Besumer and his girlfriend, Anna Harriet Lowe, were attacked with an axe at their shop on Dorgenois Street and La Harpe Street. The couple survived the attack initially, but Lowe died on 5 August, having accused Besumer of being her attacker. He was arrested the same day. The night of his arrest the pregnant wife of Edward Scheider was attacked with an axe. Fortunately, she survived the onslaught and a week later gave birth to a baby girl.

On 10 August, the Axe Man murdered barber Joseph Romano. In all cases a panel in the back door had been removed with a chisel before the attack. On 10 March 1919, Charles Cortimiglia was attacked in his bedroom.

The Axe Man was disturbed by the screams of Rose Cortimiglia and he turned his attentions to her, striking her once and killing her two-year-old daughter, Mary. For some reason Rose accused members of the Jordano family who lived across the street of being the attacker, and Frank and his father, Iorlando, were arrested.

Despite little evidence the Jordanos went on trial on 21 May, and were convicted five days later, with Frank being sentenced to death and Iorlando life imprisonment. In April, Louis Besumer had been acquitted of the murder of his girlfriend.

On 10 August, the Axe man attacked Steve Boca and on 2 September, pharmacist William Carlson saw a chisel being put through his door and fired at the door, scaring off the Axe Man. The next night Sarah Laumann, nineteen, was attacked as she slept but she survived. The last attack came on 27 October. Michele Pepitone was struck eighteen times in the head.

On 7 December 1920, Rose Cortmiglia, by now suffering from smallpox and deserted by her husband, withdrew her allegation, saving Frank Jordano from the gallows. On 2 December 1920, the widow of Michele Pepitone, the last victim, shot Joseph Mumfre dead in Los Angeles. She said that he was the Axe Man. She served three years of a ten-year sentence. The Axe Man was never identified.

Holiday Murders

Two British schoolteachers from Norfolk, Lorraine Glasby and Paul Bellion, set out on a cycling holiday in northern France in the summer of 1986. They stayed at *gîtes* in Normandy where they enjoyed relaxing in the sun and catching up on their reading. Sadly, this idyllic vacation was to end in tragedy.

The couple disappeared in August and remained unseen for six weeks. They were last seen at 1.30pm on 16 August, at the Café de Plomb in Lauziers. They spoke to the proprietor, telling him they were English teachers cycling to St Malo. Lauziers is situated on the Atlantic coast near La Rochelle.

The surrounding area is known as Green Venice on account of the network of canals shaded by trees. The area also has a reputation for superstition, including local inhabitants with a belief in *le mauvais œil* or evil eye.

The teachers were reported missing on 8 September when they failed to turn up for work at the schools in Norfolk where they taught. As the days passed with no news of the missing couple, Lorraine Glasby's parents went to France in their own bid to find them. Then, on 1 October, a local hunter out with his dog found two bodies in a maize field. They were identified three days later as the missing pair, partially clothed, bound back to back and gagged. Both had been shot in the head. There was no sign of their possessions or of their bicycles. The fact that police allowed sightseers to mill around close to the crime scene went against accepted principles of investigation.

There was criticism in the British media about the attitude of the French police and the number of tourists who became murder victims in unsolved cases. "Can Holiday Britons Really Feel Safe in France Today?" was a headline in the *Sunday Express*.

A coroner's inquest held at Diss in Norfolk in 1987 recorded verdicts of unlawful killing. The deaths were described as executions. The record of the French police in failing to identify suspects in the numerous murders of British tourists continued to be a source of comment in the press. In the space of seven years there had been fifteen murders, which remained unsolved. The deaths of Lorraine Glasby and Paul Bellion fell into that category and remained so. In 2006, the French police made the decision to close the file on the two murders that had occurred twenty years previously.

An Enduring Mystery

At 12.20pm on 20 February 1908, schoolmaster Robert George Spurgeon was walking on Southborne Cliff, Bournemouth, with some of his charges when one of the boys pointed out something in a sandy hollow abutting the cliff edge. Mr Spurgeon looked closer and made out the figure of a woman, but it was not until he went up to her that he realized that rather than drunk or asleep, she was in fact dead.

The Coastguard was summoned along with a local doctor, a physician called Facey, who performed an on-the-spot examination. She had, he opined, been dead for some hours.

In her mouth were stuffed two handkerchiefs, one of which bore the legend "E. Sherriff". Apart from a ring on the left hand there was nothing of value on the body, although she was known to wear many items of jewellery. It was when the body was stripped that the injuries became apparent. The left side of her chest had been flattened and one of her ribs broken. The internal injuries and bleeding had led to her death. It seemed that they had been caused by kicking or being knelt on.

The handkerchiefs had been stuffed in her mouth, it seemed, to quieten her. The victim was identified as 35-year-old Miss Emma Sherriff, a retired ladies' maid who was known to be timid and shy. She was described as "precise in her habits and neat in her appearance". She had no male friends apart from one – 21-year-old John Francis McGuire. They had what was called a brother and sister relationship and had never been known to have the slightest disagreement about anything. She lived above a shop at 80 Palmerston Road, Boscombe. She lived on a small investment and from dressmaking.

On 19 February, she had been reported missing by Mr McGuire who had become a picture dealer on leaving the Life Guards. Miss Sherriff was also a friend of Mrs McGuire, the former soldier's mother. A week later, Miss Sherriff's watch, chain, bangle and two rings that had vanished mysteriously turned up. Other jewellery appeared between books on the piano. The police suspected that there was more to Mr McGuire than mere concern for a friend, and he was arrested. They surmised that he had killed her for her money or jewellery. He had demanded money and when she refused he battered her to death. He hauled the body to where the schoolboys and Mr Spurgeon had found it.

After the murder McGuire had hightailed it back to his home in Denbigh Street, Pimlico, London, to establish his alibi before reporting Miss Sherriff missing. His trial began at

Winchester Assizes in May 1908. Prosecuting were Mr Radcliffe, KC, and Raymond Asquith, the son of the Prime Minister. The police believed that McGuire had left London via Waterloo at 4.10pm, committed the murder and then caught the 8.50pm return from Christchurch. Mr McGuire challenged the witnesses who had placed him near the crime scene, claiming that they were all mistaken. Prosecuting counsel summed up the case over one hour and forty minutes during which time the prisoner in the dock looked bored and uninterested, toying with a pencil and paper that he had been given, although he did not make any notes. The jury deliberated for three hours but was dismissed when it could not reach a verdict – ten being for an acquittal and only two for a conviction. A second trial was scheduled for the November assizes but the prosecution dropped the case and Mr McGuire walked free. The case remains unsolved.

The Essex Boys Murders

On Christmas Eve 1968, market trader Brian Rolfe was found dead in a grey Austin van parked in a lay-by on the A13 in Essex. His head had been bashed in and cause of death was a fractured skull.

On Boxing Day, Mr Rolfe's pregnant wife Lorraine, twenty-three, and her nineteen-year-old unemployed toyboy John Kennedy were charged with murder. The couple had run away to Birmingham some time earlier, but Lorraine, already a mother of three, had discovered that she was pregnant with her husband's child and returned to him.

Kennedy demanded that she leave her husband, but Lorraine stayed, and the night before Christmas, Kennedy crept into their home at Linwood Drive, Basildon, and smashed Mr Rolfe with a ten-pin bowling skittle that weighed almost four pounds. The couple was charged, at Maidstone in March 1969, with murder and attempting to fake a robbery.

Both pleaded not guilty. John Kennedy was found guilty of murder and given a concurrent sentence of seven years for breaking and entering and theft. On 7 June 1969, while still in

Holloway, Lorraine Rolfe gave birth to a son that she named Craig. The child grew up to fall into a bad crowd and was a juvenile delinquent. He became a drug dealer and a leading member of the Essex Boys gang.

With his friends, Pat Tate, thirty-seven, and Tony Tucker, thirty-eight, Rolfe was the supplier of the ecstasy tablet that resulted in the death of Leah Betts at Raquels nightclub in Basildon, Essex. They were also responsible for the murder of at least one man who fell foul of them.

On 6 December 1995, the three thugs were lured in their Range Rover to the deserted Workhouse Lane, Rettendon, on the pretext of a lucrative drug deal. As they sat waiting to meet a contact they were blasted to death with a shotgun. Drug dealer and friend of the trio Darren Nicholls became a super-grass and named engineer Jack Whomes, thirty-six, and mechanic Michael Steele, fifty-four, as the killers despite there being no physical evidence to link the men to the crime scene. Nicholls said that he had dropped the killers off and collected them after the deed. Nicholls and his wife were each given a new identity for his troubles. Steele and Whomes were jailed for life on 20 January 1998. They still protest their innocence. Appeals were denied in 2006, and on 29 February 2012.

"The Light That Failed"

Ronald Colman was the leading man in a film called *The Light That Failed*, screened at the Odeon Cinema in Bristol on 29 May 1946. The film had a war theme and featured a number of shooting sequences.

During the course of the evening, some real shooting took place in the cinema office. Two men bent on stealing the night's takings were surprised by the cinema manager, Robert Parrington Jackson, who unexpectedly walked in on them. The robbers' reaction was to shoot and kill the manager and escape from the scene. The gunfire in the office may well have been masked by the gunfire on the screen.

The murder remained unsolved for forty-seven years until a man walked into a police station in Salisbury and made a confession. It was a second-hand confession, because Jeff Fisher reported that his late father, Billy "the fish" Fisher, had committed the cinema murder.

The story was that Billy Fisher, accompanied by Nukey Leonard, travelled from South Wales to Bristol intent on robbery. When the plan went wrong, they fled from the scene. There were reports that the murder weapon, a .45 revolver, had been found half a mile from the cinema.

Fisher had confessed the crime to his family prior to his death in a nursing home in 1989. The police were satisfied that the admission was genuine because the report contained details not made public at the time. The cinema murder remained a mystery until the *Western Daily Press* published a report about the surprise confession in 1993.

A *Midsomer Murder*

At 8.15pm on 7 January 2004, the quiet of Furneux Pelham was shattered by the sound of a gunshot. Residents of this peaceful Hertfordshire village thought it was a car backfiring and dismissed it as such. They were shocked next morning when the pyjama-clad body of Lieutenant-Colonel Robert "Riley" Workman was discovered lying on his doorstep.

Workman, an 83-year-old man with a distinguished war record, had been killed with a 12-bore shotgun fired at close range. There were mysteries surrounding his death including an anonymous telephone call requesting an ambulance to be sent to the Colonel's home.

Enquiries into the murder victim's background revealed that he had led a secret life participating in London's gay community in the 1950s. This fuelled suggestions that his killing might have had a sexual motive. He was a widower living on his own and, as far as was known, enjoyed an uneventful life.

The identity of the mystery telephone caller was never established and the circumstances surrounding Colonel Workman's death remained unsolved for eight years. Then, in 2012, an unguarded boast by a man serving a prison sentence for murder led to the identification of the hitman.

Thirty-three-year-old Christopher Docherty-Puncheon was serving a life sentence in Bedford Prison for a killing he had committed in 2004, for which he was convicted in February 2006. His victim on that occasion was his friend, 21-year-old Fred Moss. Now, he confessed to a fellow prisoner that he had killed Colonel Workman in the Furneux Pelham shooting. He said that the colonel was a homosexual who had, as he put it, "tried it on" with Moss. He confronted Workman on his doorstep and, after an argument, shot him dead. He claimed to have had a homosexual relationship with him.

Docherty-Puncheon was a gamekeeper and he was known to have done odd jobs for Colonel Workman. After the shooting, police questioned him but there were no grounds for detaining him. In his prison cell confession, he bragged about being a hitman. The police regarded him as "cold, calculating and callous".

Charged with the Furneux Pelham murder, he was tried at St Alban's Crown Court, when he complained that he felt he was caught up in the middle of a television drama. Already serving a thirty-year jail sentence, he was convicted of killing Workman by a majority verdict and sentenced to a minimum of thirty-two years.

The case was likened to an episode of the popular television series, *Midsomer Murders*, on account of the peaceful background to a violent crime.

Billy the Cockerel

Ronald and Mavis Chambers married in 1953, moved into a bungalow in Luton and lived happily together until 1965 when Mavis's mother died. Her daughter was grief-stricken beyond measure and, increasingly, she sought refuge in alcohol. As her consumption increased, she began to experience hallucinations and became abusive. She was drunk most nights.

Matters came to a head on 30 December 1971, when Ronald returned home from his work at a local factory. There was a history of violent arguments and the police had been asked to intervene. On this occasion blows were exchanged and a fight ensued during which Ronald fatally stabbed his wife with a kitchen knife. What followed would later be described as a plot worthy of Agatha Christie.

Chambers dug a shallow grave in the garden and put Mavis's body into it. He also despatched a pet cockerel called Billy, and buried it with his wife. The next part of his plan was to sell the bungalow, telling those who enquired after Mavis that she had been admitted to a mental institution. He then moved away to Blackpool.

In the ensuing months and years, Chambers maintained the fiction that his wife was still alive. He sent a joint Christmas card to her family in 1972 and wrote letters to her sister reporting that since they had moved house, Mavis had reduced her drinking habit and lost some weight. The pretence that she was still alive was maintained until March 1976, when her sister told police that Mavis had disappeared.

Police searches were made at the bungalow in Luton and dog handlers found the shallow grave containing Mavis's body, now reduced to a skeleton. A post-mortem on the remains showed that she had died from two penetrating stab wounds to the chest.

Ronald Chambers's story was that his wife had lapsed into chronic alcoholism and became violent towards him when he tried to moderate her behaviour. On 30 December 1971, a row developed over her accusation that he was having an affair and she threatened to kill him. She was drunk and wielding a kitchen knife. He said he was forced to fight for his life when she attacked him. They lurched from the kitchen to the bedroom where he pushed her and she fell on the knife, sustaining a fatal wound. He said he buried her body and did not disclose the fact because he did not think the police would believe his account of what had happened.

The man who for five years had maintained the pretence that his dead wife was still alive, was tried for her murder in 1977. Ronald Chambers pleaded not guilty, claiming he had acted in self-defence. As the evidence against him unfolded, it became clear that his crime and subsequent deception had been discovered purely by chance. He did not cooperate with the police when questioned, but chose to engage in banter when he referred to killing "Billy, the Cockerel", an avian pet he described as "a real character, a lovely bird". Billy's fate was to be put in a plastic bag and buried with his mistress.

The jury at St Albans Crown Court found 51-year-old Ronald Chambers, a kind of lethal Walter Mitty, guilty as charged and he was jailed for life.

"There's a Man Down There – and He . . . Hasn't Got Any Head!"

The Cleveland Torso Murderer (also known as the Mad Butcher of Kingsbury Run) was a serial killer who struck between 1935 and 1938 in the Cleveland, Pittsburgh, and Youngstown areas of Ohio. He killed at least a dozen times, but some believe it may have been as many as forty.

The victims were usually homeless working-class people whose names were never known. Only two or three were ever identified for certain. The murderer cut the heads off his victims (while they were still alive), usually dismembered them as well, and poured oil or acid over the corpses. Most of the male victims were castrated.

The first victim, an unidentified man, was found on 23 September 1935, in the Jackass Hill area of Kingsbury Run (near East 49th Street and Praha Avenue) by two small boys who cried, "There's a man down there – and he . . . hasn't got any head!"

The second victim was found on the same day about thirty feet from victim number one. He was identified as Edward W. Andrassy, twenty-eight. On 26 January 1936, Florence Genevieve Polillo was found at 2315 East 20th Street in downtown Cleveland.

Five months later, on 5 June, a male known as the "tattooed man" was discovered in Kingsbury Run. He had six inkings including one with the initials "W. C. G." and another with the names "Helen and Paul". His underwear bore the initials "J. D.", but despite an in-depth investigation the victim was never identified.

On 22 July, another unknown male victim was discovered

in the Big Creek area of Brooklyn, west of Cleveland, the only victim found on the West Side. Another unidentified man, the fourth, was found dead on 10 September, at Kingsbury Run.

The first unidentified woman, nicknamed the "Lady of the Lake", was discovered on 23 February 1937, near Euclid Beach on the shore of Lake Erie. On 6 June, a woman was found beneath the Lorain-Carnegie Bridge. She was believed to be Rose Wallace, who had vanished ten months earlier. Exactly a month later, a man was found dead in Cuyahoga River in the Cleveland Flats.

The venue was the same for the next female victim found on 8 April 1938. On 16 August, another female and a male were discovered at the East 9th Street Lakeshore Dump.

There were three suspects for the murders but nothing more than circumstantial evidence was ever available and no prosecution was ever brought despite the best efforts of one detective – a chap called Eliot Ness.

The Black Sheep of the Family

Reginald Birchall was the son of the Reverend Joseph Birchall, who was rector of Church Kirk at Hyndburn, Lancashire. Unlike his father, Reginald was not a good man – in fact, he went out of his way to cause trouble.

In 1885, he went up to Lincoln College, Oxford, where he shocked his fellow undergraduates with his spending, drinking, outrageous fashions and tandem driving. He left after eighteen months without passing any exams. Birchall bought a yacht and sailed around the Mediterranean before he began horse racing and then became a theatrical manager.

On 19 November 1888, he married Florence, a London actress, and they moved to Woodstock, Ontario, where they stayed in fine hotels, calling themselves Lord and Lady Somerset.

On 15 May 1889, the day after the last of Birchall's money arrived from England, he and his wife did a bunk, leaving unpaid bills. They returned to England where he began a scheme to lure wealthy young men to Canada with a view to buying stock farms. In reality, the victims were to be robbed and murdered on the journey.

In January 1890, Birchall and his wife had interested Douglas Pelly from Saffron Walden, Essex, and Frederick Benwell in their nefarious scheme. On 14 February 1890, the four arrived in New York aboard *Britannic*. Two days later, they reached Buffalo and then went on to Niagara where Birchall intended to tip Mr Pelly into the raging water.

At 6am on 17 February, Birchall and Mr Benwell set off for the fictitious farm. At 9pm, Birchall returned alone. He said that Mr Benwell had not been impressed with the farm and had gone to visit friends. Mr Pelly continued to ask Birchall what had happened to their friend and was dissatisfied with the responses.

On 28 February, at Clifton, Ontario, Birchall showed Mr Pelly a newspaper report showing a man had been found dead at Princeton with two gunshot wounds to the head, and a cigar case bearing the legend "F. C. Benwell" had been found nearby. To stop Mr Pelly going to identify the body, Birchall told him that he had received a telegram from Mr Benwell in New York.

The Birchalls went to see the body in Princeton and identified it, Reginald Birchall saying that he thought the killers were a pair of tramps. The authorities were suspicious, and when a pair of scissors that had been used to remove labels from the victim's clothes was discovered in Mrs Birchall's luggage, the couple was arrested.

Mrs Birchall was freed before the trial opened on 22 September 1890. The circumstantial evidence was overwhelming and Birchall was sentenced to hang on 14 November. The hangman botched the job and, for ninety seconds, Birchall twitched as his body convulsed before death finally took him.

Dangerous Road Ahead

La Route de la Combe d'Ire is a narrow, twisting road which leads to the foothills of the French Alps near Lake Annecy. It is regarded as a dangerous road because its single lane makes it hazardous for those who use it, including walkers, cyclists and motorists. It lived up to its reputation in September 2012, but for a different reason – it provided a route to murder.

On 6 September, a British cyclist who lived in the area pedalled his way up towards the village of Chevaline during the afternoon. En route, he was overtaken by another cyclist going at a faster rate. A short while later, as he approached a parking spot, he saw the cyclist again. He was lying dead on the ground close to a car with its engine running.

The vehicle was a BMW with British number plates and inside were a man and two women dead from gunshot wounds in the head. He also found a seven-year-old girl with severe head injuries to whom he gave first aid before calling the emergency services. Several hours later, after crime scene officers arrived, another young girl was found in the car, deeply traumatized. She had hidden in the back of the BMW beneath her dead mother's body.

The dead man was fifty-year-old Saad-al-Hilli, an engineer of Iraqi origin who had lived in Britain for twenty years and was in France on holiday with his wife, mother-in-law and two daughters. They have been staying in a caravan on the banks of Lake Annecy. All had been shot twice in the head except the seven-year-old girl who had been struck on the head, fracturing her skull. The dead cyclist, identified as a local man, Sylvain Moliet, had been gunned down with seven shots to the head and body. He was not thought to be associated with the Hilli family but, as the police put it, was a person in the wrong place at the wrong time.

The nature of the killings suggested the work of a professional hitman. There was no evidence of theft. Twenty-five bullet casings were recovered from the crime scene and the murder weapon was believed to be a 7.65mm semi-automatic pistol.

News of a murderous attack on a British family on holiday in France caused a feeding frenzy in the media. Newspaper reports were filled with theories about the likely motive, which included security-related killings, a racial attack by a lone psychopath and family feuding. Speculation centred on Hilli's brother, Zaid, who admitted that he had been in dispute with Saad but denied the killings had been arranged. He appeared on BBC *Panorama* in October 2013, when he suggested that the reason behind the killings had local roots. Zaid was cleared of all suspicion.

Another theory put forward was that the real target of the killer was the cyclist, Sylvain Molier, while the claim by witnesses to have seen a green 4x4 vehicle in the area where the shootings took place was used to suggest a link to the UK. In November 2013, French police issued a sketch of a man spotted near the crime scene by two witnesses. He was a bearded motorcyclist wearing a distinctive helmet. Efforts to trace the individual produced no further evidence. The view of French investigators remains that a professional hitman carried out the killings.

In February 2014, a former French policeman was arrested in connection with the murder enquiry. He had been identified by witnesses who thought his appearance matched the e-fit image of the bearded motorcyclist. In the event, the man was released after questioning, the police being satisfied that he had no links with the murders.

CHAPTER 4

Double Acts and More

In crime, as in other spheres of activity, some names are recalled together, reflecting either dependency and domination or, possibly, a partnership of equals. Burke and Hare, Edinburgh's infamous nineteenth-century body-snatchers, come to mind, along with the American duo, Bonnie and Clyde. While the body-snatchers murdered entirely for gain, the "Texas Rattlesnake" and "Suicide Sal", as they chose to call themselves, made a career of holding up banks and cafés, for the joint purpose of enrichment and the pleasure of killing.

Other criminal double acts involve a degree of dependency between the partners. Myra Hindley was in thrall of Ian Brady, as Martha Beck was to Raymond Fernandez. The relationship between the Moors Murderers involved a shared appetite for sadism, while Beck and Fernandez, America's "Lonely Hearts Killers", acted out a folie à deux *scenario. This is a form of communicated insanity in which two individuals share a delusional or mental disorder. Fernandez had suffered brain damage as the result of an accident and developed the idea that he possessed supernatural powers. He believed he had the gift of hypnotizing women and compelling them to fall in love with him.*

He preyed on women who advertised in the lonely hearts magazines and met Martha Beck in 1947. She quickly fell under his spell. Martha had an insatiable sexual appetite and was only too willing to respond to his enticement. They became partners in an enterprise to lure lonely women into their orbit, providing them with sought-after affection while relieving them of their valuables.

Fernandez played the Romeo while Beck did the fleecing and, in time, what started out as trickery turned to murder.

The "Lonely Hearts Killers" were tried in 1951, when Beck's intimate account of her life with Fernandez provided lurid headlines. Where his aberrant personality had been triggered by brain damage, she was largely motivated by lust. Theirs was a folie à deux *by any other name which ended in the electric chair.*

Another kind of double act is where an outwardly ordinary life has a hidden, parallel element. When revealed, it opens up another world, which may involve criminality. Gordon Wardell provided an example in 1994, following his wife's death at the hands of the intruders who supposedly invaded their home. He put on a convincingly tearful display of grief and said he just wanted the killers to be captured.

What emerged as enquiries progressed was that Wardell had a criminal background, which he had kept secret from his wife. While posing as a respectable married man, he was, in fact practising deception, which involved theft and the use of prostitutes. After her death, he played the grief-stricken widower to the extent of feigning trauma and using a wheelchair.

Wardell was performing a double act and leading a secret life under a cloak of conventional behaviour. This was not strictly a case of an alter ego at work. The arch exponent of that form of duplicity was William Heirens, a Chicago teenager who committed burglary and arson, eventually adding murder to his portfolio. In October 1945, he shot dead a woman in her apartment and scrawled a message in lipstick on the wall; "For heaven's sake catch me before I kill more I cannot control myself". This was a moment of personal revelation when, perhaps, he realized he was lapsing into madness.

Heirens was captured in January 1946, while entering an apartment block with likely murderous intentions. When questioned by psychiatrists, he denied being a killer and said the murders attributed to him were committed by "George". This was his alter ego representing everything that was bad about his personality. He was brought to trial and judged to be insane. Both he and "George" were given life sentences.

Close bonds and criminal partnerships are never closer than those between family members. The Kray twins, Reggie and Ronnie, set the benchmark for filial devotion while furthering their gangland activities in London's East End. Ronnie was the dominant twin and had made a study of American gangland culture in Chicago in the 1930s. While he provided the drive behind "the firm", Reggie supplied the business acumen. The twins established a Capone-style grip over their fiefdom, resorting to murder when necessary to protect or further their activities. Keeping it in the family enabled them to silence any opposition and maintain control.

Double acts sometimes end in acrimony while others simply fade away. Such was the case with Colin Howell and his one-time lover. After disposing of their respective spouses to further their liaison, they parted company and established new lives. But even the best kept secrets may be revealed in time and, eighteen years after committing double murder, Howell was plagued with a guilty conscience and made a confession. This put him in the dock and also flushed out his co-conspirator. The former dentist and his Sunday-school teacher escort were each found guilty of murder.

Double Axe Murder

Paul Sutcliffe was a teacher at a school in Wiltshire, married with three children and a newly arrived baby girl. When he returned to his home at Westbury after work on 30 April 1986, accompanied by three of his youngsters, he was confronted by a grim scene. In a room that his wife, Jeanne, used for her dress-making business, he found her battered and bloodied body together with that of the baby. Both had been attacked with an axe.

Early in the investigation, suspicion focused on a fellow teacher, Heather Arnold, who had an emotional attachment to Paul Sutcliffe. He and his wife helped Arnold when her marriage broke up, leading to a divorce, and she wanted to keep close to him. He was a family man committed to his wife and children and Arnold seemed to resent that.

Police suspected that Arnold might be the axe murderer, and a watch was kept on her movements in the expectation that she would try to dispose of the murder weapon. Officers disguised as refuse collectors kept an eye open for her disposal of rubbish. Their vigilance was rewarded when they found the charred remains of an axe handle in a plastic carrier bag and also retrieved the axe head which she had kept. Forensic examination of the axe linked it to the murder scene. When she was arrested, Arnold confessed to committing the murders, although she later withdrew her admission.

Heather Arnold was tried for murder on 1 April 1987, when she pleaded not guilty. After deliberating for more than seven hours, the jury, by a unanimous verdict, found her guilty on 15 April. She was sentenced to life imprisonment and was admitted to Broadmoor psychiatric hospital. During psychiatric assessment she said that she hated Jeanne Sutcliffe and killed her because she wanted to be closer to her husband. She believed that the Sutcliffe family planned to move house and feared that she would lose contact. Interviewed by the press after the trial, Paul Sutcliffe suggested that Arnold was envious of his happy family status.

Heather Arnold lodged an appeal against her sentence in February 1996, claiming that at the time of the murders, she was subject to diminished responsibility. She said that she could remember nothing about the killings. The Appeal Court was asked to substitute the trial plea of guilty to one of not guilty of murder but guilty of manslaughter by reason of diminished responsibility.

Or, alternatively, to order a retrial. The Court rejected the appeal, stating that although the defence of diminished responsibility had been available to Arnold at her original trial, she had not used it.

"They Did an Evil Thing"

On Christmas Eve 2012, Alan Greaves, a lay preacher and church organist, made his way from his home to nearby St Saviour's Church in Sheffield to celebrate Midnight Mass. In the course of a short walk, at about 11.20pm, he was waylaid by two men who had randomly selected him as their target for a brutal attack.

Mr Greaves, sixty-eight, was battered about the head with a pickaxe handle and left lying fatally injured on the pavement. Witnesses later described seeing two men shortly after the attack, laughing and drinking beer. When help arrived, the injured man was taken to hospital where he died three days later. That the attack took place at Christmas, a time to cele-brate peace and goodwill, seemed to accentuate the shock felt by the local community.

Two local men suspected of being the assailants were arrested two weeks later. Jonathan Bowling, aged twenty-two, had a history of violent offending going back to his teenage years. He had been convicted of threatening a woman with a hammer. On Christmas Eve, he had been accompanied by Ashley Foster in what appeared to be a random attack to grat-ify their urge to commit an act of unprovoked violence. Their victim, Alan Greaves, had the gravest misfortune to be in the wrong place at the wrong time.

At a preliminary hearing, Bowling admitted murder. When put on trial, and after the jury returned a guilty verdict, the judge's direction reflected the community's sense of outrage. "Why you wished to inflict violence on another human being on Christmas Eve is known only to you." Bowling was sentenced to twenty-five years' imprisonment and Foster to nine years for manslaughter. At the conclusion of the trial, the murder victim's widow made it known that she had received a letter from Bowling. She decided to read it and then handed it on to an officer at the South Yorkshire Police.

On the anniversary of her husband's death, Maureen Greaves held a memorial service at the spot where he was attacked. In an extraordinary gesture of forgiveness, she asked those in attendance to pray not only for her husband but also for the two men who took his life. In a statement to the press, she said of them that they had done an evil thing, "I don't know why and I don't think they really know why".

What a Day for a Bank Robbery

On Tuesday, 22 August 1972, John Wojtowicz, twenty-seven, Sal Naturile, eighteen, and Robert Westenberg tried to rob the Chase Manhattan Bank at 450 Avenue P and East 3rd Street in Gravesend, Brooklyn, New York. Westenberg spotted a police car on the street and fled before setting foot in the bank.

Most robberies are for greed, but this one had a more altruistic purpose – Wojtowicz wanted the money to pay for his boyfriend's sex change operation and Naturile to get his two sisters out of care.

In 1967, Wojtowicz had married Carmen Bifuco, a typist at the Chase Manhattan Bank, and had two children by her before separating in 1969. He began calling himself Littlejohn Basso and visiting the city's homosexual bars. On 4 December 1971, in a Roman Catholic ceremony at Greenwich Village, Wojtowicz "married" the tall and demanding Ernest Aron after meeting at a party. More than 300 guests attended the nuptials, which were filmed.

Following a series of suicide attempts, Aron was sectioned in the psychiatric ward of King's County Hospital. On 21 August, Wojtowicz went to the hospital to get his "wife" released but was told that Aron would have to stay there for some time.

The next day, Wojtowicz and Naturile burst into the bank as it was closing for the day. Naturile pulled a gun on Robert Barrett, the manager, as his partner began helping himself to money – $37,951 in cash and $175,150 in travellers' cheques. They assured the staff that no one would be hurt.

The phone rang on Barrett's desk and he answered, the gun still on him. The caller was Joe Anterio who worked in personnel in head office and wanted a cashier to be moved to another branch. Desperate to give a clue, Barrett suggested an employee who had been sacked for theft a few months previously. Anterio asked if anything was wrong and Barrett said yes before hanging up the receiver.

A call was made to the police and soon FBI agents were among 200 law enforcement personnel surrounding the bank, along with a throng of curious members of the public. Wojtowicz allowed the hostages to call their families. Finally, he told police that he wanted to speak to his "wife" and Aron was brought in a dressing gown from the local asylum. In return for this, Wojtowicz released a first hostage but Aron refused to see his "husband". Another homosexual friend, Pat Coppola, came to the bank door and Wojtowicz greeted him with a kiss. The crowd booed and jeered.

Back inside the bank, Wojtowicz began giving numerous interviews over the phone to the media outside, expounding his theories on capital punishment (for), his father (hated him) and religion (firmly in favour).

By mid-evening, the FBI had decided to play for time, cut the phone lines, turned off the power for the air conditioning and switched off the arc lights that had been illuminating the bank. The hostages bonded with their captors who allowed three pizzas to be delivered to the bank. By 2am the next day, hostages and captors were tiring of the situation.

Negotiations continued and at 3am the FBI consented to a trip to John F. Kennedy Airport. They planned a journey to foreign countries and agreed to release one hostage at each stop. At 4.45am, a convoy of cars began its way along Rockaway Boulevard to JFK.

An FBI agent drove them to a dark runway where they waited for the aeroplane to freedom. Wojtowicz and Naturile were flanked by hostages for their own safety. However, as the plane arrived, the FBI had no intention of letting the kidnappers go and the G-Man pulled a gun hidden under the car mat and shot Naturile in the chest, killing him instantly. Another pulled a gun on Wojtowicz who meekly surrendered.

Wojtowicz said later that he had surrendered because he was offered a deal by the authorities – a deal that they reneged on. On 23 April 1973, he was sentenced to twenty years in Lewisburg Federal Penitentiary and served five, being released on 10 April 1978.

In 1975, Sidney Lumet made the story into the hit film *Dog Day Afternoon*. Wojtowicz was given $7,500 plus 1 per cent of the film's profits for the rights to his story. He used the money to pay for Aron's sex change surgery, and Aron became Elizabeth Debbie Eden and married someone else.

From behind bars, Wojtowicz wrote a letter to *The New York Times* claiming that only 30 per cent of what appeared on screen had any relation to the truth. In 1986, Wojtowicz violated his parole and was rearrested. The following year, on 29 September, Eden died aged forty-one of Aids-related pneumonia at Genesee Hospital in Rochester, New York. Wojtowicz died aged sixty of cancer on 2 January 2006.

"Out of His Nut"

When smoke billowed out of a ground-floor flat at New Cross in southeast London on 29 June 2008, neighbours dialled 999. Once the fire was brought under control, the flat was entered and the bodies of two men were discovered. They were not victims of the fire but of a sustained knife attack in which multiple injuries were inflicted. In addition, they had been bound and gagged.

The victims of this murderous assault were Laurent Bonomo and Gabriel Ferez, both aged twenty-three and French citizens. They had been in Britain six weeks and were intent on pursuing their studies at Imperial College. The two young biochemists were well thought of and considered to be hardworking and academically successful.

The attack appeared to be motiveless but theories began to develop that they might have been tortured to gain access to their credit card PINs. Several witnesses had seen a man running away from the scene after the fire had started, and the police issued an e-fit image. A week after the gruesome discovery of the two bodies, Nigel Farmer, described in the press as aged thirty-three, homeless and of no fixed abode, presented himself at New Cross police station.

Farmer admitted setting the flat on fire but denied any involvement in the murders. He said he had been forced to take part. Further enquiries led detectives to Dano Sonnex, a young man with a troubled history, who said he had helped Farmer murder the two French students. Farmer's account was that he had taken credit cards from one of the students and gone out to draw money on a bank ATM. When he returned, he found the two men stabbed to death.

Sonnex said that on the evening before the killings, he and Farmer had been taking drugs. Farmer was angry, saying he had been mugged and his money stolen. The burglaries were conceived to make up the lost cash. Sonnex had a history of offending and had been released from prison just five months previously following a conviction for robbery and assault in 2008.

Both men were tried for murder in May 2009. In essence, each blamed the other and the jury was asked to sit through some disturbing evidence. The families of the two dead men had been vocal in their condemnation of the British authorities, particularly failings in the Probation Service to monitor Sonnex. The Home Secretary had offered apologies to the victims' families.

The murders were described as a *folie à deux*, appropriately perhaps, bearing in mind that the victims were French. This condition has been described as shared madness where two individuals are joined by a psychotic bond. It appeared that Farmer had separated from his girlfriend and was consumed by rage.

Sonnex said he was "out of his nut". The killings had not been planned but, in the circumstances of the robbery, Farmer's rage gave vent to extreme violence which was shared by his accomplice when they inflicted more than two hundred stab wounds on their victims.

Both men were found guilty of murder and given life sentences.

"Hello Sexy"

Army reservist Nicholas Fabian, a married man whose wife was pregnant, was involved in an affair with another woman. When his wife, Victoria, learned of his infidelity, she confronted him. Fabian's response was to plan her murder using skills he had learned as a soldier.

Around midday on 5 March 2010, Victoria put her eight-year-old son by a previous relationship in her car and prepared to drive off from the family home in Vigo, Kent. As the car began to move, there was an explosion, blowing out the windscreen and severely injuring the driver.

Fabian, who had been watching the scene unfold from his car parked nearby, ran over to help Victoria and her young son escape from the wreckage. The boy was unharmed but Victoria had severe injuries to her legs and was losing a lot of blood. She and her unborn child survived the blast but she was hospitalized for two months. An hour before the explosion, Fabian had sent his girlfriend a text message with the opening words, "Hello Sexy".

Forensic examination at the scene of the explosion and of the car revealed the use of a cleverly contrived booby-trap bomb. A British army issue L109 grenade had been placed in the driver's foot well of Victoria's car. A nylon line was attached to the grenade's safety pin with a fishing hook fixed to the other end. The line was stretched taut and trailed outside the car and hooked onto one of the tyres. The effect, once the car began to move and its wheels turned, was to pull the safety pin from the grenade and trigger the explosion.

Nicholas Fabian was charged with attempted murder and tried at Maidstone in February 2011. He had stolen the hand grenade while undergoing army weapons training prior to a posting to Afghanistan. Having survived her injuries, Victoria gave evidence in court, graphically describing the explosion and recalling the moment when she lost the feeling in her legs.

Described by the prosecution as "a fantasist and an attention seeker", Fabian was found guilty and sentenced to life imprisonment.

Country Legend Murdered for His Fortune

Banjo player David Akeman was a stalwart of the Grand Ole Opry in Nashville, Tennessee, and also featured on the television programme *Hee Haw* from 1969. He was nicknamed

Stringbean because he was six foot two and skinny, and while playing a gig in the 1930s the bandleader couldn't remember his name and introduced him as "String Beans".

In 1943, he signed to play with bluegrass legend Bill Monroe and stayed with him for two years, leaving to be replaced by Earl Scruggs.

In 1952, he became a joke-telling banjo player at the Opry. Had it not been for *Hee Haw*, Stringbean would have remained an undiscovered national treasure, known only to country music aficionados. Using his skill honed by years at the Opry, he quickly became one of the most popular elements on the show.

At 10.15pm on 10 November 1973, Stringbean, fifty-seven, began his second slot at the Opry. Unbeknown to him or his sixty-year-old wife Estelle, at that moment their home was being robbed. Two young thieves had heard rumours that Stringbean eschewed banks and kept his money at home and so they broke in to steal it.

In fact, he had more than $500,000 in various accounts. They couldn't find the money so waited until the singer returned to demand it. They listened to the radio show to keep abreast of where their victim was. Stringbean and Estelle left at 10.40pm for the half-hour drive home.

As they approached, Stringbean noticed that his home-made burglar alarm – a piece of fishing line stretched across the driveway – had been activated. He pulled a .22-calibre pistol from the bag that contained his stage clothes and approached the house. He saw a man and pulled his gun.

The other thief appeared and shot Stringbean in the chest. Estelle ran back to the car but was caught and shot three times in the head as she lay helpless on the ground, forty yards from her front door. The two corpses were discovered at 6.30 the next morning.

A reward of $25,000 was offered and a con came forward with information in return for a reduced sentence. On 16 January 1974, police arrested John A. Brown and his cousin Doug Brown, both twenty-three. They had got away with $208 in cash, a chainsaw and some guns. They missed $3,182 in

Stringbean's overalls pocket and $2,150 in Estelle's bra. In November 1974, both men were found guilty and sentenced to ninety-nine years in jail. Doug Brown died in prison on 8 January 2003. John Brown is still behind bars. In 1996, the then owner of Stringbean's house found what the Browns could not – thousands of dollars had been secreted in the chimney but by that time had been chewed by mice into confetti.

A Faked Car Crash

Claire Howarth, a 31-year-old blonde beauty, had just completed her two-year probation as a student policewoman with a promising career ahead as a community officer. She lived with her fiancé, Martin Forshaw, twenty-seven, who was a tactical aid officer with Cheshire Police. The couple were engaged and, in May 2009, planned to fly to St Lucia in the Caribbean to celebrate their wedding.

They kept their wedding plans to themselves and their colleagues were unaware of their intentions. Claire, though, could not contain her excitement and, on 7 May, sent a text message to a friend expressing her joy at the forthcoming event. But, within hours, Claire would be dead. Martin Forshaw was leading a double life, still seeing a former girl-friend, and had told Claire that the wedding was off.

She was distraught and an argument ensued. He attacked her with a hammer, beating her around the head and causing multiple injuries. Forshaw carried her, still alive, downstairs and placed her in the passenger seat of their BMW. He then contrived to drive through country lanes before running the car off the road and into a hedge in a simulated accident. He called the emergency services and Claire was taken to Royal Bolton Hospital where she died the same day.

Forshaw explained that Claire had not been wearing a seat belt at the time of the crash while driving at between 50 and 60mph. His account of what had occurred did not match the scene of the crash in which the car was hardly damaged. The windscreen was intact and the air bags had not been activated.

And it soon became clear that the severe injuries sustained by the dead woman had not resulted from the car crash.

Forshaw, who was known at work by his middle name Alex, was arrested on 9 May, on suspicion of murder, and he resigned from the police force on the same day. He had been in the force for six years and was regarded as an expert in self-defence. When questioned about the injuries inflicted on Claire Howarth, he said he defended himself when she attacked him with a mallet. Like his explanation of the car accident, this did not conform to the facts. His one-time fiancée had sustained fourteen blows to the head and neck.

When brought to trial, Forshaw pleaded guilty to murder, admitting that he had struck Claire twice with a hammer during a stop on their fateful journey because he wanted to "put her out of her pain". In his defence, it was argued that he had remained loyal to the mother of his child and, consumed by doubts, had opted to stay with her and cancel the plans he had made to marry Claire Howarth.

So, the policeman who killed his fiancée with a hammer and faked a car crash was sent to trial at Manchester Crown Court. He pleaded guilty to murder and, on 23 November 2009, was sentenced to eighteen years' imprisonment for what Justice David Clarke called a "brutal killing".

Trio of Traitors . . . or a Quartet?

Treason is regarded by many as the worst crime anyone can commit short of physically harming someone. In 1929, Harold "Kim" (after the character in the Kipling novel) Philby went up to Trinity College, Cambridge (to read history and economics), followed a year later by Guy Burgess (history; and a member of the Cambridge University Socialist Society) and in October 1931 by Donald Maclean (modern languages).

The trio were to become the most notorious spies in British history. Maclean wrote an article calling capitalism a "crack-brained criminal mess", yet in 1935 he joined the Foreign Office. Burgess became personal assistant to Tory MP Captain Jack Macnamara and later worked for the BBC.

He also variously worked for the Foreign Office's Far Eastern bureau and in the Washington Embassy, where he shared a flat with Philby.

In 1935, Burgess recruited Anthony Blunt, a fellow homosexual, to their espionage network. Philby turned traitor the previous year and covered the Spanish Civil War for *The Times*, where he escaped death when a Russian-made shell hit his car.

In January 1939, Burgess began working for MI6 and in August 1940, he hired Philby. In 1939, Blunt had joined MI5. In April 1944, the bisexual Maclean worked as Second Secretary at the British embassy in Washington DC. By the time he left in 1948, he had been promoted to First Secretary. In September 1948, Maclean was appointed head of Chancery at the British embassy in Cairo. The pressure of his double life grew on Maclean and he turned to drink to cope. One night he smashed up the home of an American diplomat and was sent back to London for psychiatric evaluation. Once "cured", he was promoted to head of the American Department in the Foreign Office in November 1950.

In August 1945, a Soviet defector had offered to name three moles working inside the British establishment – the man sent to arrange his defection was Kim Philby. He was also asked to find the traitor known only as Homer from a field of 700, but Philby already knew his identity – Donald Duart Maclean.

On Friday, 25 May 1951 – Maclean's thirty-eighth birthday – Herbert Morrison, the Foreign Secretary under Clement Attlee, authorized the interrogation of Maclean for the following Monday. After eating a birthday dinner prepared by Mrs Maclean, Burgess and Maclean fled England at 11pm that Friday night although there is still a mystery as to why Burgess went – Philby told him not to and it threw suspicion on others including Philby himself. Philby was tried secretly in June 1952, but the evidence against him was circumstantial. On 7 November 1955, Harold Macmillan, the Foreign Secretary under Winston Churchill, said in the House of Commons, "I have no reason to conclude that Mr Philby has at any time betrayed the interests of this country."

Remarkably, Philby continued to work for MI6 until 1962, when the CIA provided definitive evidence of his treachery. In January 1963, he, too, fled east.

In 1956, Burgess and Maclean were publicly paraded by the Soviets. Burgess was unhappy behind the Iron Curtain and died a hopeless alcoholic on 30 August 1963. Maclean lived almost another twenty years, dying on 6 March 1983, of throat cancer. He worked as a teacher and then as a foreign policy specialist but he, too, drank too much. Philby was very happy – he became a senior KGB officer and on a ski trip in 1964 began an affair with Donald Maclean's wife. Philby died on 11 May 1988.

In April 1964, Blunt (Sir Anthony from 31 May 1956) confessed his treachery but was allowed to keep his job as Surveyor of the Queen's Pictures for fifteen more years until his public exposure on 15 November 1979, when he was stripped of his knighthood. He died on 26 March 1983. There have been various candidates for a fifth man but no substantive evidence.

Double Squaddie Murder

Hotel chambermaid Mabel Bundy was murdered and her body dumped near a footpath in Hindhead, Surrey, on 4 July 1939. Thomas Mitchell, who worked as a kitchen porter at the Moorlands Hotel, the same establishment that employed Miss Bundy, found her corpse at 6.20am the next day. He spotted a bunch of carnations below her right arm.

Pathologist Eric Gardner autopsied the body at 8.30am and estimated that death occurred between 10.30pm the previous day and 12.30am. He noted a large amount of bruising to Miss Bundy's face and body. A punch to the jaw had been forceful enough to force bones of the face into her brain and kill her.

Alice Dopson came forward to say that she had been with 42-year-old Miss Bundy in the bar at the Royal Huts Hotel from 7.30pm on the fourth. Mrs Dopson's husband, William, joined them, but Miss Bundy left them when she was chatted up by one of three soldiers from the Second Battalion North

Staffordshire Regiment. Before closing time she left arm-in-arm with one of the young squaddies.

At 10.15pm Randall Snelling saw Miss Bundy and the soldier on Portsmouth Road and spotted that the soldier was carrying a bunch of carnations. He also noticed that two other soldiers were trailing the couple at a distance. At 10.50pm at the corner of Portsmouth Road and Tower Road, Walter Hack saw three soldiers who looked to be in a hurry – there was no sign of Mabel. Police visited the Army camp and the three squaddies were identified as 26-year-old Arthur Smith (who had left with Mabel), Stanley Boon, twenty-seven, and Joseph Goodwin.

The soldiers' uniforms were taken to be examined by the Metropolitan Police Force at Hendon, and the men were brought to Farnham police station where it was spotted that Smith had scratches on his face. He said that they had been caused by manoeuvres that morning. Bloodstains were found on Boon and Smith's clothing and the three were sent for trial at the Old Bailey. Smith confessed that he had had consensual sex with Miss Bundy and said Boon had suddenly appeared at his side and punched the woman in the face.

Boon then had sex with Miss Bundy and said he had put his hand over her mouth to stop her spitting at him. The two men each laid the blame squarely on the other. Goodwin was acquitted, but Smith and Boon were found guilty of murder and sentenced to death. Boon was hanged at Wandsworth on 25 October 1939, Smith a day later at the same prison – Thomas Pierrepoint dispatched both men.

Broken Silence

Colin Howell, a dentist with a practice in Coleraine, Northern Ireland, met Hazel Buchanan at the local Baptist Church where they both worshipped. Indeed, Hazel was a Sunday-school teacher there and also looked after Howell's children.

Both were unhappy in their marriages and they gravitated towards each other during attendance at church and began an affair in 1990. They engaged in sexual activity at Hazel's house when her husband, a policeman, was out, and used the pretext that Howell was teaching her to play the guitar. It later emerged that he sedated Hazel with laughing gas before having sex so that her religious principles would not be too compromised.

When Hazel became pregnant, she had a secret abortion and, inevitably, in a tight-knit community, rumours started to get round and hints of Howell's liaison with the Sunday-school teacher reached the ears of Mrs Howell. In her distress, she attempted to commit suicide. Then, in May 1991, Colin Howell called the police to inform them that his wife was missing. She was found dead in the back of the family car with the body of Hazel's husband slumped in the driving seat on 19 May. The vehicle was parked in a garage close to some houses on the Antrim coast.

Carbon monoxide poisoning was given as the cause of the two deaths and the inquest treated the case as a suicide pact. Colin Howell went on to build a lucrative dental practice and, when his relationship with Hazel ended, he remarried. Hazel also married again, taking a retired policeman as her husband. They embarked on their reconstructed lives, having put the tragic deaths of their former spouses behind them.

In November 2009, Colin Howell walked into a police station, and, no doubt to the considerable astonishment of the officers on duty, made a confession to double murder. He explained that God had told him to admit to the murders of his wife and his lover's husband. During the course of questioning, he implicated Hazel in the plot to stage a double suicide.

Howell said he gassed his wife while she was asleep at home while Hazel dosed her husband's meal with sleeping pills. With both victims incapacitated, Howell drove them to his late father-in-law's house where he rigged the suicide by connecting a hose to the car's exhaust.

On 18 November 2010, he confessed to the crimes when he appeared at Belfast Crown Court, claiming to be ravaged with guilt. The 51-year-old father of ten was jailed for life. The judge said the truly heinous crimes had been carefully planned and ruthlessly executed to eliminate two people whom he saw as obstacles to his adulterous affair.

In March 2011, Hazel Stewart (formerly Buchanan) was put on trial at Coleraine. In interviews with the police she had claimed that she was too afraid of Howell to stop him carrying out his murder plan. She claimed to be another of his victims. The jury, after two hours' deliberation, found her guilty of a double murder and she, like her co-conspirator, was sentenced to life imprisonment.

Thus, after twenty years the silence was broken and justice was served. The *Daily Mail* headline was "Life for Killer Sunday-school teacher sedated for sex to ease her guilt".

The Terminator

The "Terminator" broke into the Zaichenko family home at Garmarnia, Ukraine, slaughtered father, mother and two sons with a sawn-off shotgun and then set fire to the house on 24 December 1995.

Eleven days later, he murdered four more people and then, on 17 January 1996, the Pilat family at Bratkovychi, then one at Enerhodar before returning to Bratkovychi – in less than a month he had murdered four families comprising twenty people. He usually kept to a pattern of killing the oldest adult male first, then the female and then the children before setting the house alight to destroy any evidence.

Any witnesses were also killed to prevent them speaking out. The police determined to catch the killer and began a massive operation that finally led them to Lviv on 16 April 1996, where they arrested 36-year-old Anatoly Yuriyovych Onoprienko. He was living on Ivana Khristitelya Street, Yavoriv, with his cousin, and although he had once been treated for schizophrenia, to all outward appearances seemed totally normal apart from his collection of weaponry, some of which matched the ballistics of evidence taken from victims.

Police also found 122 items belonging to numerous unsolved murder victims. The authorities were surprised when

Onoprienko confessed to forty murders in four months in 1995 and 1996 and asked for another twelve killings beginning in June 1989 to be taken into consideration. He showed no remorse and added "There is no better killer in the world than me." He said that he regarded his killings as "a kind of experiment".

The son of a decorated Second World War hero, Onoprienko was sent to an orphanage after his mother died. He claimed that 70 per cent of all inmates at orphanages end up in prison. Onoprienko said that his last murder occurred on 22 March 1996, when he went to the small village of Busk, just outside of Bratkovychi, and murdered four members of the Novosad family.

Psychiatrists deemed Onoprienko fit to stand trial, though he claimed to have been told by voices to kill. His trial opened in the city of Zhytomyr, ninety miles west of Kiev on 12 February 1999. Onoprienko sat in a metal cage for his own protection but it did not stop the public spitting at him and verbally abusing him. Serhiy Rogozin, who was also on trial for aiding and abetting Onoprienko, described him as a "kind, intelligent man. He seemed good-natured. I cannot say anything bad about him."

After deliberating for just three hours on 31 March, Judge Dmytro Lypsky found Onoprienko guilty and sentenced him to death by firing squad. Since Ukraine has a moratorium on capital punishment, Onoprienko was sent to prison. He died of heart failure in Zhytomyr jail on 27 August 2013, aged fifty-four. Rogozin was sentenced to thirteen years behind bars.

Handyman Wanted . . . in Bed

Francis Mawson Rattenbury was a distinguished architect living in Canada – where he designed landmarks such as the British Columbia Parliament Buildings, the Empress Hotel in Victoria, and the Vancouver Courthouse – when in 1923, he met Alma Pakenham, a glamorous divorcée with one son, Christopher, and twenty-eight years his junior.

They married in April 1925, returned to England four years later and moved into the Villa Madeira in Manor Road, Bournemouth. They had a son, John. They were initially happy, but cracks soon began to appear in their relationship, not helped by him being reclusive, impotent (they did not have sex following the birth of John) and drinking too much whisky.

On 25 September 1934, they advertised in the *Bournemouth Daily Echo* for a "Daily willing lad, 14-18, for house-work; Scout-trained preferred. Apply between 11-12, 8-9 at 5 Manor Road, Bournemouth".

George Stoner applied for the job and began work. He moved in and, on 22 November, he and Alma had sex for the first time.

Francis drank whisky and slept on the settee downstairs while his wife entertained her lover. Despite his age and infirmity, Rattenbury became the object of Stoner's jealousy and the younger man was furious when Alma spent time with her husband.

On the weekend of 23/24 March 1935, Stoner and Alma enjoyed time away in London. On the Sunday evening, Stoner bashed Rattenbury over the head with a wooden mallet he had borrowed from his grandparents supposedly to erect a screen in the garden. The blows were so savage that they removed the back of the 67-year-old architect's head. Francis Rattenbury was taken to hospital where he hovered between life and death. Early the next day, the police arrived at the Villa Madeira and, finding Alma incoherent through drink and babbling that she had "done him in", arrested her for attempted murder.

On Wednesday, 27 March, Stoner confessed to Irene Riggs and he, too, was taken into custody. The next day, Francis Rattenbury died of his injuries and the charges were altered to murder.

They went on trial at the Old Bailey before Sir Travers Humphreys on 27 May 1935, for the murder of Alma's elderly husband – both pleaded not guilty.

Alma was portrayed as an immoral woman who had "ensnared a hapless youth" while Stoner was apparently "a poor lad cajoled into the vortex of this illicit love". Stoner refused to say anything at the trial other than answer to his name, while Alma put up a robust defence.

On 31 May, after the jury had deliberated for fifty minutes, Stoner was found guilty of murder and sentenced to death but Alma was released. As she left the Old Bailey, the crowd booed her. On 4 June, she took the train to Three Arches Railway Bridge in Christchurch where she stabbed herself six times in the breast with a knife. She left a note, "If I only thought it would help Stoner I would stay on. But it has been pointed out to me too vividly that I cannot help him. That is my death sentence."

After more than 300,000 people signed a petition, Stoner was reprieved on 25 June 1935, and the Home Secretary commuted the sentence to penal servitude for life. He spent just seven years in prison. He served in the Army fighting on D-Day.

In September 1990, Stoner was again in the news when he was given two years' probation for indecently assaulting a twelve-year-old boy in a public lavatory. He died in Christchurch Hospital on 24 March 2000, aged eighty-three, around half a mile from where Alma died and on the sixty-fifth anniversary of Francis's murder.

Murder in Paradise

When holidaymakers noticed the sixty-five-foot racing yacht anchored offshore with no signs of life on board, they decided to investigate. Boarding the vessel, they found a scene of carnage. Two crewmen and an American couple were found dead, shot and stabbed after being bound and gagged.

Computacentre Challenger had sailed from the island of Antigua during the last week of January 1994. There were two British crew members, Ian Cridland and Thomas Williams, and American company executive John Cleaver and his wife, Patty, whose home was in the Channel Islands. The grim discovery of the four bodies was made at Barbuda, an island some twenty miles north of Antigua. Local police ruled out piracy and suspected there was a drugs connection.

Detective Superintendent Mickey Lawrence, one of Scotland Yard's finest, and who was already in Antigua on police business, was asked to take charge of the investigation. His enquiries on Barbuda led to the discovery of a sail boat hidden in the undergrowth and a trail where it had been dragged across the ground. This, in turn, led to a stolen Boston whaler motorboat. A search on board turned up some cigars that had clearly been stolen from *Challenger*.

A nearby house was entered by the police and the occupant, Mel Harris, a local man, was arrested. He was found to be in possession of a bundle of Bank of Guernsey currency and was ready to make a full confession about his part in the violence that took place on *Challenger*. He implicated Marvin Joseph in the crime and explained how they boarded the yacht at 1am on Friday, 28 January. They believed the boat had drugs and cash on board.

Harris said they kept the four occupants of the boat below deck, tied their hands behind their backs and gagged them with insulating tape. Having relieved them of anything of value, they then shot their captives as Harris put it, so "there would be no witnesses". Superintendent Lawrence believed three other men were involved in the crime.

In February 1996, Harris and Joseph were put on trial for murder, and a third man, Donaldson Samuel, changed his plea to one of manslaughter and gave evidence to assist the prosecution. The month-long trial was big news in Antigua. There was much debate in the media about the island's possible links with drug trafficking and strong denials from the authorities.

Harris and Joseph were sentenced to hang, which was commuted to life imprisonment on appeal. Donaldson was sentenced to fifteen years' hard labour. For John and Patty Cleaver, their snorkelling holiday in paradise had ended in death and disaster.

The Trash Bag Murders

The Trash Bag Murders came to an end on 13 March 1977, when Patrick Wayne Kearney murdered a pick-up of his boyfriend's. The killings began in 1965 and became known as the "Trash Bag Murders" because the victims were often found in bin liners. Texan Patrick Wayne Kearney was twenty-five years old when he committed his first killing, a hitch-hiker he murdered in Orange, California.

Two years later, after more killings, Kearney relocated to Redondo Beach, near Los Angeles, with his new boyfriend David Douglas Hill, whom he had met five years earlier. The pair had a tempestuous relationship, and after an argument Kearney would get in his car and find a man to kill.

His victims, primarily gay, would be collected from gay bars or would be hitch-hikers he saw on the roadside. Kearney shot his victims without warning and then had sex with the corpse. The case officially began on 13 April 1975, when the body of 21-year-old Alberto Rivera was found near San Luis Capistrano.

In the next seven months six more bodies were discovered in Los Angeles, Riverside, San Diego and Orange counties. All the victims were gay and all had been shot in the head and were found nude.

At 5.30pm on 13 March 1977, seventeen-year-old John LaMay told his neighbour that he was going to Redondo Beach to meet "Dave", a man he had met at the gym. He arrived at Kearney's home and was invited in. Without warning, Kearney shot the homosexual LaMay in the back of the head and then hid the corpse in the desert.

LaMay's mother called the police but they did not take the report seriously. Five days later, LaMay's dismembered corpse was found south of Corona. He had been drained of blood, washed, put into five industrial bin bags and then placed in an empty eighty-gallon oil drum. "Dave" was soon identified as David Hill and he and Kearney fled. They surrendered on 1 July 1977.

Hill was cleared of involvement in his boyfriend's crimes and was released on 14 July. That day Kearney was charged with two murders and the next day he confessed to twenty-eight murders. On 21 December, he was sentenced to life imprisonment after pleading guilty to three murders. In February 1978, he was charged with eighteen more murders and pleaded guilty on 21 February. Kearney is in jail at California State Prison, Mule Creek.

Final Solution

A tube led from the garage, where it was attached to the car exhaust, through a hole in the bedroom wall, and into a hooded facemask. This was a home-made gas chamber and the intention was to make murder look like suicide.

The designer of the gas chamber was Cranog Jones, aged forty-four, a Gloucestershire magistrate, and his aim was to cause the death of his wife, leaving no injuries and with the appearance that she had taken her own life. The couple had been married nearly twenty years and lived in Cheltenham. Jones was an obsessively ambitious man who wanted to scale the social ladder. In this endeavour, he felt hampered by his wife, Margaret, who was an intensely shy person and was uncomfortable in social settings. She would say later that she was afraid of using the wrong knife and fork at dinner parties.

Jones's exasperation grew as he saw no inclination on his wife's part to improve her social skills. In short, he saw her as a handicap to his career. They drew apart and he had a number of affairs, finally leaving Margaret in May 1990. While divorce proceedings were under discussion, he decided to move back to the family home. It was then that he hatched his final solution.

Cranog Jones put together his do-it-yourself gas chamber and, one night in 1991, while in bed, Margaret heard the sound of the car engine running in the garage and woke up. Her husband's lethal apparatus was in place and he was crouched at the end of the bed. She screamed and Jones collected up his death-dealing equipment and ran from the house. A subsequent press report said that Margaret Jones "was nearly put to sleep like an unwanted pet".

It was clear that Cranog Jones, the magistrate and social climber, was prepared to kill his wife so that she would no longer embarrass him with her lack of social skills. When he was tried for attempted murder at Winchester Crown Court in 1993, it came out in evidence that he had tested his infernal death-dealing apparatus on the cat.

Once he had completed part one of his plan, he would have carried his wife's body down to the garage and put it in the car, giving every indication that she had committed suicide. It would have been the perfect murder. Cranog Jones was convicted of attempted murder and given a sentence of nine years.

Bigamist Murders Wife

Arthur Andrew Clement Goslett worked in a government-owned aircraft factory, living in a nice flat on Golders Green Road, London, with his wife, Evelyn Mear, and their child (she had three by her first husband).

At 8pm on 1 May 1920, Evelyn had eaten supper with their lodgers Daisy Holt and Marjorie Orell and then went out. They never saw her again. The next morning, the police were called and Goslett freely admitted to killing his wife. He told police that he had arranged to meet her at the Prince Albert pub at 9.15pm so they could look at a house he was thinking of buying in Hendon, Middlesex. They left the pub arm in arm and walked by the River Brent.

As they reached a desolate spot, he produced a tyre lever and hit her over the head three or four times. As she lay unconscious, he knelt and kissed her hand, apologized for his actions and gently lifted her into the water. Her body was found the next day near some allotments. A post-mortem examination showed that she had been alive when she went into the water and the cause of death was drowning.

When interviewed, he told police that Daisy had told him to do it. He added that he had spent the night of the murder in Daisy's bed. She denied everything. At his trial, which opened on 21 June at the Old Bailey, he maintained his story.

To support the accusation, he produced two marriage certificates – one dated 12 June 1914, for the dead woman, while the other on 7 February 1919 was for a wedding to Daisy Holt, who was apparently pregnant at the time. She gave birth to Goslett's baby in July 1919, at which time he revealed that he was already married but said that she could move in, pretending to be the widow of his brother Percy who had died in the Great War. He also told her his real name – he had been using the name Godfrey.

Reluctantly, Daisy became her lover's lodger. He told the court that she put pressure on him to get rid of Evelyn, something that Daisy vehemently denied, although she did admit to sleeping with him under the marital roof. The jury did not believe him and he went to the gallows at Pentonville.

The Good and Bad Girl of Ice Skating

Brunette Nancy Kerrigan, five foot four and twenty-four, and blonde Tonya Harding, five foot one and twenty-three, were portrayed in the media as the good girl and bad girl of ice skating. Both had high hopes for the 1994 Lillehammer Winter Olympics and both were featured endlessly in television and radio programmes as well as magazines and newspapers. Kerrigan bore a slight resemblance to Katharine Hepburn while Harding was shorter, smoked and swore a lot.

In the first week of 1994, Nancy Kerrigan was practising before about 200 people at the ice rink at Cobo Hall in Detroit. As she left the rink Kerrigan said hello to a few familiar faces and then stopped to talk to journalist Dana Scarton of the *Pittsburgh Post-Gazette* about her hopes and chances for Lillehammer and what she thought of her competitors as her proud parents, Dan and Brenda, stood watching nearby.

Such was the interest in Kerrigan that no one noticed a shadowy figure dressed in black hovering in the background – then suddenly he rushed forward and hit the back of the skater's legs with a twenty-one-inch retractable baton. She fell to the ground crying, "Why me? Why me? Why now? Help me! It hurts so bad. Please help me." Her father, Dan, rushed to Nancy's side and picked up his injured daughter as her attacker made good his escape. When she was examined, it was discovered that the attack had failed – the thug had hit half an inch too high to fracture the leg – but he had still done enough damage to temporarily rule her out of competitive skating.

The next day, her main rival Tonya Harding took the US Ladies' Figure Skating Champion's title (for the second time) as Kerrigan could only look on helplessly from the stand of the Joe Louis Arena. The United States Figure Skating Association wanted Kerrigan on the plane to Lillehammer and said that as long as she was fit she would be included in the team.

A few days later, the police received a tip-off that a woman had heard a tape of three people, all from Portland, Oregon – Harding's hometown – discussing an attack on Kerrigan. One of them was Jeff Gillooly, Harding's ex-husband with whom she still lived; another was Shawn Eckhardt, her 25-stone bodyguard.

The FBI placed Eckhardt under surveillance and he obligingly lead them to Derrick Smith, the driver of the getaway car, and then to Smith's nephew, Shane Stant, the man who had wielded the baton. The FBI quickly discovered that none of the men had the intelligence to arrange the plot and the evidence for that quickly pointed to Jeff Gillooly. At first he denied any involvement in the attack but then broke down and confessed. He believed that with Kerrigan out of the picture, Tonya Harding's chances would be improved and also it might scare other skaters and sports stars into hiring bodyguards – perhaps from a company like the one owned by Gillooly.

Harding professed ignorance of her ex-husband's scheme and on 18 January, after the police had spoken to her for ten hours, she announced that the on-off, on-off marriage with Gillooly was over. Her estranged husband claimed that, far from knowing nothing of the plot, on 27 January, Harding had actively encouraged it.

Desperate to compete in the Olympics, Harding then admitted that she had learned about the attack a few days after but had done nothing with the information. Both skaters were included in the American team, and on the first day at Lillehammer they took to the ice at the same time. Neither acknowledged the other. During practice Harding fell and the footage was screened endlessly.

On 26 February 1994, both women competed for the gold medal – the blonde "bad girl" and her cool brunette competitor.

Unfortunately, the fairytale did not have a happy ending: Harding finished eighth and Kerrigan finished second to Oksana Baiul, the Ukrainian.

On 1 February 1994, Jeff Gillooly agreed to testify against his ex-wife. On 16 March 1994, Harding pleaded guilty to felony on a count of conspiring to hinder prosecution. She was sentenced to three years' supervised probation, a $100,000 fine, and forced to resign from the United States Figure Skating Association. She was also told to create a $50,000 fund for the Special Olympics, reimburse the District Attorney's Office to the tune of $10,000, serve 500 hours' community service and undergo psychiatric evaluation and treatment.

Sex and Sacrifice Down Mexico Way

In Mexico in 1963, the brothers Santos and Cayetano Hernandez managed to persuade the villagers of Yerba Buena that if they participated in orgies and gave them money then the Inca gods of the mountains would bestow riches upon them. Santos's tastes ran to seducing women while his brother preferred men.

The ignorant villagers were unaware that Incas lived in Peru and if any god were going to enrich them it would be an Aztec one. When no riches appeared, the villagers complained so the brothers went to Monterey where they persuaded Eleazor and Magdalena Solis to pretend to be gods.

Eleazor Solis, like Cayetano Hernandez, preferred the company of men, while his blonde sister – for whom he pimped – was a lesbian prostitute. One night the Hernandez brothers performed one of their rituals before throwing flash powder onto a fire and out of the smoke the gods appeared.

The peasants believed that Eleazor was St Francis of Assisi. A young girl, Celina Salvana, was much taken by Santos and she was regularly "purified" by having sex with him. She also had sex with the lesbian Magdalena until she got jealous and Celina stopped being purified by Santos. Eleazor and Cayetano worked their way through the handsome young men of the village, purifying as they went.

When the riches still did not appear, Magdalena decreed that unbelievers must be sacrificed. Two of the most prominent doubters were butchered and their blood added to the chicken blood that was drunk during the ceremonies.

Over the next eight weeks, six more "unbelievers" were sacrificed and many fled to neighbouring villages. Celina Salvana began to tire of lesbian sex with Magdalena and longed for the touch of a man, Santos being that man. When Magdalena found out her disciple had been unfaithful she had her tied to a cross on 28 May 1963, knocked her unconscious and then watched while the villagers beat her to death. Sebastian Gurrero, fourteen, saw what happened and ran to the police in Villa Gran to report what he had seen.

Patrolman Luis Martinez accompanied the boy back to the village and both promptly disappeared. On 31 May, police and soldiers raided the village and after a firefight they found the remains of the teenager and the policeman. Both had been hacked to death and Patrolman Martinez's heart had been ripped out.

A villager who hoped to take on his godly mantle had murdered Cayetano. Magdalena, her brother and twelve cult members went on trial on 13 June, and were sent down for thirty years.

The Manacled Mormon

It was a tabloid reporter's dream: sex, religion, crime – the story had it all. On 15 September 1977, Scotland Yard announced that the Mormon missionary Kirk Anderson had disappeared in "most unusual circumstances". The day before, 21-year-old Anderson had received a telephone call from a man calling himself Bob Bosler. Bosler wanted to convert to the Church of Jesus Christ of Latter-Day Saints and he hoped Anderson would be able to help. Anderson agreed to meet Bosler and his female friend at a church in East Ewell, Surrey.

None of the trio had been seen since and the police were worried. The British police had been advised by their counterparts in Salt Lake City, Utah, that prior to his leaving for

Britain, Anderson had been stalked by an obsessive woman. She had even hired a private detective to follow him wherever he went. She paid for the detectives by posing for bondage porn magazines and working as an escort.

The headquarters of the Church of Jesus Christ of Latter-Day Saints confirmed the stalking and said that they had told Anderson it would be better for him if he left on missionary work for a while. He had chosen England and arrived at East Grinstead, Sussex, in September 1976.

Three days after his kidnapping, Kirk Anderson reappeared claiming that a woman and two male accomplices had held him, tied and handcuffed, in a remote cottage in Okehampton on the edge of Dartmoor. Detective Chief Superintendent William Hucklesby asked the public for help in tracking down two Americans portraying themselves as man and wife. They were 24-year-old Keith May (aka Bob Bosler; aka Paul Van Deusen) and 28-year-old Joyce McKinney (aka Cathy Vaughn Bara; aka Heidi Krazler).

The Devon and Cornwall Police arrested the two within hours of Anderson's reappearance and found the cottage where he had been held. They examined the room where Anderson was kept and found an array of bondage items.

DCS Hucklesby said off the record, "I can't go into details but I'll tell you what; I've never been lucky enough to have something like this happen to me." On 22 September, McKinney, a former Miss Wyoming beauty queen, and May, an assistant architect, appeared in court charged with kidnapping and illegal possession of an imitation .38 revolver. They were remanded in custody for a week by magistrates at Epsom, Surrey. As McKinney arrived at the same court on 6 October, she struggled with a female prison officer and tore her cheesecloth blouse thus exposing a portion of McKinney's generous embonpoint to the press photographers. She also held up notes written on pages torn from the Bible that read "Ask Christians to pray for me"; "Please tell the truth. My reputation is at stake"; "He had sex with me for four days" and "Please get the truth to the public. He made it look like kidnapping".

As the police spent more time investigating the case, it became obvious that it was not a straightforward kidnapping. Indeed, Anderson and McKinney had been shopping in London together and had eaten at various restaurants. At a hearing on 13 October, DCS Hucklesby told the court that McKinney had entered Britain on a false passport and forged papers in eight fake names. He said McKinney had confessed her intention to use handcuffs, leg shackles, an imitation gun and a mixture of ether-chloroform in the kidnapping. For the defence Stuart Elgrod said, "Passion was the motive."

McKinney and May were held in custody for a second time after police opposed bail. DCS Hucklesby told the court, "I believe Miss McKinney would attempt to interfere with Anderson." At the hearing on 23 November 1977, prosecuting counsel Neil Dennison QC said that from their first meeting in Provo, Utah, there had been a strong sexual attraction between the two, but after a number of sexual encounters Anderson had been racked with guilt for going against the teachings of his church and tried to end the affair.

McKinney and May had kidnapped Anderson outside the Mormon tabernacle in Ewell and then driven him to Okehampton where she had sex with him while he was chained to a bed. At first she had oral sex with him and then the next day full intercourse took place although it was against Anderson's wishes, he said. Anderson admitted that he had asked McKinney for a back rub but said that did not mean he wanted sex with the former beauty queen. "My mom gives a pretty good back rub, but that does not mean I want to have sex with her."

At a hearing on 30 November, the court referred to a previous statement by McKinney in which she said that all the activity with Anderson was consensual and the bondage and oral sex were to help out with his difficulties. "Kirk cannot have an orgasm unless he is tied up," she said. On 6 December 1977, she told the court "I loved Kirk so much I would have skied down Mount Everest in the nude with a carnation up my nose."

Magistrates decided that McKinney and May had a case to answer and both were committed for trial and then released on £3,000 bail after three months in Holloway Prison. A date for the court case was set for the Central Criminal Court on 2 May 1978, but on 12 April both May (calling himself Richard McGrory) and McKinney (Darleen O'Connor) – heavily disguised and pretending to be members of a deaf and dumb acting troupe – jumped bail and fled to America via an Air Canada flight. After thirteen months, the FBI found McKinney and she was found guilty of using forged passports and given three years' probation.

In June 1984, McKinney was once again in court accused of continuing to harass Kirk Anderson. The case was dismissed. On 14 July 2004, she was arrested for communicating threats and cruelty to animals. In August 2008, calling herself Bernann McKinney, she was again in the news after she paid $50,000 to South Korean scientists to have her dead Pitbull dog, Booger, cloned. Five puppies were born on 28 July 2008.

Extraordinary Cunning

Andrew Lindo was a man of many gifts. He taught music, was an accomplished lothario and managed to lead a successful double life. He met Marié Stewart while studying music at Huddersfield University. At the time, he was working as a music teacher at a local school where he was regarded as something of a charmer. He certainly charmed Marié, who left her husband in order to live with him.

The couple had a child, and neighbours at Holmfirth, Yorkshire, thought they were the perfect family. But concerns arose in December 2010, when Marié's absence was noticed. Lindo said she had left the country and this seemed to be supported by messages left on her mobile phone.

Marié's family, concerned about her disappearance, alerted the police and a search was made of the couple's house. They found her strangled and battered body in a suitcase in the garage on 13 February 2011. Lindo admitted killing her after an argument over her alleged mistreatment of their daughter. He claimed to have lost control and admitted strangling her with a belt and finishing her off by stabbing her twelve times with a kitchen knife.

Lindo's behaviour created a sense of revulsion even among seasoned policemen. The master of deception had invited his latest girlfriend to stay overnight at the house, knowing that Marié's body was hidden in the garage. Before that, he had been in the habit of clearing away evidence of Marié's presence in their home so that he could entertain his girlfriends on the pretence that he was a bachelor boy.

Lindo, twenty-nine, was put on trial for murder at Bradford Crown Court in September 2011. The jury were treated to some remarkable insights into the life of a serial philanderer who pleaded guilty to manslaughter. He did not give evidence in court, leaving it to his counsel to argue that his brutal attack on Marié was due to a freak loss of control.

In his summing-up, the judge told him that he had reached "new depths in accusing her (Marié) of mistreating her own daughter . . . it was a deliberate and despicable fiction", he said. He also said that Lindo had demonstrated "extraordinary cunning".

The jury clearly agreed when it took them less than an hour to find him guilty. The judge, Mr Justice Andrew Smith, sentenced him to a prison term of twenty-two years on 21 September.

A Stolen Car and Mass Murder

On 6 August 1969, police arrested Bobby Beausoleil for driving a stolen car at San Luis Obispo, California. As the police investigated they learned that the car, a Fiat, belonged to 34-year-old music teacher named Gary Hinman who had been murdered on 27 July 1969.

Beausoleil, twenty-one, an aspiring musician and actor, was a member of Charles Manson's Family and had been due to appear in underground film-maker Kenneth Anger's *Lucifer Rising*, but the two men had fallen out before much footage could be shot.

On 25 July, Beausoleil, Susan Atkins and Mary Brunner went to Mr Hinman's to seek $2,000 retribution over some poor-quality drugs (mescaline) that the teacher had supposedly sold to the Straight Satans biker gang.

When Mr Hinman refused to return the money, Beausoleil, Atkins and Brunner held him prisoner in his own home at 964 Old Topanga Canyon Road, Malibu. Beausoleil had with him a 9mm Radom pistol which he pulled out and used to threaten Mr Hinman. The teacher made a grab for the gun and the two men fought. Mr Hinman won, but, rather than calling the police, he simply handed the gun back to Beausoleil and told the trio to leave. It was a mistake that was to cost him his life.

Manson arrived around midnight in a temper and cut Mr Hinman's left ear with a sword before leaving. Beausoleil later stabbed him to death and wrote "Political piggy" on a wall using Mr Hinman's blood. Had Beausoleil not been arrested, he would probably have taken part in the Tate–La Bianca murders that shocked Hollywood and America just a few days later.

Beausoleil was found guilty of first-degree murder and sentenced to death on 18 April 1970. In 1972, the California Supreme Court ruled the then-prevailing death penalty statutes unconstitutional and the sentence was commuted to life imprisonment. The other members of the Manson Family were also saved from the death penalty by the same ruling.

While in prison from 1976 to 1979, Beausoleil wrote and recorded the soundtrack to *Lucifer Rising*, which was finally released in 1980. The following year, on 18 December, Beausoleil married divorcée Barbara Ellen Baston and, thanks to California's overnight conjugal rights facility, has fathered four children.

On 13 December 2010, Beausoleil's appeal for probation was refused.

A Cuckold's Rage

Chris Little, a fibreglass salesman, had been married to Julie Crocker for ten years and they had two children. She became disenchanted with her husband and had an affair with Rick Ralph, a sports broadcaster whose estranged wife was Paula Menendez. These were the essential characters in a love triangle that went tragically wrong.

On 12 February 2007, Little made a 911 call from his home in Markham, Ontario, saying that he had found his wife with her throat cut in an upstairs room. The operator talked him through resuscitation procedures but to no avail, and then Little claimed to have found Paula Menendez's body hanging from a beam in the garage.

The initial supposition was that Menendez took her own life after killing Julie Crocker in revenge for breaking up her marriage. But, as more details emerged of the relationship between the parties involved, another explanation came to light.

Crocker, bent on developing a new life with Ralph, thought she could part amicably from Little with a negotiated settlement. What she had not reckoned with was the anger and humiliation this aroused in 38-year-old Little. Seething with rage, he resorted to stalking his wife to the extent of fitting a GPS device to her car so that he could plot her every move.

Over the months, resentment boiled over into rage and Little devised a plan which involved murder and a staged suicide. In February 2007, he called at Paula Menendez's home where she lived alone following her marital separation, and strangled her. He then put her body into his car and drove to Markham where he stage-managed a hanging in the garage. Then he went upstairs where he confronted his wife as the children lay sleeping down the hallway, and cut her throat. He called the emergency services, explaining that he had discovered two deaths.

In November 2009, Little appeared before a Newmarket jury charged with double murder. The case aroused considerable interest among the Canadian public in a country with a high incidence of domestic homicide. One in five of all homicides involved the killing of a spouse or lover.

Little's defence, that he had stumbled across a murder/suicide plot, carried no weight with the jury who heard the full extent of his calculated stalking and saw him as a cold-blooded killer consumed by jealousy. On 25 November, he was convicted on two counts of first-degree murder and sentenced to twenty-five years in prison. The *Toronto Sun* carried the headline "Monster gets life in jail". Ironically, Little was sentenced on a day marking The Elimination of Violence Against Women.

Daughter Discovers Double Homicide

At 6.40pm on 6 June 1945, a month after the end of the war in Europe, seventeen-year-old trainee hairdresser Eva Lucas arrived home from the salon where she worked in Leytonstone, Essex. She was surprised to find the doors locked at the bungalow in Leigh-on-Sea, so Eva forced a window open in her parents' bedroom. She climbed in and the house was strangely quiet – there was no sign of the pet cocker spaniel.

Eva walked into the hallway and found her mother, Cissie, aged fifty, lying on her back, a coat over her head and an eiderdown covering the rest of her body. Her mother's body was cold to the touch.

Eva ran out the front door into the street to seek help and bumped into the local postman. They went back into the house and found her jeweller father, Fred, fifty-two, lying on the dining-room floor, a cushion on his head and his body covered by a rug. The home had been ransacked and the walls and ceiling were smeared with copious amounts of blood. Later that day, John Young, a builder who had done some business with Mr Lucas over sovereigns, tried to gas himself at his sister's home in Barking and then slit his wrists. He was taken to Oldchurch Hospital in Romford, Essex, for treatment.

At 9am, Young was visited by several policemen and confessed to the murders. At Young's home, police found a bundle of fivers, twenty-one rings, half a dozen packets of gems and sundry other items that had belonged to Mr Lucas.

At the inquest Eva explained that the family had only moved to Leigh the previous month, expecting peace and quiet. Home Office pathologist Dr Keith Simpson testified that both Lucases had fractured skulls, the result of blows to the head. Death had occurred around 9am, that being the time Mr Lucas's wristwatch had stopped.

On 9 November 1945, Young went on trial at the assizes and pleaded not guilty. He claimed that he suffered from mental illness and, as a result, was not responsible for his actions. The jury took an hour to discount this defence and Albert Pierrepoint hanged Young at Pentonville on 21 December 1945.

Double Trouble

Lawyer Jereboam O. Beauchamp murdered love rival Kentucky politician Solomon P. Sharp, a former attorney-general, at Sharp's home in Frankfort in the early morning of 7 November 1825, after being egged on by the woman they had both bedded.

The story began when Sharp supposedly fathered a child with Anna Cooke, but it was stillborn. Indeed, Sharp denied that he was the father and claimed the baby was a mulatto. Nonetheless, Beauchamp began an affair with Cooke but she refused to marry him unless he murdered Sharp. He agreed and they tied the knot in June 1824.

Seventeen months later, Beauchamp murdered Sharp. It did not take long for him to be apprehended, and both he and his wife were arrested. He confessed, "At 2am I put on my mask, drew my dagger and proceeded to the door; I knocked three times loud and quick . . . I advanced into the room and with my left hand I grasped his right wrist . . . I stripped my hat and handkerchief from over my forehead and looked into Sharp's face. He knew me the more readily I imagine, by my long, bush, curly suit of hair. He sprang back and exclaimed in a tone of horror and despair, 'Great God it is him,' and as he said that he fell on his knees. I let go of his wrist and grasped him by the throat dashing him against the facing of the door and muttered in his face, 'Die you villain'. As I said that I plunged the dagger to his heart."

Cooke was acquitted at the trial, which began on 8 May 1826, but Beauchamp was found guilty and sentenced to death. Despite her acquittal, Anna Cooke was allowed to stay in the death cell with her husband, and shortly before the execution they both attempted suicide by drinking laudanum.

On the morning of 7 July 1826, the day of the hanging, the couple again tried to kill themselves, this time by stabbing themselves. Guards found a bleeding Beauchamp and dragged him to the gallows before he could bleed to death. He was the first person legally executed in the state of Kentucky and his wife died of her injuries before the noose finished off her husband. They were buried in the same coffin at Maple Grove Cemetery, Bloomfield, Kentucky.

The murder became the inspiration for Edgar Allan Poe's unfinished play *Politian* and Robert Penn Warren's *World Enough and Time*.

Escape from Alcatraz

Frank Lee Morris was a career criminal beginning his wicked activities when he was just thirteen. On 20 January 1960, he was sent to Alcatraz and immediately began planning an escape. The brothers John and Clarence Anglin and Allen West joined him in his plan.

The Anglins had been sent to the Rock for bank robbery. John William Anglin arrived at Alcatraz on 21 October 1960. His brother Clarence, a year younger, arrived on the Rock on 10 January 1961. Allen West was a car thief, sent to Alcatraz in 1957. For two years the men plotted and planned. They created a six-by-fourteen-foot raft and life-like dummies to leave in their beds when they escaped. They also began to dig behind the six-by-nine-inch ventilation holes in their cells, taking it in turns while one kept watch.

On the night of 11 June 1962, without West who had been slow to dig in his cell, they made their break for freedom. They went down the tunnels they had made and onto the roof of Alcatraz where they set sail onto the bay.

The FBI began one of the biggest manhunts since the Lindbergh kidnapping in 1932 but only found parts of the raft and a waterpoof bag containing the Anglins' letters. The official verdict was that the men had drowned in their attempt.

On 17 July 1962, a Norwegian freighter spotted a body floating face down twenty miles northwest of the Golden Gate Bridge, but did not report the sighting for three months. The FBI pointed to the fact that the men were habitual criminals and yet were never again arrested. They closed the case officially on 31 December 1979.

The Anglin family believe that the brothers died, and another, Alfred, was electrocuted while trying to escape from Kilby Prison in Montgomery, Alabama, in 1964. Allen West left Alcatraz on 6 February 1963, when the prison closed. He was released in 1967 but was arrested again in 1968. In January 1969, he was jailed for life. On 30 October 1972, he stabbed a black prisoner to death. He died in jail of acute peritonitis on 21 December 1978.

The story was made into a film, *Escape from Alcatraz*, starring Clint Eastwood as Frank Morris. Allen West's name was changed to Charley Butts in the film.

A Fall Down the Stairs

Janet Masterman was found seriously injured, lying at the bottom of the stairs in her Nottingham home on 27 May 1965. She died in hospital a few days later and the inquest recorded a verdict of accidental death. Mrs Masterman was aware that her husband, Bryn, a senior prison officer, had begun an intimate relationship with a woman colleague at work. Her reaction to this was a threat to move with their two children to live with her mother. The real cause of Janet Masterman's death would remain a closely guarded secret for more than twenty years.

Less than a year after his wife's death, Bryn Masterman married his lover, Selina. He boasted that he had got away with murder, describing how he hit his wife over the head with a stool and pushed her down the stairs. This admission, in the fullness of time, would come back to haunt him.

Moving forward some twenty years and following the breakdown of his marriage to Selina, Masterman deserted her. Feeling betrayed, she decided to share the secret which

Masterman had imparted to her with the police, whom he had previously described as being "as thick as two short planks". This was his critique for their failure to rumble his perfect murder.

Selina agreed a plan with officers to trap Masterman in a conversation that would be recorded. In the ensuing encounter, he admitted responsibility for killing his first wife. As a result, he was arrested, twenty-one years to the day after her death, and charged with manslaughter.

He appeared on trial in 1987, when he pleaded guilty to the charge of manslaughter. He testified that he had boasted about killing his first wife in order to make his second wife feel indebted to him. The jury listened to a playback of the tape-recorded session in which he made these admissions.

His claim that his wife's death had been accidental was not borne out by a review of the forensic evidence. She had died from a fractured skull caused by a single blow to the head. The absence of other injuries, particularly to the limbs, suggested it was unlikely she had fallen down the stairs.

Sentencing Masterman to six years' imprisonment, Mr Justice Boreham told him his act was one of the worst possible cases of manslaughter.

Crime Solved

With a population of under 30,000, the Western Isles of Scotland enjoy a crime-free existence. Rates of offending have steadily declined and the police can boast a clear-up rate of 85 per cent. But this crime-free haven was shattered by a murder in 2011, the first violent killing for forty-three years.

Coastguards found the body of sixteen-year-old Liam Aitchison on 29 November, in a disused military facility close to the village of Steinish on the Isle of Lewis. He had died from wounds inflicted with knives and a blunt instrument. The youth was last seen alive a week earlier standing outside the local store.

Liam was a relative outsider, having been on the island for only two months. He drifted from lodging to lodging and became involved in the local teenage culture. In a short time he had acquired a reputation for involvement in minor disagreements with authority and was due in court to be sentenced for committing an assault.

Rumours were rife in the wake of the murder with tales of drinking, skirmishes with other teenagers and a dispute over a girlfriend. The police had focused their enquiries on three young men wearing hoodies who had been seen near the crime scene. In December, two men in their twenties were charged with Liam's murder.

Jonathan MacKinnon and Stefan Millar appeared on trial at the High Court in Glasgow in June 2013. Both pleaded not guilty. They were believed to have killed Liam after a violent confrontation during a drinking session at Millar's house and then to have taken his body to the place where it was discovered a few days later.

Millar testified on his own behalf, but his statement was undermined by a fellow remand prisoner who said that Millar had boasted to him about the murder. This was a key piece of testimony in the absence of forensic evidence linking the two defendants to the crime. Despite extensive searches of Millar's home, which involved inspection of the drains, no murder weapon was found nor any linking evidence.

Millar and MacKinnon were found guilty of murder, a verdict which was greeted in court with shouts of "Yes" from Liam's family. The two young men were sentenced to eighteen years' imprisonment. Thus ended an incident which shocked the local community, whose senior members recalled the last murder in the islands when an eighty-year-old crofter was killed in 1968. The two killers appealed their conviction but in February 2015 their appeals were dismissed.

The West Campus Murders

Recent graduates Johnny Goosey (history and English) and Stacy Marie Barnett (architecture) had been courting for two years after meeting at the University of Texas at Austin. Unbeknown to 22-year-old Miss Barnett, her boyfriend, twenty-one, was a mid-level drug dealer, specializing in marijuana.

One of Goosey's foot soldiers was nineteen-year-old high school dropout Ricky Thompson III (according to his prison record, not Jr as some sources have it). He owed Goosey $8,500, part of a drug deal – money that he did not have.

At 9.50am on 21 July 2009, Thompson arrived at Stacy Barnett's second-floor maisonette, at 904 West 21st Street, Austin, Texas, where he shot Goosey several times in the head before going upstairs and putting two bullets into Miss Barnett's head. He picked up the bullet casings and smashed both their mobiles in a misguided attempt to hide the fact that he had rung Goosey before the murder.

Thompson left at 10.12am in a car driven by Roy M. Renick, who with Samuel Hadden Gifford helped plot and cover up the murder. The three men even went as far as arranging Thompson's apartment to resemble Stacy Barnett's so he would be able to commit the murder – they decided that Stacy would be killed only if she was at home – and escape easily. Renick also made a silencer for Thompson to use.

The police received anonymous tips that led them to Thompson and he was arrested on Friday, 24 July, and charged with two counts of capital murder the next day. On 23 August 2010, Thompson pleaded guilty to killing Stacy Barnett. He was given a life sentence and told he must serve at least twenty-nine years before being eligible for parole.

To avoid the death penalty and/or life without parole, he also agreed to plead guilty to the murder of Johnny Goosey and testify against Renick and Gifford, for which he received another life sentence on 20 May 2011. Both accomplices had no option but to plead guilty, and on Friday, 8 April 2011, Renick, twenty-two, was imprisoned for thirty-five years while Gifford, twenty, received two concurrent fifty-year sentences. Goosey and Miss Barnett were buried together at the Glenwood Cemetery, Houston.

Thatcher Wrecks Political Career With Murder

Colin Thatcher, the son of the former prime minister of Saskatchewan, Canada, was a millionaire businessman, a successful rancher who had himself become Minister of Energy and Mines in the provincial government.

On 12 August 1962, he had married JoAnn Geiger but they began growing apart, and oddly the split became more serious in 1977 when he defected to the Progressive Conservatives from the Liberal Party. He began having affairs and did little to hide them, but his constituents did not seem to mind and he was re-elected in 1978.

The Thatchers divorced in 1980, and the following year, on 17 May, someone shot and wounded Mrs Thatcher as she stood in her kitchen. The relationship became even more acrimonious and the couple battled over custody of their three children.

Mrs Thatcher was awarded custody of two of the three children and $820,000 for her share of the family home. Thatcher told Lynne Dailey, thirty, his American new girlfriend, that he wanted to kill his ex-wife and contemplated hiring a professional hitman.

Instead, on 21 January 1983, he waited in her garage at 2876 Albert Street, Regina, Saskatchewan, having made sure the interior lights were disabled. As she got out of her car he grabbed her and stabbed her in the head several times.

As she cried out, her screams were heard by passer-by Craig Dotson, thirty-eight, who went to investigate. Then the screams died as a gunshot rang out. As Mr Dotson approached the garage, a man walked out hiding something under his coat. When Mr Dotson peered into the garage he saw Mrs Thatcher lying in a pool of blood on the floor. When he looked for the attacker, the man had vanished.

The police found a credit card slip dated three days before in the snow near the garage. It was wet and soggy but it was possible to decipher "W. C. THATCH" printed on it. Colin Thatcher's full name was Wilbert Colin Thatcher. The police continued to investigate his harassment of his ex-wife, and on 7 May 1984, Thatcher was arrested for her murder. He went on trial on 15 October, and was belligerent on the stand. Lynne Dailey, by now separated from Thatcher, testified against him. On 6 November, he was found guilty and sentenced to twenty-five years to life. He was paroled on 4 December 2006, still protesting his innocence.

Golden Gate

The 10th Earl of Shaftsbury was, from all accounts, a man who craved affection. He had married twice but remained unfulfilled so he moved to France and set up home in Cannes. He became a regular at the local bars, especially the Golden Gate, where he could drink and pick up girls.

Through an escort agency, he met Jamila M'Barek, a 45-year-old mother of two, and soon proposed to her. They were married on 5 November 2002. He lavished money on her and set her up with a flat in Cannes. When she told him she was pregnant with his child, he changed his will, leaving her assets worth some £4 million.

But the earl grew tired of Jamila and spent more time drinking at the Golden Gate. Then he met another prostitute, mother-of-two Nadia Orche, and proposed marriage to her. This was the spark that would lead to tragedy. He decided to leave Jamila and visited her at her apartment to tell her that their marriage was finished. This was on 5 November 2004, two years to the day since they had married. The earl was not seen alive again.

Five months later, on 7 April 2005, his decomposed remains were found in a gully used as a fly-tip near Theoule-sur-Mer. His clothes were in tatters and a double fracture of the larynx suggested he had been strangled. The initial reaction of the police, bearing in mind the earl's reputation for using escort agencies, was that he had been a victim of one of the gangs controlling prostitutes.

But Jamila M'Barek soon became the prime suspect when she entered a psychiatric clinic and her conversations were recorded. She supposedly told her sister that her brother, Mohammed, was present in her flat when the earl came to visit her. She said that she had paid Mohammed £100,000 to strangle her husband. On the strength of these admissions, the police charged Jamila and Mohammed M'Barek with murder. They believed she had lured the earl to her flat with the intention of killing him and had then dumped his body.

The pair went on trial for murder on 22 May 2007, in Nice. Both denied the charges. In court, Mohammed took the blame and sought to exonerate his sister. He claimed the earl's death was an accident. The story was that a scuffle had broken out when the earl turned up the worse for wear with drink. Mohammed claimed he did not strangle him but that he fell down after being hit and died of a heart attack.

Jamila, now a widow, stood to gain £2 million by inheritance. Those who knew her said she had a harsh upbringing and her principal aim in life was to make money. When operating as a call girl at the Riviera's nightspots, she could earn £1,000 a night. A key element in the prosecution, despite her denials, was that Jamila had visited the spot where the earl's body was dumped, two days before he was killed. Mobile phone records confirmed her presence at the location.

The M'Bareks were found guilty and each sentenced to twenty-five years' imprisonment. In February 2009 Jamila's sentence was reduced to twenty years on appeal.

The Cheating Major

Game shows have been a staple of television on both sides of the Atlantic for many years, with prize money rising to a million pounds on shows like *Red or Black*.

Unlike in England, quiz show contestants in America have to pay tax on their winnings. One of the most popular shows in recent years on both British and American television has been *Who Wants to Be a Millionaire*. The first edition of the show was broadcast on 4 September 1998, and its last on 11 February 2014. Presented by Chris Tarrant, it was based on a format by David Briggs.

The first winner of the million pound prize was Judith Keppel, a garden designer, who triumphed on 20 November 2000. David Edwards won the top prize on 21 April 2001, and then, on 8 and 9 September 2001, a show featuring Major Charles Ingram was recorded.

Ingram went through all the questions to reach the million pound teaser, "A number one followed by one hundred zeros is known by what name?" He was given four options A: Googol, B: Megatron, C: Gigabit, D: Nanomole. After some deliberation, Ingram chose A and Tarrant awarded him a cheque for £1 million.

Then the television company became suspicious and withheld the cashing of the cheque while they investigated a theory that a confederate in the audience had helped Ingram by coughing every time Ingram was unsure of an answer or confirming a correct one.

However, Chris Tarrant said that he had not heard any untoward coughing and nor did the audience at home. It was only after the coughing was amplified by the TV company for the criminal prosecution that anyone became aware of it.

In answering the last question, there were two coughs in quick succession after Ingram read out the word Googol, and there were two more shortly after this without any mention of this word, and there were another couple of coughs in rapid succession again when Ingram decided to go for it and without any mention of the word.

In any case, Ingram, his wife Diana and Tecwen Whittock, the alleged cougher, were all arrested and charged. After a four-week trial at Southwark Crown Court, all three were convicted by a majority verdict on 7 April 2003, of "procuring the execution of a valuable security by deception".

The Ingrams were sentenced to eighteen months in jail and Whittock was sentenced to twelve months, all suspended. The Ingrams were also each fined £15,000, and each ordered to pay £10,000 towards prosecution costs.

On 19 August 2003, the Army Board ordered Ingram to resign his commission as a major. On 19 May 2004, the Court of Appeal denied Ingram leave to appeal his conviction and upheld his sentence but agreed to quash his wife's fine and prosecution costs.

"Best Friends" Sentenced for Murder

Missy Avila was a popular seventeen-year-old; easy on the eye, she made friends easily. Her closest friend was Karen

Severson. Severson, also seventeen, towered over her five-foot-two pal and was overweight. She also got into fights regularly. Another chum was Laura Doyle who worked in a supermarket bakery.

On 1 October 1985, Missy and Doyle went to meet Severson and Eva Chirumbolo at Stonehurst Park in Sun Valley. Later that day, Laura Doyle's mother, Barbara, telephoned Irene Avila asking if Missy was home yet. The next morning when she had still not returned, Irene reported her daughter missing to the police.

On 4 October, hitch-hikers discovered Missy's remains at Big Tajunga Canyon in Angeles National Forest. Her long hair had been hacked off; she was lying prone and a log had been placed on top in a clumsy attempt to hide the body. Animals had been feeding on her corpse. Severson was so distraught over her friend's murder that she moved in with Irene Avila and even slept in Missy's bed and wore Missy's clothing. She was a great comfort to Irene Avila.

Meanwhile, Doyle said that she had seen Missy talking to two young men in a blue Chevrolet Camaro. When the police failed to make an arrest, Mrs Avila and Severson began their own detective work, hassling drivers of blue Camaros.

For three years, the case dragged on, and then, on 27 June 1988, the police made two arrests – Karen Severson and Laura Doyle. The trial began on 8 January 1990. In her testimony Eva Chirumbolo claimed that Doyle attacked Missy, accusing her of sleeping with Victor Amaya, Doyle's boyfriend. The four girls then went for a walk and Doyle and Severson began pulling Missy into a creek. Miss Chirumbolo said that she became scared and ran back to the car. Doyle and Severson returned without Missy and in the car laughed about killing their friend. They held her head under eight inches of water until she drowned.

Doyle's lawyer, Charles Lloyd, alleged that Eva Chirumbolo only came forward when she was linked to the murder. "It's obscene that Chirumbolo is not charged with this killing," he raged. The jury found problems with Miss Chirumbolo's evidence and after a day's deliberation convicted Doyle and

Severson, on 31 January, of second-degree murder not first-degree as the DA had wanted.

On 9 March 1990, both were sentenced to fifteen years to life in prison. Severson was denied parole in June 1997. A second bid six years later, by which time Severson was even heavier and suffering from multiple sclerosis, was also refused. Doyle was denied freedom in June 2002. Severson, forty-four, was paroled in December 2011, from California Institution for Women, in Corona, after serving twenty-one years. Doyle, forty-four, is now serving time at Valley State Prison for Women, in Chowchilla. Doyle was released from prison in December 2012, after serving twenty-two years.

Rubber Stamped

Two ladies, both in their seventies, Helen Golay and Olga Rutterschmidt, devised a murderous scheme to enrich themselves. The two women became firm friends after meeting at a health spa in Santa Monica, California. They looked up various money-making schemes based on theft and pretence and then graduated to more serious crime.

In 1997, they befriended Paul Vados, a 71-year-old Hungarian immigrant in Los Angeles, and helped him find a place to live. Having done their "do good" bit, they next persuaded him to take out life insurance. He agreed and supplied his signature from which the two women had a rubber stamp made so that they could authenticate further life insurance policies.

Two years later, on 8 November 1999, they took the formerly homeless man in their car to a secluded back street near 307 North La Brea Avenue in Hollywood where they ran him over and left him for dead. A few days later, posing as the dead man's cousins, they made a claim on his eight insurance policies amounting to $750,000.

Their murderous scam would probably have remained a secret had they not become too greedy. They befriended Kenneth McDavid, and from November 2002 to March 2003, Golay and Rutterschmidt took out thirteen policies on Mr McDavid worth

$3,700,000. On 21 June 2005, CCTV showed Mr McDavid being hit by a silver 1999 Mercury Sable station wagon.

Los Angeles police investigating the death of a homeless man made a connection with the earlier case. What appeared to be a hit-and-run incident took on a new dimension when it was learned that two women claiming on the insurance were the same pair as in the previous case.

Before their arrest, Golay had received a total of $1,540,767.05 in insurance proceeds from Mr McDavid's death, and Rutterschmidt a total of $674,571.89.

The pattern of injuries in the two deaths was similar, with damage to the upper body, suggesting the victims had been immobilized and laid on the ground before being run over by a car in a darkened alleyway.

Golay and Rutterschmidt were arrested and charged with conspiracy and murder. They pleaded not guilty and, at their trial in 2008, a damning tape recording made after their arrest was played to the jury. In the recorded conversation, Golay questioned her friend about the extra insurances she had arranged; "You were greedy," she said, "that is the problem."

After a five-week trial, the two septuagenarians were convicted on two counts of murder on 18 April 2008, and sentenced to life imprisonment. The scheming pair had netted more than $3 million through their murderous activities and achieved comparison with the two sisters in the Frank Capra film, *Arsenic and Old Lace*, who considered it an act of charity to poison lonely old men by giving them drinks laced with arsenic.

A Walk in the Woods

Sandra and Bob Wignall had been married just over a year. They had both been widowed and met while out walking their dogs in the woods near their homes in Surrey. Romance followed and they were married on Christmas Eve 1991.

Sandra had recently broken off a relationship with Terence Bewley, which prompted her to seek romance elsewhere. But she soon tired of her new husband and began to lead a double life. Bob Wignall worked as a painter and decorator and she would drive him to work and then, secretly, meet Bewley.

Wignall, who had taken out a life insurance policy worth £21,000 to his wife in the event of his death, grew suspicious of Sandra's comings and goings. For one thing, the mileage on their car far exceeded his estimates. Sandra, meanwhile, was telling friends that she now regretted rushing into marriage.

On 5 September 1992, the Wignalls went for a walk in the woods to feed the foxes. When they reached a secluded spot in Sayes Wood, Bob Wignall was attacked, as Sandra later reported, by three men. He was fatally stabbed in the heart while his wife ran off for help.

A bracelet bearing the letter H found at the crime scene led police investigators to Harold Moult, known as H to his contemporaries, and a friend of Terry Bewley. Under questioning, Moult said he might have stabbed Bob Wignall but it was only intended to be "a frightener". In expectation of cashing in on her late husband's life insurance, Sandra was busy telling friends about her spending plans, which included a holiday in Tenerife and buying a horse.

Sandra Wignall, Terence Bewley and Harold Moult were charged with murder and conspiracy to murder. The prosecution case was that Sandra had lured her husband into the woods where he was set upon by Bewley and Moult. All three denied the charges when they were brought to trial at the Old Bailey in 1993.

The case against them centred on Sandra's promiscuity and her attachment to Terence Bewley whose bidding she was keen to follow. He was heavily in debt and Sandra had discussed the possibility of selling her house to raise money on his behalf. But, following her marriage to Bob Wignall, another avenue opened up and she conceived the plan to kill him, aided by Bewley, her lover, and his friend Moult. The trio waylaid Wignall and despatched him to his grave to secure his life insurance entitlement. All three were found guilty and sentenced to life imprisonment on 19 November 1993.

"I Shot Them Out of Love"

The man clinging to a gargoyle on the roof of the cathedral in the French city of Amiens in September 1986 was a British solicitor. Ian Wood was talked down by French police and taken into custody. He had gone on the run after his mistress and her three-year-old child were found dead in the home they all shared in Sheffield. Wood, thirty-seven, was extradited to Britain to face murder charges. An extraordinary story was about to unfold.

A former public school boy, Wood had built up an aura of professional achievement as a solicitor and maintained a wealthy lifestyle. But behind this façade of respectability lurked a very different personality. He destroyed his image as a family man when he walked out on his wife and three children to live with Danielle Lloyd. The French woman, thirty-eight, had lost her first husband in a plane crash and had been deserted by her second husband, leaving her with two children. She fell for John Wood's charms and he called her "My eyes, my life, my love, my wife". They seemed ideally suited to each other.

But there was another, secret, side to Ian Wood's life. He was fleecing his clients and perpetrating swindles and embezzlement schemes. He used his ill-gotten gains to finance his lavish lifestyle, buying Danielle expensive gifts while embarking on other relationships.

His complicated affairs made heavy financial demands and he resorted to borrowing and stealing his clients' money. Inevitably, he accumulated large debts and, as he slipped towards ruin and disaster, he turned to alcohol for salvation. His life was beginning to fall apart. September 1986 proved to be a turning point. He went to Paris in the hope of setting up a financial deal that would give him breathing space. He failed to secure the result he wanted and lapsed into despair. On returning home to Sheffield, he confessed the extent of his difficulties to Danielle, including an admission that he had stolen £180,000 of his clients' money.

While she was contemplating their miserable state of affairs, Ian Wood armed himself with a .38 revolver, catching Danielle unawares and firing two shots into the back of her head. He then shot and killed three-year-old Stephanie and left her brother, Christopher, severely wounded. Hastily packing a bag, Wood headed for France and spent a week on the run. During that time, he telephoned friends and colleagues saying he had fulfilled a suicide pact with Danielle. Of the shootings, he said, "I shot them out of love". He claimed that the suicide pact had been forced on them by Danielle's former husband. The last act in this part of the drama was his threat to throw himself off the top of Amiens Cathedral.

During his seven-day trial for murder at Sheffield in June 1987, Wood used all his skills as a solicitor to excuse his actions. He was innocent of any misdemeanours and blamed others for plotting against him. The jury did not see it that way and found him guilty of murder. The only good thing that came out of the whole sordid business was that five-year-old Christopher, whom Wood had shot twice in the head, made a miraculous recovery.

A Double Life

What appeared to be a tragic accident occurred on a remote Cumbrian farm on 1 December 2007, when Jane Wilson fell under the wheels of a tractor driven by her husband, Robert, and was killed. He dialled 999 and when paramedics arrived at the scene Wilson was in a state of hysteria and kept repeating, "I've killed her". The fatality was treated as an accident.

What was unknown at the time was that forty-year-old farmer, Robert Wilson, was leading a double life. Three months earlier, while in Spain, he met Cathy McNeil who was separated from her husband, and the couple established a relationship. He traded on her sympathies, telling her that his wife had died leaving him a grieving widower. At the time he was making this statement, Jane Wilson, fifty-three was fit and well and working on the farm.

Wilson increased his wife's life insurance and paid regular visits to Cathy McNeil who was living in Spain, during the early months of 2007. He explained that the secrecy which shrouded his movements was because he did not want to upset his late wife's family. Although burdened with debts, he took out a £15,000 loan to pay for a luxury holiday in the Maldives during which he proposed marriage.

Back in Cumbria, suspicions were aroused when the late Jane Wilson's children found a card from "Cathy" in their mother's room three weeks after she died. The police were advised and Wilson was arrested after questioning in April 2008. A fresh look at the accident evidence revealed some inconsistencies with the account given by Wilson and he was charged with murdering his wife. He denied the accusation.

At Carlisle Crown Court in November 2008, the jury heard details of his secret life and his profligate spending when he was heavily in debt. The prosecution alleged that Wilson ran his wife down in his tractor, having doubled her life insurance to £400,000, so that he could start a new life with his lover. He was found guilty and the judge imposed a sentence of life imprisonment.

Too Clever By Half

Gordon Wardell led a secret life, hiding a violent past and resorting to prostitutes, while playing the role of a respectable married man. This deception disintegrated on 12 September 1994, following the death of his wife, Carol Heslop, thirty-nine.

The building society manageress to whom he had been married for twelve years was found dead in a lay-by on Weddington Road (the A444) after being reported missing from her home in Nuneaton. She had been suffocated. Wardell said that he and his wife had been attacked in their Meriden home by a gang who abducted her and forced her to open the office safe where she worked and then killed her. Wardell had been found by police in his underpants, tied and gagged on the living room floor. His clothes and shoes had been placed carefully to one side near where he was found.

Wardell made a tearful appearance in front of television cameras in a news interview. He was in a wheelchair, wearing sunglasses and appeared visibly shaken. Seeking information to help the police he said, "I just want my wife's killers caught".

Investigators were already scrutinizing inconsistencies at the crime scene and also began looking at Wardell's background. It came to light that, as a seventeen-year-old, he had attacked a woman with a knife and sexually assaulted her. He served a term in prison for this crime but he kept his violent record a secret from his wife.

Gordon Wardell, forty-one, was now a prime suspect and, six days after the murder, was placed under 24-hour surveillance. After two days in Coventry and Warwickshire hospital and making use of a wheelchair, he adopted the role of someone recovering from pain and shock. Looking frail and using a walking stick when he thought he was being observed, he otherwise got about normally and unaided.

On 21 October 1994, Wardell was charged with the murder of his wife and the theft of £14,126.67 from the firm she worked for. One of the detectives on the case was reported as saying of Wardell that, "He's a clever man who thinks he's a lot brighter than he really is."

The depth of his deception was revealed by the records of ambulance staff who examined him after his ordeal with the gang that he claimed had killed his wife. Remarkably, they said, for someone who was supposed to have suffered a traumatic experience, his pulse and blood pressure were normal and he had shown no clinical signs of trauma.

Police believed that Wardell killed his wife and, the next morning, put her body in their car and drove to the office where she worked and robbed the safe. Wardell held a job as a warehouse manager and had studied books on the psychology of being interviewed. No doubt he thought this would hold him in good stead during his interviews with the police. In the event, he proved too clever by half.

When he was put on trial at Oxford Crown Court in November 1995, the jury gasped when they heard evidence of the scale of his deception and depraved existence. After a trial lasting six weeks, Wardell was found guilty of murdering his wife and given a life sentence four days before Christmas.

"Trying to Kill Me"

Paul Solomon, a school teacher, and his wife, Betty Jeanne, lived in an apartment at Greenburgh in Westchester County, New York State. They led busy, but largely separate, lives embracing teaching, sports activities and work in the community. On 15 January 1989, a 911 emergency call was made from the Solomons' apartment. A woman, clearly distressed, exclaimed "trying to kill me". The operator was unable to discern whether the message was preceded by "He is" or "She is".

Paul Solomon was away that evening playing bowls and, when he returned home at 11.40pm, he found his wife dead from gunshot wounds. She had been shot nine times with bullets fired from a .25-calibre pistol. When the police arrived at the apartment they confirmed there had been no forced entry, leading to the conclusion that the victim knew the murderer or that the killer had a key to the apartment.

Paul Solomon was questioned and a great deal was learned about his private life. It emerged that he had been having an affair with 26-year-old Carolyn Warmus who taught computer studies at his school. They had enjoyed a secret liaison for two years, but there had been recent strains and Solomon decided to break off the relationship.

Warmus had an unhappy upbringing in which she felt starved of affection. As an adult, she looked to older men to satisfy her needs for love and stability in circumstances which usually led to rejection. Despite his philandering, Solomon put his family needs first and, once again, Warmus felt she had been pushed aside.

When she was questioned, Warmus said that on the night Betty Jeanne was killed she was in a different part of town, having driven to the Treetops Lounge at the Holiday Inn in Yonkers to meet Paul Solomon and later to have sex with him in her car. As a picture began to emerge of Warmus's obsessive nature and tendency to harass former lovers, it was also discovered that she had bought a gun and silencer a couple of weeks before Betty Jeanne died. What might have been a tipping point was Warmus's birthday when Soloman stood her up. She was arrested in February 1990, and charged with second-degree murder.

When the news reached the media – with the inevitable revelations about Carolyn Warmus and her background – reference was made to similarities with the plot of the film *Fatal Attraction*, which had been a box-office hit. Warmus's trial at White Plains also had echoes of a previous legal encounter in 1980, when Jean Harris was convicted of killing her lover, Dr Herman Tarnower.

The evidence against Warmus was largely circumstantial and, significantly, no murder weapon was found. After deliberating for ten days, the jury was deadlocked and the judge ordered a retrial. Second time around, a new piece of evidence emerged which appeared to link Warmus to the crime scene. It was a glove which had been apparent in a photograph and seen lying next to the victim's body. What proved to be a decisive forensic item had been found in a closet in Betty Jeanne's bedroom. It bore traces of blood and was sufficient to seal Carolyn Warmus's fate. A guilty verdict was returned and her punishment was a sentence of twenty-five years' imprisonment.

The Serial Lingerie Fetishist

When his uniform was shredded and his medals destroyed, former Colonel Russell Williams had reached the abyss. He had been a rising star in the Canadian Air Force, had piloted royalty and ministers on official flights and was commander of CFB Trenton, his country's largest air-force base.

Williams's world fell apart in February 2010, when his secret life as a burglar, thief, sex offender and murderer came to light. The list of his crimes practically filled a catalogue. His downfall was brought about by chance when he was stopped at a police road block near Tweed, his home town in Ontario. He was pulled over routinely by officers investigating the disappearance of a local woman, Jessica Lloyd.

Jessica had gone missing from her home in Belleville on 29

January. Tyre tracks found close by captured the attention of investigators because they showed an unusual tread pattern. When the tyres on Colonel Williams's vehicle were examined they were found to match. He was questioned about his movements and his house was searched. After confessing to numerous crimes, he led officers to the body of the missing woman whom he admitted having murdered.

His confession opened up a veritable Pandora's Box of criminal activity. The Canadian public were shocked to learn that such a high-ranking and respected officer had been leading a secret, crime-strewn life. He admitted two murders, that of Jessica Lloyd and also of Marie-France Comeau who had been a non-commissioned officer serving at his air base. In addition, he had committed two sexual assaults in 2009, when he broke into properties close to his home town, overpowered the female occupants, sexually abused them and tied them to chairs in order to photograph them.

While these were the worst of his crimes, he also owned up to eighty-two occasions when he forced his way into houses to steal women's underwear and personal items. He had a collection of thousands of photographs he had taken, some of which depicted him wearing female lingerie. In addition, he kept a written record of some of his crimes.

The military authorities lost no time in relieving Williams of his duties after he was placed under arrest. Meanwhile, the police were widening their investigation by backtracking to all the places where he had been based as an air force officer. He waived his right to a preliminary hearing and went straight to trial at Ontario's Court of Justice in October 2010. He pleaded guilty to all charges which, by this time, amounted to eighty-eight separate indictments.

Details of his assault on Marie-France Comeau in January 2010 made grim listening for those present in court. As her base commander, he was aware of her duty roster and used that knowledge to break into her house while she was absent and lay in wait. Wearing a mask, he ambushed her when she returned. He overpowered her, stripped her clothes off and taped over her mouth and nose. Having tied his victim to a chair, he took photographs and departed with her underwear while she suffocated to death.

Williams, forty-seven, a man who once had the world at his feet, sat in the dock, head bowed, as his catalogue of crimes unfolded. The "serial lingerie fetishist", as he was described, had attempted to commit suicide while in custody and, later, went on hunger strike. On 22 October 2010, having been found guilty of first-degree murder, the former air force colonel was sentenced to two concurrent terms of life imprisonment.

"Criminal Genius"

When Malcolm John Webster crashed his car on a rural road in Scotland in 1994, the vehicle caught fire and his wife, Claire Morris, died in what was regarded as a tragic accident. Webster claimed that he had driven off the road in his efforts to avoid an oncoming motorcycle. He lost no time in making a claim on Claire's life insurance, acquiring £200,000 as a payout.

Five years later, and having remarried, Webster was involved in another car crash, this time in New Zealand. Neither he nor his new wife, Felicity Drumm, was harmed. What might have been seen as an unfortunate coincidence inspired searching questions after Webster emptied their joint bank account and returned on his own to Scotland. He then embarked on a biga-mous relationship and tried to persuade his new consort to take out a substantial life insurance policy.

Felicity's family reported their suspicions about Webster's actions to the New Zealand police in 2006, and their investiga-tive trail led back to Scotland and the death of his first wife. Beyond the coincidence of two remarkably similar car crashes and Webster's deceitful behaviour, investigators had little to go on and attempts to bring a case against him came to nothing.

Then, in 2007, new evidence came to light in the form of toxicological analysis of Claire Webster's body tissues which showed the presence of temazepam in her system at the time she died. This is a hypnotic, sleep-inducing drug used for treating insomnia and this new information gelled with Felicity's account of Webster's practice of giving her drinks which made her very sleepy. He was, after all, a qualified nurse and, hence, possessed knowledge about drugs and their effects.

As fresh enquiries intensified, it became known that when Webster crashed his car in 1994, he told motorists who stopped to help that there was no one in the vehicle. The strong presumption was that he had drugged his wife, driven the car off the road with her unconscious inside and then set fire to it. In light of this, the police in Scotland, prior to arresting Webster, alerted the women with whom he was socializing, that their lives might be in danger.

When arrested and questioned, he denied the charges but the evidence against him had been slowly building up. In 2011, he appeared on trial at the High Court in Glasgow, charged with murder and attempted murder. In what proved to be the longest ever criminal trial in Scotland involving a single accused person, the full extent of his crimes was exposed. He was referred to as a "skilled conman" who staged two car crashes in order to secure insurance payments intended to finance his extravagant lifestyle.

On 19 May 2011, Malcolm Webster, described in court as a "brilliant criminal genius", was found guilty and sentenced to thirty years' imprisonment. His conviction was upheld following an appeal in 2013. In March the following year, ITV screened a programme, entitled *The Widower*, based on Webster's criminal career. The families of his two wives had endured a long wait for justice, seventeen years in the case of Claire's death and twelve years after the attempted murder of Felicity.

CHAPTER 5

Spare Parts and Bits & Pieces

Most histories of famous murder cases contain accounts of murderers decapitating their victim. The reason for this practice is to prevent identification, on the grounds that a headless torso does not give anything away. While this was true in the age before fingerprints and DNA, it is no longer the case, although headless torsos still make good news stories.

Another reason for decapitation lies in the process of dismemberment which is intended to make it easier to transport a body in pieces. Moving a corpse, typically weighing around 160 pounds, presents a number of challenges. The task is made easier if there is an accomplice on hand but, even then, there is a chance of being observed in the process. Hence, cutting up the body and rendering it into manageable portions means that one person can carry and transport it to the disposal site.

The act of dismemberment calls for a degree of planning, including access to appropriate butchering implements, such as knives, saws and cleavers. It is also a messy business involving considerable blood-letting if the corpse is still fresh. It is time-consuming and, not to be discounted, is the need for a method, knowing where to cut and how to disarticulate limbs.

When it comes to technique, doctors should have the edge, based on their knowledge of anatomy and surgery. But, very often, medical murderers are betrayed by their own skill. Such was the case with Dr Westlake, a Californian doctor, when he killed and dismembered his victim prior to disposing of the body parts. It became clear that surgical instruments had been skilfully employed to dissect the corpse, leading to Westlake who had a background as a surgeon.

A practical reason for separating the head from the body is to conceal the victim's identity. For this to work, the torso and head need to be disposed of separately. This was the intention of the killer of Adnan Abdul al Sane in Manchester in 1993. While the headless torso was discovered at the crime scene, it remained unidentified for several weeks until the head was found some sixty miles away buried in a shallow grave. The gruesome artefact was located by a man out walking his dog. A special tribute might be appropriate to walkers and their canine companions, who occasionally uncover human remains to the detriment of those who believed they had got away with murder.

Chance discovery of body parts by animals and those who forage for a living has proved the undoing of numerous killers who saw dismemberment as a convenient means of escaping detection. The two detached legs of one of Anthony Hardy's victims were found in 2002, in a wheelie bin, by a tramp searching for food. Other body parts were found scattered around north London in a kind of game of hide and seek. Destruction and mutilation of the victim's body is, for some killers, their final act of desecration, a statement of hatred and revenge against society. When he was arrested, Hardy joked with detectives about newspaper reports comparing him with Jack the Ripper.

Perverted self-indulgence motivates another pattern of victim disposal, or, in some cases, retention of the bodies. John Christie kept some of his victims walled up in his house at 10 Rillington Place, and both Dennis Nilsen and Jeffrey Dahmer kept corpses and their body parts close to hand. These killers' objectives were summed up by Brian Masters in his highly recommended biographies. For Nilsen, it was Killing for Company *(1985), and for the Milwaukee serial killer, it was* The Shrine of Jeffrey Dahmer *(1993). It was believed that Dahmer used all his collection of trophies for sexual gratification. The book titles say it all.*

Jack the Ripper usually secures at least a walk-on part in any discussion about violent aspects of murder. A letter "From Hell" in 1888, purporting to be from Jack the Ripper, accompanied half a kidney supposedly removed from his fourth victim. The unfortunate recipient of this missive was told that the organ had been kept for him, adding, "tother piece I fried and ate it was very nise (sic)".

If this was an example of cannibalism it was followed up in due course by Fritz Haarmann who set up as an entrepreneurial butcher in Hanover at the end of World War One. The local population was suffering a food shortage to the extent that cats and dogs were slaughtered for their meat. Taking advantage of an opportunity, Haarmann set about supplying the town's market with freshly butchered meat. No doubt the townspeople were suitably grateful just so long as they did not question the origin of what they were buying for their dinner tables.

Haarmann sourced his supplies by preying on young refugees who came to Hanover seeking work. In the space of six months, he killed at least twenty-four times, cutting up his victims and selling their flesh to unsuspecting housewives. For good measure, he drank his victim's blood and pitched their unwanted bones into the river.

This was murder for profit as set out in William Bolitho's book of that title published in 1926. He noted that the purveyor of human flesh wished to be recognized with an inscription on his tombstone which read, "Here Lies Mass Murderer Haarmann". This tended to bear out the adage that "murder must advertise".

While eating human flesh unknowingly was one thing, consuming it in full knowledge of its origins was something else. This was the particular perversion of Albert Fish. In 1928, he abducted a young girl in New York whom he killed and dismembered. Having mutilated her body, he stripped off pieces of flesh which he cooked with vegetables and made part of his diet. His "instruments of hell", as he described them, consisted of a knife, cleaver and saw, the butcher's tools. Fish admitted killing at least four children, mutilating their bodies and engaging in acts of cannibalism.

A master class in the business of farming body parts for profit was provided by Michael Mastromarino in America during the early 2000s. He conspired with two brothers who ran funeral homes in Philadelphia to acquire access to the bodies of recently deceased individuals for the purpose of stealing their organs. These were then sold through Mastromarino's biomedical business to doctors needing human organs for transplantation. He was believed to have provided the input for thousands of surgical procedures.

Severing the head of his victim is possibly the most extreme dehumanizing measure undertaken by a murderer. Dr Buck Ruxton worked hard to reduce the bodies of his two victims to fragments which he parcelled up and scattered about the Scottish countryside around Moffat in 1935. Recovery of the detached heads of his wife and her friend enabled them to be identified using ground-breaking forensic methods. And, once again, it was the murderer's medical skills which betrayed him. The sum of the parts to which he reduced his victims' bodies amounted to seventy separate pieces.

Parts Master

Plundering body parts on an industrial scale was a profiteering scheme masterminded by a New Jersey dentist, 44-year-old Michael Mastromarino. He was aided by Louis and Gerald Garzone in a devilish plot targeting funeral homes in the northeastern USA. They conspired to remove and sell body parts gleaned from corpses and sell them to doctors who were unaware of their provenance. The parts were used for transplant procedures on live patients.

The Garzone brothers ran funeral homes and a crematorium in Philadelphia, delivering more than 200 corpses to Mastromarino's company, Biomedical Tissue Services. The bodies were then cut up to retrieve body organs for sale to doctors carrying out surgical procedures in Canadian and US hospitals. Some 10,000 such procedures were performed using material supplied by Mastromarino. During the course of their joint enterprise, he and the Garzones netted $4.6 million.

The scandalous practice came to light in 2006, when Mastromarino and his associates pleaded guilty to abusing corpses, and offered apologies in Court. The mastermind was sentenced to twenty-five to fifty-eight years in prison and the Garzones eight to twenty years. In 2008, Mastromarino pleaded guilty to further charges, including body stealing and reckless endangerment. This related to the risks involved supplying possibly diseased body parts for transplantation. He apologized for the distress caused and was sentenced to fifty-four years' imprisonment.

Soap Star's Headless Torso

A headless torso was found by a passer-by, floating in the Regents Canal in Hackney, east London, in March 2012. The gruesome discovery was thought to be the remains of 29-year-old Gemma McCluskie who had been reported missing.

The young woman, who had achieved a degree of minor celebrity as an actress in the television soap opera *EastEnders*, was last seen on 1 March, during a function at the Royal London Hospital in Whitechapel.

The torso had been placed in a suitcase, which had burst open after being dumped in the canal. The limbs were found in plastic bags a week later but it would take six months for the head to surface. Suspicion fell on the dead woman's brother, Tony McCluskie, with whom she shared a flat in Shoreditch.

After his sister's disappearance, McCluskie sent her text messages and reported her as a missing person. Police were suspicious because in a text he sent after he knew she was dead, he finished off with the salutation "Love ya", something that he had never done before. He also joined in neighbourhood searches organized by a group of friends. It emerged that the McCluskies, brother and sister, had a somewhat stormy relationship with arguments fuelled by Tony McCluskie's addiction to cannabis. Crime scene investigators searched the flat, finding blood traces in the bathroom and also recovering a blood-stained knife in the kitchen.

McCluskie was arrested and charged with murder, appearing in due course at the Old Bailey when he pleaded guilty to manslaughter. It appeared that he had rowed with his sister when she told him to clear out of the flat after he had caused a flood by turning on all the taps. He told the court that he had lost control in the ensuing argument but had no recollection of having killed her.

Gemma sustained fatal blows to the head, after which her body was cut into six pieces and put into a suitcase. Her brother hired a cab from a local taxi firm to take him and his luggage from the Shoreditch flat to the canal side at Hackney. He was seen dragging the suitcase to the canal.

McCluskie claimed that, during their row, his sister approached him wielding a knife. He grabbed her wrists but had no recollection of what happened next. When questioned by police he said that Gemma had been seen in a local shop after she was supposed to be missing and also visited her mother. These allegations appeared to be an attempt to divert suspicion from himself. The prosecution referred to the heightened acrimony between brother and sister which was not helped by his drug habit. Gemma had told a friend, "He's permanently stoned" and "doesn't know what he's doing".

The jury found 36-year-old Tony McCluskie guilty of murder on a majority verdict on 30 January 2013. Sentencing him to life imprisonment, Mr Justice Fulford referred to his action as "utterly cold-blooded and determined".

Fredericka the Fence

Films and TV usually portray fences – the receivers and sellers of stolen goods – as seedy, rat-faced, little men. Fredericka "Marm" Mandelbaum was different if for no other reason than that she was a woman. Born on 27 February 1818 (some sources say 1827), as Friederike Henriette Auguste Wiesener at Goslar, Hanover, Germany, she married Wolf Israel Mandelbaum and they moved to New York in 1850, where they purchased a home and dry goods store at 79 Clinton Street.

In the following decade "Marm" Mandelbaum found her vocation as a fence and trainer of apprentice thieves. In 1867, she avoided prison when Moses Ehrich, a fellow fence, bribed the authorities. Her notoriety grew and George Washington Walling, the chief of New York City's police, said that Mandelbaum had "no peer in the United States" as a receiver of stolen property.

She paid fines for criminals who stole the items she fenced but she also never paid more than 10 per cent of any item's worth to the thief. One thief, "Banjo Pete" Emerson, said, "She was scheming and dishonest as the day is long, but she could be like an angel to the worst devil as long as he played square with her."

In 1875, Wolf Mandelbaum died from tuberculosis but it seems that he had no part in his wife's criminal activities. On 27 October 1878, she was behind the Manhattan Savings Bank robbery, described by *The New York Times* as "one of the most daring and successful burglaries ever perpetrated". The thieves handcuffed the caretaker, forcing him to hand over the keys to the safe and tell them the combination. They got away with around $2.7million in cash and securities. She was arrested in July 1884, along with her eldest son Julius and her clerk Hermann Stoude, on charges of grand larceny.

District Attorney Peter B. Olney was determined to bring her down and could not be bribed. He hired the Pinkerton Agency rather than using the police to catch her. She spent a single day behind bars before posting her bail at $21,000.

Scheduled to stand trial in December 1884, instead she fled to Canada where she lived the remaining ten years of her life. Fredericka Mandelbaum died at her house in Hamilton, Ontario, on 26 February 1894, surrounded by family and friends. She was buried in New York and, reported newspapers, several mourners had their pockets picked at the funeral.

Meek and Wild

Robert George "Joe" Meek was a record producer who was ahead of his time. He was born on 5 April 1929, at 8 Market Square, Newent, Gloucestershire, and because his mother had wanted a girl was dressed in female attire until he was four.

After a stint in the RAF as a radar technician, Joe started to record local musicians and singers. He moved to London in 1953 or 1954, as much for his safety – he had been beaten up several times in Gloucestershire because of his homosexuality – as to further his career.

Meek landed a job in a studio but was difficult to work with, such was his insistence on perfection and a diet of pills. He also had a propensity to violence. In January 1960, he created his own label, Triumph, and recorded the first concept EP *I Hear a New World*. At the time space travel was capturing the public imagination and Meek jumped on the bandwagon.

Tracks on the album included such out-of-this-world titles as *Entry of the Globbots* and *March of the Dribcots*. Meek included sound effects such as bubbling water, lavatories flushing, radio interference and speeded-up voices over weirdly distorted Hawaiian guitar and layered, shifting spookiness.

Only 100 copies of the album, finished in May 1960, were pressed. With the help of a mysterious backer named Major Wilfred Alonzo Banks, a maker of Christmas decorations, Meek set up RGM Sound in a flat above A. H. Shenton, a leather-goods shop in Holloway, next door to Lloyds Bank and owned by his landlady Violet Shenton, where he would create some of his most lasting music. And he would murder her there, too.

The flat for which he paid £17 10/- a week was rather small, so string sections played huddled together on the stairs, singers recorded their vocals in the bathroom, and whole bands crammed into the minuscule recording room. Loose wires were held in place with chewing gum and matchsticks, and some of the equipment was home-made. Meek once threw the young Rod Stewart out with a well-timed raspberry because he thought the London-born Scot was rubbish, and he didn't rate The Beatles either. Meek tried to launch Geoff Goddard to fame as Anton Hollywood but discovered that Goddard's real talent lay as a songwriter and in 1961 he wrote *Johnny Remember Me* "off the top of my head in ten minutes", a melodramatic song about a man hearing the voice of his dead lover. The song, performed by John Leyton, entered the UK Charts on Thursday, 3 August 1961, and spent fifteen weeks there including three at Number 1. The bass was played by Chas Hodges, later to find fame himself in Chas'n'Dave. When the song appeared on *Juke Box Jury* the panel voted it a miss.

Meek also recorded Screaming Lord Sutch, but it was his own penned *Telstar*, composed after watching the first transatlantic broadcasts from the Telstar satellites on television, that was his biggest hit. Performed by the Tornados, it topped the charts on both sides of the Atlantic, selling more than four million copies and making the Tornados the first all-British band to reach Number 1 in the USA. Meek, who, remarkably, was tone deaf as well as being dyslexic, would probably have been horrified if he had learned that Margaret Thatcher would reveal that *Telstar* was one of her favourite records.

Meek hired Heinz Burt as lead singer of the group and persuaded the German-born former bacon slicer from Southampton to dye his hair peroxide blond. Heinz moved in with Meek but denied that they were lovers. On Monday, 11 November 1963, Meek was arrested for cottaging in the gents in Madras Place, London (another regular was Joe Orton). He was fined £15 on 12 November for "persistently importuning for an immoral purpose". Meek believed that he had been set up, not least because his accuser was an old man. He moaned, "I don't go chasing old men with watch chains dangling from their waistcoats – I go after young trade. Who wants a fucking old man?" Meek soon fell victim to several blackmailers as word got round that he would dish out fivers and tenners when accused of sleeping with someone, usually someone he had never even met. The hits continued but Meek became more and more paranoid, convinced that he was being spied on by other record companies. On 16 January 1967, the dismembered body of rent boy Bernard Oliver was found in a suitcase on a farm in Tattingstone, Suffolk. Meek had been a client and was convinced that the police would try to blame him for the murder. The hits were drying up and he faced financial worries. He was beaten up and left unconscious in his car. On 3 February, Meek burned several paintings and documents. His friend Patrick Pink visited him and while he was there a young boy called Michael who often helped out turned up but Meek told Pink to tell him to "Fuck off" and to send up Violet Shenton from her flat downstairs. She went upstairs and Pink said that he heard shouting and scuffling. He said, "I was in the office when I heard a big bang. It was such a fucking big bang. I was stunned. I rushed out and Violet was falling downstairs and I sort of grabbed her as she came to the bottom, and felt her. I was sitting on the stairs with her flapped over me . . . I saw the blood pouring out of these little holes in her back. And she died in my arms – I'm bloody positive she went still. I had quite a bit of blood over me. Her back was just smoking." Then Meek reloaded the gun and shot himself. Police found barbiturates, amphetamines and dexadrine in the flat. At his inquest, which recorded a suicide verdict, it was revealed that traces of amphetamines had been found in his body. Meek was buried in Newent cemetery on 10 March. Despite interviewing more than 100,000 people, the Suffolk police never caught the suitcase murderer.

The Goriest Killing

Two inmates of Frankland Prison in Durham found that they shared a common ambition. They had a desire to kill a fellow inmate, cut his body open and eat his liver. Michael Parr was serving a life sentence for attempted murder and Nathan Mann was jailed for life having been convicted of two murders.

In 2011, the two men found themselves occupying neighbouring prison cells. They targeted a fellow inmate, 23-year-old Mitchell Harrison, who was serving a sentence for rape. He became the focus of attention for Parr and Mann because they thought he was arrogant and they didn't like him anyway.

On 1 October, they lured their victim into Mann's cell and Parr pinned him down while Mann stabbed at his throat with an improvised knife fashioned from plastic cutlery and a razor blade. Harrison was also stabbed in the eye with a pen. With their victim dead on the floor, the killers cut open his body with the intention of taking out his liver and eating it. At this point, they hesitated to commit an act of cannibalism and just settled for disembowelment. Harrison's body was found next morning by prison warders.

Mann admitted to prison staff that they had attacked Harrison and said he and Parr had planned the assault because they fancied doing it. The two men had shared their thoughts about killing and were resolved to carry out their fantasy. Beheading and disembowelling fellow prisoners was a conversational topic. Mann had written a note to prison staff saying that if he was not put into solitary confinement, he would commit "the most goriest killing ever seen".

Mann and Parr were tried at Newcastle Crown Court on 12 July 2012. Mann was described as a remorseless and callous psychopath harbouring cannibalistic impulses. A psychiatrist said he was a "homicidal psychopath" who nursed a compulsion to kill. His counsel told the court that Mann accepted full responsibility for what had happened but pointed out there had been no cannibalism. Mann's plea of manslaughter on the grounds of diminished responsibility was accepted by the court.

Parr, who had been a willing assistant in the act of killing, took his share of the blame. Describing the pair as a "gross and obvious danger to the public", the trial judge Mr Justice Openshaw added further life sentences to those they were currently serving.

The Head at the School Gates

In February and March 1997, three young girls were attacked in Kobe, Japan. On 15 March, ten-year-old Ayaka Yamashita was bludgeoned to death with a steel pipe in the same area. On 27 May, some time before pupils were due to arrive at Tainohata Elementary School, the caretaker found the head of eleven-year-old Jun Hase, a retarded boy who had been missing for three days, in front of the school gate.

He had been decapitated with a handsaw and in his mouth was a note in red ink reading, "This is the beginning of the game . . . You police guys stop me if you can . . . I desperately want to see people die, it is a thrill for me to commit murder. A bloody judgment is needed for my years of great bitterness." It was signed The School Killer.

Later the same day the rest of the boy was found under a house in woods near the school. The killer also wrote a symbol similar to one used in San Francisco by the Zodiac killer. On 6 June, the newspaper *Kobe Shimbun* received a 1,400-word letter, purporting to be from the killer. It read in part, "I am putting my life at stake for the sake of this game. If I'm caught, I'll probably be hanged . . . police should be angrier and more tenacious in pursuing me . . . It's only when I kill that I am liberated from the constant hatred that I suffer and that I am able to attain peace. It is only when I give pain to people that I can ease my own pain." The letter was signed "Seito Sakakibara" with a PS, "From now on, if you . . . spoil my mood I will kill three vegetables a week . . . If you think I can only kill children you are greatly mistaken."

On 28 June, a fourteen-year-old boy was arrested for the murders and assaults. He had kept a diary detailing his exploits and in his bedroom police found thousands of comics and pornographic videos. Japanese law at the time meant that no one under sixteen could be charged as an adult so he was sent to a reformatory for treatment. In 2003, he was pronounced cured and he was paroled on 10 March 2004, aged twenty-one. His supervised parole ended on 31 December 2004, and he is now free, with a new identity.

Playground Fight Ends in Murder

Schoolgirls Diane Watson and Barbara Glover did not like each other, but when they faced up to fight each other in the playground of Whitehill Secondary School in Dennistoun, Glasgow, on 10 April 1991, no one realized it would end with one of them dead.

Diane, sixteen, pulled up Glover's blouse to expose her bra, and even when Glover pulled a knife from her bag, Diane stood her ground. Glover had assumed that Diane would flee and she would strut around the playground in triumph.

However, Diane did not move and even told Glover to put down the knife. Rather than losing face, Glover thrust the knife into Diane's body. The school crowd gasped and then vanished, many of them later questioned denying that they had been there or had seen anything. One boy ran to a nearby shop to ring 999 but when he learned that the phone was out of order, he fainted. Diane pulled out the knife and collapsed into the arms of her best friend Pauline Lowe. She helped her mortally wounded pal to her home 100 yards away but could not manage the two flights of stairs.

Diane's father heard the commotion and rushed down to give his daughter the kiss of life. Before she could be taken to Glasgow Royal Infirmary she was dead. Glover was tried at Glasgow Sheriff Court, and after three days, on 25 July 1991, was found guilty of murder. She was sentenced to be detained in a secure institution without limit of time, with a recommendation she serve at least twelve years. She was released on 26 January 2000, after serving just eight years.

There were to be further tragedies for the Watson family. Without any evidence, the media portrayed Diane as a bully, and on 5 December 1992, her brother Alan committed suicide, aged fifteen. Around his body were copies of the articles defaming his sister. Diane's parents, Margaret and Jim Watson, had also contemplated killing themselves.

In November 2011, they appeared before the Leveson Inquiry to speak about the mis-reporting of their daughter's murder. They were critical of one particular report by Jack McLean, published on 2 August 1991, in the *Glasgow Herald*. "They must get their facts before they delve into a final case. He's no right painting Diane as something she wasn't. He tore everything we had of Diane apart . . . We didn't even have a memory of her left because of him."

One of the World's Fastest Murderers

Born in France, 31-year-old Antoine LeBlanc moved to Germany and then left for the New World. He arrived in New York on 26 April 1833, and moved to New Jersey where he was offered a job working on the farm of Judge Samuel Sayre and his wife Sarah. His job was to chop logs and look after the pigs.

However, LeBlanc hated the fact that he was a lowly worker and had to sleep in a woodshed. On 11 May 1833 – just over a fortnight after he had arrived in America – he visited a local pub and told Samuel Sayre that there was a problem with the horses. The judge went out to the stable, where LeBlanc hit him over the head with a shovel. He used the same ploy on Sarah Sayre and he buried their corpses under a pile of manure.

LeBlanc discovered the Sayres' black maid, Phoebe, asleep in her second-floor bedroom and murdered her as well. Ransacking the house for valuables, he put everything he could carry into pillowcases and left the house on one of the Sayres' horses. Unbeknown to him, LeBlanc had overfilled the pillowcases, and as he galloped away, part of his booty fell to the floor leaving a trail.

The next day, Lewis Halsey, a friend of Judge Sayre, spotted some artefacts bearing the judge's monogram in the road. Believing that the house had been robbed, a posse went up to the house and found the bodies. Sheriff George Ludlow set off in pursuit and found LeBlanc drinking in the Mosquito Tavern in Hackensack Meadows. LeBlanc's trial opened on 13 August 1833, and was a foregone conclusion. He was convicted after just twenty minutes' jury deliberation. He was hanged on the village green on 6 September 1833, before a crowd of 12,000 people. The gallows shot him into the air rather than dropping him.

After death his body was taken to a local doctor who, with a colleague, performed some very unusual experiments including trying to reanimate LeBlanc by hooking him up to a battery. Then a death mask was made after his ears had been removed and LeBlanc was flayed and his skin made into purses, wallets and other knick-knacks, each coming with a personally signed letter of authenticity from Sheriff Ludlow.

The Sayre home is now a restaurant and is said to be haunted by the ghost of the slain maid Phoebe.

"I Hate Myself . . . Please Still Love Me. I Can't Live Unless You Love Me"

A lesbian pass led to a cheerleader murder. Orinda is a wealthy, white suburb of San Francisco. Kirsten Costas, fifteen, lived in the town with her parents, Arthur and Berit Costas, and her brother, Peter, and attended Miramonte High School. She was a pretty, petite and popular cheerleader. At school, the most sought-after sorority was the Bobbies, and when, on 21 June 1984, Kirsten received a call inviting her to a Bobbies initiation dinner she was overjoyed.

Two days later, a blonde girl picked up Kirsten, but less than an hour later, Kirsten was knocking on the door of the Arnold family telling them that her friend had "gone weird" and could she have a lift home.

Alex Arnold agreed and drove her to the Costas home. A tatty gold Pinto followed his car. As Kirsten got out, a "chunky, not fat, blonde teenage girl" jumped out of the Pinto and there was an argument followed by a fight. There was a flash of blade and Kirsten fell to the ground. Taken to Kaiser Hospital at nearby Oakland, Kirsten was pronounced dead at 11.02pm from five stab wounds – including two foot-long gashes in her back and two to Kirsten's front, one of which was a fifteen-inch slashing wound that penetrated her left arm, chest and left lung.

It was assumed that the killer must be a girl who was jealous of Kirsten, who did not conform to the Orinda ideal. Two girls – one a punk and the other a heavy metal fan – were questioned. Rumours spread of their guilt and their family homes were vandalized, they received death threats (from adults) and both moved out of the area.

When the local police drew a blank, the FBI was called in, and using profiling, they settled on one suspect, Kirsten's classmate, Bernadette Protti. On 11 December 1984, she confessed to her parents by letter. Protti was a member of the Bobbies but not as socially popular as Kirsten. She wanted to be Kirsten's friend so had made up the story of the dinner. The two girls sat in the car and smoked joints, after which it seemed likely that Protti made a pass at her friend, causing the other girl to label her "weird".

Protti agreed to plead to second-degree murder, but a publicity-seeking District Attorney wanted to go for first-degree even though the punishment was the same. At the trial, he tried to claim that Kirsten would never take drugs and that this was another lie by her killer. The defence produced two witnesses to say that they had seen Kirsten snorting cocaine at parties.

On 13 March 1985, Protti was convicted of second-degree murder and, on 1 April, sentenced to the maximum term: nine years in the custody of the California Youth Authority. She was released on parole on 10 June 1992, left California and changed her name.

In her letter to her parents eight years earlier she had begged, "I need you. I'm so sorry that I've been a disappointment to you in every way . . . I hate myself . . . I need your love, please still love me. I can't live unless you love me."

Police Chief Murdered in Own Office

Henry Solomon joined the Brighton police force in 1821 after a career as a watchmaker. He rose through the ranks to become joint chief of police in 1832 with William Pilbeam.

Four years later, Mr Pilbeam resigned because of poor health and Mr Solomon took sole control. On the evening of 13 March 1844, Chief Solomon was interviewing a 23-year-old suspect named John Lawrence, a ne'er do well and former juvenile delinquent. He had twice been convicted of felonies and had stolen £25 from his parents. He had arrived in Brighton in December 1843, and quickly fell in with a band of thieves and prostitutes. He even lived with a prostitute nicknamed Hastings Bet until they had a quarrel after he pawned some of her clothing. The quarrel turned violent and he beat her up so badly that she asked for police protection.

Three months later, Lawrence was arrested after, with another man, he stole a roll of carpet from Caleb Collins's shop at 47–48 St James's Street. The other thief made good his getaway but Lawrence was stopped by PC John Barnden and taken to the police HQ at Brighton Town Hall. Lawrence was taken for questioning into the office of Chief of Police Solomon.

Three other people were present in the room while PC Barnden waited outside the door. It was decided that Hastings Bet needed to corroborate some of Lawrence's story so the interview continued while other policemen went to find her.

Suddenly, Lawrence asked for a knife, adding that he wanted to kill himself. Then he grabbed the poker from the fireplace and struck Mr Solomon on the head with such force that the poker bent. The policeman fell to the ground before being helped to a chair by the others in the room. Lawrence gloated, "I hope I have killed him and I hope I shall be hanged for it."

Mr Solomon was taken to his home in Princes Street where two doctors attended him, but the situation was hopeless and he died at 10am the following day, leaving a widow and nine children.

Lawrence went on trial on 21 March 1844, before Lord Denman, the Lord Chief Justice, and the jury found him guilty without retiring. While awaiting death, Lawrence found God. He was executed at noon on 6 April – Easter Saturday – 1844, the last to be hanged at Horsham Jail. Henry Solomon's ghost is said to haunt the basement of the Town Hall in Bartholomew Square.

Jealous Husband Shoots Prostitute Wife

Percy Clifford did not fit into the English world he was born into – "half-caste, thirty-two, a theatrical artiste who became an engineer". Clifford saw service in the Boer War and was wounded in action.

Unable to find any regular work on demob, he drove a cab and bet on horses. In 1909, he met Maud Wilton, an attractive nineteen-year-old prostitute. She continued to ply her trade even as he courted her and they married on 7 January 1911, the day before her twenty-first birthday. They lived in various rooms around London and much to Clifford's annoyance his wife continued to sell her body. They split in October 1912, but continued to see each other.

On Saturday, 4 April 1914, the couple arrived in Brighton and at 1.45pm they took for four days the front room at 57 North Road, the home of Mary and Tom Upton. The couple did not give a name to their new landlord.

The Cliffords went out for the rest of the day, not returning till 11pm. The next day they stayed in bed till noon and then went out for the afternoon and evening. The Monday followed a similar pattern, the Cliffords returning at 11.15pm.

At 8am on Tuesday, 7 April, the fourth day, Mrs Upton left two cups of tea outside the Cliffords' door and Mrs Clifford called out her appreciation. The occupants of the room were silent till about half past noon when two loud bangs were heard. Mrs Upton assumed that it was a car backfiring or tyres bursting and thought no more of it. She became concerned by 3pm when the Cliffords still had not surfaced and went into their room. She screamed when she saw blood on the man's face and called for her husband who kicked something as he entered the room. He summoned a policeman who discovered what Mr Upton had kicked – a loaded pistol.

A local doctor pronounced Maud dead at the scene, but despite being shot in the head Percy Clifford was still alive, although he did not come round for ten days. Meantime, a search of the room revealed the couple's identity.

An inquest deemed that Clifford should stand trial for his wife's murder and he appeared at the Lewes Assizes on 8 July. Clifford pleaded not guilty and his barrister claimed that he was insane at the time of the shooting. The jury took just twenty-five minutes to find him guilty, and on 11 August 1914, after a last meal of three eggs, two rashers of bacon and a pint of beer, Clifford went to meet his maker – he was the last person to be hanged at Lewes Jail.

Butchery in Brixton

Dr David Napier Hamilton was a highly respected civil servant who had held a number of senior positions. Educated at Eton and Oxbridge, he numbered Princess Margaret among his friends. He kept his sexual preferences – he liked young black men – secret from his colleagues. While working in the Caribbean as private secretary to the Governor of Trinidad and Tobago in 1960, he met Kingsley Ignatius Rotardier, a youth who aspired to be a male model. The two began a homosexual relationship, which continued when Hamilton returned to London.

Rotardier moved in with Dr Hamilton at his flat at 164 Brixton Road, Brixton, and became involved in the older man's social circle. Strains began to show, though, and on 18 November 1985, the couple argued over Rotardier's newly established relationship with Carl Andrews, a black actor who appeared in *Crossroads*. The next day, Dr Hamilton disappeared and Rotardier used his boyfriend's credit card to buy a butcher's cleaver and saw. He followed this by systematically milking Dr Hamilton's bank account.

As part of their enquiries, the police interviewed Rotardier. He said that Dr Hamilton had left home on 19 November, to travel to Germany where he planned to visit a doctor for a consultation about his Aids, leaving Rotardier to deal with his affairs. A letter was received by Dr Hamilton's employer, the Greater London Council, informing them that Dr Hamilton was being treated for an illness and that he would not be able to return to work. Rotardier followed this up by claiming a severance payment due to Dr Hamilton following the abolition of the GLC and his £6,000-a-year pension.

By now Scotland Yard had put David Hamilton on their list of Missing Persons and began to focus suspicions on Kingsley Rotardier. In December 1986, he was charged with fraudulent use of Dr Hamilton's credit card and given a nine months' suspended sentence.

Detectives and forensic experts examining the circumstances of Dr Hamilton's disappearance came to the conclusion that he had probably been murdered. Rotardier's purchase of butchering implements led them to believe that he had killed Dr Hamilton and cut up his body in the bath. Pieces were kept in the fridge and, then, systematically destroyed in the garden incinerator. Neighbours in a nearby apartment recalled the nuisance experienced by smoke drifting into their rooms from Dr Hamilton's garden.

The missing man's colleagues and peers spoke of his cheerful disposition on the day before he disappeared. Not the outlook of a man who, according to his lover, was suffering a serious illness and intent on going away to die to spare the embarrassment of his family and friends. Letters and postcards, purportedly written by Dr Hamilton to his friends, showed anomalies in language and structure far removed from the communication skills of a man who had, at one time, been considered a potential private secretary to Prince Charles.

Rotardier denied the allegations made against him, but the circumstantial evidence was compelling. He was duly charged with the murder of David Hamilton, which he strongly denied. At the memorial service for the missing man, held at Southwark Cathedral in 1987, the cards of sympathy included one signed "Kingsley".

The trial judge Sir James Miskin, at the Old Bailey on 11 January 1988, passed a life sentence on Rotardier who had maintained an unemotional stance in the dock. The convicted man's verdict on the proceedings was to call the members of the jury "Bastards". No vestiges of David Hamilton's mortal remains were ever found.

Go West, Young Woman

Actress Mae West became famous for her "harem" of hunks and her sayings, such as "It's not the men in my life, it's the life in my men"; and, when someone commented on her jewellery "Goodness, what lovely diamonds" the riposte, "Goodness had nothing to do with it". She never did say "Come up and see me some time" however. She began writing her own risqué plays using the pen name Jane Mast. Her first starring role (as Margie LaMont) on Broadway was in a play she titled *Sex*, which she wrote, produced and directed. One of the show's angels was the gangster Owney Madden. Critics hated the show, which opened at the Daly Theatre in New York on 26 April 1926, and so did city officials. The première attracted just eighty-five patrons but the next night was packed thanks to the fleet being in town.

The mayor of New York at the time was James J. Walker and he was known to enjoy the company of gangsters and showbusiness folk. One of his friends was Owney Madden. His deputy Joseph V. McKee did not have such a laissez-faire attitude, and when Mayor Walker went on holiday in February 1927, McKee struck. The theatre was among three raided on 9 February, and West was arrested along with everyone else in the cast.

She was prosecuted on moral charges and appeared before the General Sessions on 19 April 1927, where Judge George E. Donnellan sentenced her to ten days in jail for public obscenity and a fine of $500. While incarcerated on Welfare Island, she was allowed to wear her silk panties instead of the scratchy prison issue, and Henry O. Schleth, the warden, reportedly took her to dinner every night. She served eight days, with two days off for good behaviour.

Too Cocky for His Own Good

The man who established the Mafia in America was born on 2 May 1867, and murdered on 15 August 1930, at 3.45pm. Giuseppe Morello was nicknamed "Clutch" because he had a deformed right arm with just a little finger, but that didn't stop him becoming one of the most brutal and feared figures in American crime history.

He personally murdered two people and ordered sixty others to be put to death. He was sixty-three, and he was at his office, the second floor of a four-storey brownstone at 352 East 116th Street in Italian Harlem, when two killers drove up armed with .32- and .38-calibre pistols. One of the killers was Bastiano Domingo, known as "Buster from Chicago", a relatively new arrival on the scene whose mother had been disfigured in a car bombing in September 1927, and whose father was murdered two years later, shot nine times as he sat in a cafeteria.

Joseph Valachi – who would later turn against the Cosa Nostra – described Domingo as looking "like a college boy", while Joseph "Joe Bananas" Bonanno said that he was "a virtuoso" with a machine gun. The identity of the other killer remains a mystery, although the names of Albert Anastasia, the Lord High Executioner of Murder Inc, and Frank Scalice have been suggested.

Morello had become over-confident, cocky even, and there were no guards to protect him either inside or outside his office. The killers mounted the stairs unseen and unheard. Inside they found Morello, Gaspare Pollaro and his 26-year-old nephew Giuseppe Perriano.

The assassins forced their way into the room and let fly with a fusillade of bullets. Perriano was shot twice and staggered towards a window trying to escape, fell out and died from the injuries he received in the fall rather than the bullets.

Pollaro died from a bullet in the chest. Morello was harder to kill and stumbled into a room next door where he collapsed, a grey fedora still on his head. He had seven bullet wounds and lived long enough to bleed to death.

Pregnant Teen Murdered by Boyfriend

Becontree Heath in Essex was built to accommodate an over-spill from the East End of London and as part of London County Council's Homes for Heroes programme. Fireman Charles Kirby and his wife, Hannah, moved into one of the new houses in Valence Circus.

His younger brother, Bob, and their mother, Sarah-Jane, later joined them. Bob Kirby began courting teenager Grace Newing who lived at 28 Stevens Road, a mile from the Kirby household, with her mother Rosina and eleven-year-old brother, George.

Grace worked in a sweetshop, but her beau was unemployed and he would either wait at her home for her or outside the shop. On 5 July 1933, five days after Grace's seventeenth birthday, Kirby arrived at her home at 8.45pm to wait for her. Mrs Newing went to bed two hours later.

On 2 July, he had told Mrs Newing that he thought Grace might be pregnant but that he would do the right thing. At 1am, Kirby woke his mother in her room. He was deathly pale and cold to the touch. "I have done Gracie in," he said to her.

The disturbance roused the rest of the house and Charles Kirby came into the room to find out what was happening. Kirby repeated what he said, "I have done Gracie in" before saying "I am going to Ilford to give myself up." Charles dressed and cycled to Green Lane, which led to Ilford, but could not find his brother so he went to Chadwell Heath Police Station.

PC John Bird went with Charles to Stevens Road where the body of Grace was discovered in the sitting room-cum-kitchen.

She had been strangled with a green cord. A post-mortem confirmed that she was four weeks' pregnant. Kirby was arrested at the home of another brother just before 7am that day. He told the police that Grace had asked him to kill her and even carried the murder weapon in her handbag.

On 21 September 1933, Kirby was tried at the Central Criminal Court. The jury found him guilty of murder after fifteen minutes' deliberation but recommended mercy. Mr Justice Rigby Swift passed sentence of death. The recommendation to mercy was ignored and Kirby went to his death on the gallows at Pentonville Prison on 11 October 1933.

Lovers' Tiff Ends in Murderous Rage

On 9 June 1851, Catherine Morris was sitting in the Brown Bear pub in Lichfield Street, Wolverhampton, with two new friends. She was a prostitute who lived with 26-year-old James Sones in a nearby brothel.

Catherine Morris also had a drink problem. Some time before, she had been so drunk that she allowed one of her children to burn to death. On the day she was in the pub she and Sones had had a stand-up row in the street over her desire to carry on being a prostitute and his equal desire that she now had him to look after her and should stop.

She stormed off to the pub where she met her two new friends. She downed a few drinks that they had bought for her but her alcohol tolerance was so high that she was not drunk. At 7.30pm, Sones came into the pub looking for his lover and was angry to see her being chatted up by two strange men.

He went up to the table and demanded she return his property. Loftily, she pulled out a handkerchief and threw it towards him. Sones said that he meant that he wanted her out of their home. He stormed out of the pub and his girlfriend ran after him, followed by one of the men, a Mr Lawson, with whom she had been drinking. He watched as they went down an alley near the pub.

There Sones raised his right hand to his girlfriend and pulled her head back, and as he did so he slit her throat with a knife in his left. She fell to the ground and Mr Lawson rushed over to see a seven-inch-wide and one-inch-deep wound in her neck.

Sones watched as she was carried to the Black Horse pub in Berry Street, ironically the street in which they lived. As she was being treated, Sones approached her and apologized. He was arrested for attempted murder, which charge was changed to murder when Catherine Morris died on 12 June.

Sones was tried on 30 July 1851, at Stafford Assizes, and he pleaded not guilty. An ex-employer paid for his barrister and the lawyer's skill got the charge reduced to manslaughter. Rather than the death sentence, Sones was deported to Australia where he lived the rest of his life.

The Monocled Mutineer

Francis Percy Toplis was a conman who was the subject of the television show *The Monocled Mutineer* (1986) that made a star out of Paul McGann. Percy Toplis began his criminal career aged eleven, in 1908, when he conned a tailor out of two suits and was sentenced on Friday, 6 March, at Mansfield Petty Sessions to six strokes of the birch.

On leaving school in 1909, he became a blacksmith at Blackwell Colliery, but did not like the work and was sacked after being found drinking in the Blackwell Arms when he should have been on the night shift. He moved to Scotland where he was imprisoned for ten days after travelling on a railway without a ticket.

In 1912, he was sentenced to two years' hard labour for the attempted rape of a fifteen-year-old Lincolnshire girl. He served his sentence in Lincoln Jail, was released in August 1914, and the following year joined the Royal Army Medical Corps (RAMC) as a stretcher-bearer and served with B section, 39 Field Ambulance at Torquay until Thursday, 17 June 1915, when they were sent to Gallipoli.

Unable to go straight even in the Army, he was given compassionate leave after he claimed that his wife had died in childbirth – he was a bachelor. In September 1917, Toplis was seconded to the troopship *Orantes* en route for India. He stayed in Bombay for several months.

Back in Britain, he went to RAMC Blackpool, but deserted shortly after the death of his father in August 1918. Several frauds later, including obtaining a watch by false pretences, Toplis was sent down again in November 1918. Following his release in 1920, and though still a deserter (the end of the Great War seems to have waned Army interest in such matters) he joined the Royal Army Service Corps (RASC) and, as part of No. 2 Depot Motor Transport (Bulford), he became heavily involved in the black market sale of Army petrol.

On Sunday, 25 April 1920, Toplis shot and killed Sidney George Spicer, a young Salisbury taxi driver, on Thruxton Down near Andover, and stole his car. Toplis spent the next fortnight in London living the high life dressed as a decorated and monocled officer. Press coverage of the case made Toplis flee to Scotland where he took refuge in a remote gamekeeper's bothy.

On Tuesday, 1 June, Toplis lit a fire to keep warm, but the smoke was seen by a hill farmer who returned at 11pm with the gamekeeper and the local bobby, PC George Greig. Toplis fired several shots, wounding the policeman in the shoulder and the farmer in the stomach, then made off on a bicycle.

Abandoning the bicycle at Aberdeen, he got a train to Carlisle, arriving on the afternoon of Saturday, 5 June. There he had the audacity to seek food and drink from the Army occupying the Castle. At 4pm the following day, PC Alfred Isaac Fulton of the Cumberland and Westmorland Constabulary questioned a man wearing partial military dress sitting by the side of the Carlisle to Penrith road at Low Hesket. PC Fulton was not satisfied by the replies he received and when he checked back at the station became convinced that the man was Percy Toplis.

The constable reported his suspicions to his superiors in Penrith. Fulton returned to look for Toplis accompanied by Inspector William Ritchie and Sergeant Robert Lewis Bertram who were issued with .45 Webley Mark VI revolvers and six rounds of ammunition.

Norman de Courcy-Parry, the son of the chief constable, armed himself with a small automatic Belgian pistol and joined the three. He rode his motorbike. They soon found Toplis who was walking south toward Plumpton. They drove past until their car was out of sight. De Courcy-Parry was the first to return, feigning a break-down ahead of Toplis, and spotted a gun in his coat pocket.

Further down the road the three policemen took cover behind farm buildings at Romanway, and when five-foot-eight Toplis approached Ritchie challenged him. He ran, but when he turned to shoot at the police they returned fire with three shots, one of which was fatal. The Penrith Board of Guardians, a charitable organization, buried Toplis in Penrith's Beacon Edge Cemetery, at 9am on Wednesday, 9 June.

The only witnesses were the gravedigger, one Board representative, two senior policemen, and the Reverend R. H. Law, the vicar of Christ Church, who, despite strong opposition, insisted that Toplis was entitled to a full Christian burial stating, "This man was violently removed from this life before he could be judged on earth."

Oddly, Toplis is famous for something he had nothing to do with. According to the television series, in 1917 he was sent to the British army base camp at Étaples where, despite being a private in the medical corps, he passed himself off as an officer with a monocle. On Sunday, 9 September, the soldiers at Étaples mutinied and Toplis was one of the ringleaders. The mutiny lasted six days, and when it was over Toplis went missing. However, the Percy Toplis who wore a monocle was nowhere near France during the mutiny – he was onboard the *Orantes* on his way to India.

The Shot Heard Around Westminster

A shooting in a quiet Marylebone mews, on 14 December 1962, had unintended consequences for almost everyone involved. Seventeen months earlier, John Profumo, the War Minister in Harold Macmillan's administration, had begun an affair with Christine Keeler, a nineteen-year-old showgirl, after encountering her swimming nude in the pool at Cliveden, the Buckinghamshire estate of Lord Astor.

Accounts vary – it was either a full-blooded affair with Profumo considering setting up his young *inamorata* in her own flat, or a quick fling that was over almost as soon as it begun – but whatever the case, Keeler was an equal opportunities girlfriend and she also shared her favours with a number of men who would have looked out of place in the rarefied corridors of Westminster.

Four months after meeting Profumo, she encountered Aloysius "Lucky" Gordon (who had a brother, the charmingly named "Psycho" Gordon) at the El Rio café at 127 Westbourne Park, Notting Hill. Keeler was with her friend Dr Stephen Ward, a society osteopath who mixed in grand (the Duke of Edinburgh, Marquess of Milford Haven, Lord Mountbatten) and not so grand (West Indian hoods and drug dealers) circles. Keeler, Ward and Gordon began seeing each other regularly, although Gordon was jealous and violent – he raped Keeler at knifepoint but also had consensual sex with her.

Keeler moved out of Ward's Wimpole Mews home and into a flat with her friend Mandy Rice-Davies in Dolphin Square, Pimlico. One night after Rice-Davies had found alternative accommodation, Keeler invited some friends back, including Gordon. Once there, he held her and another woman prisoner for two days. When they finally made their escape, they called the police. Remarkably, Stephen Ward stood bail for Gordon, and his brother managed to persuade Keeler to drop the charges. Terrified, she bought a Luger pistol.

Mandy Rice-Davies was the mistress of slum landlord Peter Rachman, and one of his henchmen was another West Indian called Johnny Edgecombe. He met Keeler in July 1962, and sensing that she was upset asked her what the matter was. She told Edgecombe about Lucky Gordon and he promised to sort things out.

On 27 October 1962, the two men clashed at the All Nighter Club in Wardour Street, Soho. Edgecombe slashed Gordon's face, leaving him needing seventeen stitches. Two months later, Edgecombe turned up at 17 Wimpole Mews, the home of

Stephen Ward (although he was living at Bryanston Mews West, the former home of Mandy Rice-Davies), in a minicab looking for Keeler who used to live there.

She was visiting her friend Mandy Rice-Davies who opened an upper-floor window and called down to Edgecombe that Keeler was not there. Edgecombe was about to get back into the cab when he spotted Keeler peering out of a window. Losing his temper, he pulled a gun and fired seven shots at the door before escaping in the cab. Arrested at his Brentford flat, Edgecombe was charged with wounding Lucky Gordon and the shooting at Wimpole Mews.

When Gordon came to trial on 14 March 1963, Keeler did not turn up to give evidence but had been more forthcoming about her lovers to anyone who would listen. (Edgecombe was sent down for seven years.)

On 15 March 1963, the *Daily Express* published a front-page story revealing that Profumo had wanted to resign "for personal reasons" but had been persuaded to stay on by Prime Minister Harold Macmillan. The story was not true, but also on the page was a report about the disappearance of Christine Keeler – it was a subtle way of linking the War Minister to the call girl and would have been missed by all but the very few in the know. Roger Wood, the editor of the *Express*, later claimed that it was a coincidence and not an attempt at subtlety.

On 22 March, at 11.08am, Profumo made a personal statement in the chamber of the House. He claimed that "There was no impropriety whatsoever in my acquaintanceship with Miss Keeler". It was a lie that was to do for his political career. The rumours would not go away, and while on holiday he confessed the truth to his wife, who stood by him, and to the Conservative Party, which did not. Profumo confessed that he had misled the House and resigned on 5 June.

As the police investigated, the media became interested and the names Ward, Profumo, Rachman, and Astor were mentioned more and more.

The Home Secretary Henry Brooke summoned the head of MI5, Roger Hollis, and Sir Joseph Simpson, the head of the Metropolitan Police Force. In short, he told them to get Ward.

Hollis told Brooke that Ward had done nothing illegal. Simpson, the Met Commissioner, was more accommodating and put his resources behind finding trumped-up charges to bring down Ward.

On 8 June 1963, Ward was arrested at Watford and charged with living off immoral earnings. As the scandal broke, his wealthy, powerful and influential friends deserted him one by one. His trial began at the Old Bailey on 22 July 1963.

Before a verdict could be reached, Stephen Ward took an overdose of thirty-five grains of Nembutal. On 31 July, the jury returned a guilty verdict. Ward died at St Stephen's Hospital without regaining consciousness on 3 August 1963.

The matter might never have come to the public's notice had it not been for a hot-tempered West Indian with a gun.

Keeler later summed up the liaison as "a very well-mannered screw of convenience; only in other people's minds, much later, was it 'An Affair'."

The Banker Who Lost His Head

The gruesome discovery on 17 December 1993 of a partially burned headless body, naked apart from underpants, under a railway arch near Piccadilly Station in Manchester raised immediate concerns about identification. The question was solved several weeks later when the missing head was reunited with the torso. A man walking his dog in Cannock in Staffordshire came across a severed head in a shallow grave.

The head was practically featureless because the skull had been smashed to pieces and the face mutilated beyond recognition. But, thanks to some inspired forensic reconstruction, identification was made possible. Richard Neave, who had worked in the 1970s with a team in Manchester restoring Egyptian mummies, was a specialist in facial reconstruction.

Using the remains of the battered head, Mr Neave constructed a model showing what it might have looked like in life. Police investigators issued photographs of the model and these were published in the press with a request for anyone who recognized the face to come forward. When a lawyer reported that she believed the photograph was of a man who had been her client, identification became possible.

The severed head was that of Adnan Abdul Hameed al Sane, a wealthy Kuwaiti businessman who lived in London. The lawyer made it known that she had represented Mr al Sane in a civil action in the courts. DNA testing showed that the head belonged to the torso found in Manchester and further confirmation came from a match with fingerprints found at al Sane's home in London. The businessman was last seen on 15 December 1993, at the Britannia Hotel in Grosvenor Square, and his headless body was found the next day in Manchester.

Enquiries into the dead banker's background showed that he had left Kuwait in 1986 following the collapse of his country's stock market. Mr al Sane, forty-six, came to Britain and lived the life of a retired millionaire. In London, he maintained a business relationship with Haj Hassan, a Jordanian financier, and lived in a flat at Hassan's home in Bayswater.

It was here that the next dramatic development took place when on 16 April 1994, two gunmen entered the house, shooting and seriously injuring Hassan and a friend. It seemed that Hassan and al Sane had a difficult relationship, mired in lawsuits over financial dealings. Hassan had been charged two years previously for theft but the case against him collapsed. It looked as if he had made some dangerous enemies.

The Wrong Man Murdered in Revenge

Roy Farran was a war hero who won the DSO, MC and Two Bars for heroism and escaped from a prisoner of war camp despite being badly injured. At the end of the Second World War, Farran went with 2 SAS to Norway where, in 1946, he was awarded the Croix de Guerre.

After brief service in Syria and British Mandate Palestine, he became an instructor at Sandhurst before volunteering for the Palestine Police Force. The area was awash with Jewish terrorist groups of which the Irgun was the largest.

On 2 March 1947, martial law was declared in Tel Aviv and the Jewish sector of Jerusalem and a counter-terror force was created to give the terrorists "a bloody nose". Roy Farran was appointed one of the commanders.

On 6 May, Alexander Rubowitz, sixteen, disappeared while putting up posters for the Jewish resistance organization, Lehi. He was seen being bundled into a car by a man wearing an army shirt and trousers. The man supposedly dropped a hat and inside was written Far-an.

At the time of the disappearance, Major Farran, disguised as an Arab, was having dinner with two Arab friends – but the story was soon put about that he had murdered Rubowitz with a rock after torture had failed to elicit any information.

Major Farran, fearing that he was being framed, fled to Aleppo hoping to reach Greece, which had no extradition treaty. Major Farran was persuaded to return voluntarily, but when he was arrested, he fled again, this time to Jordan. He returned when he heard of Jewish reprisals against British forces including his friends.

Major Farran was court-martialled in Jerusalem on 1 October. His defence was paid for by a fund to which his fellow officers contributed. At his trial, it was maintained that no body had been discovered and that those who claimed to have seen the boy taken away in a car had not identified Farran in a line-up. The case was dismissed because of lack of evidence – to the fury of the Rubowitz family.

On 3 May 1948, a parcel arrived at Major Farran's home in Codsall, Staffordshire. It was addressed to "R. Farran" and contained a copy of the complete works of Shakespeare – but the book had been hollowed out and filled with explosives. The bomb went off, fatally injuring 25-year-old Rex Farran, the major's youngest brother. A Lehi cell in Britain led by Yaakov Heruti had sent the bomb.

Murder Macabre

Sonia McCaskie left Britain with her widowed mother and siblings in 1946 to live in the USA. At the age of sixteen, she married an American and started a family. Sonia developed an interest in skiing and, having retained her British citizenship, was chosen to represent her country in the Winter Olympics held at Squaw Valley in 1960.

She separated from her husband and had a second child in another relationship. Her passion for skiing remained and she worked as an instructor in Reno, Nevada. She was last seen alive on 6 April 1963, when she drove her distinctive white convertible to her apartment. When she failed to collect her ten-month-old son from the friend who had been looking after him, the alarm was raised.

Police found the door to her apartment unlocked and when they looked inside were confronted with a scene described as "the work of a professional butcher". The young woman had been tortured, her head severed and body parts scattered about the apartment. Her torso was found with three knives protruding from it. Seasoned police officers were sickened by the spectacle. One said, "I have never seen anything so terrible".

There were no immediate leads as to the identity of the killer, and detectives questioned more than thirty people who had known the victim and submitted them to lie detector tests. All were cleared, but routine police work paid off when a camera stolen from Sonia's apartment was traced to a pawn-broker's shop. The owner described the seller as in his late teens, a youth of eighteen who was identified as Thomas Bean.

Bean, who lived less than a mile from the murder scene, was arrested at his home. He admitted prowling around the neighbourhood looking for opportunities to steal women's underwear from washing lines. When he found the door to Sonia McCaskie's apartment unlocked, he let himself in and killed her. He readily confessed to his crime.

Bean was taken back to the murder scene where he described raping and strangling his victim. He spoke about playing music on her record player while he cut up her body with a butcher's knife. A loaded handgun and rifle were found in his car.

When he was subjected to further questioning at a police station and was having his footprints recorded, Bean managed to break free. A chase ensued as he made a bid to escape, with a posse of policemen in hot pursuit. He was overwhelmed by determined police who quickly recaptured the teenage prowler turned murderer. During his confession, he boasted, "I killed to music."

Murder and Attempted Suicide

Pretty eighteen-year-old Alice Beetham worked at Jubilee Mill in Gate Street, Blackburn. She had much going for her – as well as her looks, she had a sunny disposition that made her popular with her workmates. She had been seeing a fellow worker named Arthur Birkett who was four years older than her.

At 8.45am on 20 May 1912, Alice was on her way back from the weft room (weft are the horizontal threads interlaced in a woven fabric) and was walking through the weaving shed when Birkett grabbed her, and before anyone could do anything, he slit her throat with a razor which he then turned on himself, inflicting two wounds. It took three workers to drag Birkett away from Alice and to stop him killing himself.

By the time Mr Smith, the mill manager, arrived from his office, Alice was dead – her head nearly separated from her body. Mr Smith examined the wounds on Birkett's throat and saw that they were not too serious. He ordered that Birkett's wounds be attended to and then summoned the police.

Birkett was taken to the local hospital and the mill closed for the day. Mrs Birkett soon learned of her son's behaviour and rushed home where she was doorstepped by the press. She told them that her son was deeply in love with Alice and had even given up drinking during his courtship.

However, something had occurred the previous weekend that had upset him, and, although she did not know what that was, it was serious enough for Alice to dump him on 16 May. Alice was buried on 25 May, in a ceremony according to the rites of the Roman Catholics. Birkett's trial began on 5 July 1912, at Manchester Assizes. He pleaded not guilty to murder but it took the jury just fifteen minutes to find him guilty and Mr Justice Bucknill sentenced Burkitt to death.

Within a short while, more than 66,000 people had signed a petition pleading for Burkitt's life to be saved, including, remarkably, Alice Beetham's mother. Mrs Beetham even visited him in prison as he awaited execution. The Home Secretary announced that he saw no reason to interfere with the course of justice and Arthur Birkett was hanged at Strangeways at 8am on 23 July 1912. Almost six thousand people waited outside the prison as the notice of death was pinned to the gate.

Errand Boy Kills Master

Walter Neilson was a chemist who lived with his mother, Janet, at 14 Shearbrow, Blackburn, less than a mile from the shop at 40 Whalley Range. Mr Neilson was twenty-eight years old, stood just five foot four and was in poor health.

At the end of 1892, he mistakenly issued a poison instead of Epsom Salts, an error that preyed on his mind. In the weeks after, his trade began to suffer. He put his fifteen-year-old errand boy, Edward Williams, on notice. The teenager was lazy, indolent and showed a lack of respect for his boss. In spite of that, Neilson wrote the boy a good reference.

At 4.30pm on 22 February 1893, the body of Walter Neilson was found in the rear of his shop, a large, bloody wound in the middle of his forehead. Forty-five minutes before his death, Mr Neilson had sent his errand boy to fetch two soda siphons from Mr Griffith's chemists at Salford Bridge, Blackburn. The boy returned at 4.15pm and found the shop shut. He waited outside, reading the paper for a few minutes before trying the door again. This time it was open; he went in and found the body and screamed that his boss had shot himself.

Oddly, the two siphon bottles had been taken into the shop by the boy and placed on the counter, which meant that he would have to pass the body to do so. A post-mortem examination was carried out at 8pm but not finished until the following afternoon. Three more wounds were spotted on the back and side of the head.

Edward Williams gave a statement to the police but Detective Sergeant Langstaff did not caution him beforehand. It also seemed apparent that Mr Neilson had been dead for some time and that the only key to the front door had been on the victim's body. The next day Williams was charged with the murder of Walter Neilson. In December 1891, Williams had been convicted of theft and fined forty shillings.

The chemist was buried on 25 February. On 1 March, Williams confessed to the crime. He had argued with Mr Neilson and it became physical; he pushed the chemist who fell and hit his head. It was when he returned to the shop that he said that he found Mr Neilson dead. On 23 March 1893, Williams appeared at Liverpool Assizes. Mr Justice Wills made it clear that he disapproved when the jury returned a verdict of manslaughter and regarded the case as one of murder. He sentenced Williams to penal servitude for fifteen years. He was released in January 1901, after serving less than half his sentence.

The Cashpoint Killer

Murderer William Josef Berkley was executed by lethal injection at a prison in Huntsville, Texas, ten years after he raped and killed eighteen-year-old schoolgirl Sophia Martinez at a cashpoint as she withdrew $20.

On 10 March 2000, German-born Berkley shot Sophia in the head at the machine in east El Paso. He forced her to withdraw $200 and then to drive to northeast El Paso, where he raped her and shot her four more times. Her remains were discovered three days later ten miles from the scene.

The crime featured on the television programme *America's Most Wanted* and El Paso locals raised a reward fund totalling $50,000. Berkley, twenty at the time of the murder, was arrested seven months later after his friend's girlfriend saw the programme and learned about the reward money. He confessed twice to the murder but recanted both times. There was also a great deal of DNA evidence linking him to the crime.

A jury of seven women and five men convicted him of capital murder and sentenced him to death after an eight-day trial in 2002. At the trial, two of his friends described him as an outcast who often lied. He told people he was a gang member until actual gang members beat him up.

Friends also testified that Berkley often used drugs, including crack. According to court records, he frequently told friends that the "best way to relieve stress was to unload a clip into someone's head".

In February 2004, Berkley, a self-professed marijuana-smoking, baggy-jeans-wearing, "sarcastic smart ass", advertised for pen pals on a prison website and again protested his innocence. He said that he was "very, very honest, sweet and constantly joking around. I am looking for a pen friend who is in it for the long run. I like all things and love all people".

Berkley was the sixth prisoner put to death in Texas, the state that executes more people than any other, in the first four months of 2010. Before his death, Berkley thanked his parents, girlfriend, Samantha Ann Gray, and spiritual adviser. Then he told prison staff to "Let her rip". Sophia's family and El Paso District Attorney Jaime Esparza, who prosecuted Berkley, witnessed the execution.

Three drugs were used in the execution on 22 April 2010, at 5.09pm. The first, sodium thiopental, sedated Berkley; the second, the muscle relaxant pancuronium bromidehim, collapsed his diaphragm and lungs, and the final drug, potassium chloride, stopped his heart. The cost per execution for the drugs was $86.08. Berkley was pronounced dead after nine minutes.

Toyboy Marries and Kills for Money

The body was badly decomposed when it was found in a ditch near Hall Farm in Cardiff on 3 June 1874. It was only the clothes that kept it in one piece. The weather, rats and insects had been at work, but it was just possible to see the remains of a large gash in the throat.

The body was identified as that of 43-year-old Susan Gibbs, a native of Jersey. She worked as a lady's maid in Lymington and it was there that she met James Gibbs, twenty years her junior and a footman. They became close despite the age gap and talked of marriage but split in 1871.

Gibbs later found a job as a butler to the owner of the stately Llanrumney Hall, St Mellons, near Cardiff. Gibbs soon gained a reputation for seducing the maids, one of whom went to work with Susan. She began writing to Gibbs seeking a reconciliation. Even though he had a girlfriend, Mary Jones, he encouraged her affections. His behaviour was no doubt affected by the knowledge that she had some money.

Indeed, she paid for their wedding on 30 July 1873. He then went back to Mary and told his new wife that his boss did not approve of employing married men so she must stay away from Llanrumney Hall and not use her married name. Still in love, she moved into a hotel nearby and continued to finance her husband's life. When money ran low she worked as a barmaid, hoping that one day circumstances might change.

Gibbs was unpopular with the other staff at Llanrumney Hall, and one day Miles the footman decided to tell Susan what her husband was really like. Furious and humiliated, Susan went to Llanrumney Hall to confront him.

Gibbs managed to placate her and wrote love letters. He arranged late-night rendezvous in locations that, picturesque by day, were quite dangerous at night. She soon tired of these, returning to her lodgings cold, wet and dishevelled.

On 10 May 1874, they slept together and he told her that he would arrange a cottage for them on the Llanrumney Hall estate. She was overjoyed, her friends sceptical. Two days later, she set off for this new life. At 11pm that night, he returned to his room, but, rather than sleeping, he spent the time washing his clothes. Four days later, he visited his wife's landlady to say that Susan was happy but unwell and he searched her belongings.

As soon as his wife's body was identified, Gibbs's arrest quickly followed. An inquest revealed that Gibbs had attacked his wife with a walking stick. He left her still alive before fetching a razor and virtually severing her head before dragging her body to the ditch where he dumped her. Gibbs continued to protest his innocence all through his trial and up to his death. He broke down and wailed when the hangman James Marwood came for him, and he had to be held up by two assistants before the execution could proceed.

Killer Arsonist

To many it seemed the height of kindness, but there was an ulterior motive. Virginia and Billie Joe McGinnis took Deana Wild, their twenty-year-old future daughter-in-law, on holiday to tourist resort Big Sur, California, in the spring of 1987.

On 2 April, Deana posed for pictures on the 400-foot drop overlooking Seal Beach and the Pacific Ocean. The next moment, she was hurtling to her death on the rocks below. The spot was called Lovers' Leap because so many distraught people had decided to end it all there. The police investigated but ruled the fall nothing more than a tragic accident.

However, Deana's mother, Bobbie Roberts, did not believe that her educationally subnormal daughter would have killed herself. If nothing else, Deana was getting married. After a brief first marriage, she had become engaged to James Coates, Virginia McGinnis's son by her first marriage. It did not bother Deana that her intended was in prison for second-degree murder, and she stayed with her future in-laws at their home in San Diego.

Mrs Roberts had taken out an insurance policy on her daughter to pay for funeral expenses but was unable to claim on it so she asked Steve Keeney, a family friend and a lawyer, to investigate. His discoveries shed new light on the character of Virginia McGinnis. Over the years, her homes had an unfortunate propensity to burn down and she made seven insurance claims. A removals truck containing her goods was even stolen en route to a new house and she claimed for that.

In April 1972, her three-year-old daughter Cynthia had died in a tragic accident and her mother claimed on insurance for that too. Two years later, her second husband Sylvester Rearden died of cancer. The nurse in charge of his medication had been his wife. Mary Hoffman, Virginia McGinnis's mother, died a little while before Deana fell to her death – Mrs Hoffman had been nursed by her daughter.

The McGinnises also took out a life insurance policy on Deana with the beneficiaries being Coates and then the

McGinnises themselves. The couple divorced but the circumstantial evidence built against them and they were both charged with murder. On 1 December 1991, Billie Joe McGinnis died of Aids in prison before the start of the trial, but his ex-wife went on trial on 6 January 1992. She was found guilty and sentenced to life without parole on 30 March 1992.

"Please Help Me – I Can't Stop Stealing"

Isobel Marshall became a doctor, married solicitor (Sir) Geoffrey Barnett, became a magistrate in 1948 and went on to become a television and radio personality in the 1950s and 1960s. Lady Barnett's life was one of middle-class prosperity. In 1953, she was one of the original panellists on BBC's *What's My Line?* and stayed with the show for ten years.

As television changed and deference disappeared so did Lady Barnett's media career. She became rather eccentric and reclusive. She took to stealing from the local shop owned by Roger Fowkes – she would hide a bag under her coat and slip pilfered items into it.

In 1980, she was caught, and in court on Thursday, 16 October, was found guilty by a jury of stealing a tin of tuna fish and a carton of cream worth a total of 87p from Mr Fowkes's shop.

Outside the court, she begged *The Sun* reporter Mary Griffiths, "Please help me – I can't stop stealing." Four days later, she committed suicide in her bath – clad in a floral nightgown with her head under the water. She was sixty-two and had taken between twenty and twenty-six Distalgesic tablets that had been prescribed for her arthritis. There was no alcohol in her body and a two-bar electric fire found in the bath with her had played no part in her death.

Of all her showbiz friends only David Jacobs turned up to her funeral on 24 October, at St Mary Magdalene Church, Knighton, Leicestershire. Lady Barnett's ashes were scattered over the grave of her husband who had died ten years earlier. Thieves ransacked her home shortly after her death.

The Bowler That Gave it Away . . .

On 24 December 1938, Ernest Key, a 64-year-old jeweller, was discovered bloodied and unconscious in the back room of his shop in Surbiton, Surrey, which he had run for more than twenty years. He had been stabbed more than thirty times in the course of a robbery, receiving wounds to his head, face and neck. He died on the way to the hospital.

A bowler hat was found at the scene and was examined by the pathologist Eric Gardner, who was able to give the police some information about the owner from the size of the hat and the hairs inside. Sir Bernard Spilsbury, the Home Office pathologist, then arrived. The hat was found to belong to William Thomas Butler, a 29-year-old unemployed man who lived in Teddington, Middlesex, with his wife and two children.

Further investigation revealed that Butler had a criminal record for house-breaking, and an hour after the murder he had visited Kingston hospital to get cuts on his hands treated. He gave Dr Day a false name (Charles Jackson) and address and told them he had cut his hands on a wood-chopping machine. A fortnight later, he was arrested and claimed that the injuries had been caused when he was knocked down by a motorbike. He said that he had given the hospital a false name and address to avoid having to pay for his treatment.

Butler was charged with murder and went on trial at the Old Bailey on 15 February 1939. He claimed that he had acted in self-defence and thus should be tried for manslaughter and not murder. The trial lasted two days before the jury found him guilty of murder.

Butler was sentenced to death and went to the gallows at Wandsworth Prison on 29 March 1939, despatched by Thomas Pierrepoint. The press went over the top in the coverage of the case and exaggerated the part of Eric Gardner, as did a German report of the case. In fact, Scotland Yard later even received a request from the German police asking for the assistance of "the clairvoyant Erich Gardner" who could apparently solve a murder by looking at a hat.

"I Use Marigolds"

A tramp rummaging for food in a wheelie bin in a suburban street at the end of December 2002 found more than he had bargained for. Opening a plastic refuse sack, he was first overwhelmed by the stench and then by the spectacle of two decomposing human legs. This was the prelude to a number of gruesome discoveries.

Earlier in the year, police had been called to a block of flats in Camden, north London, after complaints that a resident had scrawled an obscene message on a neighbour's door. Anthony Hardy harboured a grievance against Sally White following a disagreement over a leaking water pipe.

When officers knocked on the door of Hardy's bedsit, they interrupted him in the process of photographing Sally White's naked body. Pathologists determined that she had died of a heart attack. It appeared that Hardy was using her as a prop for some kind of sex ritual. There was insufficient evidence to charge Hardy with murder but he was sectioned under the Mental Health Act.

He was released from hospital on 4 November 2002, and, in December, killed two women – 29-year-old Elizabeth Valad and 34-year-old Bridgette MacLennan. It was parts of Valad's dismembered body that the tramp discovered during his wheelie bin foraging on 30 December.

The next day, police were at Hardy's bedsit intent on questioning him, only to find him missing. What they did discover, though, apart from the appalling smell, was Elizabeth Valad's torso. When arrested a few days later, he joked with officers saying, "They're calling me the Ripper".

The scope of Hardy's depravity slowly unravelled in the seven weeks it took to examine his bedsit. Among the revolting discoveries were dried skin and flesh smeared on the walls, which were also covered with satanic symbols. When he saw a forensic officer putting on rubber gloves prior to making searches, he quipped, "I use Marigolds".

A former engineer and separated from his wife, Hardy settled in London, taking the bedsit in Camden, roaming around the neighbourhood and drinking heavily. He was regarded as a strange individual and fellow residents were often disturbed at night by the noise of an electric saw. This was when he was cutting up his victim's bodies, having engaged in sadomasochistic rituals with them.

Parts of his third victim, Bridgette MacLennan, were found by bin men months after he had killed her. Hardy disposed of his victims piece by piece in plastic sacks, which he dumped, and other parts were scattered around Camden. The heads and hands of his victims were not recovered. His weird rituals involved taking pornographic photographs of his victims. Police recovered over forty photographs of his last victims, together with a collection of films and videos. He told police investigators that it was all just a sex game and he did not intend to kill.

Hardy pleaded guilty to murder at his trial in May 2010 and was given three life sentences for killing three women to "satisfy his depraved and perverted needs".

A Vampire Calls

A teenage art student had an interest in vampires; some might say it was an obsession. Matthew Hardman lived on Anglesey and attended Menai College. He was dyslexic and left school when he was sixteen.

He demonstrated his leaning towards Dracula during a visit from a German exchange student whom he invited to bite his neck. This episode was drawn to the attention of the police but Hardman said he could not remember such an incident taking place.

Six weeks later, in November 2001, he broke into the bungalow of Mabel Leyshon, aged ninety. She lived alone and was hard of hearing. Hardman knew her because at one time he delivered her newspapers.

He surprised the old lady while she was watching television and subjected her to a horrific ordeal, stabbing her twenty-two times and cutting out her heart. He placed it in a saucepan to which he added blood drained from wounds in her leg. Then he drank from the saucepan. He also placed pokers on the floor in the form of a cross, together with candles in a representation of a black mass.

When the seventeen-year-old was put on trial for murder at Mold Crown Court, he had not been publicly named. The prosecution said that the youth was fascinated by vampires and accessed websites such as the Vampire Rights Movement which gave directions on conducting a black mass and cooking human flesh. Books found in his possession included a copy of *Dracula* by Bram Stoker.

Crime scene evidence, including his DNA and a footprint, placed him at Mrs Leyshon's bungalow. When questioned by police, he showed little emotion and, asked if he needed anything, requested a burger and fries. In court, he denied any obsession with vampires, dismissing the idea as a passing interest.

The trial judge lifted the ban on identifying Hardman and the jury brought in a unanimous guilty verdict. Sentencing him to be detained at Her Majesty's pleasure, the judge told him the evidence indicated that he believed he could attain immortality by drinking his victim's blood.

One Law for Men and Another for Women

In fourteenth-century England, wives had no virtually no rights, and indeed on marriage their goods became the property of their husband, thanks to an interpretation of St Paul's first letter to the Corinthians.

With no recourse to divorce, some women took extreme measures to rid themselves of unwanted husbands. The wealthy Sir Thomas de Murdak visited Stourton Castle near Stourbridge with his wife, Juliana, and servants at Easter 1316. On 12 April – Easter Monday – Sir Thomas was asleep when he was murdered by his servants and those of Sir John de Vaux, the steward of the castle. After he was stabbed to death, Sir Thomas was decapitated and dismembered and his body parts dumped in the grounds of his home.

Three days later, Juliana – who was wealthy in her own right thanks to inheritances from her father and a brother – married Sir John de Vaux. An inquest was held on 29 June 1316, but no one was brought to trial until the following year.

On 30 September 1317, Robert Ruggele, a lead assassin and servant of Sir Thomas de Murdak, was put on trial although no one seems to know how or what evidence implicated him. He implicated six other people in the crime and Juliana was sent to Marshalsea Prison in London on 4 October 1320, to await trial.

Less than a month later, on 2 November 1320, John de Vaux was arrested and sent to the Tower of London. On 20 January 1321, Juliana went on trial before a jury of twenty-four, including a dozen knights. Three days later, she was found guilty of petty treason and ordered burned at the stake. Sources vary as to her eventual fate – some say that she was burned at the stake on 20 May 1321, while others say she suffered execution by hanging.

Her husband was found guilty of bigamy on 23 January, but pleaded benefit of clergy, being able to recite Psalm 51. He spent some years in the Tower before being acquitted of all charges and freed in 1325. He died around four years later. The fate of the servants who actually carried out the killing remains a mystery to history.

"What Do You think Would Have Happened If You'd Been Single?" . . .

Susan Christie was born in August 1968, to a member of the Ulster Defence Regiment (UDR). She lived on Army bases around the world until she was twelve, when her father was stationed in Belfast. In November 1986, she joined the UDR as a part-timer and went full time in July 1989.

A teetotaller, she disapproved of the hard drinking among her colleagues. She also had a hang-up about her height (just five foot) and what she saw as a large behind and fat legs. To make up for these deficiencies she often went braless in tight jumpers or low-cut tops, her 38C breasts straining against the material. She was still a virgin at twenty-two, although not by choice. She made allegations of sexual harassment against two soldiers, one of whom was demoted.

On 11 July 1990, she met Captain Duncan McAllister of the Royal Corps of Signals who in 1984 had married the stunningly attractive Penny. Two days later, they met at a local beauty spot. He recalled, "A shiver went down my spine as I looked at her. The see-through material of her blouse stretched across her breasts. I was filled with sexual excitement."

On 23 July, they had sex for the first time. Christie's behaviour became extreme, accusing soldiers of making passes, bullying and hitting her. None of it was true. On 2 November, when Captain McAllister told her that he wanted to end the affair, his lover said that she was pregnant. On 5 December, she said that she lost the baby. There never was a child.

Captain McAllister told her that he was being posted to Germany in the following June. On 16 March 1991, the lovers had sex for the last time. Ten days later, Christie rang Captain McAllister and asked, "What do you think would have happened if you'd been single?"

The next day, Penny McAllister and Susan Christie met to walk their dogs in Drumkeeragh Forest. At 1.30pm two boys met Christie rushing out of the woods claiming that she and her friend had been attacked by a wild, bearded man who had stabbed Penny to death. Christie was crying and her clothes were covered in blood.

Four days later, Captain McAllister admitted the affair and the police charged Christie with murder. Christie's trial opened at Downpatrick Crown Court on 1 June 1992. Thanks to an overly sympathetic judge, Lord Justice Kelly, Christie was found "guilty of manslaughter with diminished responsibility" and he sentenced her to five years.

In October 1992, the sentence was increased to nine years.

Christie served her sentence at the maximum security Maghaberry Prison near Belfast and was released in December 1995.

A Murder Shopping List

Benjamin Laing, a 25-year-old delivery driver, made an appointment, using a false name, to visit Matthew Manwaring at his home in Barking, Essex, on 23 April 1992. His ostensible purpose was to view a car that Mr Manwaring was selling.

Once admitted to the house, Laing killed Mr Manwaring with a 12-bore shotgun and then waited for the return home of Alison, Mr Manwaring's daughter, who had been out with her boyfriend. When she returned, Laing attacked her, committed sexual assault and strangled her. Then he took both bodies to the bathroom where he dismembered them using a knife and hacksaw. Next, he drove home to Abbey Wood where he unloaded ten plastic bags filled with body parts and buried them in the garden of his girlfriend's house.

Manwaring, father and daughter, were reported missing, probably kidnapped. There was extensive media speculation about the possible outcome. In the meantime, Laing used one of his victim's cash cards to draw money and spent a day at Alton Towers amusement park where he boasted to friends about his new car.

Then, Laing brazenly walked into a police station and stated he had bought the car from Mr Manwaring who was in good health when he left him. Laing had done enough to draw suspicion to himself and he was taken into custody. A search of his girlfriend's house and garden revealed the grave. A neighbour recalled seeing a man using a pickaxe and shovel in the garden during a period of heavy rain. A search of Laing's house produced two notebooks, one of which contained "a murder shopping list". The items listed included a tool kit, black bags, change of clothes, and glasses. "Hcuffs" and "gloves" were listed but crossed out.

Laing was tried for murder at the Old Bailey in February 1993. He claimed that the murders had been carried out by the Fijian Freedom Fighters who employed him as a gun-runner. They then tried to pin the blame on him. It was shown in court that Laing had sent a bogus letter to Alison Manwaring's brother in a move to wrong-foot the police by telling him his father and sister were going away for a while. The letter was signed "Love Always in God", the letters of which spelled LAInG.

The prosecutor said it "illustrated the total arrogance of the man" who killed two people and "believed he could get away with it". When he gave evidence in court in his own defence, Laing dissolved into tears. There was applause and cheering in the public gallery when the jury returned a guilty verdict. Benjamin Laing was sentenced to life imprisonment.

Jigsaw Man

Police were mystified when human body parts started to turn up in Hertfordshire and Leicestershire during the spring months of 2009. First, it was a forearm found on a grass verge by walkers and then, some weeks later, a leg was discovered in a holdall. In the ensuing weeks, a severed head and another forearm and leg turned up, with the discovery of a torso on 12 April. But the hands remained missing.

The parts all belonged to the same individual, but DNA profiling failed to find a match. From the dismembered parts it was possible to define the likely stature of the unidentified person. The remains belonged to a male aged between forty and sixty, weighing around sixteen stone and of about average height. A breakthrough came when links were made to a man reported missing late in March.

He was 49-year-old Jeffrey Howe who ran a company that fitted kitchens, and he lived in a flat in north London. Investigators found that the victim of the "Jigsaw Murder", as it was referred to in press reports, shared his flat with two others. They were Stephen Marshall and Sarah Bush. Marshall admitted lying to the police about the whereabouts of Jeffrey Howe and pleaded guilty to charges of perverting the course of justice. Bush pleaded not guilty to all charges.

The couple were charged with killing Howe and appeared in St Albans Crown Court in January 2010. While pleading not guilty to murder when he first appeared on trial, Marshall subsequently changed his plea and said that he killed Howe, dismembered his corpse and scattered the remains around the countryside.

During the trial, it was alleged that Marshall and Bush had set out to steal Jeffrey Howe's identity. They were intent on milking his bank account and taking over his house and possessions in what was described as a sophisticated plot. Initially, Marshall claimed that his girlfriend committed the murder while he helped with dismemberment and disposal of the body. Subsequently, he admitted stabbing Howe, assisted by Sarah Bush who later told friends she had put a pillow over the victim's face "to stop the noise".

It was alleged in court by an unnamed witness that Marshall claimed to have cut up bodies for a criminal gang in London in the late 1990s when he worked as a club doorman. The corpses of four unidentified victims of gangland crime were said to have been dismembered and the remains taken to Epping Forest for burial. These allegations prompted the police to open a number of cold case reviews.

Having accepted full responsibility for killing and dismembering Jeffrey Howe, Marshall was found guilty and given a life sentence. His 21-year-old girlfriend was judged guilty of helping to cover up the crime and received a sentence of three years' imprisonment.

Poetic Listomaniac Seeks Revenge

Many people compile a list of friends, family, even celebrities who annoy them for some reason or other, but rarely do they do anything about it. David Schoenecker, fifty, was different. His list contained fifty-four names and he wanted revenge.

Schoenecker became more obsessed with the list, and what he wanted to do with the people on it, to the extent that he told his second wife, Gail, a forty-year-old teacher, all about it.

Rather than understanding his thinking and consoling him, she was horrified.

Fearing she would go to the police, he decided to murder her at their home at East Amanda Circle, Anaheim Hills, California. On 5 May 1989, he prepared a romantic candlelit dinner for her and then as she lay dozing on the settee afterwards, he shot her in the head with a .357 Magnum.

He then wrote some doggerel, which he left on the table: "I made my list,

I'm checking it twice,

I'm going to find out who's naughty, not nice.

All I seek is revenge.

I want to make it very clear

They have taken things from me that I've held very dear.

This plan has taken three years to prepare.

I've hidden money and weapons everywhere.

. . .

All on the list will go to their grave,

All with the help of friendly old Dave."

Schoenecker took $4,000 and set off for Montana and his next victim. However, he was unable to resist boasting about what he had done and wrote to his local newspaper, *Orange County Register*, who informed the police. They broke into the house on 10 May, and found Gail's rotting body. They also discovered the list and alerted the potential victims. Schoenecker was caught when his car had a flat tyre and he had to hitch-hike. He was found guilty of murder in August 1989, and two months later Judge Robert Fitzgerald had some sentencing words of his own:

"You killed your sweet wife who loved you so dear.

For that you're being punished, let me make that fact clear.

The sentence I've chosen for you may seem cold.

You'll pay, and you'll pay all the while you'll grow old.

One day you will die, a funeral your warden will hold.

For you will serve your entire natural life and not be paroled."

Slicing and Dicing

If ever a man's destiny shaped him to be a criminal, it must be the self-styled "Crossbow Cannibal", Stephen Griffiths.

Griffiths, a forty-year-old psychology graduate, enrolled as a PhD student at Bradford University intent on studying criminology, and became a practitioner of the black arts. He had a public school education but was subjected to psychiatric assessments from his late teenage years. He had convictions for possessing weapons and was obsessed with murder, particularly serial killers. In 1991, he was described as a schizoid psychopath and adopted Peter Sutcliffe, the Yorkshire Ripper, as a role model.

Griffiths had lived for fifteen years in a flat close to Bradford's red-light district. This was his centre of operations. On 21 May 2010, the caretaker at the block of flats was routinely examining security camera footage when he saw some shocking scenes. A woman ran out from number 33, followed by a man who grabbed her, shot her twice in the head with a crossbow and dragged her back into the flat. Thus was the violent death of Suzanne Blamires, a local prostitute, recorded.

When he was arrested, Griffiths was ready to talk, claiming that "I've killed a lot more than Suzanne Blamires", boasting that he had eaten flesh from her body; "That's part of the magic", he declared. Dismembered pieces of her body were dumped in the River Aire in bin bags, one of which, containing her head, was discovered by a shocked member of the public.

In Griffiths's flat there were bloodstains on the walls and forensic evidence that both Susan Rushworth (forty-three, last seen on 22 June 2009) and Shelley Armitage (thirty-one, last seen on 26 April 2010), local prostitutes who had been missing for months, had been there. Indeed, images on his computer showed one of the women trussed up in the bath and another lying on the floor of the living room. Griffiths described the bathroom as "just a slaughterhouse". He claimed to have cooked and eaten some of his victim's body parts.

Tried at Leeds Crown Court in December 2010, the enormity of Griffiths's killing activities was laid before a shocked jury. His videos and collection of weapons, which included thirty knives, spoke eloquently of what he called "slicing and dicing". The judge told him that "It was one thing to terrorize and kill but to dismember and eat parts of the victims takes it to another level of the exertion of power".

Griffiths, who had pleaded guilty to murder, was convicted on three counts on 21 December. Describing him as "wicked and monstrous", the judge sentenced him to life imprisonment. Newspaper reports speculated that he could continue his criminology studies for a PhD while in prison.

CHAPTER 6

The Coward's Weapon: Method and Opportunity

We owe the term "coward's weapon", with reference to premeditated poisoning, to the English poet, Phineas Fletcher (1582–1650). Its sinister reputation lies in the secrecy and planning which accompany its use. Poison is administered unemotionally, using stealth and the exploitation of everyday situations. The poisoner can doctor food or drink with fatal consequences or contrive to deliver a fatal dose in the guise of medicine. There is no need for a knife, gun or bludgeon. No blood is spilled and there is an absence of injuries.

The world abounds in poisonous substances, from natural plants with a deadly reputation, such as aconite and belladonna, to chemical elements such as arsenic and cyanide, and many more besides. Added to nature's dispensary full of poisons are those that are man-made, including ricin, polonium and bacterial cultures.

Terence McLaughlin, in his book, Coward's Weapon, *published in 1980, made the point that poisoning is often resorted to by individuals who have been cast as underdogs in the way life has treated them. This includes hen-pecked spouses and family members aggrieved by being overlooked in the division of family spoils. "Revenge is a kind of wild justice," wrote Francis Bacon (1561–1626), which comes in many forms including death by poisoning.*

Elimination of an unwanted relative or rival has been a key feature in murders involving the administration of poison. Thus emerged the wife killers, Dr Crippen in 1910 and Major Armstrong in 1920, the doctor using hyoscine and the solicitor, arsenic. This process has run the full gamut of many centuries, and arsenic was known as "inheritance powder" for very good reasons. And, in the modern era, poisoning has taken on a political dimension with the removal of dissidents and defectors using sophisticated toxins and methods to match.

Thus, in September 1978, Georgi Markov, a Bulgarian dissident, was made the victim of the "Umbrella Murder" as he walked in a London street. A lethal dose of ricin was injected into his leg with fatal consequences by an unknown assassin using a modified umbrella to implant the poison in his body. Almost thirty years later, Alexander Litvinenko, a former KGB officer who defected to London, died after being plied with Polonium 210, a so-called "designer drug", probably dispensed in his coffee. What distinguished these murders was the level of sophisticated planning that went into them backed up by laboratory facilities. These were not off-the-shelf poisons.

Fate plays cruel tricks on victims whose tormentors are members of the medical profession and, thereby, legally entitled to keep and administer drugs. Physicians have the capacity to become silent killers but their boldness sometimes leads to mistakes. Dr Robert Clements murdered his wife in 1947 by dosing her with morphine and diagnosing her as a leukaemia sufferer. What he failed to realize was that this drug has the effect of reducing the pupils of the eyes to pinpoints. When an observant pathologist noted this tell-tale sign of poisoning, the game was up.

Those who nurse the sick in hospitals and in their homes also occasionally resort to poisoning to terminate an unwanted life. Such was the case with Kenneth Barlow, a male nurse who grew tired of caring for his sick wife. He dosed her with insulin and pretended that she had drowned in the bath. Again, it was the victim's eyes at post-mortem which spoke to the pathologist when he noted they were widely dilated. Injection marks were found on her body and insulin in the bloodstream. As a nurse, Barlow had access to drugs and was heard to have boasted that insulin could be used to commit the perfect murder.

Working as an intensive care nurse in a hospital in Indiana, USA, Orville Lynn Majors also had access to drugs and medication. He put on a caring front but had been heard referring to the elderly patients in his care as "trash". A rising death toll at the hospital caused concern and a common feature in many of the deaths was that the victim had been in the care of Majors. He had been seen tampering with patients' intravenous drips, and potassium chloride had been discovered in some of the dead patients. The "Angel of Death", as he was quickly named in the media, was judged to have committed six murders by poisoning.

Poisoners are entrepreneurs, always looking for more novel and sophisticated means of achieving their lethal aims. Their guiding philosophy is that poison can make murder look like accident or suicide. Carbon monoxide is well known for its death-dealing potential, and Cranog Jones embraced it in his cunning plan to gas his wife and make her death appear to be suicide. To this end he constructed a home-made gas chamber designed to channel car exhaust fumes from the garage to the bedroom. His plan was to gas his wife by placing a hood over her head while she slept, then take her body down to the garage and simulate a tragic suicide. Fortunately, the intended victim fought off her husband and survived his murderous intentions.

The use of germ cultures as a poison medium was pioneered in 1910 by Dr Henri Girard, a French medical practitioner with designs on a friend's financial assets. He experimented with typhoid cultures and induced the disease in his intended victim by means of a fatal injection. Girard also saw possibilities in the use of poisonous mushrooms and earned a reputation as the first so-called "scientific murderer". Where he led, others followed, including Ma Anand Sheela, who, driven by religious sectarianism, doctored food served in an American restaurant in the 1980s with salmonella to create a food poisoning scare.

An out-and-out extremist was Johnson Aziga who contracted HIV and deliberately set out to pass on the disease to his sexual partners, resulting in a landmark trial in Canada in 2003. By this means he killed two of his lovers and became the first individual known to use a viral infection as a murder weapon. It seems that there are no lengths to which a committed murderer will not go to secure his objectives.

Apart from being seduced by their own cleverness, the poisoner's greatest enemy is the science of toxicology. James Marsh made his

*historic breakthrough in 1836 when he discovered a means of iden-
tifying arsenic. This heralded the beginnings of forensic toxicology,
which advanced rapidly during the nineteenth century. Nearly
half of the pages in Dr William Guy's book* Forensic Medicine,
*published in 1861, were devoted to toxicology. In his comprehen-
sive text, he covered everything from arsenic to zinc in what he
called "the most important division of forensic medicine".*

*Of course, each new technical advance tests the ingenuity of the
determined poisoner to devise new methods to avoid detection and
outwit the scientists. It is a mind game that has been played out
over centuries.*

Folie à Deux

Press reports of the trial of a doctor and his mistress accused
of murder read like the plot for a novel. Paul Vickers was an
orthopaedic consultant, whose wife, Margaret, suffered from
paranoid schizophrenia. He offset the role of carer by engaging with Pamela Collison as his mistress.

Margaret Vickers died in hospital on 14 June 1979, from the
debilitating effects of aplastic anaemia, aged forty-three. It was
later revealed that, believing his wife had a malignant brain
tumour, Dr Vickers was treating her with CCNU, a cancer
drug. It was also the case that this particular drug could induce
aplastic anaemia and leave no traces in the body.

The drug had been administered in capsule form over a
four-month period in 1978 and 1979. None of the doctors
treating Margaret Vickers at that time had been advised that
she was taking CCNU. Her husband persuaded Pamela
Collison to collect the prescriptions, which were not made out
to Mrs Vickers but used up to twelve false names. Paul Vickers
and Collison broke off their liaison in the spring of 1978 before
Margaret Vickers died. The deception over the prescriptions
came to light when Pamela Collison informed the police.

When questioned, Vickers admitted giving his wife CCNU,
saying "All I wanted to do was to make her well". He thought
she had a brain tumour, "I wanted to help her, not kill her", he
said. He agreed that he had been guilty of gross medical

negligence. Enquiries into Margaret Vickers's death led to charges of murder brought against her husband and Pamela Collison.

During their trial at Teesside Crown Court in October 1981, some extraordinary allegations and statements were made about Paul Vickers's affair with Pamela Collison. He claimed they were both being treated for venereal disease and blackened her name by claiming she was hysterical and indiscriminate in her sexual liaisons.

The prosecution said that Collison had mesmerized Vickers and was a "relentless, blackmailing Boadicea". She denied all the allegations made against her, saying, "I never met, saw or spoke to Mrs Vickers". As far as the prescriptions were concerned, she believed they related to clinical drug trials being carried out by Vickers. She said all her relationships had been properly conducted and she resented attempts to sully her character. The prosecution case was that Margaret Vickers had died because of a "joint determined and skilful enterprise undertaken equally" by Vickers and Collison. Both denied the charges.

In his summing up, the judge reminded the jury that, "This is not a court of morals. It is a court of law. The charge is murder, not committing adultery." The jury found Paul Vickers guilty and he was sentenced to life imprisonment on 21 November 1981. Pamela Collison was acquitted of the murder charge but given a six-month suspended sentence for obtaining drugs by deception.

Dr Vickers had appeals against his sentence rejected in 1983 and again in 1994. It emerged during his trial that he had been seeing a psychiatrist who diagnosed induced psychosis, known as *folie à deux*, a delusional disorder shared by two people.

The Female of the Species

In 1929, a body washed up on the shores of the River Tisza near Nagyrév in Hungary. It was examined by a medical student who found a large amount of arsenic in the stomach.

This aroused the suspicions of the police who were already interested in two recent mysterious deaths, of Josef Nadarasz and Michael Szabo. Both corpses were exhumed and autopsies performed. Both bodies were found to contain arsenic.

Further investigations uncovered a local midwife named Susanne Fazekas who for the previous twenty years had been performing illegal abortions and supplying arsenic to women who wanted to get rid of the unwanted men in their lives, be they husbands, brothers or fathers.

Nine women confessed that they had bought arsenic from Fazekas, but before she could be brought to justice she committed suicide. When her cottage was searched, police found piles of flypapers, from which she had extracted the arsenic.

Police began the task of exhuming fifty corpses from Nagyrév Cemetery. They had to post guards because some of the women, determined to obstruct justice, began defacing gravestones so no one would know who was buried there. They also tried to remove incriminating evidence from their homes.

Police arrested dozens of women aged from twenty to seventy, and fifty-three were sent for trial. The first trials began on 13 December 1929, and it was discovered that most had poisoned their husbands either to benefit financially or to take a new one. Of the thirty defendants, all were found guilty and sent to prison for life, apart from one who was sentenced to death.

A second trial began on 17 January 1930, and among the defendants was Maria Szendi who had murdered her 23-year-old son Hardor (because she did not like him playing cards and drinking) and her husband. Hardor's dinner was poisoned while his father had his brandy and later food dosed with arsenic. Szendi was sentenced to death.

On 7 February 1930, a third batch of trials began. Maria Varga, forty-one, was accused of poisoning her husband (who was blinded during the First World War), her lover and his grandfather. She was found guilty and sentenced to hard labour for life. Maria Kardos, also on trial, was found guilty of murdering her second husband and her eldest son and was sentenced to death.

In addition, five of the accused women committed suicide before the trials began.

"Are You Sure It's Safe?"

Spoiled by his mother after the death of his father (when the son was thirteen), William Palmer was sacked from his first job for stealing when he was seventeen. Despite his bad character, he became a doctor's apprentice, during which time he sired fourteen illegitimate children and worked as an abortionist. He landed a job at Stafford Infirmary where he poisoned a man with strychnine just to see what would happen, before relocating to London to complete his studies.

He qualified in 1846 and began to practise in Rugeley, Staffordshire, and although he was quite a successful doctor he also gambled, a habit he could not break. Palmer lost a £9,000 inheritance through gambling.

In October 1847, he married Anne Thornton, the illegitimate daughter of an Army officer who had killed himself, at St Nicholas in Abbots Bromley, and fathered five children by her. Four died in infancy and it is a matter of dispute whether he had a hand in their deaths. His mother-in-law, Mary Thornton (who hated Palmer), came to visit in December 1848, and a fortnight later, in January 1849, she was dead.

In May 1850, Palmer murdered Leonard Bladon, to whom he owed a considerable sum of money. Another creditor who was owed £800 also died. An uncle died after a heavy drinking session.

By 1854, Palmer was heavily in debt and so insured his wife's life for £13,000. He paid the first premium and then she died in September of cholera – according to the death certificate. Later it was established that she had in fact died as the result of poisoning by antimony. Palmer insured his alcoholic brother Walter for £82,000, hoping he would die of the drink, but years of drinking had strengthened his constitution so Palmer killed him with prussic acid in August 1855.

To Palmer's annoyance, the insurance company refused to

pay out. Palmer next poisoned John Parsons Cook after Polestar, a racehorse he owned, won several thousand pounds at Shrewsbury races. Cook died six days later on 19 November 1855, but his family insisted on his body being exhumed and examined.

No evidence of poison was found, but Palmer was arrested for murder on 15 December. The bodies of Walter and Anne Palmer were exhumed, but it was impossible to determine Walter's cause of death. Palmer was the first Englishman convicted of a strychnine murder, albeit on mainly circumstantial evidence, and was sentenced to death.

He was hanged outside Stafford Prison on 14 June 1856. As he stepped onto the gallows, Palmer is said to have looked at the trapdoor and exclaimed, "Are you sure it's safe?"

Not So Lucky

Aconite is an unusual choice of poison for a prospective murderer. It is a plant poison derived from Monksbane and, once ingested, depresses the central nervous system, causing death if the dose is sufficiently large. The poison featured in the prosecution of Dr George Henry Lamson in 1882, when an Old Bailey jury found him guilty of fatally poisoning his brother-in-law.

One hundred and twenty eight years later, and standing trial at the Old Bailey, was Lakhvir Kaur Singh who doctored her ex-lover's curry with aconite. The 45-year-old woman's passage to her trial for murder had been a colourful one.

Married with children, Singh lived in Southall with a chronically sick husband. She was related to 39-year-old Lakhvinder Cheema, known as Lucky, who moved into her home when his marriage failed. She seduced him and, for sixteen years, they conducted a secret affair.

When Lucky moved to his own accommodation, Singh visited daily to cook, clean and do the laundry. She had two pregnancies both of which were aborted on his insistence. Then, in 2008, "Lucky" met Gurjeet Choongh, a 21-year-old illegal immigrant, and when the couple announced they planned to marry in 2009, Singh begged Lucky to call it off, but he declined. At that point, her indignation turned into something more vengeful.

On a visit to India, Singh acquired a quantity of *Aconitum ferox*, a variety of aconite and an extremely powerful poison. On 27 January 2009, she let herself into Lucky's house and opened the fridge. Among its contents was a plastic container of chicken curry into which she sprinkled her aconite.

That evening, Lucky and Choongh ate a curry supper. He was hungry and had a second helping. Soon afterwards, both became ill. Parts of his body became numb and he was nauseous. He called 999 saying he suspected he had been poisoned. Soon after being admitted to hospital he died; Choongh became comatose but survived.

Suspicion fell on Lakhvir Singh and police found traces of aconite in her handbag. She was charged with murder and the trial jury heard the full story of her scheming. Choongh watched proceedings from the public gallery, perhaps contemplating her narrow escape from death. Singh was found guilty of murder and, sentencing her, the judge said, "You set about a cold and calculating revenge." She was given a life sentence with a minimum of twenty-three years.

Disputed Verdicts

When it comes to poisoning, most minds turn to arsenic or cyanide. But succinylcholine? Well, that's another story. Two cases, over thirty years apart, shared a number of unusual and controversial features. Both involved doctors charged in Florida courts with using the drug, succinylcholine, to murder their wives. In 1967, Dr Carl Coppolino, at his second trial for murder, was found guilty, and, in 2001, a Florida jury also convicted Dr William Sybers. Both received life sentences after extended legal proceedings involving questionable medical evidence.

Succinylcholine is a drug used in anaesthesiology as a muscle relaxant before surgery. In high doses it can cause widespread paralysis, resulting in breathing failure and death. Once introduced into the body, the drug breaks down rapidly, forming succinic acid and choline, compounds normally found in body tissues.

Dr Sybers was the medical examiner for Bay County in 1991 when his wife died, on 30 May, apparently of a heart attack in the Syberses' Panama City home. He did not call for an autopsy and sent her body for embalmment the day after her death. Needle marks found on her arms raised concerns and led to a charge of murder. He said that he had taken blood for testing purposes and in a moment of aberration had thrown away the syringe.

Kay Sybers's death was treated as suspicious and her husband was charged with murder. In 2001, he was found guilty on the basis that he had injected her with succinylcholine to eliminate her and make way for his mistress. Dr Sybers was spared the death penalty and sentenced to life imprisonment.

In both cases, there was the complication of extra-marital affairs, which provided possible motives for murder. And in both cases controversial medical evidence guided the prosecution. F. Lee Bailey, the celebrated attorney, described the Coppolino verdict as "a terrible mistake". A scathing comment on the Sybers verdict attributed the outcome to "voodoo science".

In 2003, an appeal court reversed the Sybers conviction on the grounds that the scientific evidence presented in court was based on new analytical tests that had not been independently verified. The doctor pleaded guilty to manslaughter and received a reduced sentence. But the case did not stop there. The State Governor appointed a special prosecutor to help a grand jury evaluate the substance of the scientific evidence given by their expert witness.

Dr Sybers maintained that the needle marks on his dead wife's arm resulted from his using a hypodermic syringe to withdraw blood for testing purposes. The succinylcholine products found after death and attributed to poisoning were judged to be uncorroborated results. All of this raised questions about the presentation of scientific evidence to juries who might be swayed by the charisma of a good witness rather than the quality of the arguments.

Dr Sybers died on 19 April 2014, from lung cancer, in Central Florida. He was eighty-one. Perhaps the last word in a case that proved difficult to unravel lay with Dr Sybers who maintained his innocence throughout. He was quoted as saying, "If I had truly killed my wife, I would have ordered a cremation."

Matricide and the First Criminal Executed at Walton Jail

Elizabeth Berry, a 31-year-old widow, worked at the Rochdale Road workhouse in Oldham on a salary of £25 a year. She had two children but one died in infancy and the other, Edith Annie, eleven, lived with her sister Ann Sanderson in Manchester.

Berry paid 3s a week for Edith's keep plus a further 6d a week for schooling and 1d a week for insurance plus clothing. However, she was much better off than the workhouse inmates and was allocated two servants to help her. On 27 December 1886, Berry visited her sister and stayed two days, returning with Edith and her thirteen-year-old Sunday-school friend Beatrice Hall. The two girls played during the day and all three slept in Berry's bed at night.

At 10.45am on 1 January 1887, Edith began vomiting. The workhouse's surgeon, Dr Patterson, examined the girl and prescribed a mixture of iron and quinine. Edith was taken to her mother's bedroom where she was nursed through the night by Berry.

The next morning, Dr Patterson noticed a slight improvement, although when he sniffed one of the towels used to mop the vomit, he noticed that it had an acidic odour. However, when he next saw Edith she had taken a turn for the worse. Edith died at 5am on 4 January.

Berry claimed to have no insurance and bemoaned the fact that she would have to meet the funeral expenses herself. However, on 6 January, she received an insurance payout of £10. Meanwhile, back at the workhouse, Dr Patterson believed that foul play was afoot and went to see Charles Hodgkinson, the Chief Constable of Oldham, with his suspicions. He visited Berry at the workhouse and was shown into her bedroom where Edith's corpse lay on her mother's bed. He told her that there was a suspicion that her daughter had been poisoned.

A coroner's inquest opened on 7 January, and Ann Sanderson testified that her sister told her that Edith had been suffering from "acute stoppage of the bowels". Another witness said that when she had seen Edith she was fine but shortly afterwards was being violently sick.

The inquest was adjourned for further medical tests and Dr Charles Estcourt reported that he had found nothing that could account for Edith's death. Despite this, the jury returned a verdict of murder and Berry was held for the next assizes.

At the trial the insurance evidence weighed most heavily against Berry and she was sentenced to death. She was hanged at Walton Jail, Liverpool, on 14 March 1887, by her namesake James Berry who cut off a lock of her hair that he kept for luck . . .

"Now She's Acquitted, She Should Tell Us . . . How She Did It"

The Pimlico Mystery began when Edwin Bartlett died on 1 January 1886. Adelaide Blanche de la Tremouille was born at Orleans, France, illegitimately, on 19 December 1855. She married the wealthy grocer Edwin Bartlett, ten years her senior, on 6 April 1875. Their marriage was reasonably happy, although Edwin believed that every man should have two wives – one for companionship and the other for sex.

Adelaide was to be the wife for companionship but she claimed Edwin did not seek a second wife for sex. However, the fact that contraceptives were found in his wardrobe made this claim dubious.

In 1885, they met the Reverend George Dyson, a 27-year-old Wesleyan minister and a friend to both who had long conversations with Edwin about sex, marriage and relationships.

During one chat, Edwin told the Reverend Mr Dyson that in the event that he (Edwin) died he would like to "give" Adelaide to the clergyman. In the months leading up to his death Edwin took vicarious pleasure watching his wife and Dyson kissing.

In August 1885, Edwin and Adelaide moved to two rooms in Pimlico but they no longer shared a bed. Edwin was suffering from halitosis caused by rotting teeth and tapeworms. He also believed that he had syphilis and took mercury to cure it. In December 1885, he fell ill with gastritis and a dentist removed his rotten teeth.

On New Year's Day 1886, Edwin was found dead in bed. According to the post-mortem examination he had swallowed chloroform. When the police learned of the relationship with George Dyson, Adelaide was arrested and charged with Edwin's murder. The trial of Adelaide Bartlett began at the Old Bailey on 12 April 1886. The case was prosecuted by the Attorney General (Sir Charles Russell) and Edward Clarke QC defended Adelaide.

It was revealed in court that on 28 December 1885, at Adelaide's urging, Dyson had bought four small bottles of chloroform from chemists in Putney and Wimbledon, but Adelaide claimed that these were to dampen Edwin's suddenly discovered ardour.

However, rather than a drop or two it was a mystery how a whole bottle of chloroform had found its way into Edwin's stomach without burning his throat or mouth and without any screams of agony being heard. The jury returned a verdict of not guilty on 17 April. Sir James Paget, surgeon to Queen Victoria, commented, "Now she's acquitted, she should tell us, in the interests of science, how she did it."

Bengal Tigress

It could be said that it all started with The Beatles. In the Sixties they went to India to find spiritual enlightenment. Thus was started a whole procession of middle-class Westerners searching for themselves.

Chandra Mohan Jain was born in 1931. After university, his career was immediately controversial when he criticized socialism and Gandhi and called for carnal freedom – leading him to be called the "sex guru".

On 26 September 1970, he initiated his first group of disciples, whom he called sannyasins. In December, at Bombay, he began giving lectures to Westerners for the first time. The following year he adopted the name Bhagwan Shree Rajneesh.

Apart from their sexual freedom, the sannyasins believed that they could fly. They moved to an ashram in Pune. By the late 1970s, the group had outgrown the ashram and sannyasins were sent out to find new premises. However, they had become so controversial that they were unable to buy anywhere and the Indian government refused admission to all Westerners who indicated that their destination was the ashram.

On 10 April 1981, Rajneesh began a period of three and a half years of silence in public. Around this time, Ma Anand Sheela (Sheela Silverman) became his secretary. They decided to move their commune to America.

He went to America supposedly to seek medical treatment for various ailments but was never to see any doctors during his time in the States. In 1984, he pleaded guilty to immigration fraud.

On 13 June 1981, Swami Prem Chinmaya (Marc Harris Silverman), Sheela's husband, bought the Big Muddy Ranch, a 64,229-acre farm near Antelope, Oregon, for $5.75 million. Rajneesh moved in on 29 August, and the venue was renamed Rancho Rajneesh.

In May 1982, the residents of Rancho Rajneesh voted to incorporate it as the city of Rajneeshpuram and that was when trouble with the locals really began. The townspeople combined to stop the incorporation.

Sheela was the real power in the commune as Rajneesh maintained his public silence (until November 1984). The only time the sannyasins saw him was on his daily drive-by in one of his ninety-three Rolls-Royces. Sheela relayed all of "his" utterances, announcing in 1983 that he spoke only to her. (He was later to say that he was ignorant of the things that she did and said in his name.)

Sheela, thirty-six, and her two cohorts, Ma Anand Puja and Ma Shanti Bhadra, ruled over the 500 members of the commune. Sheela lived in style, jetting around the world and using expensive hotels. The commune acquired a poor reputation locally and stories circulated about orgies. Some sect members were recipients of hate mail and death threats.

Sheela was determined to keep the sect together and countered criticism by appearing on television and in the media. She also picked up any perceived threats from within and protected herself with armed bodyguards. She managed to create an atmosphere of hysteria at the commune in 1985 at a time when the guru was expelled from the USA.

In March 1984, Sheela announced that Rajneesh had predicted that two-thirds of mankind would die from Aids and that sannyasins must use condoms during sex and must not kiss.

Meantime, having lost their bid to incorporate Rajneeshpuram, they decided to take over the city of Antelope, Oregon, and on 18 September 1984, Antelope's charter was amended by a vote of fifty-seven to twenty-two to change its name to Rajneesh. (It was changed back on 6 November 1985.)

Sheela and her gang made an attempt on the life of Swami Devaraj (Dr George Meredith) by injecting him with poison. They were jealous of the special position the doctor enjoyed with the guru and wanted to eliminate him. He was made seriously ill and hospitalized but survived the attempt to kill him.

The trio's next move was bizarre in the extreme. A vote was due to be staged in the confrontation between the commune and local people represented by their county council in November 1984. In a bid to win local elections, Sheela and her cohorts bussed in thousands of tramps from across America to vote for them. When the local district attorney was successful in preventing them from voting, they were returned to their original locations at state expense.

As a measure to incapacitate voters and prevent them from taking part, Sheela and her gang doctored food served at several local restaurants with salmonella. As a result, hundreds of people were taken ill with food poisoning. It was the first act of mass bioterrorism in the United States. In the mayhem that followed, Sheela absconded to Germany with her two accomplices on 13 September 1984.

The trio were arrested in Germany on 28 October 1985, and returned to the USA in February 1986. At their trial in Portland, they pleaded guilty in a series of plea bargains. Apart from attempted murder, there were charges for wire-tapping and attempted arson. Court reports referred to the isolation fostered by some religious communes which distorted reality and led to a kind of hot-house politics.

Sheela was sentenced to twenty years' imprisonment, which would be followed by expulsion from the USA.

On 13 December 1988, Sheela was released for good behaviour after serving twenty-nine months. She moved to Switzerland where she ran two care homes.

A Poisoning in Balham

Florence Campbell, born in New South Wales, Australia, was sixteen days past her nineteenth birthday when she married Captain Alexander Ricardo (two years her senior) in 1864. Despite her vivacity he preferred drinking himself to oblivion at home and spending time with his mistress when he was out. The relationship made Florence ill and she went to Malvern to recuperate on 28 April 1870.

On 2 May she met the elderly Dr James Gully. Alexander Ricardo tried to effect a reconciliation and Florence rented Orwell Lodge in Malvern for them, but when he arrived he was drunk.

On 31 March 1871, Florence's solicitor, Henry Brooks, arranged for a legal separation. Less than three weeks later, at 1am on 19 April 1871, Captain Ricardo died of alcoholism at 6/8 Frankenplatz, Cologne, while living with a mistress. The affair with Dr Gully became sexual despite his being married (his wife was in a mental asylum).

Florence's parents disapproved of her affair and refused to have anything to do with her while it continued. With an income of £4,000 from her husband's estate Florence lived her life her way. She moved to Stokefield, Leigham Court Road, Streatham.

In December 1871, Dr Gully retired and moved to a house also on Leigham Court Road and their affair continued. They scandalized their friends and family by going on holiday for six weeks to Italy.

Back in England, Florence took on an unattractive middle-aged woman called Jane Cannon Cox as her companion. Mrs Cox had been the governess at the home of Henry Brooks and, in August 1872, moved into Stokefield at a generous salary of £80 per annum (the normal companion wage was £30).

In the summer of 1873, Florence and Dr Gully went to Kissingen, Germany, on holiday. Florence suffered a miscarriage, although some believe that Dr Gully performed an abortion on her.

In March 1874, she moved to The Priory in Bedford Hill Road, Balham, and Dr Gully bought a house a few minutes away, which he named Orwell Lodge after Florence's Malvern residence. They spent the night together at The Priory whenever Mrs Cox was away. Eventually, the affair began to peter out. Friends of Mrs Cox were the Bravo family and their son, Charles, a lawyer, who was born on 30 May 1845.

One day he met Florence, but their acquaintance really took off when they met by chance on a trip to Brighton. In October 1875, Florence told Dr Gully that she wished to reconcile with her parents and thus end the relationship with him. He bowed out with grace. The following month Charles Bravo proposed and Florence accepted. His mother thoroughly disapproved of the match. In those days a woman's property became her husband's on marriage, but Florence did not want to give up her house and furniture so Charles threatened to call off the marriage if she did not acquiesce. She consulted Dr Gully who told her to let Bravo, who had a temper, have his way, and she married him on 7 December 1875.

Florence paid all the expenses for the house, but under Bravo's "guidance" she began cutting back on spending. In January 1876 she miscarried again and on 6 April she lost another baby. Mrs Cox asked Dr Gully for help and he prescribed a medicine.

At 9.45pm on 18 April, Charles Bravo complained of feeling unwell. By this time the Bravos were sleeping in separate bedrooms due to her recuperation. At bedtime he began to vomit and doctors were called. The next day, Bravo's condition was worse and he was in constant pain. Florence sent for Sir William Gull, a friend of her father's and later an unlikely Jack the Ripper suspect. Gull was one of seven doctors attending Bravo and they all believed that he had been poisoned, but he insisted that he had taken nothing more than laudanum for toothache. At 4am on 21 April, Charles Bravo died.

On 30 April, a day after the funeral, Florence and Mrs Cox moved to 38 Brunswick Terrace, Brighton. A second inquest opened on 11 July, and the remains were disinterred. Mrs Cox insisted that Bravo had committed suicide, jealous of his wife's former lover Dr Gully. A pathologist revealed that Bravo had taken forty grains of antimony and that he must have ingested the poison in a drink after 7.30pm on 18 April.

It was probably in the water jug by his bed but no trace could be found of it to examine it. The verdict was one of murder by person or persons unknown. Did Mrs Cox murder Charles Bravo because he threatened to sack her in his economy drive? Or did Florence murder her husband because she was about to lose her boon companion? Or was it because she wanted to dampen his sexual ardour and gave him too much poison, killing him rather than just making him ill?

Florence Bravo drank herself to death, dying at Coombe Lodge, Southsea, on 21 September 1878 – she was just thirty-three. Dr Gully died on 27 March 1883, at Orwell Lodge, Bedford Hill Road, Balham, London. Jane Cox died in 1917 at 19 Cambridge Road, Lee, south London. Authors are divided on who was Charles Bravo's killer.

Bernard Taylor and Kate Clarke point the finger at Mrs Cox who was caught out in several lies. John Williams writes that Florence murdered *both* her husbands. She wanted Ricardo out of the way so she could have Dr Gully and her husband's money. She murdered Bravo simply because she was tired of him. Or did she? The case remains unsolved.

"He Wanted Complete Control Over Life and Death"

We place our trust in members of the medical profession and so it is much more of a shock when we learn that that trust is misplaced. Arnfinn Nesset was born illegitimately on 25 October 1936, at Trøndelag, Norway, and raised by his mother. By 1976, he was the manager/head nurse of the Orkdal nursing home for old-age pensioners at Sør-Trøndelag. During his time in charge, larger numbers than usual of old people died.

A routine police investigation revealed large quantities of curacit (a derivative of the poison curare) in his office. He told them it was to put down his dog. The police immediately found two problems with this explanation: the amount was far greater (180 doses) than would be needed to kill a dog and, in any case, he did not have a dog.

Nesset was arrested in 1981 and he confessed to killing twenty-seven of his patients. He said that he murdered them by injecting them with suxamethonium chloride, a muscle relaxant.

Before he could be brought to trial, he retracted his confession and professed his innocence. His trial began in October 1982, and his defence team claimed that he was practising euthanasia. However, since curacit results in a painful demise, it was not the sort of drug that would be used in euthanasia. The chief prosecutor, Olaf Jakhelln, described Nesset as "an ambitious man, who wanted complete control over life and death [of his victims]".

On 11 March 1983, after the longest trial in Norwegian legal history, he was found guilty of killing twenty-two of his patients (the actual figure could be as high as 138) between May 1977 and November 1980, and given the maximum sentence permissible under Norwegian law – twenty-one years in jail.

He served a dozen years of the sentence before being released for good behaviour.

Murder for Gain

Loose-lipped Louisa May Merrifield murdered her mistress for gain at 1.50pm on 14 April 1953. By March 1953, Merrifield, forty-six, was married to Alfred, seventy, her third husband. She had been employed in around twenty jobs in just three years and was seemingly unable to settle. Then she and her husband were given the job of housekeepers to Sarah Ann Ricketts, a four-foot-eight 79-year-old widow, who lived in The Homestead, a bungalow at 339 Devonshire Road on the North Shore of Blackpool.

Less than a fortnight after she had started the job (on 12 March), Merrifield went to see a solicitor, supposedly on the old lady's behalf, and told him to draw up a new will naming her (Merrifield) as the sole beneficiary.

On 26 March, she also began telling friends that she had inherited a bungalow worth £3,000. Mrs Ricketts was a difficult, cantankerous mistress with a fierce temper and a drink problem, which may have gone some way to explaining why both her husbands had committed suicide by putting their heads in the oven at The Homestead.

When Mrs Ricketts died, an autopsy revealed that cause of death was phosphorus poisoning, probably derived from rat poison. The police arrived to search the house and Merrifield insisted that the Salvation Army Band that she had arranged to be outside play *Abide with Me*.

No traces of phosphorus were found in the bungalow, but on 20 July, Alfred and Louisa Merrifield went on trial for murder. Her comments about the bungalow counted against her, but she put gossip about her role in the death down to spite and jealousy.

The jury returned a guilty verdict on Louisa Merrifield but was unable to decide if Alfred had had a hand in the murder, and he was released. On 18 September, Louisa Merrifield became the fourth and last woman to be executed at Strangeways. Alfred Merrifield continued to live in the bungalow until 1956, and after a fight with Mrs Ricketts's relatives inherited a sixth of its value.

He died, aged eighty, in 1962, having for a time worked as a circus sideshow on Blackpool's Golden Mile. Louisa Merrifield offered no confession. Her husband may well have been her next victim – she had secretly taken out a number of insurance policies on his life . . .

Thrice a Medical Murderer

Dr Alfred William Warder was a respected expert on poisons. He had been a lecturer on the subject at the Grosvenor Place School of Medicine in London and was a witness in the trial of the poisoner William Palmer (see page 278).

On 23 May 1866, Warder and his wife Ellen took rooms at 36 Bedford Square, Brighton, the home of Charlotte Landsell. She was impressed by her new tenants, little knowing of Warder's rather unusual private life, although she noticed that Mrs Warder was not in the best of health. Mrs Warder's brother, Richard Branwell, was a prominent local surgeon.

Not long after they moved in, Mrs Warder fell ill. Her brother was so concerned that he called in Dr R. P. B. Taafe, but his work did nothing to help Mrs Warder. Before his arrival, Dr Warder had been treating his wife. He had given his wife twenty drops of Fleming's Tincture of Aconite as the only remedy that helped her pain.

Dr Taafe believed that this was the wrong treatment and insisted on giving his own medicines. Mrs Warder seemed to rally until Warder told him that she was unable to keep down the tonics. Mrs Warder was given further medicines and briefly rallied, before again vomiting and again complaining of agonizing stomach pains.

On 30 June, her condition took a turn for the worse. When Mr Branwell called at the house at 5.30am the next day, his sister was dead. Dr Taafe conducted an autopsy and was not convinced that Mrs Warder's death was natural so an inquest was called. The inquest opened on 7 July, and after hearing some testimony the coroner David Black adjourned for six days. Later that day Mrs Warder was buried and Warder fell ill.

On 9 July, he travelled to London and then back home where he asked Miss Landsell to settle his bill. He left and booked into a hotel on the seafront. When he did not come down for breakfast the next morning, staff went to his room and found him naked in bed, quite dead. An empty bottle lay on the nightstand – it had contained prussic acid.

When the inquest reconvened later that month, it returned a verdict that Mrs Warder had died as a result of aconite administered with malice aforethought by her husband. It was then revealed that Mrs Warder was the doctor's third wife and that both his first two wives (in 1863 and 1865) had died under mysterious circumstances ...

Unrequited Love Turns to Poisoned Confections

Christiana Edmunds was a spinster in her forties (although she claimed she was in her thirties) when she became obsessed with her doctor, Charles Beard. She was known locally in Brighton as a shrew; she lived with her mother and suffered from a number of illnesses.

Dr Beard looked upon her kindly, realizing that most of her behaviour was caused by psychological rather than physical ailments. It was this kindness that led to her sending him love letters and assuming that he would leave his wife for her. When this didn't happen, Edmunds decided that she had to eliminate Mrs Beard.

In the summer of 1870, she gave Mrs Beard a box of chocolates laced with strychnine. Mrs Beard put one in her mouth but spat it out immediately. Dr Beard analysed the sweet and discovered the poison. He accused Edmunds of attempting to kill his wife and unsurprisingly told her that he could no longer treat her.

Edmunds developed a plan to divert attention from herself by trying to discredit the confectioner John G. Maynard of 39, 40 and 41 West Street, Brighton, who had sold the chocolates. She managed to get access to the chocolates by bribing children to buy them and then having them sent back but with added poison.

Sidney Barker, four, died on 12 June 1871, after he was given a chocolate cream by his uncle during a day trip to Brighton, and others were taken ill. At the inquest of Master Barker, Edmunds even testified that she and a friend were victims of poisoned chocolates themselves.

However, it was discovered that she had bought strychnine on at least two occasions, supposedly to kill stray cats and dogs. Thus the poisoning was traced back to Edmunds and she was arrested. She declared her love for Dr Beard and revealed that she had poisoned the chocolates for him. She went on trial on 15 January 1872 – at the Old Bailey because it was thought she would not get a fair trial at Lewes. She pleaded insanity. Her father had died in Peckham Lunatic Asylum in 1847. Her brother Arthur had died at Earlswood Asylum for Idiots and both grandfathers and a cousin were educationally subnormal. Her plea was rejected and she was sentenced to death.

However, the sentence was commuted to life in prison and she was sent to Broadmoor Lunatic Asylum where she died on 19 September 1907, aged seventy-eight.

Murder Virus

Johnson Aziga achieved the distinction of being the first individual to be convicted of causing murder by passing on the HIV virus. The 52-year-old former civil servant of Ugandan origin, living in Canada, was a man of considerable sexual appetite. He had been diagnosed as HIV positive in 1996 and been warned by public health officials about the dangers of spreading the virus through unprotected sexual activity.

While receiving antiretroviral treatment, he engaged with numerous lovers and persuaded them to abandon the protective use of condoms. Aziga was arrested in August 2003, after several women brought charges against him of aggravated sexual assault. Two of his lovers subsequently died of Aids-related lymphoma and five others tested positive for HIV. Following his arrest and publication of his photograph by the media, several more women came forward with complaints against him.

After due process, he was charged with two counts of first-degree murder and ten of aggravated sexual assault. These were described as sexual activity deliberately pursued without the use of prophylactics in the knowledge that he might infect his partners with HIV.

Aziga took a defiant stance on the issues at stake and was allowed to make a statement in court during the early stages of the legal process. He made it clear that his belief was that HIV transmission should not be criminalized. He hired and fired a number of lawyers before finally appearing on trial at Hamilton, Ontario, in October 2009.

Prosecutors said that all the women named in the indictments had contracted HIV from a shared source of a viral strain rare in North America but prevalent in parts of Africa. One of Aziga's lovers had spoken to police about her relationship with him and the fact that he never told her that he had HIV. She allowed the interview to be videotaped while in a bedridden state and died three weeks later. The tape was played during the trial, creating a considerable impact on all present.

Johnson Aziga was found guilty of murder in the first degree, having decided not to give evidence on his own behalf. The *Toronto Star* reported that he was "dishonest and duplicitous, thinking only of his immediate sexual gratification ... knowingly and intentionally exposing his unsuspecting lovers to the HIV virus."

"Gastric Fever"

Thief and murderer Mary Ann Cotton went to the gallows at Durham County Jail on 24 March 1873. Born in County Durham, she married William Mowbray and moved to Plymouth where she gave birth to five children, four of whom were dead before the family returned to the northeast. Back home, she gave birth to three further children but the one survivor from Plymouth died of "gastric fever" aged four in June 1860. The child's death led to Mowbray taking out life insurance on his life and those of the children. In September 1864, another child died, after suffering diarrhoea.

On 18 January 1865, Mowbray lost his job and that day came down with such a severe bout of diarrhoea that he died the same day. The British and Prudential Insurance Company paid Mary Ann £35 on her husband's policy. Another child died and the insurance paid a further £30 on its death.

Moving to Seaham Harbour with one child, Mary Ann fell in love with Joseph Nattrass, but he was already married and refused to leave his wife. She landed a job at the Sunderland Infirmary, House of Recovery for the Cure of Contagious Fever, Dispensary and Humane Society.

She fell for ex-patient George Ward, and they married at Monkwearmouth in August 1865. Fourteen months later, he was dead from "fever". He left everything to his widow and she also received an insurance payout.

In August 1867, Mary Ann married shipyard foreman John (or James) Robinson. Not long afterwards, her daughter and two of his children were dead from "gastric fever". She stole £50, ran up debts of £60 and insisted that James Robinson insure his life – he threw her out. She met widower Frederick Cotton and married him bigamously in September 1870. He died a year later, followed by his sons.

She took up again with Nattrass – he died on 1 April 1872. She was offered a job as a nurse by a parish official, Thomas Riley, but her stepson Charles Edward Cotton was "in the way", and shortly after a workhouse rejected him, he died.

Riley was shocked by the boy's sudden death and complained to the police. Mary Ann was arrested for his murder. The trial was delayed until 5 March 1873, after the birth of her twelfth child. She claimed that Charles had died from exposure to arsenic in the wallpaper. After ninety minutes, the jury found her guilty.

"Gentlemen, Do Not Hang Me Too High for the Sake of Decency"

Born about 1718 at Henley-on-Thames, Oxfordshire, Mary Blandy was spoiled by her doting parents. It was said of her father Francis that his "whole thoughts were bent to settle her advantageously in the world". He let it be known that he was worth £10,000 when in fact he had less than £3,000.

However, every boyfriend was put off because Mary's father refused to spend his "fortune" on her but promised to "leave her his All at his Death". In the summer of 1746, a new suitor appeared in the form of Captain William Henry Cranstoun.

When Francis Blandy discovered that his daughter's new boyfriend had a wife and child he forbade the relationship to continue. Cranstoun was not easily dissuaded and continued to court Mary, telling her that his marriage was illegal.

In June 1751, Mary began – perhaps at Cranstoun's urging – to put arsenic into her father's tea and later his gruel. She called it a "love powder" and said that she hoped it would lessen his contempt for her boyfriend. Two months later, Francis Blandy fell ill, and on 14 August 1751, he died.

Almost immediately, Mary was arrested for murder. Her trial opened in the Divinity School at the Oxford Assizes on 3 March 1752, and family servants testified that Mary had called her father "a rogue, a villain, a toothless old dog" and said that she wanted him "dead and at Hell". A servant testified that Mary had told her father that she had been giving him arsenic but only "to make him love Cranstoun". Mary implored her father not to curse her and he replied, "My dear, how couldst thou think I could curse thee? No, I bless you, and hope God will bless thee and amend thy life."

The jury took just five minutes to pass a guilty verdict and the judge sentenced her to death. Protesting her innocence, Mary Blandy was hanged outside of Oxford Castle Prison at 9am on Easter Monday (6 April) 1752. Her last words were, as she ascended the scaffold, "Gentlemen, do not hang me too high for the sake of decency."

The Agra Poisoning Case

In pre-First World War India, Britons lived a life of luxury in large houses populated with servants. Lieutenant Henry Lovell William Clark, forty-two, employed by the Indian Subordinate

Medical Service in Agra, was an unhappily married father of four children. He met and fell in love with Augusta, the 35-year-old daughter of a Bengal river pilot and wife of Edward Mckean Fulham, a government military accounts assistant examiner who lived at 9 Metcalfe Road. The couple decided that they had to be together and the only way to achieve this was to get rid of her husband.

A plot was hatched to make it appear that Mr Fulham had died of heat stroke, and Clark gave his lover arsenic to administer to her unsuspecting husband, which she did. On 10 October 1911, Edward Fulham died of heat stroke – the attending doctor was Henry Clark, who signed the death certificate.

Next, the lovers decided, they had to do away with Louisa Amelia Clark, and to this aim they hired four assassins, who broke into the family home at 135 Cantonments on 17 November 1912, and attacked and killed her.

Police, aware of her affair with Clark, interviewed Augusta Fulham and under her bed they found a stash of 370 love letters written to her lover. They contained incriminating evidence including a passage where she asked, "Please send me the powder next week."

Her husband's body was exhumed and a post-mortem examination revealed traces of arsenic. Dr Clark and Augusta Fulham went on trial at the High Court in Allahabad, firstly charged with the murder of Edward Fulham and then for the contract killing of Mrs Clark. Fulham, pregnant with Clark's child, turned King's Evidence, but it was not necessary as he confessed in the dock.

On 26 March 1913, Henry Clark was executed, as were three of the four Hindus he had hired. One, like Fulham, turned King's Evidence. Augusta Fulham's condition prevented her from facing the gallows and she gave birth to a son in prison. Ironically, she was to die aged thirty-eight, on 28 May 1914, from heat stroke in Naini Prison. The home where the Fulhams lived is said to be jinxed and the woman of the house invariably falls ill, recovering only when she leaves . . .

Death on the Nile

"My wife needs a doctor, I think she's dying." These were the words used by John Allan when he spoke to the receptionist at the hotel where he was on holiday. Standing by the desk was an American tourist who offered to help. She accompanied him to room 508 in the New Winter Palace at Luxor, Egypt. There, lying on the bed, was Cheryl Lewis, sweating profusely and foaming at the mouth. She was past help and died where she lay. A doctor called to the scene believed the 43-year-old woman had succumbed to a heart attack, but forensic tests showed that she had died of cyanide poisoning.

John Allan, an unemployed industrial chemist, and Cheryl, his girlfriend of seven years, had travelled to Egypt for a holiday on the Nile in October 1998. Cheryl worked as a senior partner for a Liverpool law firm, and the reality of her relationship with Allan was that she supported him financially. Within weeks of her death he was propositioning one of her friends, a 53-year-old divorcée, to whom he gave a gold bracelet that had once belonged to Cheryl.

In February 1999, Allan's new girlfriend was taken ill with severe stomach pains but made a full recovery in hospital. The cause of her sudden illness was not ascertained but the symptoms suggested cyanide poisoning. The poison acts rapidly once it enters the body by interfering with the oxygen-carrying capacity of the blood. The respiratory centre of the brain is affected and convulsions and unconsciousness result. Death may occur within five minutes. Cyanide is quickly altered by the metabolism of the body and is converted into compounds normally present. Hence, the poison may have disappeared from the body before it is possible to make an analysis.

The circumstances of Cheryl Lewis's death and the illness of her friend suggested cyanide poisoning. John Allan was arrested on suspicion of committing murder and attempted murder. A search of the home that he shared with Cheryl revealed his addiction to pornography and it seemed that he was in the habit of consorting with prostitutes.

Also found in his home were computer disks carrying different drafts of Cheryl's will. These provided key evidence showing that Allan had forged her will in the expectation of inheriting more than £400,000 on her death. Suspicions of cyanide were confirmed by the discovery of traces in Cheryl's body at post-mortem and a quantity of poison found in her car.

Allan had led a colourful life, with two failed marriages and a faltering career which meant he had not worked for seven years. He lived in a fantasy world, claiming that he had been an arms dealer in Africa and feared that hitmen were out to get him. He blamed Cheryl's death on his past life, which he said had come back to haunt him.

A reconstruction of the crime painted a scenario of the occupants of room 508 enjoying a nightcap. Unbeknown to Cheryl, her gin and tonic had been laced with cyanide by her boyfriend who witnessed her agonizing death.

Standing trial in March 2000, John Allan denied murder. The jury's guilty verdict was greeted with approval by Cheryl Lewis's family. Allan was sentenced to life imprisonment for what the judge called, "a cruel and premeditated killing".

Gin and Atropine

An epidemic of sickness struck a number of people who had recently shopped in a supermarket at Hunters Tryst in Edinburgh during the last weekend in August 1994. A common factor was that they had all bought tonic water and had used this as a drinks mixer, precipitating varying degrees of sickness.

Several of the sufferers went to hospital, including the wife of an anaesthetist who determined that the tonic water had been contaminated with atropine, which is a derivative of deadly nightshade. It is used medicinally as a muscle relaxant before surgery but in large doses it can have fatal consequences by paralysing the heart and lungs.

As word spread about the phantom poisoner who was doctoring bottles of tonic water, an employee at the supermarket involved told police of an incident he had witnessed. He saw a man who he thought was a shoplifter replace two bottles of tonic water on the shelves which he withdrew from a shopping trolley covered with a jacket.

The man was identified as Dr Paul Agutter, a biochemist and senior lecturer at Napier College in Edinburgh. It was revealed that he had visited one of those affected by the poisoned tonic water and mentioned that his wife had also been affected.

Enquiries into 48-year-old Agutter's background revealed that he had begun an affair with a mature student who was separated from her husband and they planned to live together. Suspicion now settled on the biochemist who it was conjectured devised a scheme to murder his wife so that he would be free to move in with his mistress. As part of his plan, and using his knowledge of poisons, he doctored bottles of tonic water in the supermarket as a kind of smokescreen. He was, accordingly, charged with attempting to murder his wife and endangering the lives of others. He denied the accusations.

Dr Agutter appeared on trial at Edinburgh High Court in February 1995. His knowledge of, and access to, atropine went against him, as did the witness who had seen him in the supermarket tinkering with bottles of tonic water. Neither his wife nor his mistress believed he was capable of committing the crimes.

The jury took three and a half hours to bring in a majority guilty verdict. Sentencing him to twelve years' imprisonment, the judge said, "This was an evil and cunningly devised crime which was not only designed to bring about the death of your wife, but also to cause great alarm, danger and injury." The *Daily Mail*, in its report of the trial, headlined it, "Poison on the Rocks".

Take Your Medicine

When the deputy mayor of a small town in Normandy was arrested on suspicion of murder, a controversy began which fuelled fierce loyalties and passions. Jean-Marc Deperrois, forty-three, was a popular figure in Gruchet-le-Valasse, although there were some disapproving rumours about his relationship with Sylvie Tocqueville, a secretary who worked in the town hall.

On the evening of 11 June 1994, the town was in buoyant mood, primed to hold its annual medieval fair. Nine-year-old Emilie Tanay was one of those looking forward to the big event. As her parents had another commitment that evening, they asked Sylvie and Jean-Michel Tocqueville to take Emilie to the fair and look after her.

Emilie had been suffering from bronchitis for which she had been prescribed an antibiotic, syrup-based medicine. She took the syrup with her and left it at the Tocquevilles' house when they all went off to the fair. Her mother had impressed on her that she must take her medicine as soon as she returned. This she did at around 8pm and promptly collapsed in severe pain. She was taken to hospital where she died a couple of hours later. It was suspected that her medicine had been contaminated with cyanide.

News of Emilie's death spread like wildfire and attention focused on her medicine. The manufacturer of the syrup was contacted and the company's processes reviewed. As a result, the medicine was removed from pharmacy shelves throughout France. The police inclined to the view that Deperrois had let himself into the Tocquevilles' house with the intention of contaminating Jean-Michel's medication, not realizing that the syrup was actually being used by Emilie. The reasoning was that Sylvie's husband was an obstacle to his affair with her. That Jean-Michel was a sickly man given to dosing himself with medicines was possibly relevant.

When it was learned that Deperrois had recently acquired a supply of cyanide in connection with his thermal-imaging business, the accusations against him intensified. He did not deny buying the chemical but said he panicked about the inferences that would be drawn with the news that cyanide poisoning had caused Emilie's death. Consequently, he disposed of the cyanide by dumping it in the River Seine.

The arrest of the deputy mayor triggered shock waves in the local community. The town divided into two camps; those who saw Deperrois as an upright citizen and totally blameless, and others who scented the whiff of scandal in his relationship with Sylvie Tocqueville. The man at the centre of the breaking storm strongly protested his innocence.

The whole farrago was put to the test at Rouen in 1997, when Deperrois appeared in court to answer the charges against him. While it was not doubted that cyanide poisoning had been the cause of Emilie's death, it was not satisfactorily proved that the cyanide used to kill her was the same as that bought by the defendant. Much of the evidence was circumstantial and the scientific testimony was inconclusive. Nevertheless, Deperrois was found guilty and sentenced to twenty years' imprisonment.

In the aftermath of the trial, bitter passions spilled over. Sylvie Tocqueville and her husband were targeted with death threats, and Emilie's family were forced to move away due to social harassment. There was strong support for Deperrois and many believed that he had been made a scapegoat. Theories abounded about what had happened on that fateful night in June 1994, one of which was that the victim's death was an accident made to look like a bungled murder.

A higher court declined to overturn the verdict of the Rouen trial and requests for a retrial in 2001, based on new evidence, were also rejected. Jean Marc Deperrois steadfastly maintained his innocence.

CHAPTER 7

Among the Missing

When thirteen-year old Genette Tate went missing while out on her bicycle delivering newspapers in 1978, her disappearance prompted a huge public response. Seven thousand members of the public volunteered as searchers, backed by unprecedented police activity and media coverage.

Witnesses who had seen the youngster riding her bicycle on the afternoon of 19 August were subjected to hypnosis in the hope of enhancing their recollections. Police frogmen searched nearby water courses, "Missing Girl" posters bearing her photograph were widely distributed and thousands of people were interviewed by the police. But, all to no avail, as Genette had simply disappeared without trace.

Comparisons were made with the case of April Fabb, also aged thirteen, who went missing in Norfolk in 1969. In both instances, bicycles were involved. Genette was cycling on her newspaper round and April was riding home. Neither girl was seen again, and, despite similarities in the circumstances, no links between the two disappearances were ever proved.

Another girl called April went missing in 2012. Five-year-old April Jones was abducted close to her home in Machynlleth, North Wales. Despite the most extensive investigation involving a missing person in the UK, no trace of her whereabouts was found. Justice was served when a local man, Mark Bridger, was convicted of abduction and murder. He claimed not to know where the girl's body was and, in 2013, the police decided to call off further searches.

Abduction is often a prelude to murder but people go missing for a variety of reasons. Some individuals, unable to cope with life's trials, or in the grip of mental breakdown, decide to opt out of normal society. Once they are reported missing, increasingly well-coordinated responses come into play. These typically involve fingertip searches of local terrain, enhanced by aerial surveys, ground-penetrating radar and investigation of water courses.

Public response is important, particularly recent sightings of the missing individual. This, in turn, places an emphasis on the recording of data and cooperation between agencies. The UK Missing Persons Bureau plays a fundamental role in collating information in what has become a huge task, faced with an estimated 250,000 people reported missing every year. The charity, Missing People, was established in 1994 to support these activities with a helpline and to reinforce public awareness with a National Missing Persons Day.

While some missing persons are reported as such very quickly, others simply vanish without trace and few questions are asked. Rosemary and Fred West, the villains of 25 Cromwell Street in Gloucester, spirited away twelve young women in the 1970s including two of their own daughters. Some of the victims had remained buried for twenty years before being discovered in 1994.

A disappearance that led to concerns about the personal safety of young professional women was that of estate agent, Suzy Lamplugh. She went missing in London in July 1986, on her way to keep an appointment with "Mr Kipper" to view a house for sale. Suzy disappeared without trace and was presumed to have been murdered. Her body has not been found. Her mother, Diana Lamplugh, established a trust with a view to making vulnerable women aware of the dangers to which they might be exposed in carrying out their professional duties.

Some murderers, especially serial killers, choose to keep their victims' bodies close to hand. The Wests and John Christie, the infamous Rillington Place murderer, opted for garden burials or walled-up remains in the house, while Dennis Nilsen preferred to place his victims' bodies under the floorboards. When twelve-year-old Tia Sharp went missing from her home, Stuart Hazell made an emotional appeal for her to return in the knowledge that he had killed her and hidden her body in the attic. Plastic bin bags have become an essential item on some criminals' shopping lists to parcel up body parts and corpses ready for disposal.

Shallow graves in some remote area of countryside have proved popular as disposal sites, with the idea that nature will destroy criminal evidence. This practice has prompted new scientific developments, such as forensic biology and forensic anthropology, which enable investigators to solve crimes. In addition, DNA and fingerprint databases, together with the use of dental evidence, have prompted major advances in identification and crime scene interpretation.

E-fit facial likenesses, compiled from descriptions, and facial reconstruction have added to the resources available to crime investigators. A severed head found in a field in 1993 with its features mutilated was matched to a torso discovered earlier in Manchester. Using the latest reconstruction techniques, the face was remodelled and photographed. The result was that someone who knew the dead man came forward to make an identification.

Many of those who join the legions of the missing, at the rate of around ten a month in the UK, end up as unidentified corpses. In 2010, the Missing Persons Bureau had a backlog of over seven hundred such cases. Not all of these are due to foul play; traffic accidents, homelessness, vagrancy and mental illness account for many of these. But, the facts are that some 250,000 individuals are reported missing every year, of which over half are under the age of eighteen.

One of the most hostile environments for the missing are the world's oceans. Rebecca Coriam worked on the cruise ship Disney World during a week-long cruise from Los Angeles to Mexico. She went missing from the ship on 22 March 2011, and has not been seen since. This young woman was one of 165 people who have disappeared from cruise ships since 1995.

Historically, one of the most famous disappearances from an ocean-going vessel was that of the actress, Gay Gibson, in 1947. During the voyage from Cape Town to Southampton, off the coast of West Africa, she was reported missing on 18 October. One of the ship's stewards, James Camb, was convicted of murdering her and pitching the body out of a porthole and into the sea.

There was a presumed sexual element to the incident, with allegations of rape and strangulation. Doubts cast on the verdict *suggested that 21-year-old Gibson had died of a heart attack in the course of sexual activity and that Camb was panicked into disposing of the body. Indeed, rape aboard cruise liners is one of the most frequently encountered crimes.*

Disposal at sea is also an option open to a murderer who seeks oblivion. After killing his wife and daughter in 1931, and burying their bodies in the garden, Charles Lewis boarded a steamer heading for Scotland. At some point on the voyage, one of the ship's officers heard a splash and suspected that a passenger had gone overboard. Lewis was reported missing and an unidentified body was seen in the water but it quickly disappeared beneath the waves. Lewis was not seen again. At the very least, it is an intriguing incident, which poses the question of whether he jumped, fell or was pushed?

Arguably, the most celebrated disappearance was that of Lord Lucan in 1974, which remains a mystery. On 7 November of that year, Lady Lucan discovered the body of her children's nanny, Sandra Rivett, in the basement of their London home. She had been beaten to death and her body placed in a canvas bag.

Lady Lucan reported how she had been attacked by her husband who then left the house. It was known that he called on some friends and then drove down to the south coast where he conceivably took a ferry across the English Channel to France. Despite unverified sightings and a great deal of speculation, the aristocrat and presumed murderer has not been seen since. Which makes him a highly successful fugitive from justice or, possibly, a victim of fate.

A Judge Vanishes

The childhood ambition of Joseph Force Crater was to be a judge. Nothing was going to get in his way and in 1916 he graduated from Columbia Law School and joined a Manhattan firm where his colleagues believed he was on his way to a seat on the United States Supreme Court. The following year, on 16 March 1917, he married Stella Wheeler whose divorce he had negotiated exactly a week earlier.

Crater took cases that other lawyers refused and wrote complicated briefs. In 1920, he became secretary to Judge

Robert Wagner of the New York Supreme Court. By 1927, Crater was earning $75,000-a-year and bought a luxury flat at 40 Fifth Avenue and a summerhouse at Belgrade Lakes, Maine.

Crater was a womanizer but kept one special mistress, an ex-model called Constance Marcus. He acted in her divorce case, part-paid her rent and gave her money to run a dress shop. Keeping two expensive properties, a wife and a mistress did not come cheaply so Crater began dealing on the dark side.

In 1930, he ran for the seat of the retiring New York Supreme Court Justice Joseph M. Proskauer, despite the 75 per cent drop in salary that sitting on the bench would entail. On 8 April, Governor Franklin D. Roosevelt appointed Crater. With his new position, Crater looked forward to the November election and confirmation to the fourteen-year post with a possible eye on the Supreme Court.

In June, Judge and Mrs Crater went to their Maine summerhouse, and while he was away, his political opponents began investigating some of the deals he had brokered. After a break in Atlantic City, New Jersey (with his latest mistress, showgirl Sally Lou Ritzi), he returned to Maine and then went to New York on 3 August, promising his wife that he would be back in Maine for her birthday in six days' time.

At 11am on 6 August, he was working hard in his office and sent an assistant to the bank to collect $5,150 (more than $72,000 in 2015 values). He left the office for lunch, taking the money and some files. At 8pm he went to Billy Haas's Chophouse restaurant at 332 West 45th Street for dinner. At 9.15pm he jumped in a taxi for a trip to the theatre (or possibly walked up the street).

Judge Crater was never seen again. The City of New York offered a $5,000 reward for information but nothing substantial was offered. Crater was declared legally dead on 6 July 1939. In 1985, the New York Police Department officially closed the case.

In August 2005, Stella Ferrucci-Good died aged ninety-one, leaving a note claiming that former NYPD cop Charles Burns and his cab-driving brother, Frank, were responsible for Crater's death and his corpse was buried under the pavement on Coney Island beneath what is now the New York Aquarium.

What Happened to the Trade Union Leader?

Jimmy Hoffa, who was perceptively given the name James Riddle Hoffa by his parents, was the head of the powerful Teamsters Union in America. He was also in the pay of organized crime.

In 1931, Hoffa began organizing a union among the workers of a grocer's. He won a 40 per cent pay rise for his men and earned himself a full-time job with the International Brotherhood of Teamsters. However, the only money Hoffa then earned was a percentage of the subscriptions from members he had personally recruited.

At a time when employers would think nothing of settling an industrial dispute with violence, Hoffa encouraged his members to reciprocate in kind. As times changed and employers became more enlightened, Hoffa began to intimidate other union leaders and in 1946 was investigated for extortion.

On 4 October 1957, he was elected the head of the Teamsters after his predecessor, Dave Beck, decided not to stand for re-election. By 1964, virtually every lorry driver in America was a member of the Teamsters.

It was rumoured that Hoffa was stealing a portion of the union funds for himself and his criminal chums. The government stepped in and in August of that year Hoffa was jailed for thirteen years for jury tampering, conspiracy, and mail and wire fraud.

Bobby Kennedy, the Attorney General under his brother President John F. Kennedy and briefly his successor Lyndon Johnson, had said, "Hoffa is a very evil influence on the United States and something has got to be done about it." However, due to various legal challenges the crooked union leader did not start serving his sentence until March 1967, and was freed on 23 December 1971, when President Richard Nixon commuted his sentence.

On his release, Hoffa was given a pension pot of $1.7 million in a lump sum. Coincidentally, the Teamsters supported Nixon in his bid to be re-elected in 1972. As part of his freedom Hoffa was banned from participating in union activities until 6 March 1980.

Never one to obey the law or know when he was beaten, Hoffa began moving to regain control of the Teamsters. Others preferred that he remained "retired" – including New Jersey union leader Anthony "Tony Pro" Provenzano, who also happened to be a made member of the Genovese crime family. The Mafia liked working with Hoffa's successor, Frank Fitzsimmons.

On 30 July 1975, Hoffa made arrangements to meet Provenzano and another mobster, Anthony "Tony Jack" Giacalone, in Machus Red Fox Restaurant at 6676 Telegraph Road in Bloomfield Township, Detroit. When his guests did not show, Hoffa made two calls from a payphone in the restaurant. He was never seen again. The next day Hoffa's green 1974 Pontiac Grand Ville was found unlocked in the restaurant car park.

Questioned by police, Provenzano and Giacalone swore they knew nothing about a meeting with the former union leader. Some claim that Hoffa was seen that day in the back of a maroon 1975 Mercury Marquis Brougham, and in 2001 a DNA match was made to him with a hair found in the car. Hoffa was legally declared dead in 1982. Machus Red Fox Restaurant closed in 1996.

In 2005, a book named Frank "The Irishman" Sheeran, a mob hitman, as Hoffa's killer. The following year, the *Detroit Free Press* published an FBI memo that indicated that the Mafia murdered Hoffa because his attempt to retake control of the union threatened their control of the union's pension fund.

In 2009, another mob hitman, Richard Kuklinski, claimed to have murdered Hoffa with a hunting knife before burning his body and burying it in a scrapyard. When it was thought that the authorities might dig up the area, the body was apparently exhumed, put in the boot of a car and transported to Japan.

In 2012, police dug up a driveway in Detroit after someone came forward to say that they had seen someone being buried there around the time Hoffa vanished. Scientists from Michigan State University examined the soil and found no trace of human remains. A similar wild goose chase took place in June 2013, in a property in Oakland Township. The FBI dug for three days before abandoning the idea as a waste of time. Jimmy Hoffa remains missing.

Hoffa's only son, James, became president of the Teamsters in 1999, a position he still holds, while his sister, Barbara Crancer, was a judge.

Where Is Our Diplomat?

Benjamin Bathurst was our man in Vienna, where he was envoy. On 25 November 1809, he was travelling to London when he stopped for dinner at the White Swan, a pub in Perleberg, Germany. England was at war with France and Bathurst was concerned for his safety.

During the course of the evening, he went outside to check on something with his coach and was never seen again. Rumours were rife: he had committed suicide; French agents had murdered him; he had died during interrogation by the French at Magdeburg Castle; and he had drowned when his ship went down in the Baltic.

The government offered a reward for information leading to his whereabouts, as did Prince Frederick of Prussia and Bathurst's own family. No more details were forthcoming.

Benjamin Bathurst was born on 18 March 1784, into a large family – his grandfather had twenty-two children by his first wife and fourteen more by his second including Bathurst's father, the Bishop of Norwich.

Bathurst was appointed to the embassy at Vienna in 1804. The following year, he married and was sent to the legation in Stockholm. However, after three years he regarded it a dead-end job and his health – physical and mental – suffered.

In March 1809, George Canning, the foreign secretary, appointed him envoy-extraordinary to Austria. His job was to persuade the Austrians to join the English in the war against Napoleon. Austria declared war on France in April 1809, but did not prove an effective ally and in May Vienna surrendered. In July the Austrians signed an armistice and in October broke off diplomatic relations with Britain. Bathurst and the Austrian court had already fled to Hungary.

Bathurst believed that Napoleon had a special hatred of him personally for persuading the Austrians to fight. He claimed to be a German called Koch but his entourage and fine clothes made him stand out. He travelled through Berlin without contacting the British envoy there and stopped at Perleberg, halfway between Berlin and Hamburg.

He asked the military governor for two bodyguards as he had heard that there were French soldiers nearby. For some reason he dismissed his guards around 8pm and later went out to his coach. At 9pm, the time of departure, his servants looked for him but there was no sign.

On 16 December, his trousers were found. They contained two bullet holes but no bloodstains. *The Times* accused the French secret service of murdering Bathurst, but Napoleon wrote personally to Bathurst's widow assuring her that he had had nothing to do with her husband's disappearance.

What happened to our man in Vienna? Did the French murder him? Did he commit suicide? Or is there a more prosaic explanation? One of his servants said that, in the pub, Bathurst had been flashing his money around and shown off his expensive watch. Was he just a victim of a robbery?

Cinematic Mystery

Many regard Louis Aimé Augustin Le Prince as the true father of the cinematic film. Born in France, he moved to Leeds in 1866. In 1881, he emigrated to America to work and began representing several French artists. He patented in 1888 in America a combined camera-projector. On 14 October of the same year in Roundhay, Leeds, he filmed *Roundhay Garden Scene* (lasting 2.11 seconds, it shows his son Adolphe Le Prince, his mother-in-law Sarah Robinson Whitley, Joseph

Whitley and Harriet Hartley walking around in a garden) and later that month *Traffic Crossing Leeds Bridge* using his single-lens camera and paper supplied by George Eastman, the founder of the Eastman Kodak Company.

Le Prince's films were shown privately but never publicly. In 1889, he took dual French–American citizenship so that he could work in New York. In September 1890, he planned to exhibit the fruits of his work and research at Jurnel Mansion in New York. However, he disappeared before he could make the presentation.

On Tuesday, 16 September 1890, he boarded the Paris–Dijon Express at Dijon. From the French capital he was due to return to London. However, when the train pulled into Paris there was no sign of Le Prince or his luggage. A search of the track provided no clues.

There were various theories as to what had happened to Le Prince. In 1928, one author suggested that Le Prince had committed suicide because he was on the verge of bankruptcy and arranged for neither his body nor his luggage ever to be found. Le Prince's widow believed that he had been murdered and his son Adolphe Le Prince also died under mysterious circumstances after losing a lawsuit against Thomas Edison. Adolphe Le Prince was found dead in 1900 on a duck shoot on Fire Island, New York.

Another theory that was aired in 1985 had Le Prince disappearing voluntarily because of his family's shame over his homosexuality. In this theory, Le Prince died in obscurity in Chicago in 1898. There is no evidence, however, to suggest that Le Prince was anything other than heterosexual. Another theory has a suicidal Le Prince being murdered by his brother.

In 2003, a photograph of a drowning victim was discovered in the Parisian police archives and the man looked very much like six-foot-three Le Prince. It seems likely that Le Prince was murdered for his invention and his body and luggage were thrown from the train as it passed over a river. However Le Prince died, it was the Lumière brothers and not he who got the credit for inventing the cinematic film.

"I Feel Trapped"

Seventeen-year-old Shafilea Ahmed lived with her parents and siblings in Warrington, Cheshire. She wanted to be free to dress and socialize as she pleased, but her parents had other ideas. They wanted her to forsake her chosen way of life and marry a cousin in Pakistan. She resisted the idea to the extent of attempting suicide by drinking bleach.

Following a family visit to Pakistan in 2003, her parents Iftikhar and Farzana Ahmed used every means at their disposal to coerce their daughter to conform to their wishes. It was made clear that her refusal to marry her cousin brought shame and dishonour to them and she was punished. Her mother kept her confined in the house at different times and starved her. The teenager was constantly threatened and slapped and her father told her that, if anything happened to her, no one would ever know.

In September 2003, Shafilea went missing. Her disappearance was not reported by her parents but by a teacher. Five months later, her decomposing remains were discovered on a riverbank in Cumbria. She was wearing white stiletto shoes and Western-style clothing, symbols of the life of which she wished to be part.

The Ahmeds came under suspicion and a listening device was planted in their house. Conversations were recorded of the dead girl's parents discussing what kind of proof was needed in a murder case. Their guilty secret which they had kept hidden for six years finally came apart through the revelations made by Alesha, the dead girl's sister. Alesha, now aged twenty-one, was arrested and questioned following a robbery at her parents' home in which she was complicit. Observing the family protocol of "silence and denial", she kept quiet about what she knew of her sister's disappearance. But she was a disturbed personality and found some consolation by confiding in school friends.

Rumours began to circulate and Alesha was questioned by the police after her parents were arrested on suspicion of kidnap. At first, she denied any knowledge of what had happened but, ultimately, she unburdened herself. She had witnessed her parents acting together to suffocate her sister. They held her down on a settee after an argument about her boyfriends and the clothes she wore. Shafilea struggled and was slapped in full view of her brother and sisters.

Then a plastic bag was thrust into the teenager's mouth and her father held her down while she gasped for air. Once the life had been squeezed out of his daughter, Iftikhar Ahmed prepared to dispose of her body, assembling bin bags and rolls of adhesive tape. Later that evening, Alesha saw her father carrying a bulky bin bag to the car and then driving off. Her mother told her that if anyone asked after her sister she was to say that she had run away.

Iftikhar and Farzana Ahmed were finally charged with murder in September 2011, and brought to trial the following year. They denied any involvement in Shafilea's death, but Alesha's graphic and harrowing account of her sister's final moments told otherwise. Midway through the trial, Farzana changed her story and put the blame on to her husband.

While Shafilea's parents had crushed her power to resist their abuse and manipulation, her spirit remained strong. A poem she had written was read out in court – its title was "I feel trapped". The Ahmeds were found guilty and sentenced to life imprisonment.

Neighbours from Hell

We cannot choose our neighbours, but given the choice most would prefer not to live near a Mafia don. Such was the misfortune of John Favara, who lived on the street behind Gambino crime family mobster John Gotti in Howard Beach, New York.

Mr Favara, fifty-one, worked as a manager in a furniture shop, Castro Convertibles in New Hyde Park, New York, and was a close friend of Anthony Zappi, the son of Ettore, a member of the Gambino crime family, despite the two men operating on opposite sides of the law. Scott Favara, John's adopted son, was very friendly with the Gotti children, especially the eldest boy John, and often slept over at the family home at 85th Street.

On 18 March 1980, Mr Favara was driving home to 86th Street after work, the sun was low in the sky and he was not too far away when twelve-year-old Frank Gotti, the youngest son of the gangster, darted into the street on a motorized minibike from behind a dumpster. Because of the sun, Mr Favara did not see the boy and ploughed into him, killing him instantly.

The police investigated and ruled the incident an accident and no charges were filed against Mr Favara. The Gottis did not see it that way and his life became a living hell. His car was stolen on 13 April, and, when it was found, the word "Murderer" was written on the bonnet. A funeral card was posted to him. On 28 May, Victoria Gotti put him in hospital with an aluminium baseball bat but Mr Favara refused to press charges. He asked friends of the Gottis what he should do. He was told he had two choices: move, or get a gun and kill John Gotti. He decided to move from Howard Beach.

In the summer, Gotti and his family went to Fort Lauderdale for a holiday – and an alibi. On 28 July 1980, two or three days before he was due to exchange contracts, John Favara was abducted as he was leaving work. Three men – Willie Boy Johnson, Funzi Tarricone and Tony Roach Rampino – part of a seven-man hit squad, pulled up in a van and jumped Mr Favara who had taken to carrying a gun but was unable to get off more than one off-target shot before Johnson hit him with a two-by-four and, unconscious, he was bundled into the boot of his own car.

There are various theories as to what happened to John Favara after that, including one that he was held prisoner until the Gottis returned from holiday. Then John Gotti personally dismembered Mr Favara with a chainsaw while still alive before he was put into a barrel, which was filled with concrete and thrown into the ocean off a Sheepshead Bay pier. Another theory is that he may have been dissolved in acid.

John Gotti told the police, "I'm not sorry the guy's missing. I wouldn't be sorry if the guy turned up dead." His wife

Victoria, when questioned, said, "I don't know what happened to him, but I'm not disappointed he's missing. He killed my boy."

John Favara remains missing and was declared legally dead in 1983. His wife, Janet, died in 2000, unable to provide a burial for her husband.

"Take Care"

The thought that might have passed through the mind of Robert Baltovich as he stepped into the Ontario courtroom where he would be tried for murder in 1992, cannot be divined. It is conceivable that he might have believed the lack of a victim's body would work in his favour.

The popular belief is that murder cannot be proved unless there is a body; what many people conceive of as the corpus delicti. But this concept embraces more than just the body, particularly when the presumption is that a known person has been killed in circumstances amounting to unlawful violence.

When he appeared on trial in 1992, Robert Baltovich knew that the supposed victim's body had not been found. The whereabouts of his girlfriend, 22-year old university student, Elizabeth Bain, had not been discovered despite intensive searches over twenty-one months. The young woman went missing on a summer's evening in June 1990, when it was believed she intended to visit tennis courts near her home in Scarborough, Ontario.

The alarm was raised when she failed to return home and, a few days later, her bloodstained car was found. A witness alleged that he had seen Elizabeth talking to a man believed to be Baltovich. Suspicion quickly focused on him and it was believed Bain had broken off their relationship and that he had killed her in a fit of jealous rage and then hid the body. Baltovich strongly denied this.

In due course, he was charged with second-degree murder and sent for trial. The jury sat through eight weeks of legal representation in proceedings that depended entirely on circumstantial evidence, there being no witnesses and, crucially, no body. What they had to decide was whether Baltovich committed a murder beyond reasonable doubt. After sixteen hours of deliberation, the jury found him guilty which meant that he would automatically receive a sentence of life imprisonment. Baltovich had consistently protested his innocence and, as he was escorted from the dock and taken down to the cells, he seemed relaxed and acknowledged a press reporter, winked at him and said, "take care".

In its report of the trial, the Toronto Globe & Mail expressed concern about the validity of the verdict, chiefly due to the reliance on circumstantial evidence. "We are not confident, at the end of this trial, of either Mr Baltovich's innocence or guilt", reported the newspaper.

This unease about the verdict was underlined twelve years later when, in 2004, Baltovich secured a retrial which resulted in the original conviction being set aside. He then faced a new trial in 2008 to answer a further charge of second-degree murder which led to a not-guilty verdict after the prosecution's case collapsed. To the distress of her family, Elizabeth Bain, believed to have been murdered, remains among the missing.

Posh Totty

When a 47-year-old woman living on her own was seeking excitement, she set herself up as a prostitute on a website called AdultWork using the pseudonym, poshtottyfun. It was a recipe for disaster. In May 2012, Carole Waugh, who lived a solitary existence in a flat in Marylebone, central London, was reported missing.

There were concerns that a man posing as her brother was trying to defraud her. She was a wealthy woman owning a property worth more than half a million pounds and known to possess expensive Cartier jewellery. Police enquiries revealed that a man had been seen outside Waugh's flat discussing its sale with an estate agent. Reporting her disappearance, the newspapers carried a compelling photograph of a smiling woman with a mass of auburn hair and sparkling blue eyes – every bit a "posh totty".

Carole Waugh had worked for an oil company in Libya and liked to boast about her friendship with Colonel Gaddafi and his family. She led a lonely and secretive life in London and, craving attention, sought sexual excitement by offering her services as an escort. Her wealth and social circumstances attracted some unsavoury characters who set out to befriend her and then to commit fraud, and worse.

Police investigators learned that large sums of money had been extracted from Waugh's bank accounts and that several women had impersonated her in order to make unauthorized withdrawals. A search of her flat showed that several pieces of expensive jewellery were missing. All of this tended to confirm the view that she had probably been abducted by a gang who had stolen her identity. Her disappearance was now treated as a murder enquiry.

By this time, police were homing-in on two men who were known conmen, one of whom had borrowed money from Waugh. Rakesh Bhayani was arrested, suspected of murder and conspiring with Nicholas Kutner to carry out fraud and abduction. Several women were also detained on suspicion of identity theft. Then, on 2 August, Carole Waugh's decomposing body was found in a zipped-up holdall in the boot of a car parked in a quiet suburban area of London. It was evident that she had been stabbed in the neck.

Rakesh Bhayani and his co-conspirator were professional conmen and gamblers sharing a string of convictions for fraud aimed at producing funds to feed their addiction to gambling. It was revealed that Waugh had loaned £40,000 to Bhayani after meeting him through her escort activities. When the relationship cooled off, she demanded the return of her money but, by then, he knew enough about her to see an opportunity for exploitation.

He killed her in her flat on 16 April 2012, and planned to burn her body. This idea was abandoned and he chose instead to dump her corpse in a car boot, the vehicle being secreted in a lock-up garage. At his trial for murder, the Old Bailey judge described how Bhayani had "ruthlessly targeted" Carole Waugh and "left her body to rot". In November 2013, Bhayani was found guilty and sentenced to life imprisonment. His conspirator, Nicholas Kutner, was judged not guilty of murder but was sentenced to thirteen years' imprisonment for helping to cover up the crime or, in legal terms, perverting the course of justice.

The "Cinderella" Mystery

On 5 November 1994, privately educated dancer and model Revelle Balmain vanished from a Sydney street just before she was due to leave for a six-month dancing tour of Japan.

That night she was due to meet a friend for a drink but failed to show. Neither did she keep a date with her boyfriend, Piers Fisher-Pollard, the same night.

The alarm was raised officially when the next morning the 22-year-old failed to catch the 9.30am train from Sydney to Newcastle to meet her mother to say goodbye before the trip to Japan.

A search of Kingsford, a south-eastern suburb of Sydney, two days later turned up her cane make-up bag, diary, keys to her Bellevue Hill home and one cork-heeled platform shoe – the items found dotted around four streets.

Further investigation showed that the blue-eyed five-foot-eight model had been working as an expensive prostitute for two agencies.

On the day she vanished, Revelle had seen a client, Gavin Owen Samer, at a house on McNair Avenue, Kingsford. After they had sex, he drove her to the nearby Red Tomato Inn at 7pm that evening, but no one there remembered seeing her. Mr Samer explained away the scratches on his neck, chest and hands by saying they had been caused when he was surfing.

A coroner's inquest named him as a person of interest but no charges were ever laid against him.

Deputy State Coroner John Abernethy said he could not identify any motive. "While Mr Samer certainly had the opportunity to kill Miss Balmain, and rightly in my view is the main person of interest to police, there is no plausible motive proved."

Revelle had been working for the escort agency Select Companions for six weeks before she disappeared. However, having fallen in love with Piers Fisher-Pollard, she decided to stop working as a prostitute and Mr Samer was to be her last client.

In 2008, Detective Superintendent Geoff Beresford revealed that new evidence showed Revelle had been murdered at a house in Kingsford.

"A full forensic search was carried out of the crime scene at Kingsford during the last twelve months," Det Supt Beresford told *The Australian*. "We are able to say we have fresh evidence as a result of those investigations."

It was at this time that the *Sydney Daily Telegraph* reported that Mr Samer had vanished from the city. A $250,000 reward offered for information leading to an arrest remains unclaimed.

The Naval Disappearance

The 1950s was a decade when the Cold War became deadlier than ever. Western Europe and the Soviet bloc lived in an era of mutual suspicion constantly spying on one another. Following the death (murder?) of Stalin in March 1953, Nikita Khrushchev took over running the Soviet Union and it was hoped that there would be a thawing of relations.

In 1956, it was announced that Khrushchev and Soviet Prime Minister Nikolai Bulganin would be visiting Britain on a diplomatic mission aboard the cruiser *Ordzhonikidze* and it would berth in Portsmouth Dockyard.

Lieutenant Commander Lionel "Buster" Crabb, a dapper five foot tall, was an experienced Second World War Navy diver who, after his retirement in March 1955, was recruited by MI6. On 19 April 1956, Crabb was paid sixty guineas to dive into Portsmouth Harbour to examine the propeller of *Ordzhonikidze*, a new type that the security services wanted to learn about.

It was not the first time that he had spied on a Soviet vessel. In 1955, Crabb investigated the hull of the cruiser *Sverdlov* to evaluate its superior manoeuvrability.

His mission to look at *Ordzhonikidze* did not have a similar successful outcome and Crabb was never seen again. Ten days later, the Admiralty announced that Crabb had vanished while partaking in trials of secret underwater apparatus in Stokes Bay on the Solent. The Soviets said that the crew of *Ordzhonikidze* had spotted a frogman near the vessel.

On 9 June 1957, a body in a frogman suit was found floating off Pilsey Island in Chichester Harbour. It was headless and handless, making identification impossible. A scar was found on the left knee, making it likely that the corpse was Crabb's. An inquest jury returned an open verdict but the coroner announced that he was satisfied that the body was that of Crabb.

What did happen to Buster Crabb? One theory posits that Crabb was captured and died during interrogation by the Soviets. Another has him murdered by Eduard Koltsov, a Soviet diver, who slashed Crabb's throat. Koltsov claimed that he knew Crabb was trying to place a mine on the ship and killed him to save the ship. A third has him spotted by an *Ordzhonikidze* crew member (which the Soviets admitted) and shot by a sniper (which they did not). Possibly, there was nothing suspicious about Crabb's death. He was in poor health through smoking and drinking and it is possible that his body just gave out. If that is the case, however, why are official government documents under lock and key until 2057?

Fit for Trial

Career criminal Henry Colin Campbell was arrested for murder on 11 April 1929. On 23 February 1929, next to a motorway in Cranford, New Jersey, police found the burnt body of a woman who had been shot in the head. It was six weeks before the remains were identified as Mildred Mowry, a local woman, who had gone missing at the start of the month after joining a lonely hearts' agency.

Investigators discovered that in August 1928, Mildred had married sixty-year-old Dr Richard Campbell who then disappeared to California with her life savings of $1,000. Her increasingly desperate letters went unanswered, probably because "Dr Richard Campbell" was not in the Golden State but much closer to home in Elizabeth, New Jersey, where he was living with his real wife, Rosalie, and family under his true name Henry Colin Campbell. When the lack of replies finally got to her, she decided to look for her errant spouse. Then she vanished.

The murder trial of Henry Colin Campbell began at Elizabeth, New Jersey, on 9 June 1929, before Judge Clarence E. Case. Two court-appointed psychologists – Dr Gus Payne and Dr Lawrence Collins – had examined Campbell and declared him fit to stand trial despite an addiction to morphine.

Campbell did not deny that he had shot Mildred Mowry with the .38 automatic found in his home or that he had burned her body afterwards. His defence was based on him claiming to be an amnesiac, saying that he had no memory of having done so.

Prosecutor Abe J. David read Campbell's confession in which he said he had murdered Miss Mowry to cover up his bigamous marriage but also put into evidence seventeen letters written by Campbell to his victim. They showed how he had manipulated her, playing on her loneliness, and when she finally discovered where he was he murdered her. Judge Case summed up, "If the defendant was conscious of the nature of his act he cannot be acquitted. The law does not recognize that form of insanity in which the faculties are so affected as to render a person suffering from it unable to control those urges."

On 13 June 1929, the jury found Campbell guilty of murder and he was sentenced to death. On 17 April 1930, he was electrocuted.

"Still Missing"

Described as a "real estate scion", Robert A. Durst is a member of a New York family with a rich real estate portfolio. He is also a man dogged by the aftermath of violent events and unanswered questions. In 1982, his wife, Kathleen, went missing and her disappearance has never been explained. Her family directed pointed questions at Robert Durst, as did the New York police. Nothing came of these enquiries and she remained a missing person.

Nineteen years later, Durst was arrested and charged with murdering his neighbour, 71-year-old Morris Black, in his apartment at Galveston, Texas. The elderly man's body had been dismembered and beheaded. The torso was found floating in the Bay in September 2001. A witness had seen Durst loading plastic bags into his station wagon, and a .22-calibre handgun, the same type of weapon used to kill Morris Black, was found in a nearby trash heap.

While free on bail, pending enquiries, Durst went on the run, resulting in a nationwide manhunt. He was a wealthy man and had resources to follow any action he chose. In another startling development, Susan Berman, a long-time friend of Durst's, was shot dead at her home in Los Angeles. Investigators had made it known that they wished to question Berman about the disappearance of Kathleen Durst.

The fugitive was now wanted for questioning about his missing wife and the killings of Morris Black and Susan Berman. After being on the run for forty-five days, Robert Durst was arrested for shoplifting at a supermarket in Bethlehem, Pennsylvania, where he stole a chicken sandwich. As soon as he was recognized as one of America's Most Wanted, the questions followed thick and fast. He had in his possession nearly forty thousand dollars in cash, two handguns and a driving licence belonging to Morris Black.

In 2003, Durst was put on trial for Black's murder. He pleaded self-defence and admitted using a knife, two saws and an axe to dismember the body. The jury acquitted him of the charge of murder. In further court proceedings in 2004, he pleaded guilty to two counts of jumping bail and one of tampering with evidence. Following a plea bargain, he was given a sentence of five years' imprisonment.

He was paroled in 2005 but, following an unauthorized visit to the site of Morris Black's murder, he was convicted of parole violation and returned to prison for a year. In 2011, at the age of seventy-one, Robert Durst was reported to be living in New York. Questions remained about the disappearance of his wife and the violent death of his friend, Susan Berman.

"Taken"

Sian O'Callaghan worked as an office administrator in Swindon. On the evening of 19 March 2011, she visited a nightclub in the town and left in the early hours of the morning to walk the short distance to her flat. When she did not return, her boyfriend tried to contact her by mobile phone. Failing to gain any response, he called the police and reported that she was missing.

Suspecting that the young woman had been abducted, police set about examining her mobile phone records. They learned that at the time her boyfriend's call was sent, her phone was located in Savernake Forest, some twelve miles from Swindon. Search teams, aided by sniffer dogs and volunteers from the public, began to comb the 4,500 acres of woodland.

Following other leads, the police were keen to establish the whereabouts of a green Toyota taxi which had been seen in the Savernake Forest area. Public interest in the missing woman was very high and the sought-after vehicle was quickly located in a supermarket car park in Swindon.

The driver of the taxi was 47-year-old Christopher Helliwell, who told officers the location of two bodies. He guided them first to a spot near Uffington in Oxfordshire where he had moved Sian O'Callaghan's body after killing her in Savernake Forest. Helliwell also gave police the location of a second grave, a young woman he said he had "taken" from Swindon in 2003 or 2005 and later killed.

O'Callaghan's body, partially stripped, was found lying face down in a shallow grave. She had been stabbed and traces of her DNA were found in Helliwell's car. The body of Becky Godden-Edwards, who had been officially missing since 2007, was found in a field at Eastleach in Gloucestershire. Once again, Helliwell led officers to the spot. The young woman had actually been missing since 2003 but had not been reported as such.

Helliwell told detectives that when he finished work at night he roamed around Swindon in his taxi looking for likely victims to kidnap. At his trial for the murder of Sian O'Callaghan, he pleaded guilty and was given a life sentence. A second murder charge implicating him in the death of Becky Godden-Edwards was dropped when the judge ruled his confession was inadmissible due to discrepancies in police procedure.

Body in the Loft

With the London Olympic Games in full swing in the summer of 2012, came news of a missing schoolgirl. Tia Sharp, twelve, was reported missing from her grandmother's home in New Addington, Surrey. It was believed she had gone shopping in Croydon. Police officers were diverted from duties at the Olympic Park to search for her, and local volunteers also helped.

On 6 August, her family made an impassioned appeal for the youngster to return home. Stuart Hazell, thirty-seven, who lived with Tia's grandmother, Christine Sharp, was the last person to see her. He too made an emotional appeal for her return, describing Tia as his "golden girl". Her family affairs were complex – following the separation of her parents, her mother lived with her boyfriend at Mitcham, Surrey, while her father was based in Northampton. In consequence, Tia spent a great deal of time at her grandmother's home.

Detectives made three searches of the house at New Addington, including the loft in the roof space. Nothing significant was found until 10 August, when a fourth search located Tia's body hidden in the loft. The search procedures would become the subject of much recrimination later.

It appeared that Tia, whose body had been concealed in a plastic sack, was smothered. The police decided to question Stuart Hazell, only to find that he had absconded. He was located after a tip-off from a member of the public and arrested. Later, he was charged with murder. Hazell had form, including convictions for racially aggravated assault, drug offences and possession of an offensive weapon. It also appeared that he had visited child pornography sites online.

Hazell denied killing Tia, saying that she had fallen down the stairs. The prosecution case put forward at his trial, which began on 7 May 2013, was that he had assaulted the girl before smothering her and hiding the body. This put his emotional appeal on television for her safe return home into a cynical perspective.

He had experienced a troubled childhood and grew up in care. At one time he lived on the streets, existing on the proceeds of petty crime and suffering depression. When he met Tia's grandmother, he found some respite from hard times. Perhaps in recognition of this, he changed his plea to guilty on 14 May, at the Old Bailey. The jury convicted him of murder and he was sentenced to life imprisonment with a minimum term of thirty-eight years.

No Body, No Proof, No Justice

Kate Prout was last seen alive on Bonfire Night in 2007. She was the estranged wife of millionaire landowner Adrian Prout, whom she had married in 2000. The couple lived at Redhill Farm at Redmarley near Tewkesbury and, at the time she disappeared, were involved in an acrimonious divorce settlement.

Police carried out extensive searches of the farm but could not find a body. They were convinced, nevertheless, that the 55-year-old former teacher had been murdered. Adrian Prout was the chief suspect and he was duly charged and tried. He was convicted of murder at Bristol Crown Court in February 2010, and given a prison sentence.

Prout protested his innocence and his friends claimed that a miscarriage of justice had been perpetrated. They formed a support group with the slogan, "No body, no proof, no justice". His fiancée, Debbie Garlick, who had moved into the farm, led a campaign for his release and arranged for him to take a poly-graph test in prison.

The results of the test indicated that he was lying about the circumstances surrounding his late wife's death. He then made a confession to Garlick and, subsequently, to the police. He admitted he had killed Kate and said he would show officers the place where he had buried her body.

Taken back to his farm, he indicated an area of woodland where he said the body lay. A large-scale search ensued, involving ground-penetrating radar and the latest forensic archaeology techniques. After a week, human remains were uncovered on 24 November 2011. Prout admitted that he had strangled her and expressed remorse. He had misled family members for four years over the circumstances of his wife's death and the location of her body. The judicial authorities were vindicated in their prosecution of him despite the lack of a body.

What Happened to Claudia?

Blonde, beautiful and popular Claudia Elizabeth Lawrence, thirty-five, worked as a chef at the University of York's Goodricke College at the Roger Kirk Centre. On 18 March 2009, she vanished and has not been seen since.

On that evening she rang her parents, sent a text message to a friend at 8.23pm and then simply disappeared. Her passport and bank cards were left at her home in Heworth Road, York.

The alarm was raised when she failed to turn up for her 6am shift at work on 19 March, and had still not made an appearance by Friday, 20 March. She had agreed to meet her close friend Suzy Cooper on the Thursday night for a drink at the local pub The Nag's Head (four doors up from Claudia at 56 Heworth Road).

The police were called on the Friday at 2.07pm and it would appear they initially worked on the premise that five-foot-six Claudia was promiscuous and had had secret affairs with numerous men from her locale and further afield, including some who were married – although her father, Peter, said that he did not recognize that description of his daughter.

In May 2009, the case was upgraded from that of a missing

person to one of suspected murder. The following month, on 2 June, the story was featured on *Crimewatch*, and although this generated more than sixty calls there were no firm leads. The case was again featured on the BBC programme on 19 March 2014.

In December 2010, the body of a young woman was found in the southwest, and Peter Lawrence wondered for a time if it was his daughter, but it turned out to be that of Joanna Yeates (see page 331).

On 13 May 2014, 59-year-old Michael Snelling was arrested on suspicion of the murder of Claudia Lawrence. He was released without charge two days later and freed from bail in October.

The case remains open.

"Summer Jumbo"

Hisako Yoshida, a 42-year-old unattached lady living in Iwate Prefecture in Japan, won 200 million yen on the "Summer Jumbo" lottery in 2005. She kept her win to herself and the first her family heard about it was when she went missing in May. She was last seen in the previous month when she signed a deal to buy a new car which she never collected.

Police enquiries revealed that Hisako had been dating Jinichi Kumagai, a newspaper delivery agent. He was believed to be the only person who knew that she had won the lottery prize. He was suspected of being involved in her disappearance. Kumagai had started a new business dealing in electronic components and at the time he was seeing Hisako, he was living with another woman.

Progress was slow but police enquiries led to a search of Kumagai's former house where he had lived prior to divorcing his wife. There, detectives found Hisako's savings book. It appeared that he had borrowed money from her before she won the lottery and he admitted using some of her winnings to repay his business debts.

Kumagai was arrested in October 2008, on suspicion of

murdering Hisako. Police believed the couple had quarrelled over money matters prior to his business becoming bankrupt. Faced with these allegations, the 51-year-old confessed to strangling her and burying her body in the yard of his former home. Her remains were recovered after being in the ground for three years. It was later revealed that Kumagai had also confessed the crime to his current girlfriend.

Those who knew him described Kumagai as a popular individual and expressed their shock over what had happened. The "Summer Jumbo" lottery win proved a mixed blessing for both him and his one-time consort, Hisako.

"Burn in Hell!"

Catherine Ayling, an English student, met Curtis Howard when she was studying in Boston, USA, in August 1989. He became infatuated with her and, although she did no more than treat him as a college friend, he began to pursue her relentlessly with letters and phone calls.

When Catherine's father died, later that year, she returned to the UK. What she did not realize was that Howard was intent on stalking her. He travelled to England in June 1990, and broke into her sister's house in Sussex in the hope of finding her there. He was disappointed but left his mark by scratching a reverse swastika symbol on a door, accompanied by the words, "Catherine is dead". He also desecrated the grave of Mr Ayling and made menacing phone calls to the family.

Howard was arrested for committing these offences and convicted of burglary. In due course, he was deported to the USA, informing one of his police escorts that "Catherine will join her father in hell". Catherine, twenty-four, took up her studies at Crewe and Alsager College in Cheshire in May 1991, but was later reported missing, having last been seen on her way to the college library.

A few days later, her body was found in the boot of a car left in the long-term car park at Gatwick airport. She had been killed with multiple stab wounds, and Howard, who had hired the rental vehicle, had fled back to the USA. He was picked up two days later and charged with passport violations. As he was *persona non grata* in the UK, he had stolen the identity of a dead child in order to create a travel document for himself. It was using the name Dwayne Williams that Howard regained entry to the UK.

Curtis Howard, twenty-seven, was extradited to the UK to stand trial for murder. He appeared at the Old Bailey in October 1994, and pleaded guilty to manslaughter on the grounds of diminished responsibility. His counsel argued that he had no previous record of violence and had been stricken by mental illness.

The judge said he had examined reports on the defendant's mental status and was satisfied that Howard was "a cunning, devious, violent and dangerous man". He was a danger to the public and the family of his victim. Curtis Howard was convicted on 26 October, and sentenced to life imprisonment, which the judge said was unusual for manslaughter but justified in this instance. Several members of the Ayling family were present in court to hear the sentence and, when it was delivered, Catherine's sister shouted out "Burn in hell, you bastard!"

"A Detached Crazy Person"

The disappearance and murder of Joanna Claire Yeates in Bristol in late 2010 sparked off a storm of media interest. The young landscape architect left her flat in Clifton on the evening of 17 December, leaving behind her purse, mobile phone and keys. She did not return and was reported missing.

She was last seen at around 8pm that evening when she joined friends for a drink at a pub in the city centre. On the way home, she stopped at a store to buy a pizza. Joanna shared the flat with her boyfriend who was away visiting his parents before Christmas. When he returned, he was alarmed not to find her at home and, on 19 December, she was reported missing.

Six days later, on Christmas Day, a man out walking with his dogs found a corpse covered in snow lying on a grass verge near a quarry. The discovery of Joanna's body prompted a massive police enquiry involving seventy detectives. Her body was clothed, although her shoes and one sock were missing. There were no obvious injuries but it was established at post-mortem examination that she had been strangled.

Detectives found no sign of a break-in at the flat. Their searches including sifting through nearly 300 tons of domestic refuse from neighbourhood bins in the hope of finding clues, such as the missing pizza box, which might bear fingerprints. Increasingly, the feeling was that Joanna had been murdered by someone known to her. Suspicion began to settle on Chris Jefferies, aged sixty-five, a retired teacher who lived in the same building as Joanna. He was also her landlord.

What followed amounted to character assassination by the tabloid press of a man respected by the local community while being regarded as quietly eccentric. Mr Jefferies was arrested on 31 December, on suspicion of murder. The level of accusation and finger-pointing he suffered at the hands of the media led to intervention by the Attorney General and, in due course, to legal proceedings.

In fast-moving developments, attention was quickly redirected to another of Joanna Yeates's neighbours. Dutch architectural engineer Vincent Tabak, thirty-nine, who had moved to Bristol in 2009, lived next to Joanna. He made what proved to be a fatal mistake by calling the police and giving them information about Jefferies's movements. This action simply drew attention to himself.

Tabak was interviewed and, following a search of his flat, he was arrested on 23 January 2011, on suspicion of murder. Traces of blood were found in his car and it became evident that he had searched for pornography online and took an interest in sites discussing strangulation and bondage. He had also followed the police investigation, which he discussed with friends, voicing the opinion that the murderer must be "a detached crazy person". Officers were satisfied there was sufficient forensic evidence to link Tabak with Joanna and he was charged with murder. While in custody, he confessed to the prison chaplain that he had killed Joanna.

At his trial in Bristol on 4 October 2011, Tabak pleaded guilty to manslaughter but denied murder. The evidence showed that as well as being strangled, Joanna had sustained forty-three other injuries including cuts, bruises and a broken nose. It was revealed that after killing the young woman Tabak went shopping for beer and crisps while her body lay in the boot of his car. He also found time to send a text message to his girlfriend, telling her that he was bored.

Tabak said in his defence that he had not intended to kill Joanna. His explanation of events was that they had a chance meeting when she invited him into her flat for a friendly drink. He said that she was flirty and he attempted to kiss her. At this point, things got out of hand. She resisted his advances and began to scream. He panicked and attempted to silence her by putting his hand over her mouth. When this failed to quieten her, he applied pressure to her throat. He maintained that he had not intended to harm her. When the jury were shown photographs of Joanna's body, Tabak broke down. The question for the jury was to decide whether he had intended to kill her.

With a ten to two majority, the jury returned a verdict of guilty of murder on 28 October. Mr Justice Field said he believed the killing of Joanna Yeates had been a sex crime which he described as "a dreadful, evil act against a vulnerable young woman in her own home". He sentenced Vincent Tabak to a minimum of twenty years' imprisonment.

CHAPTER 8

By Design

Most categories of crime contain a strong element of premeditation, although opportunism also has a part to play. By definition, murder is a matter of design and intention. Distinction has to be made between murder and manslaughter, the distinction hinging on malice aforethought, the evil intent that must be proved beyond a reasonable doubt.

In some jurisdictions, allowance is made for the crime passionel *when impulse overrides intention. This demonstrates the human capacity for committing unthinking and irrational acts. In this context, the killing of her husband by Marguerite Fahmy in 1923, and the shooting of her lover by Ruth Ellis in 1955, are instructive. While Fahmy was acquitted, Ellis paid the ultimate price after being found guilty.*

The intention to commit a crime may evolve over a considerable time-span which encompasses careful planning. If the prime objective is to execute the crime successfully, a secondary ambition is to avoid capture and punishment. This brings into play the concept of the perfect crime, so smoothly conceived and carried out as to create no suspicion. The planning process calls for a strategy, which embraces motive, method and opportunity. These are the three essential components of premeditated crime: why, how, and when.

H. H. Holmes, properly known as Herman Webster Mudgett, is one of America's most infamous mass murderers with a tally of victims numbering at least twenty-seven. He had a motive for killing, devised intricate methods and created opportunities to secure victims. He devoted a great deal of time and energy to achieve his ambitions and put murder onto a more or less industrial scale. In the 1890s, he had a hotel built in Chicago, which was a veritable death factory.

"Holmes's Castle", as it was called, was equipped with a number of guest rooms fitted with airtight doors and windows and fed with a gas supply. Guests selected as murder victims were exterminated in these rooms and conveyed by chutes down into his basement crematorium. There, the corpses were dismembered and either put into vats of acid, or lime pits, or destroyed by fire.

He murdered chiefly for gain and, apart from stealing his clients' valuables, offered their bones for sale to medical schools as teaching exhibits. His forward planning involved advertising jobs that attracted numerous applicants. He carefully vetted their financial prospects before offering a position, and then it was a short cut to one of his airtight death rooms.

Not many murderers go to such lengths, but some like to make lists. Benjamin Laing, who planned two murders in 1992, in the furtherance of theft, drew up a modest shopping list. This included a tool kit, change of clothes and a supply of black bin bags. Having despatched his victims, he dismembered their corpses and filled ten plastic sacks with their remains, ready for burial. Bin bags have become an important requisite for those dealing in body parts and disposal of corpses.

A favoured tactic employed by some killers is to disguise murder as accident or suicide. Making the distinction poses taxing problems for the forensic pathologist. A prime exponent of this form of duplicity was George Joseph Smith, the "Brides in the Bath Murderer". He drowned three wives from 1912 to 1914 and, having secured verdicts of death by misadventure in each instance, collected on their insurance policies. His cunning plan involved prior consultation with his victim's doctor, suggesting that his wife was subject to fits or fainting spells. With such a background, drowning in the bath hardly seemed remarkable.

A classic ploy to disguise murder as accident is the push down the stairs or the fall off the top of a cliff. To ensure his wife's death, Bryn Masterman first hit her over the head, cracking her skull, before staging her apparent fall down the stairs. The coroner's inquest recorded a verdict of death by misadventure, but eventually

Masterman was undone by bragging that he had got away with murder. A re-examination of the evidence by an astute pathologist showed that the fatal injuries had been caused by blunt force trauma and not by a fall down the stairs.

When a pair of newlyweds had a tiff during a cliff-top walk, the result was the death of the young man after he had tumbled over the edge. His widow's explanation was that she had fended him off during their argument and he accidentally fell over the precipice. A court in Montana, USA, listened to opposing arguments about pushing and falling and concluded that his death was murder and not an accident.

Murder scenarios involving cars and faked accidents came into vogue after Alfred Arthur Rouse immolated his passenger in the "Blazing Car Mystery" in 1930. It was really no mystery at all as Rouse had tampered with the carburettor and laid a trail of petrol, which he ignited from a safe distance. The identity of the victim was never established.

In more recent times, Malcolm Webster became the master of the faked car crash and got away with killing his wife in what he thought was a perfect murder. But justice finally caught up with him several years later when he staged a second faked car crash. On this occasion, his intended victim survived, and justice beckoned.

The "no body – no crime" argument, while it might seem a logical defence, does not stand up in court, as John Haigh discovered to his cost in 1949. The "Acid Bath Murderer" taunted the police that a murder charge could not be made against him when there was no victim's body. When Kate Prout disappeared in 2007, her husband claimed to be ignorant of her whereabouts and proclaimed his innocence on the basis of, "no body, no proof, no justice". Thanks to the use of ground-penetrating radar, the missing woman's remains were found four years later. And, in Haigh's case, his plan was undone by the discovery of a set of his victim's dentures, which survived the acid bath.

The emergence of the hired killer came about in the 1930s in America's criminal underground. Using contract killers to dispose of their rivals was a favourite tactic adopted by gangland bosses. The idea was to put distance between the crime and its true architect. The hired killer acted without real motive, apart from being paid, thereby affording protection to the mastermind.

But this ploy, of murder by proxy, was not the sole preserve of the underworld, as any intending murderer with money to spare could put distance between himself and the act of killing by hiring an assassin. Contract killers frequently work in pairs, as in the case of the elimination of Nishal Patel Basri in 2006. When he became disenchanted with his wife, Fadi Nasri hired two hitmen to kill her while he was away, protected, as he thought, by a perfect alibi – playing snooker.

Women who enlist the services of a contract killer to eliminate a husband or boyfriend are not unknown. But a rarer phenomenon is a woman fulfilling the role of hired killer, or hit woman. One such was a lady of Maori descent, Rangimaria Nagarimu, who was hired by two men in 1992 to kill a business associate who, at the time, was in hospital. Armed with a photograph to identify her target, she entered the hospital and fatally shot him, all for a pittance as payment.

Architects of the perfect murder frequently resort to the use of poison, the so-called "Coward's Weapon". Historically, poison trials have been among the most celebrated annals of crime. Its use by medical practitioners has been significant. Doctors with access to the sick and the elderly have been tempted to administer over-doses of prescribed drugs, thereby creating the appearance of death through illness or natural causes.

Dr John Bodkin Adams, during the course of thirty-five years' medical practice in Sussex, was widely believed to have killed eight or nine elderly patients with drug overdoses. Some said he murdered them for gain while others believed he merely practised euthanasia, what the practitioner himself described as "easing the passing". Either way, he benefited from numerous legacies and retired a wealthy man.

Two other practitioners, one in France and the other in America, perverted their skills to serve ambitions of greed. Dr Henri Girard dosed his victims with specially cultured bacterial agents. Already weakened by illness, his victims died of typhoid and tuberculosis. Dr Arthur Waite, a New York dentist, followed the same course, *cultivating death-dealing germs in the laboratory. Girard eluded justice by taking his own life using one of his infernal toxic concoctions.*

While the murder tally of H. H. Holmes was impressive, that of Dr Harold Shipman was in a class of its own. He was the arch-exponent of murder by design over twenty years, murdering more than two hundred people who had the misfortune to be treated by him at his surgery in Hyde, Greater Manchester.

He killed terminally ill patients and those he regarded as a nuisance, using lethal overdoses of diamorphine. His planning involved persuading grieving relatives to have the body of their departed loved one cremated, thereby destroying evidence of his murderous activities. He also backdated medical records to suit his purpose.

In the end, it was his own cleverness that brought him down when he forged the will of a lady who became his last victim in 1988. An astute undertaker had also noted the abnormally large number of patients who died during visits to Shipman's surgery. The practitioner exhibited no signs of being mentally unstable, giving no cause for alarm or suspicion. Indeed, he was regarded by his patients with considerable esteem. In his book, What Is Madness?, *published in 2011, psychoanalyst Darian Leader wrote that Shipman was "a study in quiet madness". Unrepentant to the last, he committed suicide in prison in 2004.*

Though design and careful preparation may be seen as the route to committing the perfect crime, it is also amply demonstrated that even the best-laid criminal plans can go awry.

Fashion Victim

Andrew Phillip Cunanan was born into a middle-class family at San Diego, California, on 31 August 1969. Gianni Versace was born at Reggio di Calabria, Italy, on 2 December 1946. Both men were homosexuals, but one was internationally famous while the other lived a good life thanks to rich boyfriends and his good looks. They met in October 1990 in a San Francisco restaurant and Cunanan realized what fun life could be like with the gay jet set.

In 1992, to please his boyfriend, Cunanan appeared in two gay porn films; the same year Versace bought the house where he would die for $2.9 million and Cunanan first met Jeff Trail, a handsome sailor. They became firm friends in late 1995 when Cunanan had left yet another older, wealthy boyfriend, but Trail could not be persuaded to jump into bed with Cunanan.

In early 1997, Cunanan went to visit Trail in Minneapolis where he was working. Returning to California, Cunanan worked as a transvestite prostitute to support himself. On 26 April 1997, he returned to Minneapolis where, the next day at 9.55pm, he murdered Jeff Trail by smashing him over the head with a claw hammer. On 2 May, he shot architect David Madson, another friend. Two days later, Cunanan killed property developer Lee Miglin, seventy-two, at Chicago.

On 9 May 1997, Cunanan murdered 45-year-old caretaker William Reese and stole his pick-up truck. He moved to Miami where he became a regular on the gay scene until Tuesday, 15 July 1997, when Cunanan murdered Versace as the fashion designer returned from breakfast at the News Café.

The two men argued and then Cunanan pulled a heavy .40-calibre pistol from his backpack and shot Versace in the head outside his luxury home, Casa Casuarina, 1116 Ocean Drive, Miami Beach, Florida. He fell to the ground, and to make sure that Versace was dead Cunanan fired another bullet into the designer's skull.

On 23 July 1997, eight days after he murdered Versace, Cunanan shot himself in the head aboard a Miami houseboat moored at 5250 Collins Avenue, Indian Creek. The father of Jeff Trail said, "I take no joy in his death . . . Now nobody will be able to tell me why this happened."

Hair Today

Single mother Heather Barnett was murdered on 12 November 2002, in her ground-floor flat at 112 Capstone Road, Bournemouth, after taking her two children to school. A self-employed seamstress, Heather, forty-eight, worked from home, and that Tuesday was no exception.

Some time around 9am Heather was killed and left in a
bloody pool on her bathroom floor. Her throat had been cut
from ear to ear, her jeans pulled down to expose her pubic hair
and both breasts cut off and placed by her badly beaten head
(the latter injuries inflicted by a hammer). A clump of light
brown hair rested in her right hand, which was on her lower
stomach. In her left hand were about thirty hairs of a different
colour to hers. Terry and Caitlin Marsh, her children, discovered Heather's body that day when they came home from
school. As they waited for the police, a neighbour, Fiamma
Marsango, who lived at number 93 with her boyfriend Danilo
Restivo, pulled up in their car.

Restivo comforted the distraught children and took them
into his home. The police assumed that DNA on the hair and
the blood samples would lead to a quick arrest and conviction.
It was a false hope. A check of the sex offenders in the area also
came to nothing. Local hairdressers were also questioned
because of the hair left at the scene. It was only when the
search was widened to include Interpol databases that a name
sprang up.

Detectives flew to Potenza in Italy to get information on the
diappearance of Elisa Claps, sixteen, on 12 September 1993.
The then 21-year-old Danilo Restivo had been courting her. A
search of his home elicited none of Elisa's possessions or evidence
that he might have been involved in her disappearance.

Around that time there had been complaints by nine women
of having their hair cut on public transport by a stranger.
Restivo was jailed in Potenza in March 1995, for perjury relating to his statements about Elisa's disappearance. Upon
release, he moved to Bournemouth. In 2004, he married
Fiamma and in June that year was arrested. He had been
observed cutting women's hair on public transport. After three
days, the police released him but put him under surveillance.

On 17 March 2010, workmen discovered the body of Elisa
at Most Holy Trinity Church. She had been beaten, stabbed
thirteen times and sexually assaulted. A clump of her own hair
had been cut and placed in her hand. Restivo was arrested at
6.30am on 19 May 2010.

On 11 May 2011, Restivo's trial opened at Winchester Crown Court. When he gave evidence, Restivo admitted his hair-cutting fetish but denied murder. On 29 June, Restivo was found guilty after just four hours' deliberation by the jury and handed down a whole of life tariff.

Royal Robbery

On Saturday, 11 September 1971, a group of thieves broke into safe deposit boxes at a branch of Lloyds Bank on the corner of Baker Street and Marylebone Road, London, after tunnelling fifty feet into the vault from a rented shop and going under a fried chicken restaurant.

The thieves took over a leather goods shop named Le Sac, which was two doors from the bank and separated from it by a Chicken Inn. To ensure their success, they only tunnelled at weekends.

The thieves placed a lookout on the roof opposite and kept in touch via walkie-talkie. They tried to use a thermal lance to break into the bank but had to resort to explosives in the end.

Unfortunately for the crooks, at 11.15pm a radio ham named Robert Rowlands, then thirty-five and running his own financial company, had just got into bed in his fourth-floor flat in Wimpole Street, central London, with a cup of tea and an Ian Fleming novel. "I was trying to tune into Radio Luxembourg," he said in an interview years later. Instead he heard a south Londoner say, "We've got about 400,000. We'll let you know when we're coming out. Can you hear me?" The reply came, "I can hear you, how long do you think you're going to be in there, then?"

He recalled, "I knew any robbery had to be within a mile-and-a-half radius of my flat to pick up a signal and I thought it was taking place in a tobacconist shop – 400,000 cigarettes seemed the most likely theft." He called the police and was told to record "any more funny voices" if he heard them, which he did on a cassette machine he was using to teach himself Spanish.

Shortly after midnight, a man called Steve told the lookout, "We want you to mind it for one hour from now, and then stop there, and go off air, and then come back on the air with both radios at 6 o'clock in the morning, over." The lookout was unsure about remaining *in situ* while the gang went home. "Steve" said, "Look, the place is filled with fumes and if security come in and smell them we are all going to take stoppo [make a hasty getaway] and none of us have got nothing, whereas this way we've all got 300 grand to cut up."

Another thief said, "You can't go now, we're almost there" to which the lookout replied, "Money may be your god, but it's not mine, and I'm fucking off." In the end he stayed. Rowlands called the police again and a constable arrived but left thirty minutes later.

Exasperated, he called New Scotland Yard, who sent two plainclothes detectives who "sat on chairs by my bed, and we stayed up all night" listening. Two more detectives arrived at dawn. At 9am, "Steve" told the lookout, "We're going to finish off in [the bank] and we shall be coming out early this afternoon and you'll just have to bluff, bluff your way straight down off the roof."

The raid made the Radio 4 News the next day at 9am after staff had arrived to find the contents of 300 safe deposit boxes gone. To add insult to injury and incompetence, the police took Rowlands's tape recording and did not return it for six years and threatened to prosecute him for listening to an unlicensed radio station.

The thieves took £1.5 million in cash and a similar amount from safe deposit boxes. The total haul was estimated at around £3 million (approx. £35.9 million in 2014 figures). Scrawled inside the safe were the words: "Let Sherlock Holmes try to solve this."

In January 1973, at the Old Bailey, Anthony Gavin, thirty-eight, a photographer from Dalston, Thomas Stephens, a 35-year-old car dealer from Islington, and Reginald Tucker, thirty-seven, a company director from Hackney, all pleaded guilty to the robbery and were, sentenced to twelve years' imprisonment. A fourth man, Benjamin Wolfe, sixty-six, a fancy goods dealer from East Dulwich, pleaded not guilty but was convicted and was sent to jail for eight years. He had signed the lease on Le Sac.

Two other men were acquitted of handling stolen bank-notes. The robbery has taken on mythic proportions supposedly because the "real" reason behind it was that MI5 wanted to recover some allegedly compromising photographs of Princess Margaret taken on the Caribbean island of Mustique and kept in a deposit box at the bank by Michael X, a Black Power activist and pimp who became the first non-white person to be charged and imprisoned under the UK's Race Relations Act and who would be hanged for murder in 1975.

It has been reported that a D-Notice was issued to prevent the press carrying reports of the crime from Thursday, 16 September. However, *The Times* was still reporting on the case two months later. The files on Michael X are to be kept secret until 2054. The story, complete with likely royal and espionage embellishments, was made into the 2008 film, *The Bank Job*.

From the Emerald Isle to a Double Murder Down Under

Thomas John Augustus Griffin emigrated from County Antrim, Ireland (where he had been born on 27 July 1832), to Australia in 1856, taking advantage of free passage offered to former soldiers.

He had served in the Royal Irish Constabulary and then volunteered for the Crimean War, where he was decorated twice. He arrived in Victoria in early 1857, and on 29 April, at Essendon, he married Harriett Klisser, who he thought was a wealthy widow. He left her and in May 1858 joined the New South Wales police.

In February 1859, he was appointed chief constable at Rockhampton. On 18 October 1863, he was appointed police magistrate and gold commissioner on the Clermont field, but his bullying manner made him unpopular. His appointment was supposedly due to an affair with a leading politician's sister. He almost went bankrupt through gambling and, when his wife caught up with him, paying maintenance. The politician's sister dumped him when his wife turned up.

In June 1866, he was accused of theft but was exonerated. Rumours of embezzlement from local miners surfaced, but he was transferred to Toowoomba as police magistrate before the accusations could be proved; later he moved to Rockhampton as gold commissioner. His job was to buy gold from the prospectors.

With troopers John Power and Patrick Cahill guarding ten canvas bags containing notes and coins to the value of almost £8,000, he set off across the Mackenzie River to Claremont on 27 October 1867. Griffin decided to go back to Rockhampton as they approached the river. On his return, he went to the police station and asked if the rumour was true, that the gold escort had been killed. The news had just been received that Power and Cahill were indeed dead and the money had vanished.

Griffin had a number of theories about what had happened to the troopers, and when someone suggested they had been poisoned he said, "They are shot, you'll see if they aren't". A number of men including Griffin and a doctor visited the scene and Griffin's prediction came true. The troopers had indeed been shot. Unsurprisingly, suspicion fell on Griffin.

In a pub in Rockhampton, Griffin bought a round of drinks using a pound note taken from the consignment that the troopers had been carrying. Its serial number had been noted. Griffin was quickly arrested on suspicion of murder, put on trial, found guilty and sentenced to death on 18 March 1868.

As he awaited his punishment, he tried to bribe his guards to let him escape, but they refused to allow him. He was hanged in the Rockhampton jail on 1 June. To prevent a trophy hunter stealing his head from his corpse, it was ordered that another body be buried on top of his in the same grave. The safeguard was not enough and Griffin's skull was taken and later became a grisly souvenir in the office of the doctor who had accompanied him to the murder site.

Slower Than a Speeding Bullet

Long before Christopher Reeve took to wearing his under-pants on the outside of his clothes, George Reeves, a burly ex-boxer and wrestler who appeared in *Gone with the Wind*, played the Man of Steel.

The Adventures of Superman was one of the most popular television programmes in 1950s America. Reeves had been born as George Bessolo on 6 April 1914, in Ashland, Kentucky. The Second World War interrupted his career, and at VJ day he found that he had lost momentum.

Major roles were still going to the established stars like Clark Gable and Humphrey Bogart while the younger upstarts like Gregory Peck and Burt Lancaster hogged the romantic leads. Reeves was reduced to appearing in children's serials and play-ing opposite starlets during their screen tests. Although his friends knew Reeves was bitterly disappointed at being passed over for stardom, never once was he unprofessional and he always did his best to put the starlets at ease for their big chance.

In 1951, the producers of the *Superman* TV series began casting around for a new actor to don the mantle. The current incumbent, Kirk Alyn, wanted to do serious work on the New York stage and also wanted more money than the producers were prepared to pay. Later that year, six-foot-two Reeves was sent along to audition by his agent. More than 200 hopefuls had preceded him, but as soon as producer Robert Maxwell saw Reeves he knew his search was at an end. Not only did Reeves look the part but he was a good actor to boot.

Despite already having a muscular physique, Reeves's costume was foam muscles. Over the next five years, Reeves played the title role in 104 episodes of the serial. To keep costs down, each episode was shot in just two and a half days.

To escape continuity problems the characters wore the same costume in every scene. Off-set Reeves spent a lot of time helping children and children's charities. Belligerent kids often challenged him to fights but Reeves used his charm to defuse difficult situations.

One incident required all of his tact. A boy pointed his father's pistol at Reeves, threatening to see if "Superman" really could dodge speeding bullets. Reeves told the boy that although he obviously would survive, others nearby might be hurt by the ricocheting bullet.

Reeves had no illusions about his work, but if he felt anger he relied upon his wide circle of friends to remind him of his good fortune. More people were seeing that good fortune in a week than most actors achieved in a year. His financial remuneration from the series was a not inconsiderable $50,000 a year. He spent money whenever he felt like it, making his home, 1579, Benedict Canyon Road, a regular drop-in for all sorts of characters.

Reeves was sensible enough to make sure his hell-raising lifestyle was kept a secret from the ladies and gentlemen of the fourth estate. His career depended upon it. An arrest would have seen the series cancelled quicker than a producer could say charge sheet. Not only that, but Reeves's professionalism would not allow him to hold up shooting because he was hungover. He had seen that happen too often at Warner Brothers with Errol Flynn. During one off-season Reeves appeared in the US hit movie *From Here to Eternity* (1953), which won Best Supporting Academy Awards for Frank Sinatra and Donna Reed. However, Reeves's role was pared to virtually nothing when test audiences wondered aloud what Superman was doing in Hawaii.

Following the cancellation of *The Adventures of Superman*, Reeves turned down the opportunity to star in a series about that square-jawed all-American hero Dick Tracy. He also rejected the opportunity of a nationwide tour on which, dressed as Superman, he would have sparred with boxer Archie Moore. The tour would have garnered Reeves $20,000 for just six weeks' work.

Like many actors Reeves wanted to direct and had been behind the camera for the last three episodes of *The Adventures of Superman*. He had also bought the rights to two scripts, intending to direct and star in both. In May 1959, he was offered a feature role in a film to be made in Spain. Despite stories to the contrary Reeves could not have been happier, and to add to his joy the producers of *The Adventures of Superman* approached him about reprising his role, a job Reeves was happy to accept.

Personally, he was engaged to Leonore Lemon and the happy couple were due to marry on 19 June 1959. Three days beforehand, Reeves retired early, only for his front doorbell to ring. His fiancée answered the door to two friends, Carol von Ronkel and William Bliss. Reeves got up and went downstairs where he shouted at them to go away. A short while afterwards, he apologized for his uncharacteristic outburst and invited them in. The four sat and chatted for a while until Reeves went upstairs. The talk continued until Lemon suddenly said, "He's going to shoot himself." The other friends were puzzled, especially when they heard a drawer slide open. "He's opening it to get a gun," explained the future Mrs Reeves.

Within seconds a shot rang out and William Bliss raced up the stairs to find a naked Reeves with blood oozing from his left temple. The official autopsy listed the cause of death as suicide, although Reeves's mother discounted this, having received a telephone call from the actor three days before his death in which she described his mood as "splendid". His colleagues also refused to believe the coroner's verdict, and two bullets found embedded in the bedroom wall were never satisfactorily explained. Reeves's mother hired the famous Hollywood lawyer Jerry Geisler to look into her son's death, refusing to allow his cremation for three years.

Was George Reeves's death suicide? Was it a mistake, a dreadful blunder? Or was it something far more sinister?

In 1996, the truth was finally revealed. In 1949, Reeves had started an affair with Toni Mannix, the wife of MGM studio executive Eddie Mannix. The affair progressed until 1958 when Reeves met and fell for Leonore Lemon. Hell hath no fury like a woman scorned, and Mannix did not take her rejection lying down. She began to call Reeves at all hours of the day and night and hang up whenever he answered. On 9 April 1959, Reeves was involved in a car crash that could have killed him. Mysteriously, the break lines on his Jaguar had been cut.

On 12 June, Toni Mannix decided to kill what she loved and hired a hitman. She knew that Reeves kept a Luger next to his bed because she had given him the weapon. The gunman was to quietly break in and shoot Reeves using his own weapon. If the gun could not be found, then the mission was to be abandoned. In her befuddled state Mannix believed that the world would believe Reeves had killed himself if his own gun was the killing weapon. The hitman found Reeves's Luger and for nearly forty years the world believed that TV's Superman had killed himself.

Caruso the Pervert

Italian singer extraordinaire Enrico Caruso was a tenor celebrated for his strong, romantic voice. He was also the first person to understand the value of the phonograph as a means of recording voices and made a lot of money from his records.

He smoked two packets of strong Egyptian cigarettes a day but protected his voice by wearing fillets of anchovies around his neck. He once said, "I am a great singer because I have always remained a bachelor. No man can sing unless he smiles and I should never smile if I were married." When he was forty-five, however, Caruso married Dorothy Benjamin, twenty years his junior, and they were devoted to each other for the rest of their lives.

On 16 November 1906, Caruso was arrested for indecent assault in the monkey house of the Central Park Zoo in New York. He was accused of pinching the backside of a strange woman described as "pretty and plump". The newspapers labelled the singer an "Italian pervert" and he was shunned by polite society.

At his trial a white-veiled mystery figure claimed that Caruso had fondled her at the Metropolitan Opera House. A deputy police commissioner claimed that he had a dossier of women who claimed that they had been groped by the singer.

Caruso was found guilty and fined $10 despite the arresting policeman's reputation for filing trumped-up charges.

It did not go unnoticed that the policeman had been the best man at the wedding of the Monkey House victim – thirty-year-old Hannah Graham from the Bronx – who had refused to testify. Caruso claimed that his rivals in the operatic world had framed him. Nonetheless, he would not perform for some time, fearful of being hounded further by the press. When he did return to the New York stage he was greeted with a standing ovation. He died on 2 August 1921.

Cash for Ermine

The name of Maundy Gregory had been all but lost to history until associates of Labour Prime Minister Tony Blair were arrested (and later cleared) in a police probe for allegedly selling political honours. Liberal Prime Minister David Lloyd George sold honours to finance his political aims and to ensure that the House of Lords was packed with his supporters.

Arthur John Peter Michael Maundy Gregory, the five-foot-six son of a Southampton clergyman, saw what was happening and approached the Liberals and offered his services. Lloyd George hired Gregory to raise funds for his putative United Constitutional Party. Gregory set up an office near Downing Street and installed a commissionaire in a uniform very similar to those of government messengers.

Gregory used bribery, flattery and gifts to learn who was in line for an honour and then wrote to them inviting them to dinner. For a sum, he told them, he could ensure that they received an appropriate honour – he charged £50,000 for a peerage, £35,000 for a baronetcy and £10,000 for a knighthood.

As news of what Gregory was doing spread, various businessmen seeking honours approached him. Not all of them were honest – Richard Williamson received a CBE for "untiring work in connection with various charities". He was a Glasgow bookmaker with a criminal record.

There were many other instances. Gregory earned about £1.2 million for the Liberal and later Tory parties – about £45.3 million at present values. He also pocketed about £3 million annually, enabling him to buy many properties including the Ambassador Club at 26 Conduit Street in 1927, and his own newspaper which he used to spew anti-Bolshevik and anti-Semitic views, as well as acquiring *Burke's Landed Gentry* in 1929.

When Lloyd George's administration lost power to the Conservatives, they passed the Honours (Prevention of Abuses) Act on 7 August 1925, making the sale of honours illegal. The Tories also placed a spy in Gregory's organization to find out to whom he had promised gongs.

In 1932, he began to offer papal honours after being received into the Church of Rome on 22 January. Edith Rosse, Gregory's 59-year-old long-term platonic companion (he was homosexual), died at 12.55am on 14 September of the same year at their London home. She left her entire estate – worth £18,000 – to Gregory, who had her buried on 17 September, in an unsealed lead-lined coffin for one hundred guineas in a shallow grave in a cemetery at Bisham next to the Thames, which meant that it often flooded.

On 23 January 1933, Gregory met Commander Edward W. Billyard-Leake and offered him a knighthood for £10,000. Commander Billyard-Leake, an honourable man, went straight to Scotland Yard where he filed a complaint. He met Gregory again for lunch two days later and afterwards reported the event to the authorities.

The commander spurned a second lunch on 27 January, before telling Gregory that he was going to Scotland and would let him have a decision when he returned on 1 February. He telephoned Gregory on the second and told him that he "definitely [did] not wish to continue the matter", resulting in Gregory asking him to reconsider and a down payment of "£2,000 or £3,000 on account".

Thirty-six hours later, on Saturday, 4 February, Gregory was arrested at his home, 10 Hyde Park Terrace, London. The case opened at Bow Street Magistrates Court on 16 February, and

Attorney-General Sir Thomas Inskip prosecuted Gregory. Defending counsel was Norman Birkett, later a Lord Justice of Appeal.

After Inskip outlined how Gregory had approached Commander Billyard-Leake, the case was adjourned. When it resumed on Tuesday, 21 February, Gregory, after some persuasion, had changed his plea to guilty. It was the first trial under the new Act and Gregory was a first offender – he was jailed for two months, fined £50, and ordered to pay fifty guineas in costs.

On his release from Wormwood Scrubs on 12 April, Gregory moved to France where, calling himself Sir Arthur Gregory, he lived on a pension of £2,000 per annum. On 28 April 1933, Mrs Rosse's body was exhumed and examined at Paddington mortuary for evidence of poison, but the waterlogged ground prevented any conclusion being reached.

The celebrated pathologist Sir Bernard Spilsbury had been unable to find any cause of death when he performed the autopsy. Many police believed that Gregory had murdered her. In November 1940, the Germans arrested Gregory and put him in an internment camp at Drancy. He died on 28 September 1941, of heart failure.

Paying for Sex and His Life

Wealthy French banker Édouard Stern was murdered in the bedroom of his penthouse flat at Geneva, Switzerland, on 28 February 2005. M Stern, fifty, a father of three, the thirty-eighth richest man in France and a friend of French President Nicolas Sarkozy, was found the next day tied to a chair and clad in a pink latex bodysuit. He had been shot four times. The Swiss police arrested M Stern's long-time lover, Cécile Brossard, a 36-year-old prostitute, and charged her with his murder.

The two had met in 2001 when she was working at a Parisian airport shop. For four years they indulged in regular bouts of sadomasochistic sex. One day, they argued over a gift of $1 million that he had put in her bank account and then blocked the account with the words, "'A million dollars is a lot to pay for a whore."

On the day he died they were indulging in a bondage sex session in his home, which was full of sex toys and expensive antiques. She shot him between the eyes and then again in the head before firing two more bullets into his body, all from close range. It took four years before Brossard came to trial.

At Geneva High Court she said, "On the night it happened, I felt an explosion in my head and took a gun he kept in his bedside drawer. I pointed the weapon at his face and fired the first shot. The gun must have been six inches from his face. I think I hit him between the eyes. He got up, turned halfway round on himself and fell. I fired another round at his head. I am a woman who was desperately in love with a man and I remain so."

Brossard was convicted of murder rather than a crime of passion because the jury believed that her actions were motivated by greed and hatred. She confessed to cleaning up the murder scene and throwing the murder weapon into Lake Geneva before fleeing to Italy and then Australia. "Her cynical, deliberate and manipulative behaviour was not that of a reasonable woman who commits a crime under an excusable emotion or despair," the jury said.

On 18 June 2009, she was sentenced to eight and a half years in prison but was freed on parole in November 2010.

At the time of the murder M Stern was in an eight-year-long relationship with Julia Lemigova, the glamorous daughter of a Red Army colonel and the penultimate Miss USSR before the Soviet Union's collapse. At the 1991 Miss Universe pageant in Las Vegas, she came third. She had three children: daughters Victoria (born in 2001) and Emma (born in 2005) – the identity of their father is unknown – and a son, Maximilien, by M Stern in 1999. At first, Stern accepted responsibility as the child's father, visiting the boy and paying for a Bulgarian nanny. However, when a colleague suggested a paternity test, M Stern decided he could have been one of three men who were potential fathers. Miss Lemigova insisted he was the father, but M Stern rejected both mother and child. The paternity issue became irrelevant when Maximilien, not yet six months old, was rushed to a Paris hospital where he died. An autopsy revealed that he had died of a brain injury, possibly caused by excessive shaking. The child was in his father's care at the time; Maya, the nanny he had hired, had vanished.

In 2010, a previously concealed post-mortem examination report showed that Maximilien's blood had contained diazepam, an anti-depressant that can prove fatal to a small child.

In 2008, Miss Lemigova began a lesbian relationship with the former tennis player Martina Navratilova and in September 2014 accepted a proposal of marriage.

Drunken Escape

Royal favourite Ranulf Flambard was born at Bayeux about 1060. He moved to England and joined the court of William the Conqueror. Ranulf was a skilled financier, and although he enjoyed William's favour he was disliked and distrusted by other members of the court. They gave him the nickname "Flambard" which means "incendiary".

Following William's death on 9 September 1087 (possibly through rupturing himself on the pommel of a saddle), Ranulf became chaplain and treasurer to his son William (II) Rufus. Ranulf encouraged the public to support their new king and indulge his vices and schemes, however mad.

In 1089, Ranulf was put in charge of Canterbury, and in September 1093, he was appointed to the judiciary. In 1094, William Rufus summoned 20,000 men to Hastings to join an expedition to fight his brother Robert Curthose in Normandy. Ranulf also went to Hastings and there he took from each man the ten shillings that their villages had given them for their keep.

While William Rufus was fighting overseas, Ranulf ran the country. He oversaw the construction of London's first stone bridge and the king's hall at Westminster. On 5 June 1099, he became the Bishop of Durham. His fall from grace was, however, imminent.

On 2 August 1100, William Rufus died under mysterious circumstances in the New Forest – probably murdered.

William was succeeded by his brother, Henry I, the Conqueror's fourth son. Henry had Ranulf imprisoned in the Tower of London on Wednesday, 15 August 1100, for treason. Ranulf was the first prisoner in the newly built Tower, then comprising only the square keep now known as the White Tower.

On 2 February 1101, after 171 days of captivity, Ranulf became the first person to escape from the Tower of London. Friends sent in a cask of wine and Ranulf allowed his jailers to share it with him.

When they were drunk, he broke open the cask, found a rope concealed within and used it to climb down to the ground where his friends were waiting with horses. Ranulf fled to Normandy with his elderly mother where he became an advisor to Robert Curthose, Duke of Normandy. Ranulf later made peace with Henry and returned to England in 1106. As a penance Ranulf completed the magnificent nave of Durham Cathedral.

Judge Murdered by Man He Jailed

At 8.20am on 12 May 1981, Judge William Openshaw was stabbed twelve times in the head, neck and back by John Smith, a man he sent to Borstal thirteen years earlier. Judge Openshaw, the senior circuit judge at Preston Crown Court, had sent Smith down for eighteen months in 1968 for stealing.

Smith hid in the rafters of the garage of 68-year-old Judge Openshaw's home, Park House in Broughton, near Preston in Lancashire. When the judge went to the garage for his drive to work, Smith dropped down and launched the vicious attack.

Disturbed by the judge's wife, he fled and flagged down passing motorist Walter Hide and forced him at knifepoint to drive to Scotland. They drove to Hawick where Smith tied him to a tree and stole his wallet and car. Smith, thirty-one, had held a grudge against the justice system and initially went to London intending to murder Quentin Hogg, Lord Hailsham, the Lord High Chancellor. Smith decided against attacking Lord Hailsham after he realized that he had done him no personal harm and instead turned his murderous rage on the man who had sent him to Borstal.

Asked why he had done it, Smith replied, "I am not sorry for what I have done. He was a bastard. He sent me down the first time on five charges, unauthorized taking, housebreaking and shop-taking. He never gave me a chance."

Smith was given a five-year sentence for the kidnapping of Mr Hide. On 19 November 1981, as the judge, Mr Justice Lawson, passed sentence of twenty-five years at Leeds Crown Court on Smith, the prisoner in the dock yelled, "I won't forget you. I'll cut your throat when I get out."

In a chilling echo, on 7 July 2008, murderer Daniel Breaks threatened to escape from prison and kill Judge Peter Openshaw, the son of Judge William. Judge Peter Openshaw had sentenced Breaks to thirty years for the murder of his sister's boyfriend. As members of the jury gasped in shock, Mr Justice Openshaw said to them, "I very much doubt he'll have the chance."

Rapist and Killer Avenges Himself on Wealthy Women

Gertrude Robinson, a 72-year-old widow, was discovered raped and murdered in a cottage on Southlands Beach, Bermuda, on 7 March 1959. Two months later, on 9 May, Dorothy Pearse, fifty-nine, was found also raped and had been bludgeoned to death. The killings followed a series of attacks on elderly women on the beautiful islands.

The local police asked Scotland Yard for help and they instituted a large-scale fingerprinting of men from eighteen to fifty. However, the exercise produced no results and after six weeks in the sun the English policemen returned to London.

A middle-aged woman was attacked in July, and then, on 28 September, the killer murdered 29-year-old secretary Dorothy Rawlinson from Hanwell, Middlesex, who had gone swimming. Her bloodstained clothes were found on the beach and her body two miles away on a coral reef where it had been partially eaten by sharks. Had it not been for the blood on the clothes, investigators would have assumed that she had drowned while swimming.

The Bermudan police again called on Scotland Yard, and this time they found witnesses who had seen a young black man who seemed distressed around the time Miss Rawlinson disappeared and who had tried to buy something with wet money. He was soon identified as nineteen-year-old Wendell Willis Lightbourne, who worked as a golf caddie at the local club.

He was taken into custody and after denying all knowledge of the crime finally cracked and confessed to killing Dorothy Rawlinson. "I want to get if off my chest. I bashed her. I can't go to Heaven now," he said. When the police asked him about the other murders, he admitted his guilt and revealed that he had a nasty streak in him. He also said that he had feelings of inferiority and took it out on the wealthy inhabitants of the islands. Tried and found guilty on 12 December 1959 for Miss Rawlinson's murder, he was sentenced to death. His sentence was commuted to life imprisonment on 30 January 1960, to be served in Britain because Bermuda did not have appropriate facilities.

Death on the Piste

Claudine Longet was a popular singer during the 1960s, no doubt helped by her marriage to Andy Williams on 15 December 1961. They had three children, split in 1969, and divorced in January 1975.

In 1972, Longet began a relationship with the Olympic skier Vladimir "Spider" Sabich, nearly four years her junior, and she and her three children moved in with the handsome sportsman, reportedly the inspiration for the Robert Redford character in the film *Downhill Racer*. After a time, the bachelor Sabich began to tire of life with Longet and told friends he wanted to separate. However, he did not ask her to move out of their home in the Starwood district of Aspen, Colorado, because he adored her children.

On 21 March 1976, the couple was together at his house when he went to take a shower. As he was down to his blue thermal underwear, she shot him. In his autobiography, Andy Williams denies the story that Longet and Sabich were on the verge of breaking up. He also says that the gun went off accidentally when Longet asked her lover for more information about how the gun worked. That was what she told the police when they arrested her. Noëlle, her twelve-year-old daughter by Williams, witnessed the shooting and as she went to call for help, the two other children went in to see what the noise had been and saw Sabich in a pool of blood. He bled to death on the way to Aspen Valley Hospital. An autopsy showed that the skier was bent over with his back to her and no nearer than six feet away when he was killed.

Longet was arraigned on 8 April 1976, and stuck to her story that it was all a tragic accident when she came to trial. Williams publicly supported his ex-wife throughout the ordeal. A preliminary hearing was heard on 10 June, when the judge issued a gag order on the lawyers and forbade the press and public from the courtroom. Jury selection began on 3 January 1977, and the trial proper began a week later. The Aspen police had made two mistakes when prosecuting the case. They had taken a blood sample from Longet – which showed cocaine in her system – and taken her diary in which she recounted bitter arguments with Sabich. However, both these actions were carried out without a warrant, which rendered them inadmissible in court. The weapon was also unaccounted for for three days after a policeman kept it in the glove compartment of his car.

Longet threw herself on the jury's mercy, saying that they should not find her guilty because her children needed her. The jury listened, and on 14 January 1977, after forty minutes' deliberation, acquitted her of felony manslaughter but convicted her of criminal negligence, a misdemeanour. Judge George E. Lohr sentenced her to spend thirty days in jail and pay a $250 fine and even let her choose the days she served.

After the verdict, Longet went on holiday with her lawyer Ron Austin, who left his wife and children for her. They later married. Longet never performed again. She was sued by the Sabich family for $1.3 million but settled out of court for a large sum and a promise never to write or tell her story. Prosecutor Frank Tucker said, "I've always known she shot Spider Sabich and meant to do it."

Searching for Revenge

When 35-year-old Glasgow-born Jeannie Tait left her home in Southend-on-Sea, Essex, on 25 June 1901, she did not expect to meet murder on the way. That afternoon, she went out to buy some prawns and as she returned at 5pm she saw her five-foot-eight estranged husband George Facer standing near their front door with a pistol in his hand. As Jeannie walked towards him, he lifted the weapon and shot her three times.

Horrified passers-by then watched as the man turned the gun on himself – but there were no more shots. He ran off as the witnesses divided into two groups; some went to tend the injured woman while others chased her assailant. He ran faster and faster but could not shake off his pursuers. He managed to put some distance between them, and then, at Thorpe Hall, Southchurch, he raised the gun to his own head and fired. The chasers, who now numbered thirty men, found the body in a ditch behind the hall.

Meanwhile, those who went to Miss Tait were unable to help as they realized that she was dying. She was carried gingerly into a house on Brewery Road where it was discovered that she had two gunshot wounds to the head. Dr W. Cardy Buck tried to stem the bleeding, but it was hopeless and Miss Tait died twenty minutes later.

The couple had married fifteen years earlier when he was serving as a sergeant in the 15th Hussars, although the marriage was bigamous – his first wife was still alive. Jeannie Tait did not leave Facer when she learned his secret and indeed bore him two sons, who were aged three and seven at the time of her death.

However, she left him when he hit her and he was sent to jail. While he was inside, she placed the boys in a Dr Barnardo's Home for Waifs and Strays in Jersey and moved in with a female friend. When he left prison, he asked her to let his sons live with him but she refused. He traced her to her new home in Southend where he committed his foul crime. The inquest jury returned a verdict of "wilful murder" and suicide "whilst in a state of insanity".

That Money Is Mine Not the Bank's

When William Edward Hall, twenty-eight, turned up for work at Lloyds Bank on 3 April 1924, he could not know that it would be for the last time. Mr Hall was deputed to work at the bank's sub-branch, which served the Army at Bordon Camp, Hampshire, and was a few miles from the main branch.

The killer shot Mr Hall, escaped with more than £1,000 in cash and locked the door so the corpse was not found until more than an hour had passed. Pathologists found that the bullet was one used by the Army, and when the camp was searched an officer's revolver was missing. The top brass cancelled all leave and the camp was put under observation.

On 8 April, Lance Corporal Abraham "Jack" Goldenberg, twenty-two, of the East Lancashire Regiment, was spotted behaving oddly by Sergeant-Major Thomas Alliott, and a latrine Goldenberg had visited was searched. There in the roof, Sergeant-Major Alliott found a brown paper parcel containing around £500 of the stolen money.

Goldenberg had already volunteered his help to the police. He told them that he had cashed a cheque at the bank at 1.45pm on the day of the murder. He said that he had returned to the bank half an hour later to find it shut.

On 6 April, he had returned to the station and told police, "No further developments have come to my knowledge. If anything does, I will notify you at once." He was arrested after the money was found and confessed to the killing, explaining that he needed money to marry his girlfriend.

He told them where he had hidden the murder weapon and also led police to a dozen bags of silver. About his person he had £37, but he insisted that it was his own money and nothing to do with the robbery. On 19 June 1924, he went on trial at Winchester Assizes and his defence team, led by Mr

Hancock, tried to portray him as insane. The jury found Goldenberg guilty and he was sentenced to death.

Bizarrely, Goldenberg then asked Mr Justice Bailhache, "Can I be assured that the £37 found upon me will be declared to be my property?" On 30 July 1924, an appeal having failed, he was hanged by Thomas Pierrepoint at Winchester Prison.

"Herbal Remedies"

Anxiang Du and Jifeng Ding were partners in a business selling traditional Chinese medicine products. Ding and his wife, "Helen", who had studied at Southampton University in the 1990s, met Du when he came to the UK as an immigrant from China. The couple helped him to settle in to his new life and they decided to form a business partnership with him, selling herbal remedies in the Midlands.

But the early promise of working together soon became fractured when arguments developed about money. The friendship was irreversibly damaged in 2001, when Du confronted Helen Ding outside her Herb Magic shop in Coventry. He attacked her verbally and issued threats which Ding later confided to a friend included the words that he would "get her and her children".

The once promising business partnership got into financial difficulties and Du became involved in litigation. The tipping point came on 28 April 2011, when the courts ordered Du's assets to be frozen and he was faced with legal costs amounting to £80,000.

The following day, Du travelled to Northampton armed with a knife and intending to confront the Dings in their home. He arrived in the early afternoon and killed Jifeng and Helen Ding in their kitchen, inflicting multiple stab wounds to their upper bodies. Terrified by the violent commotion, the two children fled upstairs to their bedroom to hide. The eldest girl used her mobile phone to call 999. Du followed them to their room where he inflicted fatal stab wounds on both of them.

Having fulfilled the threat he had issued earlier to Helen Ding, and with their bodies lying in pools of blood, Du lay down to sleep. Once recovered from his exertions, he took the Dings' car and drove to London where he dumped it and took passage to France. From there, he made his way to Morocco. The bodies of his four victims were found two days later.

Following the issue of an international arrest warrant, Du was located in Tangier and, in due course, extradited to the UK to face murder charges. In court, accused of murdering four people as revenge for losing face with his partner, Du pleaded guilty to manslaughter due to loss of control or diminished responsibility. His attorney said he had endured a protracted period of stress due to business difficulties.

Anxiang Du was found guilty of murder in what the judge described as a desire for revenge, resulting in the savage butchery of a whole family. He was sentenced to life imprisonment with a minimum term of forty years.

RFK Must Die

Former US Attorney General turned Senator for New York Bobby Kennedy had just finished giving his victory speech at the Ambassador Hotel in Los Angeles on 5 June 1968, having unexpectedly beaten Eugene McCarthy of Minnesota in the Democratic primary.

After campaigning, Senator Kennedy had retired to the Malibu home of his friend John Frankenheimer, the film director. The senator was persuaded to go to Los Angeles because the television crews would not travel to Malibu to interview him should he win. Reluctantly, he agreed to let Mr Frankenheimer drive him to the Ambassador Hotel.

Standing on a podium in the packed hotel ballroom, Senator Kennedy brushed his floppy hair out of his face, gave a V for Victory sign and said, "My thanks to you all and now it's on to Chicago and let's win there." With some aides, Kennedy began heading for the Colonial Room where he was to give a press conference.

There was very little security around, and the Kennedy campaign team had hired a bodyguard from Ace Security, a local company. It was not Secret Service policy at the time to protect presidential candidates until they had received the official party nomination. The group moved through the crowd until press secretary, Frank Mankiewicz, took charge and headed towards the pantry, a less crowded but ultimately fatal route.

Assistant maître d'hôtel Karl Uecker moved in front of Senator Kennedy, and Thane Cesar, twenty-six, the part-time bodyguard from Ace Security, was following. Kennedy shook hands with kitchen staff as he walked. Suddenly, a brown-skinned young man moved from the vicinity of the ice machine toward the steam table where Kennedy was shaking hands. Concurrently, the young man brushed past photographer Virginia Guy, his gun chipping one of her teeth.

At 12.15am, he pulled an Iver-Johnson Cadet .22-calibre revolver from the waistband of his jeans, shouted, "Kennedy, you sonofabitch", and fired eight rounds. The senator and five other people were hit. The shooter, Palestine-born Sirhan Sirhan, was held until police arrived. He claimed, "I did it for my country."

When doctors operated on the stricken senator, they discovered that one of the bullets had penetrated the brain but did not have the power to exit the skull. (The fatal bullet entered the right rear mastoid area of the head and splintered.) Senator Robert Francis Kennedy passed away, aged forty-two, at 1.44am, a few minutes after being taken off a life support machine. Sirhan Sirhan remains in jail.

Wrong Place, Wrong Time

The killing of a young British woman while on a working holiday in New Zealand in 2008 created a storm in a part of the world unaccustomed to violence. On 17 January, 26-year-old Karen Aim was found by police officers investigating a suspected break-in. She was lying in the street severely injured with head wounds and, though only semi-conscious, she was able to identify herself. She died soon afterwards in hospital.

Karen, whose home was in Orkney, was on her second visit to New Zealand's North Island where she found a job in the resort town of Taupo. She worked in the local art gallery and made many friends. Security cameras showed that she had visited a BP service station on foot about thirty minutes before she was discovered lying in a pool of blood in the street. She had been socializing with friends until the early hours when she began to make her way home to the flat she shared with two other women.

Police were already in the vicinity responding to an alarm just after 2am at a local college where several windows had been broken. Officers wondered if the attempted break-in and murderous attack on the young woman might be linked.

The violent killing shocked the people of Taupo, a town described by its mayor as, "vibrant, friendly and safe". Police mounted an intensive investigation, including door-to-door enquiries and an appeal for residents to search their properties for any discarded weapons or clothing.

Detailed scrutiny of the CCTV footage showed the presence near the crime scene of an individual riding a bicycle. As the murder investigation progressed, an abandoned bicycle was discovered which led detectives to its owner, fourteen-year-old Jahce Broughton. A search of his home provided links to the murdered woman, including her camera and a blood-stained baseball bat.

Broughton, who could not be named at the time, was arrested and charged with murder, aggravated robbery and criminal damage. Significantly, the baseball bat retrieved from his home was not only bloodstained but also had fragments of glass embedded in it. The bat had, conceivably, been used as a tool to break into the school, an act that might have been witnessed by Karen Aim who paid the price for being in the wrong place at the wrong time.

Fourteen years old at the time the murder was committed, Broughton was committed for trial at Taupo's youth court in 2008. The following year, having confessed to the murder, he was tried at Rotorua and sentenced to life imprisonment. He was believed to be the youngest person to be given a life sentence by a New Zealand court.

The Marvellous Boy . . . Who Was a Forger

Born posthumously at Pile Street School, Bristol, on 20 November 1752, Thomas Chatterton's life was all too brief. His father, also named Thomas, was an amateur antiquarian. Despite his literary precocity, Chatterton was not a quick learner at school; a teacher described him as "a dull boy, and incapable of improvement".

He was not short of self-confidence, telling one friend, "My name will live three hundred years." When he was eight, Chatterton was already reading voraciously – at home, at school and even in the local graveyard. He lived through his books, as his sister recalled; "Once I well remember his being most severely chastised for a long absence: at which he did not, however, shed one tear, but merely said 'It was hard indeed to be whipped for reading'."

He also began to write poetry, *Apostate Will*, *Sly Dick* and *A Hymn for Christmas Day* being among his earliest efforts. On 1 July 1767, he became an apprentice legal scrivener to the lawyer John Lambert, where he spent time creating his own literary works, cultivating a taste for old English vernacular poetry inspired by all things medieval.

One day he found a box of manuscripts that had belonged to his father and spent a great deal of time poring over the ancient screeds. He began telling people that among the treasures were the works of a monk, Thomas Rowley (c.1400–1470), a priest, poet, antiquarian, connoisseur, and the literary agent, biographer, and confidant of William Canynge, five-times mayor of Bristol.

Chatterton began to produce examples of Rowleyana, earning himself the sobriquet the "Marvellous Boy". According to Chatterton, "T. Rowleie was a Secular Priest of St John's, in this City. His Merit as a Biographer, Historiographer is great, as a Poet still greater: some of his Pieces would do honour to Pope."

Chatterton – encouraged by the response he had received – wrote to Horace Walpole on 25 March 1769, enclosing some of his poetry. Walpole was impressed, but when Chatterton sent more it was denounced as a forgery. Chatterton was furious but continued to write more Rowleyana plus political letters, heroic satires and prose narratives.

By 1770, he had virtually abandoned Rowley and had earned enough money to move to London to work as a writer. Chatterton left for the capital on 24 April 1770, but he had left his Rowleyan notebook in Bristol and couldn't write any more until it arrived in July. In June, the month he had seven pieces published, he had moved into the garret of a Mrs Angell at 39 Brooke Street, Holborn. She ran a brothel and Chatterton slept with her and her prostitutes and caught a sexually transmitted disease.

On the night of 24 August 1770, Chatterton died from an accidental overdose of arsenic and laudanum. Although for many years it was thought that the seventeen-year-old committed suicide, recent research shows that is more likely that his death was an accident caused by mixing the drugs he took socially and those to get rid of his venereal disease. The Rowley poems were published in 1777, with a new edition the following year admitting the poems were Chatterton's. Romantic and Pre-Raphaelite poets added to the myth of Chatterton, a boy genius who died before he was a man.

Lady Killer

A woman's body was found by Koreans looking for herbs on 9 May 1993. They noticed a hand sticking out of the ground on scrubland near County Road 51 in Northampton, Long Island, and they called the police. The victim was identified as Leah Evans from Brooklyn.

On 24 June, Tiffany Bresciani, a 22-year-old heroin addict and prostitute from Louisiana who was also the girlfriend of Dave Rubinstein (a.k.a. Dave Insurgent, a member of the 1980s punk band Reagan Youth), was killed – as it turned out the last victim of the same murderer.

After his pop career ended because of his drug addiction, Rubinstein began dating Tiffany and she supported them by selling her body. She had been touting for business on Allen Street, Manhattan; her boyfriend waited with her when she was approached by the driver of a Mazda pick-up truck. She got in and told Rubinstein that she would be back in twenty minutes. The couple would never see each other again.

Having killed her, her murderer placed her body in the boot of his truck where he left her for the next four days. Driving on the Southern State Parkway in Nassau County, Long Island, New York state troopers Sean Ruane and Deborah Spaargaren spotted that he had no number plates on the vehicle and signalled for him to stop, an order he failed to obey.

A high-speed chase ensued, ending at Mineola only when the driver crashed into a lamppost outside the local courthouse. The police found Tiffany's rotting remains in the boot. The driver was identified as Joel David Rifkin, a 34-year-old horticulturist who had been adopted at the age of three months. He confessed to killing sixteen more women, strangling them during sex and then dumping their corpses around New York.

His crime spree had begun four years earlier, killing a woman and then dismembering her body and tossing it into the East River. When he came to trial on 20 April 1994, Rifkin claimed to be a schizophrenic and thus unable to tell the difference between right and wrong. Various psychiatrists testified – one said he was mad while another asserted that he was sane.

The jury agreed with the latter, and on 9 May, they found him guilty of murder and reckless endangerment (for leading police on the wild car chase). In November, he confessed to more murders, bringing the total to seven with ten cases outstanding. He was sentenced to one hundred and eighty-three years in prison for the seven deaths.

In handing out the jail term, Judge Robert Hanophy said, "It is not in my power to give Mr Rifkin the sentence he deserves. In case there is such a thing as reincarnation, I want you to spend your second life in prison." Rifkin will be eligible for parole on 26 February 2197. The women were not Rifkin's only victims. Unable to cope with the loss of his girlfriend and his own drug addiction, Dave Rubinstein killed himself on 3 July 1993. He was twenty-nine.

Cliff-Top Killer

Two men out walking in the Cambridgeshire village of Brampton in August 1994 saw a discarded plastic carrier bag lying in the grass. Then, looking around, they saw what they thought was a dummy hanging from a tree. They had discovered the body of Alan Conner, a self-confessed murderer and rapist.

Eighteen days earlier, a young woman had been raped and strangled on a cliff-top overlooking Salcombe in Devon. The death of 23-year-old Sandra Parkinson sparked off a nation-wide search for the man who had killed her and who was suspected of other, similar, crimes.

Within days, a woman who had survived a rape attack two years earlier came forward and appeared on the television programme *Crimewatch*, when she helped an artist create a facial likeness of the man in question. DNA tests linked her attacker with the killer of Sandra Parkinson. Police activity was scaled up as it was thought this individual might be linked to other similar crimes and that he could strike again.

Then came the discovery of Alan Conner's body. The 33-year-old drifter had hanged himself from a tree using garden twine. Prior to taking his life he had written a number of notes expressing remorse and seeking forgiveness. He confessed to killing Sandra Parkinson and noted how strongly she had tried to resist him.

The notes, which he placed in the plastic carrier bag along with his personal possessions, carried an air of sadness for a man who could no longer cope. Possibly, he was in the grip of a personality disorder when he wrote "I am sorry for what I did to her. Please believe me it wasn't me, it was the other bastard. I can't live with it . . . All I can do is kill myself. I hope it helps even if it's just a bit."

Conner was a drifter who roamed around the Midlands and southern counties, living rough and frequently in trouble. He

had served time for rape and other offences. Police believed he
might have been linked to other murders and a series of rapes
committed over a fourteen-year period.

Clinching evidence of his guilt had been the matching of his
DNA to an earlier rape victim. An inquest into the death of
Sandra Parkinson, held at Plymouth, recorded a verdict of
unlawful killing. The coroner took the unusual step of naming
the person responsible for her death – Alan Conner was the
cliff-top killer.

"I'm Duck Soup"

Duane Oswald David, regarded as a shy and retiring young
man, had problems with his family, so he killed three of them.
In April 1994, he visited the family home in Adgala Township
near Toronto, and bludgeoned his cousin, Dana Ricardo
Navarro, and strangled his mother, 46-year-old Glennie
Navarro, and her sister, Lyrister David, also in her forties. He
then disappeared. The bodies were found on 19 April. Police
reported that the Navarros had been strangled and Mrs David
had died from blows to the head with a small hammer.

Enquiries revealed that David had been missing from his
college classes and had been suspended. A search of his apartment turned up a calendar which had a drawing of a noose
next to the day the murders had been committed. It was
discovered that he had crossed the Canada/US border and
driven to Chicago and then to Los Angeles where he stayed in
a hostel using the name David Oswald.

The next that was heard of him was on 20 May, when he
telephoned his mother's workplace in Toronto. He expressed
surprise when told of his mother's demise. His call was traced
by the police and he was subsequently arrested. Admitted to
the Clarke Institute psychiatric unit, pending legal proceedings, David opened up about his personal feelings. He
resented his mother because she humiliated him, and admitted to sexual fantasies regarding his aunt. He had grown up
without contact with his father, whom he had not seen since
he was twelve.

He made what amounted to a confession to Dr Phil Klassen, a psychiatrist at the Clarke Institute. "The situation was inevitable", he said of the killings, saying basically that once he started, one assault led to the next. He confided in Dr Klassen, "If we don't win the legal arguments, I'm duck soup!"

At his trial a defence expert, Dr Ruth Bray, stated that David had a personality disorder with bouts of depression which might have made him subject to a "transient psychotic episode". His demeanour throughout the seven-week trial was impassive and unresponsive. The jury rejected a defence submission that he had a mental disorder, with the implication that either he did not commit the murders or was unaware that he had.

In a trial that left more questions than it answered, particularly about the defendant's motive, the jury convicted David of first-degree murder. He was sentenced to life imprisonment.

A Shocking Experience

When Julia Ellis took a bath at her home in Rhiwbina, Cardiff, she had a shocking experience. There was a blue flash and her leg went numb. She leapt out of the bath and her husband responded by wrapping her in a towel and testing the water with his hand. His explanation for what had happened was that the shock was due to natural static electricity.

If 32-year-old Julia had died, her husband stood to gain more than £600,000 from her life insurance. Peter Ellis, a 34-year-old property developer, had been leading a double life. He befriended a divorced lady who was unaware that he was married. Ellis managed to obtain details of her employer's bank account, which he proceeded to milk.

Ellis planned to kill his wife in what he believed would be a perfect crime. He trailed live electric wires from a kitchen extension and secretly connected them to the overflow pipe in the bathroom. Julia had a miraculous escape from death because she did not touch any surface that would have earthed the current. When Peter Ellis tested the bath water and talked about static electricity he had, of course, disconnected the wires he had rigged up.

Some time after her shocking experience, Julia received an unexpected caller; the lady her husband was seeing. The two women were completely unknown to each other and, following a heart-to-heart conversation, Julia was convinced that her husband had tried to kill her and went to the police with her account of what had happened.

Peter Ellis denied attempted murder when he was put on trial at Cardiff Crown Court in November 1993, but the jury thought otherwise and delivered a guilty verdict. He was sentenced to fifteen years on the main charge and a further three years for theft, forgery and deception. The trial judge described Ellis as "callous and scheming", a man who planned what he thought would be the perfect crime. But for the good fortune that attended his wife at bath time, he might have succeeded.

The Quiz Show Rigging

The list of quiz shows on television is almost endless, from the cerebral *Mastermind* and *University Challenge* to the populist *Bob's Full House* and *Pointless*.

In 1950s America the era of the quiz show was just beginning, but some producers decided that the format could do with a little outside help.

Nebbishy Herb Stempel was a contestant on *Twenty One*, a show that began on 12 September 1956, and was devised by the presenter Jack Barry and his partner Dan Enright. The first edition was a disaster and the show's sponsors made it clear to Barry and Enright that they did not want anything like that to air again.

As a result, the pair decided to rig the show. Barry was not involved in the initial rigging but did help later with the cover-up. The producers found Charles Van Doren, a handsome English teacher at Columbia University. Stempel was in the middle of a winning streak when it was suggested that he throw the match to boost ratings. The first three games between Stempel and Van Doren ended in a tie and the viewers clamoured to watch.

Stempel had won $69,500 when he was told that he would be losing his spot as the face of *Twenty One*. On 5 December

1956, Stempel was told to give the answer *On the Waterfront* to the question what was the best film at the 1955 Oscars. Stempel knew the answer was *Marty* (starring Ernest Borgnine) because it was his favourite movie.

Van Doren became a popular figure but the producers under-estimated Stempel's annoyance at being thrown off the show, especially having to lose on a question to which he knew the answer. He began muttering publicly that *Twenty One* was not as honest as it should be, but was initially dismissed as a bad loser.

Then in August 1958, Ed Hilgemeyer, a participant on *Dotto*, another quiz programme, said that he had discovered a notebook that contained the exact answers being given on stage by the contestant Marie Winn. Then it was discovered that *Twenty One* contestant James Snodgrass had sent letters to himself containing the answers.

As ratings for quiz shows dropped, the networks dropped the shows, all the while claiming no knowledge of the cheating. New York prosecutor Joseph Stone convened a grand jury to investigate the charges, yet many contestants claimed that they had not been coached in any way. The judge sealed the grand jury report for unknown reasons.

In 1959, the 86th Congress convened the House Committee on Legislative Oversight to investigate the claims. Patty Duke, who had been a child actress, said that she had been coached, as did Stempel, Snodgrass and Hilgemeyer.

On 2 November, Van Doren, too, confessed: "I was involved, deeply involved, in a deception. The fact that I too was very much deceived cannot keep me from being the principal victim of that deception, because I was its principal symbol."

After concluding the investigation, Congress passed a law prohibiting the fixing of quiz shows (and any other form of contest).

The Reformed Character Who Wasn't

Johan "Jack" Unterweger was released from prison on 23 May 1990, where he had been serving life for the murder of an eighteen-year-old prostitute in Vienna in December 1974.

Austria has a policy of *resozialisierung*, or re-socialization, which encourages rehabilitation rather than punishment.

The prison governor believed that Unterweger was a poster boy for proof of how well *resozialisierung* worked. In prison, Unterweger had found the ability to write and had produced short stories, plays, poems, and his autobiography *Fegefeuer* ("Purgatory"), which was later made into a film.

The liberal establishment flocked to Unterweger, fêting him as he gave readings around the country. Four months after leaving prison, Unterweger strangled a prostitute in Prague.

In October 1990, two more prostitutes disappeared in Graz, Austria. Their remains lay undiscovered until January 1991.

Police, having become suspicious that Unterweger wasn't a model citizen, questioned him, but he denied all knowledge of eight unsolved murders in Vienna and Graz. The following month, a warrant was issued for his arrest but by then Unterweger was in Los Angeles where he went to research the red-light district.

During his time there, three prostitutes went missing. He returned to Austria before police realized that they were looking for one killer. Questioned in Vienna, he again escaped detection and flew back to America.

However, he had failed to disclose the fact that he had a criminal record and was held by Customs in Florida in February 1992. While he was held in custody, Austrian and American police compared their case files and began to assemble a case against Unterweger.

On 28 May, he was extradited from America but it would be two years before he saw the inside of a courtroom. On 20 April 1994, Unterweger went on trial accused of eleven murders: seven in Austria, one in the Czech Republic and three in America. The jury retired on 28 June 1994, and returned to the courtroom at 8.50pm to announce majority guilty verdicts.

For the second time, Johan "Jack" Unterweger received a life sentence. For a poster to promote the film of *Fegefeuer*, Unterweger had posed with a noose around his neck. Six hours after the guilty verdict, Unterweger hanged himself in his cell with the string from his jogging bottoms.

Murder by the Book

Captain Shirley Gibbs Russell vanished from the married officers' quarters on the Quantico Marine Base, Virginia, on 4 March 1989. A few weeks beforehand she had separated from her husband, Robert Peter Russell, but on that day, although both living elsewhere, they both returned to clean out what had been their home.

No trace of Shirley Russell has ever been seen since. Her credit cards and bank accounts have not been touched, nor has the property she placed in storage following her marriage break-up. The year before, Robert Russell had been dishonourably discharged, and when Sergeant William Kane searched Russell's desk he discovered a computer disk.

On it was a file entitled "Murder", which Sergeant Kane opened. He was shocked to see that it seemed to be a murder manual with twenty-six topics such as "How do I kill her?" and "What to do with the body?" listed. He rang Shirley, who had not long been married, but she laughed off his fears. It was an odd coupling – he was white and racist and she was black; nonetheless, she did not believe that he would harm her. The last item on the "Murder" list was "Blame it on her own kind".

Out of the service, Russell got a job as a teacher and began an affair with Sandy Flynt, a colleague. One day after sex, she fell asleep on Russell's settee and was almost caught when Shirley came home unexpectedly. The lovers joked about the narrow escape on the phone later, Russell forgetting that he had bugged his own line because even though he played around, he was scared his wife might do the same.

On the day she disappeared, Russell called the police telling them that she had gone to buy some paint and not returned. She had, he assumed, deserted. Police searched for months for Shirley without success. The law eventually brought a case against him based purely on circumstantial evidence and he was arrested on 8 February 1991.

The prosecution claimed that he had shot her with a .25-calibre pistol that he had bought on 2 March 1989. He then, it was claimed, threw her body into a mineshaft in Pennsylvania. The "Murder" list was dismissed as preliminary research for a novel that Russell intended to write with his mother, a story she backed up. When asked where the manuscript was, Patricia Russell said that she had thrown it away. On 3 May 1991 the jury returned a guilty verdict after sixteen hours' deliberation. Russell was sentenced to life imprisonment without parole on 2 August.

Mass Killing in the Lakes

It was at High Trees Farm, Lamplugh, Workington, Cumbria, on Wednesday, 2 June 2010, that Derrick Bird, a 52-year-old self-employed cabbie, began a shooting spree that left twelve dead and eleven injured. Bird was using a licensed shotgun and a .22 telescopic rifle with a silencer.

His first victim was his semi-naked twin brother, David, who was murdered in the bedroom of his home, High Trees Farm – a farmhouse set in four acres of land, three miles from Derrick Bird's home in Rowrah. Bird let himself into the house, which was not locked, silently climbed the stairs and crept to his brother's bedroom where he shot David Bird eleven times at point-blank range at 5.30am. He then returned to his home where he was spotted washing his car, a dark grey Citroën Xsara Picasso, at 9.30am. A neighbour found David Bird's bullet-riddled body – he had suffered fifteen different entry and exit wounds – around 11am.

Bird drove to Frizington where, at around 10.20am, he murdered sixty-year-old Kevin Joseph Commons, the family solicitor, at his home, Mowbray Farm, Frizington Road. Bird shot the lawyer as he left for work, having blocked in his car. He did not use a silencer and neighbours reported hearing gunshots to the police. Bird fired twice with his shotgun at Mr Commons, hitting him once in the shoulder. Witnesses told police the terrified and bleeding man scrambled out of the vehicle and staggered back to his house, pursued by Bird. Mr Commons was found dead with two .22 rifle wounds to the head.

Bird then drove to Duke Street, Whitehaven, and at 10.33am, he shot fellow taxi driver Darren Rewcastle, forty-three, in the face as the victim smoked and drank a cup of coffee. The twice-married and twice-divorced father-of-one was a former friend whom Bird wrongly suspected of having an affair with his ex-girlfriend Linda Mills. The two men had also argued about queue jumping in the taxi rank. Bird got back into his car and shot at cabbie Don Reed, who only received shrapnel wounds. Bird called another cabbie, Paul Wilson, over and, as he leaned over to the car window, Bird shot him, but fortunately the shot only skimmed his cheek. Bird drove off, and up the road from Scotch Street he shot at fifteen-year-old schoolgirl Ashleigh Glaister as she walked back from the shops – luckily he missed. She said, "I hadn't heard at that point about people being shot and thought he was going to ask me for directions. He said something but I didn't hear him. When I turned to look at him again, he was pointing a gun at me through the car window. I put my hands over my head and ducked down to protect myself, and the gun was fired. I felt the bullet go past my ponytail. Then I ran down the hill and he fired another shot. When I got around the corner, he drove off in his car."

It was here that Bird reached Coach Road, Whitehaven, where he shot taxi driver Terry Kennedy whose right hand had to be amputated, such was the severity of his injuries. The passenger, Emma Percival, also received wounds to her neck, arm and side. Three unarmed policemen in a commandeered taxi and a police transit van witnessed the attack. After seeing to the two new victims, the police set off after Bird, but he managed to evade them. The police ordered residents of Whitehaven, Egremont and Seascale to stay indoors, and the local nuclear power station at Sellafield went into lockdown mode. Bird had been sacked from the plant for theft in 1990, for which he had received a twelve-month suspended sentence.

At Hagget End, Egremont, Bird shot 57-year-old mother of two Susan Hughes twice in the stomach at 10.55am while she was on her way home from her local Co-op with her grocery shopping.

Five minutes after murdering Mrs Hughes, Bird murdered Kenneth Fishburn, a retired 71-year-old Sellafield security guard and former soldier at Bridge End, Egremont. It is thought that Mr Fishburn was on his way to a betting shop and was killed on a bridge just fifty yards from his home. Also in Egremont, Bird shot Les Hunter, but he survived.

Bird's next target was Jason Carey, diving officer at the Solway Sub-Aqua Club, but he escaped certain death because he was still in bed, and Deborah Scott, his girlfriend, did not open the door to Bird. Isaac "Spike" Dixon, sixty-five, became the killer's next victim. A part-time mole catcher, Mr Dixon was murdered near Carleton Woods.

At 11.05am, Bird murdered James, sixty-seven, and Jennifer Jackson, sixty-eight, at Wilton. Mrs Jackson was a retired tax worker and she, too, was summoned over to Bird's car to give him directions – or so she thought. As she bent down, Bird shot her. Her husband, James, recovering from a gall-bladder operation, was chatting to new friends Steve and Christine Hunter a few minutes up the road. Bird drove past and then reversed fifteen yards to them where he opened fire. Mr Hunter tried to pull his wife away, but he was not quick enough and she was hit in the back, later causing a collapsed lung. Mr Jackson was hit in the head and died later.

It was at Gosforth at around 11.15am that Bird murdered 31-year-old Garry Purdham, the brother of Harlequins rugby player Rob Purdham, as he worked in a field. Bird left his car, walked up to Mr Purdham, who had played semi-professional rugby, and shot him in the head.

His next victim was James Clark, twenty-three, an estate agent, who was shot as he drove his Smart car in Gosforth Road. The attack caused Mr Clark, the son of a National Lottery millionaire, to crash and overturn his vehicle. It remains unclear whether the bullet or the resulting car crash killed him. His girlfriend had tried to call him to warn him that a mad man was on the loose but did not get through.

Bird reached Seascale at 11.25am and next to a tunnel at Seascale Station nearly crashed into a Land Rover driven by Harry Berger, the landlord of The Woolpack Inn Eskdale, Cumbria, who was on his way to collect a prescription for one of his employees. Bird fired at Mr Berger who later recalled, "In the first twenty seconds I had only a burning sensation. I could see bits of myself all over the car. I opened the door and stepped out and said, 'I've been shot'. The police arrived with a rifle and said, 'Move that bloody car'."

Mr Berger somehow managed to move his car. He was to lose one and a half fingers and a large chunk of his upper arm. Because of the number of casualties, Mr Berger had to wait nearly ninety minutes for paramedics. He told helpers, including two doctors, "As much as I appreciate everyone here helping me, would you mind getting me a fucking ambulance?" At 11.57am, Samantha Christie and her boyfriend, Craig Ross, pulled over so she could take a photograph. As Bird drove by he asked, "Are you having a nice day?" Before she could reply, he opened fire, inflicting multiple injuries to her jaw, palate and eye socket. Mr Ross began running to her aid, but stopped when Bird ordered him to get back into the couple's car and drive away. As he did so, the killer fired a parting shot that shattered his rear windscreen.

Bird shot Michael Pike, sixty-four, who was cycling in the village where he lived with his wife, Sheena, and son, Jason, thirty-nine. Jane Robinson, sixty-six, was shot while delivering catalogues just yards from the home she shared with her twin sister, Barrie. Both women were spinsters.

After wounding some more, Bird abandoned his car at Cockley Beck, near the hamlet of Boot – warning yet another set of passers-by not to approach him – and walked towards Low Birker Farm, leaving behind the shotgun but taking with him his .22 rifle. As he walked, he unscrewed the weapon's silencer, apparently realizing that this would make it easier to deliver a self-inflicted injury. In a wooded copse, he knelt down, placed the rifle barrel to his forehead and fired a single round. The bullet killed him instantly. His corpse was found at 1.40pm.

Bird, who lived in a two-up, two-down at 26 Rowrah Road, Rowrah, Frizington, Cumbria, left no suicide note and knew only three of his victims, so the motive for his shooting spree remains unknown.

At the inquest held in March 2011, at the Energus Centre in Workington, Detective Chief Superintendent Iain Goulding, from Cumbria Police, the senior investigating officer, confirmed that Bird was being investigated by HM Revenue and Customs for the sum of £60,000 (Bird feared that he would be jailed over fifteen years of unpaid tax. In reality, the routine HMRC investigation showed him to be "financially secure") and had had arguments with other taxi drivers over his personal hygiene, the cleanliness of his vehicle and queue jumping. His friends recalled Bird as "an outgoing, well-known guy, who everyone liked".

On 22 May 2010, Bird had become a grandfather for the first time when his son Graeme's wife gave birth to a son. Bird was cremated at a private service on 18 June 2010. His home was sold by auction at Carlisle Racecourse in October 2010, and went for £35,000. Similar houses in the village were on sale at about £70,000.

The police were criticized for their slowness to react when news of the shootings first broke. They refused to let emergency crews attend to victims until they were certain the area was safe. In some cases, this meant delays of up to an hour. They also released the following inaccurate statement: "Police are currently searching for a dark grey/silver Citroën Picasso driven by a man in his thirties with a shaven head who is believed to be involved." Bird was fifty-two and did not have a shaven head.

Betrayal of Trust

Neil and Rachel Entwistle had recently moved with their nine-month-old daughter into a rented home at Hop Kinton, Massachusetts, USA. Neil, a British computer specialist, met American student, Rachel Matterazzo, at college in the UK in 1999. They married and, after a while, moved to live in the USA. As far as their friends knew, they were a happy family.

In January 2006, Rachel's parents became concerned after they failed to get a response when calling at the Entwistle home. The police were notified and the house was entered and searched. In the bedroom, lying under a heap of bedclothes, they found Rachel's body and that of her daughter. They had both been shot. There was no sign of Neil Entwistle.

It was discovered that he had left the country, flying out of Boston on a one-way flight to the UK. He did not return to attend the funeral of his wife and child who were buried together in a single coffin. Investigators in the US speculated that Entwistle had encountered financial problems in his efforts to set up a business and that the killings, on 22 January, had been part of an intended murder–suicide plot. An extradition warrant was issued and he was returned to the US three weeks later.

Enquiries into Entwistle's background activities established that he had trawled Internet sites dealing with questions about killing and suicide. He had also looked up escort sites offering sexual services. It was known that he had taken a revolver from his father-in-law's house and subsequently returned it. Entwistle claimed he had discovered the dead bodies on the bed and covered them up before leaving. He did not call the emergency services.

At Entwistle's trial in a Massachusetts court, both sets of parents were in attendance nursing their understandable but conflicting loyalties to the accused. The prosecution case was simply that having accumulated large debts and experiencing difficulties in his married life, Entwistle opted for murder as a way out. Against this, the defence argued that Rachel had been depressed and killed her child and then herself in an act of murder and suicide.

The jury opted for murder and delivered a guilty verdict accordingly. There being no death sentence in the state of Massachusetts, the judge handed down two life sentences to be served concurrently. An appeal against conviction was heard in 2012, when the question of jury bias was

considered. The Supreme Judicial Court declined to grant
the appeal.

Design for Murder

Peter Ferry and Suzanne Robson met while working backstage
in a theatre in Newmarket, Ontario, in October 1982. The
following year they decided to live together, and the last stage
production they worked on was called, ironically as it turned
out, *Design for Murder*.

The couple married in 1989, but were beset with problems
caused by Ferry's breakdown in health. He suffered from
bowel disease, necessitating surgery and the fitting of a colos-
tomy bag. Embarrassed by his illness and the demands made
by treating it, he decided to sleep separately from his wife. In
consequence, their love life deteriorated and Suzanne began to
show signs of stress. Taken together, the circumstances led to
the gradual breakdown of their marriage.

Whatever the tensions, the couple seemed to their friends to
be happy together. Then, in 1991, the frustration which had
been kept hidden suddenly broke the surface. Following a
dispute over Peter's style of driving, the argument they had in
their car boiled over when they reached home. Peter struck
Suzanne in the face and she responded hysterically. Soon after
this confrontation, she asked for a separation.

In April, Suzanne met an old friend and they began dating.
She was still living with Ferry but spent weekends away. She
told him she was seeing someone else and he became very
angry, so much so that he told a friend, "I could kill her".
Shortly after this, Ferry went on a three-week visit to England,
perhaps hoping things would change for the better.

When he returned on 4 June, he found that nothing had
changed. Suzanne was not there to greet him, and when she
returned home after work, they retired to their respective
bedrooms.

The following morning, Ferry arose early, and after letting
the cats out, went upstairs. He was carrying a rolling pin, which
he had picked up from the kitchen.

He found Suzanne still in bed and, using the rolling pin as a bludgeon, began raining blows down on her head. In a very short time she was dead. Ferry then fetched a can of petrol and splashed it around the bedroom and over Suzanne's body. With a book of matches in his hand he leaned over to kiss her and then struck a match.

Perhaps his intention was to immolate himself in the blaze, but he survived to answer a charge of murder. If it was a "Design for Murder", it had clearly worked.

The Tart with a Heart

Julia Bulette was born in 1832 at New Orleans (some sources state London) and arrived in Virginia City, Nevada, in 1859. At the time, Virginia City was a shantytown housing about six thousand miners and very few women, so the enterprising Julia set herself up as a prostitute known as the "Queen of Sporting Row". She began work before her cabin was finished and entertained her clients as other grateful men built the walls and roof around her.

Within a year she was a madam running six girls and had opened a brothel that had daily fresh flowers sent by Wells Fargo, as well as the finest French wine and food. She charged $1,000 for a night of passion – an enormous sum at the time. She was appointed an honorary fire marshal, the only woman so honoured. Julia Bulette was probably the West's favourite prostitute – loved by rich and poor and often the subject of articles by a young cub reporter for the *Territorial Enterprise* who would go on to fame himself as the writer Mark Twain.

During the American Civil War, Julia raised money for the forerunner of the Red Cross and more than once turned her brothel into a hospital for the sick when an epidemic hit the town, even pawning her jewellery and furs to pay for much-needed medicines. After the war, a different kind of person patronized Virginia City and Julia moved from being the centre of attention to an embarrassment to the place.

On 20 January 1867, Julia Bulette was murdered, strangled in her bed at her home on D Street, and most of her valuable possessions were stolen. The miners – her original clients and supporters – were up in arms at her death and rounded up twelve suspects, all of whom, luckily for them, were able to prove their innocence.

She was given what was virtually a state funeral, with the fire brigade and a brass band leading the cortège. It was said that ladies closed their curtains lest they saw their husbands in the funeral procession.

Some months later, John Millain was arrested while trying to rob another madam, Martha Camp, and many of Julia's possessions were found on him. He was tried on 2 July 1867, and quickly convicted. He was hanged on 24 April 1868, near the Jewish burial ground one mile outside the city, such was the desire for so many people (three thousand or thereabouts) to witness justice.

"Scatty But Not Wicked"

Bankrupt Pierre René Anne Marie Paul Sarrebourse d'Audeville was estranged from his wife when at lunchtime on 4 December 1890 he arrived at the home of her parents, the Heurteaux, at Nantes, France. He shot his wife in the mouth and then aimed the gun at Mme Heurteaux, but her husband, a retired sardine salesman, saved her life by hitting Sarrebourse d'Audeville's arm as he aimed.

In March 1891, Sarrebourse d'Audeville went on trial for his wife's murder. Sarrebourse d'Audeville was around thirty but looked much older thanks to his dissolute lifestyle. He indulged in gambling, drinking, fishing and hunting, and his marriage to Felicie Heurteaux at twenty-seven was one of financial necessity rather than love. He lost money in stocks and shares and declared himself bankrupt.

In June 1890, Felicie went to court to obtain a judicial separation. This was granted and she moved into her parents' home. Sarrebourse d'Audeville begged his wife to return, more because he had no money to live on than because he had any real feelings. In November, he bought a double-barrelled shotgun and a pistol and moved into rooms on the Tue

Bonne-Louise near his in-laws' home. At his trial he claimed that the shared laughter between his wife and parents was too much and pushed him over the edge. He said that he had intended to commit suicide in front of them, but this evidence was discounted when his father-in-law took the stand. Sarrebourse d'Audeville was, he said, too much of a coward to top himself.

Another witness testified that Sarrebourse d'Audeville was cruel to his wife, that he had dragged her around by her hair and threatened to throw their four-month-old baby out of the nursery window. During the trial, Sarrebourse d'Audeville sat and cried and three doctors said that he was not in his right mind and was not sane when he murdered his wife.

Other witnesses said that Sarrebourse d'Audeville was "scatty but not wicked". The jury took thirty minutes to find him guilty of murder and he was sentenced to death. However, the president of France later commuted the sentence to hard labour for life. Sarrebourse d'Audeville died on 19 July 1901.

They Are Not Getting My Stuff

A devastating fire destroyed Osbaston House at Maesbrook near Oswestry during the early hours of 25 August 2008. The home of Christopher Foster, a millionaire businessman, was reduced to a smouldering wreck. There was no sign of either Foster or his wife and daughter. They had attended an evening barbecue party with friends and, so far as anyone knew, returned home in good spirits.

Once conditions in the wrecked house and outbuildings made it possible, forensic teams set to work sifting through the wreckage. Two sets of human remains were found, one male, the other female. They were charred beyond recognition and required identification using dental records and DNA.

The bodies were those of Jill Foster and, close by, her husband, Christopher. She had been shot in the head, while his cause of death was not immediately apparent. Further searches led to the discovery of fifteen-year-old Kirstie's body; she too had been shot. In the outbuildings, apart from the burned-out wrecks of four motor vehicles, investigators found three dead horses and four dogs – all had been shot.

Fifty-year-old Christopher Foster became the focus of the ensuing investigation. His personal life was that of a wealthy business tycoon who enjoyed driving expensive cars and taking luxury holidays abroad. The family's lavish lifestyle was based on the success of Foster's invention of a safety material used to protect oilrigs from fire risks.

But success turned to ashes when Foster over-reached himself and got into debt. Crisis came early in 2008 when he lost control of his company at a time when his financial liabilities far exceeded his assets. With debts of £2 million and the threat of liquidators on the doorstep, he confided in friends. He said that his family would not be able to cope with a situation in which their lifestyle was reduced. He hinted that he would sooner commit suicide than face the ignominy of seeing his home and possessions taken away. He said, "I would top myself before that".

Clearly in a fragile state of mind, Foster was prescribed anti-depressants and advised to seek counselling to deal with his suicidal feelings. At the Coroner's Inquest into the deaths at Osbaston House it was concluded that Foster had shot dead his wife and daughter in their respective bedrooms and then killed the horses and dogs. A .22 rifle was recovered at the scene.

CCTV footage revealed Foster at night patrolling the grounds around the house and carrying containers of kerosene. He started three fires that consumed the house and outbuildings. Foster did not use a gun to take his own life but died of smoke inhalation. He had said that the liquidators "would not get his stuff" and, as events showed, they did not.

Rape and Murder in the Deep South

Christopher Newsom, twenty-three, a talented carpenter and former high-school baseball player, was out on a Saturday night with his girlfriend, Channon Christian, a 21-year-old University of Tennessee student. They had just left a friend's home after eating at a local restaurant when they were held up at gunpoint in the car park and carjacked in the early hours of 6 January 2007.

The couple was forced to drive in their Toyota 4-Runner to a house at 2316, Chipman Street, in one of Knoxville's toughest neighbourhoods. Lemaricus Devall "Slim" Davidson rented the house. There they were subjected to a dreadful ordeal.

Mr Newsom was tied up and repeatedly raped, blindfolded and gagged, before being shot in the back of the head and the neck before they set his body on fire. Miss Christian was forced to watch her lover's ordeal before she was tortured for several hours.

She was repeatedly raped vaginally, orally and anally by the men and then with a broken chair leg. They then beat her about the head and poured bleach down her throat and over her bleeding genitals to try to obliterate any evidence of rape. Still alive, she was hog-tied with curtains, gagged with a strip of a sheet, and a plastic bag was put over her face. She was then put in five black bin liners and dumped in a large bin in the kitchen where she slowly suffocated to death.

The police arrested four black men and one black woman for the horrific crimes: Davidson, twenty-five, his brother Letalvis "Rome" Cobbins, twenty-seven, his ex-girlfriend Vanessa Coleman, twenty-one, George Geovonni "Detroit" Thomas, twenty-seven, and Eric DeWayne "E" Boyd, thirty-seven.

On 16 April 2008, Boyd was found guilty of being an accessary to a fatal carjacking and sentenced to eighteen years in prison. Cobbins was convicted of both murders on 25 August 2009, and the next day sentenced to life without the possibility of parole. On 30 October 2009, Davidson was sentenced to death by lethal injection after the jury deliberated for three hours. Vanessa Coleman was sentenced to thirty-five years in prison and is eligible for parole in December 2020. Thomas was given a sentence of 123 years to life.

The case received little comment because, according to some, the victims were white and the perpetrators black. Right-wing blogger Michelle Malkin said, "Reverse the races and just imagine how the national media would cover the story of a young black couple murdered by five white assailants." The district attorney denied a racial element to the crime.

In October 2011, the Tennessee Supreme Court disbarred Richard Baumgartner, the original judge at the trial, after it was revealed he had illegally bought prescription pain pills from a criminal under his supervision.

Two months later, Judge Jon Kerry Blackwood, a special investigator, awarded new trials to Lemaricus Davidson, Letalvis Cobbins, George Thomas and Vanessa Coleman after deciding that Judge Baumgartner had not been fit to rule at the original trial. In May 2012, the Tennessee Supreme Court overruled that decision ensued, and permitted the original verdicts to stand. More legal arguments and Thomas and Coleman were awarded new trials, but Cobbins and Davidson were not.

On 20 November 2012, Coleman was convicted a second time (on lesser charges than her initial convictions) and re-sentenced to thirty-five years in prison. On 4 June 2013, George Thomas, having been convicted a second time on all counts, was given consecutive life sentences with an additional twenty-five years.

The house at 2316, Chipman Street, was demolished in October 2008.

"The Time Has Come"

Before setting out for what was thought to be a reconciliation with his girlfriend, sixteen-year-old Joshua Davies told his friends, "The time has come". He walked to the woods at Aberkenfig near Maesteg in South Wales, to meet Rebecca Aylward, fifteen, whom he had been dating for three months before they drifted apart.

But his purpose was not one of making up but something far more deadly. He had taken their separation badly and openly discussed murdering her with his friends. He talked of making a poisonous concoction from a plant such as deadly nightshade and of finding a way to commit murder and get away with it. When he asked his friends what they would give him if he succeeded, they responded by saying they would buy him breakfast at their favourite café, not believing he was serious.

Davies met Rebecca, who was five foot two and weighed just six stone, in the woods on 23 October 2010. He crushed her skull with a heavy rock and left her body lying on the ground. He boasted to his friends about what he had done and showed one of them the girl's dead body. He also sent her a text message to cover his tracks, saying that he was worried about her. When Rebecca failed to return home, a search was organized and she was found the next day.

Following his arrest, Davies tried to implicate one of his friends as the guilty party. He was sent for trial, charged with murder, and appeared at Swansea Crown Court in September 2011. The court heard that, after he had killed Rebecca, Davies had spent time updating his Facebook page and watching television. He had been examined by psychiatrists who found nothing that seemed to predispose him to violence and he was well liked by his peer group.

Both prosecutor and judge tried to make sense of what had turned a teenage youth into a killer. One suggestion was that, after they split up, he began to talk about killing Rebecca and worked himself into a situation where he turned an empty threat into reality. The Senior Crown Prosecutor said, "Only the defendant truly knows what motivated him to commit such an act."

The jury found Joshua Davies guilty and the judge ordered his anonymity to be removed. He said that the public had a right to know the identity of the person convicted. He was sentenced to a minimum of fourteen years' imprisonment.

Rebecca's mother Sonia Oatley said that she hoped that he would suffer "pain and torment for the rest of his life. The evil-doer Joshua Davies robbed us of watching our precious and perfect little girl flourish into a successful young woman.

"We will never forgive him for tearing our world apart so brutally and I would welcome the return of capital punishment for the likes of Joshua Davies, who forfeited his human rights when he chose to take my daughter's life."

China Syndrome

Gu Kailai and her husband, Bo Xilai, were leading lights in the social and political hierarchy of China. But, in 2012, Gu would be convicted of murdering a British businessman and Bo would be in disgrace, with his political ambitions in tatters.

Neil Heywood, a 41-year-old British businessman living in China, was found dead in his hotel room in Chongqing in November 2011. The Chinese authorities said that he had died of excessive alcohol consumption. No post-mortem examination was carried out and his body was cremated. His death raised many questions and there were wide repercussions.

Heywood had worked in China since 1990, and counted among his business interests representation for Aston Martin cars and consultancy for a business intelligence company. He was on friendly terms with Bo Xilai, a politician whose ambition was to be selected to sit in China's Politburo, and also with Bo's wife, Gu Kailai, who was a lawyer.

The British expat cut a dash in Beijing where he drove around in a Jaguar with a 007 number plate, evidence of his fascination for James Bond. Heywood formed a close liaison with Gu and helped to get her son into Oxford University. Gu proved to be a controlling personality and her cosy relationship with Heywood began to wane when differences arose over money transactions. The pair parted company in 2010 and had not spoken for over a year. Heywood told friends he suspected Gu was mentally unstable.

There were rumours that Heywood had threatened to expose Gu's plans to transfer money abroad. And, at the same time, Bo Xilai was coming under scrutiny for what was termed "disciplinary violations", which, ultimately, led to his disgrace and suspension from the party. In the wake of Neil Heywood's murder, allegations of corruption and extortion, not to mention political machination, were rife. Following his death, allegedly by cyanide poisoning, Gu and an associate, Zhang Xiaojun, were charged with murder.

Media representatives were barred from the murder trial in August 2012, but details of the proceedings were widely reported. The prosecution case was that Gu had met Heywood in his hotel and they had a session drinking tea and alcohol to the point where he became inebriated. Then, aided by Zhang, she administered a poisonous concoction straight into his mouth. Those who knew Neil Heywood found this difficult to believe because he was a very moderate drinker.

Reference was made in court to Gu and her mental status – she suffered from insomnia, depression and paranoia. On these grounds, she was excused the death penalty which would normally have followed the guilty verdict. Zhang was given a nine-year prison sentence. Less than a year had passed since Neil Heywood's death, leaving many questions unanswered.

In July 2013, it was announced that Bo Xilai would stand trial on charges of corruption. In the following month, Neil Heywood's family was reported to be seeking more than £5 million compensation for his death.

"My Babies Are on Fire"

The Fire Department at Youngstown, Ohio, was called out in the early hours of 1 April 1983. It was not an April Fool's joke. The caller was Rosalie Grant, a distressed mother, who urged an emergency response, saying, "my babies are on fire!"

Arriving at the scene, the firemen found Rosalie Grant being restrained by neighbours from entering her house where a fire was raging. The seat of the blaze was a bedroom where they found two children, aged one and two, burned to death.

Grant, twenty-three, lived with the two babies after their father left her. She said that she had fallen asleep while watching television and awakened to the cries from the blazing bedroom which she tried to enter but was beaten back by the flames. She was forced to leave the house by the intensity of the fire and smoke and made several attempts to re-enter, being restrained by neighbours for her own safety.

After the fire had been brought under control, investigators searched the house. A smell of accelerant was evident, and in a shed in the yard, an empty can of charcoal lighter fluid was found. This bore fingerprints which proved to be Grant's, and it was noted that there was no barbecue on the premises.

Suspicions as to the part played by Grant in the tragic event were heightened when firefighters who talked to her at the scene observed that she bore none of the characteristic signs of someone who had been involved in a fierce house fire. Her hair was not singed and there was no evidence of soot or carbon particles on her face and hands. Police investigating the death of the two children began to think that their mother had set the fire and closed the bedroom door before leaving the house. This view was heightened when it was learned that Grant had taken out $5,000-worth of insurance on each of the two children just two weeks before their tragic deaths.

Rosalie Grant was put on trial in October 1983, charged with killing her two children. The prosecution case was that she burned Joseph and Donovan in order to benefit from their insurance. She proclaimed her innocence throughout the court proceedings but was not asked to testify. She did, though, avail herself of the opportunity to address the jury before being sentenced.

She continued to protest her innocence and said that on the night of the fire there was a man in the house who prevented her from saving the children. This had not been mentioned before and was seen as a desperate attempt at salvation. Writing about the trial in the *Sunday Sun*, veteran Canadian crime writer, Max Haines, commented that there was never any direct evidence against Rosalie and referred to her claim made to the jury as a "wild story".

Rosalie Grant was found guilty and sentenced to death by electrocution. She was taken from the court and placed on Death Row at the Ohio Prison for women at Marysville. In 1991, Ohio Governor, Richard F. Celeste, commuted eight death sentences to life imprisonment. These included four women on Death Row, one of whom was Rosalie Grant.

Fish and Chips for Supper

A fish and chips supper provided vital forensic evidence relating to time of death in a 2010 murder case. During the early hours of 23 March, tragedy struck the village shop and post office at Melsonby in Yorkshire. The postmaster, 45-year-old Robin Garbutt, called the police, saying that the post office had been robbed by armed intruders who also killed his wife in the flat above. In a state of distress, he told officers he had found the body of his wife, Diana, lying in bed with her head smashed in.

Doubts about the turn of events began to emerge as enquiries were made into the lives of Robin and Diana Garbutt. Forty-year-old Diana had been indulging in extra-marital affairs and the couple was heavily in debt, with their business making very modest returns. Nevertheless, they were planning a holiday in the USA which meant that, during their absence, a relief postmaster would be drafted in. This caused Robin Garbutt great anxiety because he had stolen large sums of money from the post office and feared that his theft would be discovered.

It was at this point that Garbutt devised his get-out plan. It involved killing his unfaithful wife and attributing her death to a raid on the post office by armed robbers which would account for the stolen funds.

The plan began to flounder at the post-mortem examination carried out on Diana Garbutt. She had been bludgeoned to death while she slept with three blows to the head which shattered her skull. Forensic pathologists examined the contents of her stomach, determining that she had eaten a fish and chip supper earlier on the night she died. Normal digestion would have been completed six to eight hours later, which gave a likely time of death at variance with Robin Garbutt's account.

He was tried for his wife's murder at Teesside Crown Court in April 2011. His story about an armed robbery was dismissed by the judge as "pure humbug". Garbutt had shown no remorse and the jury returned a majority guilty verdict. The judge, referring to Diana's death, said "This was a brutal, planned, cold-blooded murder of his wife as she lay sleeping in bed".

"I Just Pushed"

A cliff-top walk in Glacier National Park, Montana, ended in disaster for newlyweds Jordan Linn Graham and Cody Johnson. The couple had been married eight days previously and were pictured together smiling and looking happy. But, at some point during their walk along the Loop Trail in July 2013, an argument broke out and, during some pushing and shoving, Johnson fell to his death more than two hundred feet below.

The explanations given by his wife, now a widow, would come back to haunt her. She drove away from the scene without reporting the fall or even bothering to check whether Cody might have survived. She claimed later that he had sent her a text message saying that he was going on a joyride with some friends. When questioned, she was unable to prove that any such message had been sent.

Johnson was reported missing by his employers on 8 July, when he failed to turn up for work. Graham's next action was to guide a search team to the spot on the cliff-top where her husband had gone over. A helicopter was called in to retrieve his body. Graham now admitted that she had pushed him over. She said she had become unhappy about their marriage and confronted Johnson about the issues. An argument ensued during which, she claimed, he grabbed at her and she retaliated by pushing him away. Graham said she was not thinking about their precarious situation on the cliff's edge when she tussled with him; "I just pushed," she said, adding, "It was a moment of shock and panic".

Graham, twenty-two, initially maintained her innocence, implying that Johnson's death was an accident. But when her trial started in December 2013, she was charged with first-degree murder and faced with prosecution attorneys seeking a sentence of fifty years' imprisonment. At this stage, she asked to plead guilty to second-degree murder and this was accepted by the court. Prosecutors argued that she had lied consistently to cover up her crime and believed she had been thinking with a clear mind when she lured Johnson to the cliff-top and pushed him off. It was acknowledged by those who knew her that she was a normal person, at least on the surface.

Graham's counsel suggested that, while she had been reckless, the outcome was unintentional. Her attempt, as her trial progressed, to withdraw her plea of guilty to second-degree murder was rejected by the trial judge. In consequence, she was found guilty as charged.

In March 2014, Jordan Linn Graham was sentenced to thirty years' imprisonment, the judge commenting that she had shown no remorse. She did, though, offer an emotional apology to her late husband's family.

Fantasy Turns to Murder

Colin Hatch was a compulsive sexual offender who slipped through the surveillance safety net to commit murder. His biological father was an alcoholic bisexual transvestite who subjected his mother to violent beatings. He began a career of sexual assaults at the age of fifteen and, over a period of four years, between 1987 and 1991, committed five indecent assaults on young boys.

In December 1991, Hatch was sentenced to three and a half years' custody for an attack on an eight-year-old boy and was sent to Feltham Young Offenders Institution. While in detention, he fantasized about future acts that he might commit and wrote about his sexual aspirations. One story concerned a ten-year-old girl whom he would rape, choke to death and dispose of in a bin bag.

Ten months later, Hatch was granted parole. A recommendation that he be sent to Broadmoor Hospital for psychiatric assessment was not acted upon. And, as later events showed, he failed to keep his parole conditions. On 19 July 1993, he befriended a seven-year-old boy riding his bicycle near the apartment block in Finchley, north London, where he had a flat.

Sean Williams was intent on meeting up with a friend when he encountered Hatch who offered to show him the way. Hatch took the boy to his tenth-floor flat where he stripped and sexually assaulted him and then suffocated him with a plastic bag. He put the body in two bin bags sealed with tape and dumped it in a lift. All this happened just eleven weeks after Hatch was released from Feltham.

At his trial for murder at the Old Bailey in January 1994, questions were asked about the circumstances in which a known sex offender had gained parole and the freedom to kill. A major issue was why a psychiatrist's recommendation that Hatch should attend a special hospital for assessment was not acted on. There was also controversy over the apparent lapse in the supervisory regime, which prompted discussion on new procedures. A key issue was that a known sexual offender was receiving no remedial therapy.

Colin Hatch pleaded not guilty on the grounds of diminished responsibility, but the trial jury found him guilty of murder on Friday, 28 January. The verdict was cheered by those in the public gallery. The judge Nina Lowry handed down a sentence of life imprisonment.

On 22 February 2011, Damien Fowkes, a 35-year-old fellow prisoner, crack addict and robber, strangled Hatch, then aged thirty-eight, in his cell at Full Sutton Prison near York.

On 5 October 2011, Fowkes was jailed for life with a recommendation that he serve a minimum of twenty years after admitting the manslaughter of Colin Hatch on the grounds of diminished responsibility and the attempted murder of Soham murderer Ian Huntley at about 3.25pm on 21 March 2010.

The Door Keeper

The word concierge, meaning doorkeeper, is well understood, but what does "Financial Concierge" mean? This was a term which David Jeffs used to describe the function he performed for wealthy Roberto Troyan, a gay man who lived a stylish life in London's Mayfair. When Troyan's boyfriend, a successful interior designer, died he left him with a considerable inheritance.

To help him manage his newly acquired wealth, Troyan took on an accountant in 2005, to act as his financial adviser. David Jeffs assumed the role, which he described as "financial concierge" in an arrangement which, for him, meant that the door was always open. He earned £1,000 a week for managing Troyan's funds, in the course of which he defrauded his employer to the tune of £343,000.

Jeffs, aged thirty-six, used his ill-gotten gains to finance a lavish lifestyle, buying luxury cars, staying at classy hotels and taking expensive holidays abroad. But, when Troyan's pot of gold began to run down, he started to worry that the extent of his fraud and deception would be discovered. Clearly, the "financial concierge" needed to take action.

On 8 March 2013, Troyan's housemaid discovered her employer's body lying in a pool of blood on the kitchen floor. He had been bludgeoned to death in an attack so brutal that he suffered a fractured skull and other injuries. Investigators found CCTV recordings showing Jeffs entering the Mayfair apartment building and leaving fifteen minutes later. When questioned, he denied entering Troyan's flat, saying he was unable to elicit a reply from within. He also left voicemail messages.

The story changed when traces of Troyan's blood were found on Jeff's briefcase. Now, he said that he had encountered an unidentified man covered in blood at the door to the flat. He offered the opinion that this individual might have been an aggrieved pimp. He went on to trash his late employer's reputation by saying he had been in the practice of holding drug-fuelled sex parties in his Mayfair home. It later emerged that Jeffs had used the toilet at a nearby service station to change out of and dispose of his bloodstained clothing.

Already the prime suspect in what had become a full-scale murder enquiry, the extent of Jeffs's fraud became apparent. At the time of the murder, he had less than £10 in his bank account and owed the Inland Revenue some £200,000. The case against him was that he feared Troyan would discover his deception and, therefore, he decided to kill him.

At his trial for murder in November 2013, the full extent of the financial concierge's activities was revealed. Among numerous extravagances, he had bought two Lotus sports cars and blew nearly £20,000 on a stag party. This was in addition to luxury holidays in resorts such as Ibiza and Mauritius. Clearly, Jeffs had come to depend on Troyan's largesse to support his chosen lifestyle. When his deceit was in danger of being exposed, he took his trusting benefactor's life. David Jeffs was found guilty of murder and sentenced to life imprisonment.

Mince Day

Hanny Klinkhamer went missing without trace from her home in the Dutch village of Ganzedijk in 1991. Her husband, Richard, immediately came under suspicion, but nothing could be proved against him. A search of the house and garden failed to produce any evidence, and while Klinkhamer remained a suspect, under Dutch law it was not possible to mount a murder enquiry in the absence of a body.

Klinkhamer, a former member of the Foreign Legion, had begun to establish himself as an author, drawing on his military experiences and with ambitions to be a crime writer. Twelve months after Hanny had disappeared, he offered a new book to his publisher with the title *Woensdag Gehaktdag* (a Dutch saying which translates as "Wednesday, Mince Day"). His story was an account of seven ways in which he might have killed his wife. It was a gruesome narrative, and one of the scenarios he wrote about involved stripping the flesh from her body, putting it through a mincer and then feeding it to the pigeons. Unsurprisingly, his publisher was both repulsed and alarmed.

The aspiring crime writer continued to live in what had been the marital home and began to drink heavily. In 1997, he moved to Amsterdam where he built up his reputation as an author and enjoyed the social activity which went with it.

Meanwhile, new owners moved into his former home and began to make changes which involved re-planning the garden.

They set about demolishing a dilapidated shed and, in the course of doing so, broke up the concrete base on which it had been erected. Workmen with a digger were engaged for this task, in the course of which they made a startling discovery.

In a concrete-filled pit, they unearthed first a skull and then the bones of a skeleton. They had discovered the remains of Hanny Klinkhamer. Using dental records, forensic specialists confirmed her identity. Within hours, her husband was arrested, and nine years after she had disappeared, he confessed to murdering her. The police believed that on 31 January 1991, he beat her to death and buried her in a hole in the shed floor which he filled with concrete. Six days later, he reported his 43-year-old wife as missing. It emerged later that Klinkhamer had dropped a hint about his intentions. When neighbours saw him digging a hole in the garden, he quipped that it was large enough to put a body in.

In an eerie coincidence, a Polish novelist, Krystian Bala, emulated Klinkhamer's crime-writing feat of committing a murder and then writing about it. In a novel entitled *Amok*, published in 2006, he described a killing which echoed a murder he had carried out six years previously. As if one coincidence were not enough, there was a further revelation, that on 15 July 1957, Hanny Klinkhamer, as a nine-year-old, had discovered the dead body of her 46-year-old mother, Maria. Hanny's father had thrown her downstairs and then killed her with a hammer.

Richard Klinkhamer, having confessed to killing his wife and concealing her body, was convicted of manslaughter in 2000, and sentenced to six years' imprisonment. It was probably not the plot ending that the author of *Wednesday Mince Day* had intended.

Record Promoter Murdered by Jilted Girlfriend

Behind the scenes in the record business are people known as pluggers – it's their job to get radio stations to play songs by new and established artists. One of the most successful was Charlie Minor. Indeed, Bryan Adams, Sting and Janet Jackson all credited him with helping them to be successful in America.

Every Saturday night for years, Minor's rented Pacific Coast Highway, Malibu beach house would be chock-full of celebrities, music bosses and beautiful bikini-clad starlets hoping for fame or just to snag a rich lover.

Charlie Minor romanced many of the women who attended his parties. Not all realized that a night with him did not mean a lifelong commitment. One such was Suzette McClure, a 27-year-old stripper, who thought that she was something special to the plugger.

However, beginning in 1990, Minor had made drastic changes to his life – he was forty-seven and going grey, he had stopped taking drugs, started going to the gym, cut back on his drinking and reduced the number of Saturday night bashes. His marriage to Danica Perez had ended in divorce after seven years and his career was on the skids – no longer promotion chief at A&M Records where he earned $500,000 a year, he was a promotions executive at *Hits*, a music industry magazine.

He still liked to mingle with beautiful women despite cutting down on his other vices. He frequented strip clubs and he met McClure at Bailey's 20/20 Gentlemen's Club in 1994. They began seeing each other, but Minor did not take her to fancy restaurants or snazzy clubs as he usually did with lovers.

Nonetheless, McClure told friends that she was in love and wanted to marry Minor. On 19 March 1995, she arrived unannounced at Minor's house and found him entertaining his newest girlfriend, Dorothy Sowell, in the bedroom. After shouting at him McClure went downstairs but did not leave the property. She waited for Miss Sowell to go to the kitchen, whereupon she went up the stairs and shot Minor nine times in the head, neck and arms.

Miss Sowell found Minor face down in a pool of blood wearing only paisley pyjama bottoms. McClure was arrested soon after at her Santa Monica condominium. She had told her family that she was a cocktail waitress not a stripper. She was sentenced to nineteen years to life for second-degree murder.

A Lone Wolf

Pavlo Lapshyn, a 25-year-old student from the Ukraine, came to Britain in April 2013 to further his studies. Within five days of his arrival, he began a campaign of terror against the non-white population.

He set himself up in a flat in Small Heath, Birmingham, and obtained a work experience position with a local business. Late on the evening of 29 April, while roaming the streets of the city, he encountered 82-year-old Mohammed Saleem who was making his way home from the mosque where he worshipped. The elderly man was attacked by Lapshyn who stabbed him in the back and left him for dead.

During the following weeks, Lapshyn busied himself buying and assembling bomb-making materials while making plans to mount a racist terror campaign. He visited websites offering information about explosives and constructed his first device. The would-be bomber travelled by bus to his target, a mosque in Walsall, on Friday, 21 June, knowing that it was likely to be packed with worshippers. He left the bomb, complete with timer, in a child's lunch box and took the bus home. Using his mobile, he activated the timer and the bomb exploded. Fortunately, although the building was damaged, there was no loss of life.

Lapshyn's next target was a mosque in Wolverhampton where he planted a bomb which he detonated on 28 June, again a Friday. And, again, while there was structural damage, no lives were lost, but the Muslim community became fearful for their safety.

His third bomb was detonated on 12 July, at a mosque in Tipton. He timed the explosion for 1pm during Friday prayers. The bomb contained a powerful explosive charge and was packed with nails. By a stroke of good fortune, prayers were delayed, and when the bomb went off, there were no worshippers in the building.

In their search for the serial bomber, police teams scrutinized a mass of CCTV images recorded at the locations of the three explosions. They began to focus on an individual who appeared in all three places and made public appeals seeking to identify him. Enquiries at Small Heath brought a breakthrough when staff at a local business recognized their work experience student, Pavlo Lapshyn.

When arrested, Lapshyn did not hesitate to make a confession. He owned up to setting the three bombs and admitted the murder of Mr Saleem. He also boldly stated that his mission as a white supremacist was to carry out a series of terror attacks on the basis that a campaign would be more effective than a one-off event.

During police questioning, Lapshyn said that he hated anyone who was not white. He was believed to be a lone wolf acting entirely on his own without links to any other group. A search of his flat turned up three partially assembled bombs and a video game which portrayed ethnic cleansing.

When he appeared at the Old Bailey, he pleaded guilty to carrying out a racially motivated campaign of terror which included a murder and three bomb attacks. He was sentenced to life imprisonment and a minimum jail term of forty years.

Bedside Murder

A hospital bed with a witness in attendance is an unusual choice of location for a murder. But this was the scene which David Jenkins chose for his act of killing in 1987.

Jenkins, twenty-five, who lived in Stevenage, Hertfordshire, met a local woman, Carolyn Jane Myland, who was born on 8 March 1963, and worked as a waitress in a cocktail bar. He fell head over heels in love with her. They made an attractive couple and became engaged.

Their relationship was doomed to failure though because of Jenkins's obsessive and controlling personality. This was not to Carolyn's liking and she decided to call off their engagement. He reacted to this rejection by stalking her every movement. His mindset seemed to be that if he could not be the man in her life no one else would. He told friends that he intended to kill her and take his own life.

In May 1987, he turned up at her home and argued with her and her father. As a result, he was arrested and a search of his house turned up some shotgun cartridges. He told police that he no longer owned a shotgun. Magistrates bailed him on condition that he did not go near Carolyn. He unhesitatingly broke this condition by driving past her home. The police regarded him as a threat and asked for him to be kept in custody on assault charges. This did not happen.

On 19 May, Jenkins hired a car, collected his shotgun from the place where he had concealed it, clearly with sinister intentions in mind, and wrote a farewell note to his mother. Then, late at night, he presented himself at Carolyn's home and held the young woman at knifepoint. When her father intervened to free her, she was badly cut on the hand by Jenkins to the extent that she had to be taken to the A&E department at Lister Hospital where she was admitted for treatment.

Jenkins was already lying in wait at the hospital and managed to elude the police escort that had accompanied Carolyn and her mother to A&E. Holding a shotgun, he appeared at his former fiancée's bedside and shot her at close range, instantly killing her. The victim's mother was the shocked witness of his brutal crime.

At his trial for murder, Jenkins pleaded guilty to murder and received a life sentence. In his favour, it was suggested that he was not a pathological killer but a man who "cared too much".

"It's All Right Pumpkin"

The male nurse on the staff of the intensive care unit (ICU) at Vermillion Hospital, Clinton, Indiana, had a reputation for his dedication to the elderly patients he looked after. Orville Lynn Majors volunteered to work extra shifts without pay.

Worries began to emerge at the hospital in 1995, over the rising death toll of its patients. Where losses from the ICU ward had averaged two a month, the rate had shot up to around nine a month. When hospital managers began an investigation to determine the reason behind what some were calling "an epidemic", they found a common factor. At the time most of the deaths occurred, Nurse Lynn Majors had been on duty. Indeed, on seven occasions, he had been the only nursing attendant working in the ICU.

As the scope of the internal enquiry intensified, the police were brought in and the deaths of 147 patients between 1993 and 1995 were investigated. When staff and patients' relatives were interviewed, a striking picture emerged of Major's Jekyll and Hyde personality. To some, he was a caring and compassionate nurse. One visiting relative recalled him calming an eighty-year-old patient awaiting tests by stroking her hair and whispering, "It's all right, Pumpkin", in her ear.

If this was his caring side it was balanced by a darker image, according to some of his colleagues. He had been heard to refer to patients as "white trash" and expressed the view that they should be gassed. Other visitors had noticed occasions when he fiddled with patients' IV lines and used a syringe to inject something into them. While this might have been a required medical procedure, doubts were mounting about a more sinister explanation.

Police investigators compared each death in Vermillion Hospital with the staff duty roster and discovered that patients died at the rate of one a day when Majors was on duty. This compared to one every three weeks when he was not in attendance. The stark facts were that in the last six months of 1994, sixty-seven patients died, sixty-three of them when Majors was present. At this point, he was suspended from duty.

The net was tightening around the nurse and, in December 1997, Majors was arrested. A search of his home produced a cache of drugs and syringes. Following exhumation of the bodies of fifteen patients who had died at the Vermillion, analysis of some of the remains showed traces of potassium chloride, a compound known to cause cardiac arrest. Majors was now charged with seven murders, and the "Angel of Death", as he had been nicknamed by the media, was put on trial in 1999. Found guilty of six murders, he was sentenced to a total of three hundred and sixty years' imprisonment.

In the book entitled *Nurses Who Kill*, published in 1990,

Clifford L Linedecker and William A Burt gave accounts of healthcare workers who had murdered patients in their care. In a preface to the book and with a degree of prescience, Dr Stephen E. Langer noted that the cases covered were "almost certainly the tip of a deadly iceberg". Orville Lynn Majors showed how accurate that appraisal was.

A Crime of Passion

The crime of passion, or *crime passionel*, is a defence plea recognized in France as a response to betrayal and, depending on the circumstances, deserving sympathy and meriting lenient treatment in the courts. The same considerations do not usually apply in the English judicial system, although, historically, the acquittal of Marguerite Fahmy, following the killing of her husband in 1923, is an exception.

The crime committed by Pamela Megginson at Cap Ferrat in Southern France, when her lover betrayed her, had a different outcome. Sixty-year-old Pamela had lived with Alec Hubbers for ten years in London and enjoyed an expensive lifestyle. Hubbers had been a successful business-man and lavished expensive gifts on his mistress, financed her shopping at top-of-the-range stores and proposed marriage. Aged seventy-nine, Hubbers had a track record for acquiring mistresses and, in 1982, he broke some unwelcome news to Pamela.

On 14 October, the couple were engaged in a sexual encounter at Hubbers's flat on the Riviera when he told Pamela that he was deserting her in favour of another, much younger, woman. Pamela flew into a rage and, grabbing a champagne bottle, bashed him over the head three times and killed him. After the murder, she returned to London in a distressed state and received psychiatric counselling. Five months later, she made a statement to the police and was arrested.

Put on trial at the Old Bailey, she pleaded not guilty to murder, explaining that she did not intend to kill Hummers but was provoked and lost her self-control. She acted, she said, "when I was crazy and in a frenzy". Prosecution Counsel argued that if Pamela Megginson had battered Hubbers in a jealous rage out of fear that she would be undermined financially, she would be guilty of murder. In her defence it was said that Hubbers had taunted her with remarks about the youth and beauty of his new conquest. As a consequence, she struck out at him with the nearest available object, a champagne bottle, and fatally injured him. She had expressed the wish that Hubbers was still alive.

With a majority verdict of ten to two, the jury found her guilty of murder and she was sentenced to life imprisonment. While jealousy and provocation were words used in court to describe Pamela Megginson's actions, no consideration was given to the Gallic concept of the *crime passionel*.

Get Me Tom Cruise!

Sweden's tradition whereby leading politicians walked the streets of Stockholm without the protection of bodyguards was severely tested in 1986 when Prime Minister Olof Palme was murdered. Seventeen years later, history repeated itself when Anna Lindh, the country's Foreign Minister, was fatally stabbed.

On 10 September 2003, she went shopping in a popular department store in Stockholm. Several witnesses saw a man wearing a camouflage jacket chase up after her on an escalator and stab her, wounding her in the stomach. He threw the knife down as he ran away and out into the street. Medics failed to save Anna Lindh's life and she died in hospital.

The man in the camouflage jacket was arrested two weeks later. Initially, he denied any involvement with the attack but finally confessed after forensic evidence clearly linked him to the murder weapon and the crime scene. Mijailo Mijailovic, twenty-five, was a Swedish citizen of Serbian origin.

At first it was thought that Lindh's murder might have been politically motivated in light of Sweden's impending referendum on the European single currency. But, under questioning, it became clear that Mijailovic had a troubled mental history and that the killing was a random act. When asked whom he wanted as his legal representative, he answered, "Tom Cruise".

Mijailovic had dropped out of school and could not find employment. In 1997, he attacked his father with a knife, and psychotherapy was recommended. Those who knew him said he heard voices and harboured malign thoughts about politicians who he believed had failed him and people like him. There were also suggestions that he wanted to kill someone as a means of boosting his self-importance.

At his trial in Stockholm's District Court, Mijailovic admitted stabbing Anna Lindh but said he had not meant to kill her. The prosecution argued that he knew what he was doing and that there were no extenuating circumstances. His lawyer (not Tom Cruise) maintained that Mijailovic was mentally unstable and had been taking medication on the day of the attack. Moreover, he had not slept properly for several days. The court found him guilty and sentenced him to life imprisonment. An application to refer him for psychiatric care was rejected.

Four months later, at an appeal hearing, the life sentence was set aside and, on the grounds that Mijailovic suffered from a mental disorder, he was committed to a psychiatric institution.

"Kiss of Death"

A middle-aged couple met while on holiday in Portugal and, following a whirlwind romance, married six weeks later. Muriel, a former beauty queen, sold her successful fashion business in Liverpool and went to live with her new husband, William McCullough, near Peterborough.

Mr McCullough was a wealthy industrialist and the newly-weds lived in style. But the glamour quickly wore off when his heavy drinking led to bouts of rage when he beat his wife. This situation lasted for eleven months before Muriel decided to take action. Her plan was to hire a contract killer to dispose of her husband.

She confided in a friend who used his influence to enrol a couple of young men to carry out the killing. They were offered £8,000 to eliminate McCullough. On 17 November 1982, Muriel went to stay with friends in Liverpool. While there, she called her husband to make certain he was at home and on his own.

This telephone call, which included her goodnight wishes, was referred to as the "Kiss of Death" because it was the prelude to murder. Having ensured that her husband was at home and preparing for sleep, Muriel alerted her contract killer, James Collingwood. He was assisted by Alan Kay who drove the pair to her home in Peterborough. While Kay stood watch, Collingwood entered the house and fired two shots into McCullough's head as he lay asleep.

When the insurance company began to process the late William McCullough's life policy, worth around £100,000 to his widow, suspicions began to form regarding the circumstances of his death.

Muriel McCullough was tried for the crime of procuring her husband's murder by taking out a death contract on him. On 17 December 1982, she was found guilty and given a life sentence. James Collingwood, who fired the fatal shots, and his fellow conspirator, Alan Kay, were also jailed for life.

Honeytrap Killing

The murder of a sixteen-year-old boy in the summer of 2008 put a focus on the gang culture of south London. Seven teenagers aged from sixteen to nineteen were convicted of his killing.

Samantha Joseph, fifteen, led on Shakilus Townsend, letting him believe that he was her boyfriend. However, she was still seeing eighteen-year-old Danny McLean, a member of the Shine My Nine gang (the name refers to a 9mm gun).

McLean was furious when he learned his girlfriend was seeing someone else, but she offered to set up her young admirer. She had told a friend: "Either I get the beats, or he gets the beats."

She opted to lure him into a so-called "honeytrap", a gang ambush in a quiet street in Thornton Heath, south London, in

July 2008. There, McLean and five others, their faces hidden by masks and wielding baseball bats and knives, stabbed and beat Shakilus. They left him to die, calling out for his mother, while Joseph walked away with McLean.

Police urged parents to be more aware of the dangers of gang culture, especially the violence that could erupt over turf wars.

In September 2009, Samantha Joseph and six gang members were tried at the Old Bailey. In court she was adamant that she had never had sex with Shakilus, or even kissed him, but admitted she was "cheating" on McLean with the younger boy.

Joseph said under cross-examination that she was bored with McLean, who just used her for sex and never took her out or bought her presents, whereas Shakilus showered her with attention and offered to buy her gifts, including a dog.

On 2 September, Joseph and six gang members were found guilty of murder. On 4 September, she was sentenced to life with a minimum tariff of ten years. The others were ordered to serve a minimum of from twelve to fifteen years.

"An Evil Intruder"

Alun Phillips's marriage to Nadine got off to a romantic start when he proposed to her while appearing on a radio show. They became a wealthy couple with a large house near the Hurlingham Club in Ranelagh Gardens, Fulham, and a town house in west London. Already a millionaire, 36-year-old Phillips still stood to gain a £15 million share in his father's estate.

Despite their wealth and three children to care for, their relationship was full of suspicion and jealous thoughts. This came to a head when Nadine had a brief dalliance with a City trader which enraged Alun and, in front of witnesses, he said he would kill her if she was unfaithful to him.

They seemed to have put this episode behind them, but, still harbouring suspicions, Phillips confided in one of Nadine's friends that rather than go through a messy divorce, it would be easier to kill your wife and just say that someone broke in and did it. This scenario turned out to be his game plan for, on 15 May 1999, he killed Nadine at their house in Fulham.

He half-throttled his wife, hand-cuffed her wrists behind her and forced her into the bath tub where she drowned. Leaving her naked body under the water, he spent the night in a soundproof room which he used when he did not want to be disturbed by the children. The next morning, he called the police saying he had just found his wife's body and claimed that an "evil intruder" had murdered her. As there were no signs of anyone having broken into the house, Alun Phillips became the prime suspect and he was arrested.

While in custody, Phillips's father died, leaving him a share in a £30 million fortune. At his trial in November 2000, Phillips denied killing Nadine and stuck to his story about an intruder. He claimed to have loved his wife despite the threats he had made about killing her should she be unfaithful. His ploy was to pass himself off as eccentric when he made such remarks because he was dedicated to running a well-ordered life.

Phillips was found guilty of murder at his trial and, following psychiatric reports that he was not suffering from any mental disorder, he was jailed for life on 15 December 2000. Reporting on the outcome, *The Guardian* commented that he could become Britain's wealthiest prison inmate.

Playboy Killer

Photographs in the newspaper of Thanos Papalexis smilingly perched on a golden throne said everything about the playboy lifestyle he espoused. He lived in Florida where he bought the beachside mansion previously owned by fashion designer, Gianni Versace, who was murdered in 1997 by Andrew Cunanan (see page 338).

But the world of the Greek-born British property developer began to crumble in 2000, when his business interests started to fail. Faced with heavy financial losses, Papalexis came up with a scheme to raise money on a London property. He wanted to do a deal whereby he would buy a derelict plot in

Kilburn and sell it on before paying the owner. That way, he believed, he could raise the cash he needed to solve his money problems.

But the ploy faltered from the start because the property housed a long-term sitting tenant, 55-year-old Charalambos Christodoulides. He lived in a flat in a warehouse on the site and, although he was willing to move, he wanted to do so in his own time.

This delay was not acceptable to Papalexis who needed to act quickly to save his business. His solution was to dispose of Mr Christodoulides, and he hired two Albanian illegal immigrants to help him. In March 2000, Christodoulides was tied up, beaten and tortured and, finally, murdered by strangulation. His body was thrown into a car-inspection pit on the warehouse site where it was discovered two weeks later.

Papalexis's London deal fell through, leaving him with large debts, and he fled to the USA where his businesses were also failing. After years searching for a solution to Christodoulides's murder, the UK police investigation received a welcome boost from an unexpected source. In September 2009, Rebecca DeFalco, an American porn star and former lover of Papalexis, said that he had confessed to her in 2004 about killing a man in London who was causing him problems. This was timely information as new forensic evidence also linked him to the crime.

Papalexis was arrested in Florida and charged with murder. Extradition followed and he returned to the UK to face trial at the Old Bailey in August 2009. The extent of his financial manipulation, overwhelming ambition and arrogant disregard for others was put before the jury who found him guilty on 4 September.

Sentencing him to life imprisonment, the judge said, "You are a totally amoral person in the sense that you do not think twice in doing or saying anything which helps you achieve your own ends". The jury at the trial of Papalexis's two Albanian henchmen, both charged with murder, ended with no verdict. But another jury in a re-trial held in 2010 convicted both men of murder and they were given life sentences.

Licence to Kill

On 31 May 2009, Dr George Tiller, who ran an abortion clinic at Wichita, Kansas, was shot dead while he was carrying out the duties of usher at his local church. His assailant, Scott Roeder, killed him with a single shot to the head. It was a violent incident that opened up the debate about abortion in America.

Tiller had been the target of violence on two previous occasions when his clinic was bombed in 1986 and, in 1993, when he survived an assassination attempt. Such were the threats to his life that he habitually wore a bullet-proof vest.

The doctor's clinic was one of a small number of practices in the USA prepared to carry out abortions on women in the later stages of pregnancy. While there was condemnation of Tiller's killing in some quarters, justification was felt in others. Some anti-abortionists regarded him as a murderer and, indeed, referred to abortion as murder.

Scott Roeder, as a born-again Christian, believed abortion was a sin. He bought a .22 handgun and, the day before he shot Tiller, engaged in a session of target practice. Thus prepared, he approached the doctor at the Reformation Lutheran church and killed him, as he explained later, to save the lives of unborn children. Roeder was charged with first-degree murder.

Protests were staged at Dr Tiller's funeral by anti-abortionists waving placards declaring "God Sent the Shooter". Roeder confessed to the killing, saying he was "defending an innocent life". "That is what prompted me," he declared, as if he had been given a licence to kill.

In the proceedings leading up to Roeder's trial, the judge, controversially, said he would permit the defendant to argue that he was justified in his act because his intention was to protect unborn children. This ruling made US legal history and was widely applauded by anti-abortionists. Allowing Roeder to plead justification meant that he could argue a defence of voluntary manslaughter. This was all uncharted territory for the lawyers.

When the trial opened on 22 January 2010, Roeder was asked if he had shot Dr Tiller. He answered, "Yes". Despite protests from the prosecution, Roeder was allowed to make self-serving statements from the dock. He practically delivered a sermon about the taking of life and the sanctity of the unborn child even in cases of rape and incest.

The jury listened intently to the arguments and then retired to make their decision. It took them thirty-seven minutes of deliberation on 29 January to decide that Scott Roeder was guilty of first-degree murder. He was given a mandatory life sentence.

A Dark and Evil Crime

When Roger Smith told his wife, "If you divorce me, I'll ruin your father's life", he set off a chain of events that led to his murder at the hands of a hired assassin. Smith and his wife Maureen left London's East End in the 1970s to start a new life in South Africa. Her father, Harry Mullock, was an insurance assessor who specialized in dodgy dealings, making a great deal of money in the process. His legacy became a source of seething discontent in his family.

As the Smiths' marriage faltered, due to Roger's tendency towards loutish behaviour and heavy drinking, Maureen proposed divorce. He took exception to this and threatened revenge by exposing her father's shady background. The family's response was to contrive a plan to eliminate Roger by arranging his murder.

Various methods were discussed, including drowning, suffocation, drugs, tampering with car brakes and hiring a hitman. The option chosen was to pay the Smith family's chauffeur, Jack Ramogale, to find an assassin. He selected David Mnungi who would be paid 5,000 rand to make the hit. On the night of 20 July 1982, Ramogale switched off the electricity supply to the Smiths' bungalow, which prompted the intended victim to go out into the garden. There, Mnungi lay in wait and ambushed Roger Smith, repeatedly stabbing him with a seven-inch knife.

When 38-year-old Maureen Smith appeared on trial for murder with co-defendants Ramogale and Mnungi, in the Supreme Court of Johannesburg, parallels were drawn with the "Scissors Murder" case in the 1970s. Both crimes involved a woman hiring an assassin to kill an unwanted husband on Smith's part, and her lover's wife in the Maureen Lehnberg case.

The trial of Maureen Smith attracted a great deal of publicity and there were scuffles as members of the public fought to gain entry to the courtroom. The full extent of the family's background participation in planning the elimination of Roger Smith came out in evidence. There had been proposals to send a hitman from Britain to dispose of Smith with the aim of preventing his disclosures about his wife's father. In the event, Ramogale and Mnungi shared a commission of 10,000 rand to carry out the murder.

When a guilty verdict was returned, Judge Van Dyke said "No sentence other than the ultimate one would suit this dark and evil crime." All three defendants were sentenced to death.

Making a Job Offer

The possibility of a job working as an airline stewardess with a salary of £14,000 a year sounded an exciting job prospect for seventeen-year-old Lynne Rogers. She had been seeking a job for some time, sending out copies of her CV and hoping for such a call. Lynne arranged to meet the caller in anticipation of a job interview at Charing Cross railway station.

On 4 September 1991, Lynne was observed waiting outside the station by a cab driver who saw her get into a blue Vauxhall and drive off with a man at the wheel. Alarm bells started to ring when she failed to call her father and her boyfriend. Five days later, her body was found in a patch of brambles in a side road in East Sussex. She had been strangled in what appeared to be a sexually motivated attack.

The bogus job offer made to Lynne over the telephone came from a man who shared an office with a company which had received her CV. The man was 36-year-old Scott Singleton who posed as an airline executive and made the call from a post office in Crawley. He was overheard talking about salaries and working at Gatwick Airport.

Singleton was questioned and, in view of a bite mark found on the dead girl's chin, was invited to give a dental impression for comparison purposes. He declined to cooperate. A week later, when detectives visited his dentist in Crawley, they found that Singleton was registered as a patient under his former name of Andre Reich. His dental records showed a match with the bite marks left on the murder victim's face.

Singleton was tried for murder at Lewes Crown Court in July 1992. He denied the charge but vital dental evidence linked him to the crime victim. He drove a blue Vauxhall car, and his presence at the post office in Crawley on the day he made the call to Lynne Rogers was confirmed by a giro which he had cashed. Singleton was described as something of a fantasist with an obsession about flying.

When the jury delivered its guilty verdict, Lynne's father angrily faced Singleton in the dock threatening that he would kill him. Derek Rogers subsequently gave an interview to *The Guardian*, talking about the loss of his daughter and highlighting some of the inadequacies of the judicial system as he saw them.

Death in a High Place

The sound of gunfire disturbed the quiet of a Sunday evening in the Swiss Alpine village of Les Crosets on 30 April 2006. The tragic result was the death of the former Swiss skiing champion, 32-year-old Corinne Rey-Bellet, and her brother.

In May 2002, Corinne married 32-year-old Gerold Stadler, a banker, and they had a two-year-old son. The marriage came under strain and, early in 2006, Corinne obtained a legal separation from her husband. She moved with her child into an apartment at her parents' chalet in Les Crosets.

The Rey-Bellet family were like local royalty. Corinne's father was known as "Le Sheriff" in the bourgeoisie order of the local community. He headed a powerful family and managed successful business interests. In the context of the prevailing social order, it was said that "The Rey-Bellets are so powerful, they even decide the weather".

There was speculation that joining this family was too over-powering for an outsider and that Gerold Stadler perhaps felt out of place. Whatever his motivation, he drove to the chalet where Corinne was living in order to return to her their young son, whom he had spent some time with during that fateful Sunday.

He helped Corinne put the child to bed and then, at about 9.30pm, he produced a pistol, shooting his wife dead and also killing her brother, Alain, and injuring his mother-in-law. He then left the chalet and drove off at speed down the mountain road to a village some twelve miles away. A search was mounted to locate Stadler, who was the sole suspect in the murder at Les Crosets.

It was known that he was a captain in the Swiss army and, in that capacity, was allowed to own a service weapon. The murder had been committed using a 9mm pistol. After three days of searching, police found the body of Stadler whom they described as "the presumed murderer". He had committed suicide using the same weapon that had killed his wife.

It was a sad ending to a family tragedy, which made big headlines in the Swiss media due to the sporting pre-eminence of Corinne Rey-Bellet. In the aftermath, the focus was on Swiss regulations regarding firearms ownership, with an emphasis on the high rate of male suicides and the incidence of family killings involving guns.

Where There's a Will . . .

Violet Durling, aged 100, lived in a flat above her brother's workshop in Plaistow, east London. When "Siddie" Durling locked up the premises on 17 February 2006, all was well, but after the weekend it was a different story. A fire had been started in his workshop and a second blaze on the stairs lead-ing to the old lady's flat. He found her dead, overcome by smoke inhalation.

The fire had been started with an accelerant, and the lack of signs of forced entry indicated that Violet Durling had let the fire-raiser into the premises. The fact that a second fire had been set on the stairs meant that her only possible escape route was blocked.

Suspicion fell on 48-year-old Susan Turner, Mrs Durling's niece, who believed she had been unfairly treated when it came to apportioning family finances. She had left the country and was touring around Europe on what was later described as a "money-spending spree".

Crime scene investigators found DNA on the top of a bottle of accelerant, and a search of Turner's home uncovered remnants of burnt clothing in a garden barbecue. She was arrested and charged with murder as soon as she returned to England. It was learned that she had inherited more than £100,000 from her adoptive father and had made attempts to become sole heir of her aunt's property.

At her first trial in early 2007, the jury failed to reach a verdict, and she was sent for a second trial held at the Old Bailey in December 2007. Forensic evidence showed that partial DNA found on the accelerant bottle at the crime scene matched Turner's. The jury heard that she bitterly resented her siblings and believed that she had been unfairly treated in decisions about inheritance.

The judge said the murder of Violet Durling, a distinguished dressmaker, was premeditated. Turner protested her innocence and said she would never do anything to hurt her aunt. The evidence told a different story and she was found guilty and sentenced to life imprisonment by Judge John Milford QC.

Meant to Live

Abraham Rosenfield, whose home was in Manchester, checked into the Sharon Rest Home in Southport for two weeks' convalescence in June 1988. He came under the care of Deputy Matron Ruth Thomas and care assistant Sara Wrighton, whom he looked upon as friends.

One evening they joined him in his room and played poker. During the course of the card game, the two women plied him with whisky and drugs and then attacked him. They struck him over the head with a wine bottle and kicked him in the face, leaving him, as they believed, for dead.

Thomas, thirty-seven, had made a plan that involved her teenage lover, Robert Burns, as well as Wrighton. She had drugged the rest-home matron, making her so unwell that she had to take time off, leaving Thomas in charge. She charmed Mr Rosenfield into confiding that he kept his life savings at home and allowed her to have the keys so that she could keep an eye on the flat while he was away.

On the evening of the poker game, Burns used the keys to gain access to the flat and stole £19,500. The plan might have succeeded but for the fact that Abraham Rosenfield refused to die. The 67-year-old survived his ordeal and was able to provide the police with a full account of what had taken place.

Thomas and Wrighton made a run for it in their car but were stopped by police. It came to light that the pair had some "previous", when they worked at another rest home in Southport and had drugged the owner in order to steal from her.

Put on trial at Liverpool Crown Court in April 1989, Thomas pleaded guilty to attempted murder and was sentenced to ten years. Her cohorts were charged variously with endangering life and theft. Abraham Rosenfield, fully recovered, commented, "I was meant to live, that's all I can say".

Murder in Court

On 21 August 2008, a pregnant Muslim pharmacist, 31-year-old Marwa el-Sherbini, took her son to a local playground in the German city of Dresden where 28-year-old Alexander Wiens was with his niece. An argument ensued over which child should play on the swing.

Mrs el-Sherbini waited a while and then politely asked Wiens if he would mind letting her son go on the swing. The man reacted by directing a stream of racist abuse at her, calling her a terrorist and a whore. A shocked bystander called the police and Mrs el-Sherbini filed a complaint against Wiens.

In due course, Wiens, an unemployed man of Russian origin, appeared in court and was fined €330. When he refused to pay and claimed to have been unfairly treated, the magistrate increased the fine to €780. Wiens again refused to pay and the case was referred to Dresden's regional court.

On 1 July 2009, Wiens attended the appeal hearing in the presence of Marwa el-Sherbini and her husband. During the proceedings, Wiens produced a twelve-inch knife from a bag he had brought into court and violently attacked Mrs el-Sherbini, stabbing her sixteen times in the chest. Her husband, Elwi Ali-Okaz, was wounded trying to defend her, but she bled to death on the courtroom floor. Her attacker was immobilized by a security guard.

The killing of Mrs el-Sherbini, an Egyptian by birth, caused outrage in the Arab world, and a fatwa calling for revenge was issued against Wiens. The dead woman was a respected pharmacist working in the local community and her death as the "Veil Martyr" put a strain on diplomatic ties between Germany and Egypt.

Security was raised when Wiens appeared in court charged with murder and protesters demonstrated outside. When he took his place in court, Wiens obscured his head and face with a ski mask and, at one point, had to be restrained when he started bashing his head on the table.

He was described as a person harbouring a hatred of foreigners and whose activities were listed as drinking, smoking and gambling. The judge who had presided at the hearing and witnessed the attack on Mrs el-Sherbini graphically described what happened. He had been so disturbed by the incident that he had since been unable to work.

On 11 November, Alexander Wiens was found guilty of murder and sentenced to life imprisonment. What had begun as a playground tiff had ended up with a brutal killing, the destruction of an innocent life and an international outcry about racism.

CHAPTER 9

Simply Bizarre

What are the qualities of a crime that might qualify it to be described as bizarre? To a certain extent, most crimes have bizarre aspects but the overriding quality of a bizarre crime is probably that the details are so weird, it would be difficult to make them up.

The crime world of a university mortuary assistant in the Yemen offers some possibilities. Mohammed Adam Omar was arrested in 2000, on charges of having raped, mutilated and murdered five women. Under questioning, he confessed to killing fifty-one women over a twenty-five-year period in four Middle East countries. His technique was to lure his victims, usually medical students, into the mortuary where he worked and then kill and dismember them. He described his motive as one of wanting "to send them to heaven".

He admitted that he enjoyed killing beautiful women who triggered off an irresistible urge inside him. In some instances he cut off their hands and feet and kept some of the bones as trophies. He denied selling their body parts and said that his death by execution would purify his sins.

Many crimes are so off the wall that they are reported as being motiveless. This is rarely the case, for there is inevitably a trigger to violence. It may be something as trivial as a postponed medical appointment, which prompted Laith Alani to kill two hospital doctors in 1990.

Alternatively, the motive may be more deep-seated, as in the case of teenager Daniel Bartlam. He was fascinated by violence and dreamed of committing the perfect murder. He left a story he had written on his computer, in which he featured as the killer of his mother. In 2011, fantasy became tragedy when he savagely bludgeoned his mother to death with a hammer. He claimed to have heard voices urging him to commit violent acts and, when he felt in the mood, shared gruesome fantasies with his friends.

A world away from Bartlam's diet of horror films was a Japanese couple's culinary masterpiece. They conceived a plan whereby they would take out a life insurance policy for an acquaintance without his knowledge and then poison him to collect the proceeds. Spurred on by their initial success, they cooked up a plan to expand their money-making enterprise by serving curry laced with arsenic to a group attending a festival dinner. As a result, four people died and sixty-three others were laid low after eating poisoned food. This episode, in 1998, had the effect of sparking off a series of copycat crimes throughout Japan.

Totally unrelated but equally bizarre was the story of an unusual parcel sent through the Japanese postal service in 2014. A package, measuring two metres in length and purporting to contain a doll, was sent from Osaka to a township near Tokyo, a distance of 230 miles. Suspicion was aroused when the package remained unclaimed, and officials opened it to discover the body of a young woman. She was identified as a nurse who had been missing for two months and, it seemed, had been stabbed to death. The incident proved to be a novel way of disposing of a body and gave a whole new meaning to the concept of a special delivery.

Household pets, especially cats, sometimes get caught up as unlikely participants in a crime scene, through no fault of their own. After he had murdered two female acquaintances in 1990, Michael Shorey asked a friend to look after a carpet which he had moved from his flat and intended to have dry-cleaned. It was thought that he had used the carpet to conceal his victims' bodies, a theory strengthened by the appearance of bloodstains. When questioned by the police, Shorey blamed the stains on the cat, which he said had captured a bird and killed it on the mat. Possibly this was the first time a cat was made an accessory to murder.

More tragic was the fate of the moggy which was the household pet of a Chinese couple living in Newcastle. Their computer skills drew them into an international betting scam and they became targets for a gang demanding payments. In 2008, the couple were brutally murdered in their flat and investigators were mystified by *the discovery of the cat, which had evidently been drowned. One theory was that the much-loved feline had been tortured and sacrificed in order to prise information out of its owners.*

Identifying the killer at a crime scene in the Philippines proved to be easy because the victim had taken a photograph of his nemesis at the moment of death. A family group celebrating New Year 2011 assembled outside the house of Reynaldo Dagsa, waiting for him to catch the moment on camera. Sadly he did not live to see the result: a picture that showed not just his family, but also his assassin pointing a gun at him moments before discharging the fatal shots.

Another instance of the picture telling the story occurred in Guatemala in 2009. Rodrigo Rosenberg, a lawyer by profession, recorded a video message telling viewers that if they are receiving the message it is "because I have been murdered". He named his country's president as the instigator. Rosenberg had been depressed over problems in his personal life and was also upset with the government. He decided to sacrifice his life in a contrived suicide whereby he hired two assassins to shoot him dead in the street. The video played at the dead lawyer's funeral attracted hundreds of thousands of viewers.

Not to be forgotten in a narrative about bizarre crimes is the part played by victims suddenly thrust into danger and responding with resilience. A teenage girl walking home in a leafy part of Surrey was attacked by a man wielding a knife and attempting to force her into his car. She successfully fought him off and made a run for it, while making a mental note of the car's registration number. So she would not forget it, the astute young woman wrote the number down on a cornflakes packet when she reached home. As a result, her would-be abductor was quickly arrested.

"Life after death" might have been an appropriate headline to describe the experience of an Iranian man who survived execution by hanging in 2013. Following a conviction for drug smuggling, he was duly hanged and pronounced dead. His body was then taken to the mortuary prior to burial by his family. The following day, an alert attendant at the morgue noted that the supposedly dead man was still breathing. The judicial authorities' initial reaction was that he should be executed again. But this decision was overruled and the man they could not hang lived to tell the tale.

The catalogue of bizarre details of crimes seemingly has no boundaries. Certainly not for Thomas Bean who broke new ground by playing music on his victim's record player while he carved up her body. "I killed to music," he boasted.

Online Self-Hatred

In February 2014, hugely obese Michelle Chapman, twenty-four, of Par, Cornwall, became the first person in Britain to be jailed for trolling herself – she had filled her own Facebook page with fake abuse. The bizarre battle began when she had a disagreement with her father, Roy Jackson, whom she had not seen for twenty-one years, and his new wife.

After he married Louise Steen in 2010, Mr Jackson tried to effect a reconciliation and Chapman went to his house in the North of England, but they argued and on her return she vowed revenge. Chapman went online and created several fake Facebook accounts for her father, stepmother (Louise Steen) and other family members. She began by using her stepmother's "account" to send rude messages to Mr Jackson hoping to split them up. She then posted on her own page several hundred insults of a "very unpleasant sexual nature" complete with photos, supposedly sent by her family.

She then went to the police claiming that her family had been "trolling" her, and gave eight written statements between February and October 2011. In 2009, Chapman had been given a caution for sending a false message, but oddly the police still took her allegations seriously.

Louise Steen was arrested and the police issued warnings to her father and two other puzzled relatives, Angela Steen and Elaine Abrams. It was only when forensic internet experts discovered that the accounts had been created at her home that Chapman's warped plan unravelled. She was arrested and admitted doing actions tending or intended to pervert the course of justice by sending herself degrading emails between February 2011 and March 2012.

Prosecuting Philip Lee said, "She said that she wanted revenge on her father for matters in the past. She just wanted to make their life hell." In one aim she succeeded – her father's marriage broke up. At Truro Crown Court Judge Christopher Harvey Clark QC jailed Chapman for twenty months and also banned her from having computer equipment or contacting her relatives. He said, "People have suffered a great deal of distress as a result of your wicked behaviour."

Animal Husbandry

In 1750, Jacques Ferron, a Frenchman, was put on trial and hanged for having sex with a female donkey. Ferron lived in the commune of Vanvres, and Ferron came before the courts along with his co-accused. The usual sentence for bestiality was death for both parties (see page 423), but in this instance the court decided that the sex had not been consensual and that the jenny was a victim of sexual assault. Indeed, the court received an affidavit, dated 19 September 1750, that the donkey was of good character. The document was witnessed by the local priest and other community leaders and stated that "they were willing to bear witness that she is in word and deed and in all her habits of life a most honest creature".

The Butcher and Cop Killer

John Jones and his wife, Ann, left Wolverhampton in the late 1860s to move to Cardiff in South Wales where they opened a pork butcher's shop. Only they weren't Mr and Mrs Jones – he was Benjamin Swann, a slaughterman, and she was Ann Hollingsworth, the wife of his former employer – and they had left the Black Country to escape the scandal of their illicit affair. Their shop in Wharton Street was successful (they lived above the premises), and soon they also ran a market stall in nearby Canton.

Adopting a new name did not allow Jones to shed the demons of depression and alcoholism. His depression led the shop into difficulties and he believed that local rivals were out to get him; his belief was exacerbated by his drinking, which led to paranoia. He began giving away his belongings in pubs, then while at the theatre he accused the act on stage of singing about him.

In the early hours of New Year's Eve 1872, Jones jumped out of bed and ran down to the shop where he smashed the window display. He returned to sleep with the help of a drug and when he woke at 6am he was in fine fettle. He set off for their Canton Market stall at 8am, bidding his wife a cheery goodbye. Later, he invited his friend Thomas Thornton, a retired police inspector, for a drink at the Canton Cross.

Mr Thornton saw Jones put a slaughtering knife into his coat before they left for the pub but said nothing. Jones drank a peppermint cordial while his friend downed a whisky. Later, Jones saw PC William Perry on his beat and invited him for a drink at the Wyndham Inn. PC Perry said a cheery no thanks, but Jones was not one to take no for an answer and he walked alongside the policeman. They chatted amiably until they reached the Westgate Turnpike when Jones shouted at the policeman, "Damn you, you have done the worst against me!" PC Perry said that he had done what he had to do.

Jones's mood changed again and he invited the policeman for a drink at the Westgate Hotel. Once more, PC Perry declined, and then as Jones beckoned him from the doorway, changed his mind and walked over. As the two men stood in the entrance at 11am, Jones pulled out his knife and plunged it into the policeman's chest. Jones carried on into the pub and sat by the bar. There, he pulled open his coat and stabbed himself several times.

Jones lay near death as he went on trial in absentia. He was found guilty of murder but sentence was delayed until he recovered. He never did, dying of his self-inflicted wounds on 8 January 1873, three days after PC Perry's funeral.

Animal Husbandry 2

Just over one hundred years before Jacques Ferron's animal indiscretions (see page 422), on 8 September 1642, sixteen-year-old Thomas Granger (or Graunger), a servant of Love Brewster, one of the original passengers on the *Mayflower*, was hanged (the first person to suffer the fate in the Massachusetts Bay Colony and the first juvenile to be sentenced to death and hanged in what is now the USA) for having sex with Brewster's "mare, a cowe, two goats, divers sheepe, two calves, and a turkey". He confessed on 7 September, and before his execution, the animals were, as the Bible commanded in Leviticus 20:15, slaughtered before his eyes.

One Sin Leads to Another

One of the Ten Commandments – thou shalt not commit adultery – has been the subject of numerous stories and court cases over the years. In Massachusetts in 1641, adultery was a capital offence, the colony having based its laws on the Ten Commandments.

Mary Latham was eighteen, a refined young lady whose only crime was to fall in love with the wrong man at the wrong time in the wrong place. However, the object of Mary's passions did not reciprocate her feelings and so she decided to marry the first available man.

Unfortunately, he was three times her age, "had neither honesty nor ability" and the marriage was unhappy. Mary soon began seeing "divers young men" both married and single who "solicited her chastity". One was James Britton, a thirty-year-old professor and playboy, who had recently emigrated from England.

At a party they drank too much and crept away to sate their passions. After he had sex with Mary, Britton fell ill with "a deadly palsy and a fearful horror of conscience" and, believing that it was a punishment from God, confessed his "sin". The next day, the lovers were arrested. Mary claimed that Britton had tried to have sex with her but had been unable.

However, a witness soon undermined that argument and Mary confessed. In addition to her "crime", it was said that "she did frequently abuse her husband, setting a knife to his breast and threatening to kill him, calling him old rogue and cuckold, and said she would make him wear horns as big as a bull".

The magistrates decided that there was not enough evidence to convict, but the jury found against her and Mary admitted that she had had sex with twelve men (five of them married). Five of her lovers were arrested, the rest having fled, but since their accuser was herself now a felon the cases against them were dropped.

Both Mary Latham and James Britton were sentenced to death – the only couple to be hanged in America for adultery. Mary "had deep apprehension of the foulness of her sin, and . . . was willing to die in satisfaction to justice". Britton "was very much cast down for his sins, but was loath to die, and petitioned the general court for his life, but they would not grant it".

On Tuesday, 21 March 1643, they went to their deaths "both . . . very penitently, especially the woman, who . . . gave good exhortation to all young maids to be obedient to their parents, and to take heed of evil company".

"It Was the Devil in the Form of the Coachman Who Betrayed Me"

Anna Maria Schwägelin was born in poverty in 1729, and worked in service in Lachen, Bavaria, for a rich family. She had reached her mid-thirties still virgo intacta, but fell for the family's coachman who offered to deflower her. He had one condition, which was that she must give up her Catholic faith, and she agreed.

However, afterwards he wanted nothing to do with her. Anna was shocked at the triple loss – her faith, her lover and her virginity. She turned to an Augustinian friar for help, but when he became a protestant, she believed that only the devil could have so evilly double-crossed her.

Not long after, she was found in the street dressed in rags, begging for alms and spouting nonsense. She was taken to an asylum at Laneggen near Kempten where she told her fellow inmates that she was a lapsed Catholic who had abandoned her faith to a Satanist lover with whom she had attended sabats and indulged in obscene behaviour. Her constant muttering,

"It was the Devil in the form of the coachman who betrayed me," led people to believe that her lover was the Devil.

The story was relayed to the matron of the institution, Anna Maria Kuhstaller, who insisted Anna be brought before her. She beat Anna until she confessed that she had indeed had sex with the Devil. She then denounced poor Anna to local magistrates.

On 20 February 1775, Anna Maria Schwägelin was arrested and charged with being a witch. She was found guilty and beheaded on 11 April 1775.

Dirtysomething

Mel Harris, star of the 1980s show *thirtysomething*, was a key figure in one of New York's steamiest love-triangle murder cases. Not that anyone would know this from the press coverage when the beauteous green-eyed actress was at the height of her fame. Reports in the 1980s also curiously fail to mention two former husbands. One was a discredited former Green Beret and suspected explosives trafficker who had been imprisoned for fraud. The other was a highly regarded dog trainer.

Five foot nine inches tall, Harris was a 22-year-old fashion model with the prestigious Wilhelmina Agency in New York when she became involved in the so-called "Penthouse Murder Case" in 1978. The plot revolved around Mel's closest friend and fellow model from the Eileen Ford Agency, Melanie Cain, twenty-one, and her live-in lover, Howard "Buddy" Jacobson, forty-nine, once America's number one trainer of thoroughbred horses.

The murder victim was 32-year-old John Tupper, a muscular restaurateur who was heavily involved in one of America's biggest international drug-smuggling rings. On the morning of 6 August 1978, Tupper was shot, stabbed and bludgeoned to death in the hallway outside his duplex penthouse on the seventh floor of a posh Manhattan townhouse at 155 East 84th Street, a building owned by Buddy Jacobson.

The corpse was stuffed into an army gun crate that Mel Harris's then fiancé, 31-year-old David Silbergeld, had brought from Vietnam where he had served as a munitions expert. The crate was hauled from the murder scene in a van to the northeast Bronx where it was dumped in a junk-strewn wasteland and set alight.

When Melanie Cain discovered her boyfriend was missing it was Mel Harris whom she called first. A family out on a Sunday drive spotted two men in a Cadillac leaving the site of the burning crate.

Police intercepted the car and Jacobson was arrested, prosecuted for murder, convicted and sentenced to twenty-five years to life imprisonment. (He escaped, was recaptured and died of bone cancer in Attica, New York State Prison, early in 1990.) His co-defendant was found not guilty and deported to his native Sicily where he was bumped off in a Mafia feud in 1990.

Mel Harris was one of the State's chief witnesses at the trial in the Bronx County Courthouse, near Yankee Stadium and the setting for Tom Wolfe's book *The Bonfire of the Vanities*.

Before she took the stand on the twenty-seventh day of proceedings, 29 February 1980, Mel made a courtroom entrance worthy of a Cecil B. DeMille spectacular. All eyes turned to stare at the dark-haired beauty with the heart-stopping figure.

At her side, protectively holding her arm, was 26-year-old Brian Kilcommons, who in the previous year had opened a dog training school on Long Island and would soon open a Manhattan branch. His appearance at the trial caused a murmur among the press because at the pre-trial hearing Mel Harris was married to David Silbergeld.

Harris's marriage to Silbergeld was short-lived. She became fed up with him after he was arrested and jailed for signing on the dole while working for a credit rating agency.

Harris met Silbergeld in 1977, while she was living in Garden Apartment 1-A of the 84th Street townhouse with Ronnie Stone, a well-healed jeweller. Harris stayed with Stone until Silbergeld invited her to move upstairs and share his penthouse apartment, 7-C, just across the hall from Buddy Jacobson's flat, 7-D, where Melanie Cain was living with the former horse trainer. Silbergeld was not a man a nice girl would want to introduce to her mother.

Prior to Mel, he had been living with a brassy blonde and had been involved in a number of shady deals. Just before he left the army as a captain following his return from Southeast Asia, Silbergeld took part in manoeuvres at West Point and came under a cloud of suspicion when he could not account for the disappearance of eleven Claymore mines, a sophisticated explosive capable of causing damage equivalent to a dozen hand grenades.

After a time at 84th Street, Silbergeld was taken in for questioning by the Nassau County District Attorney, Denis Dillon, about the wrecking of Long Island dustman Harvey Hochlerin's 1974 Peugeot. A thug named Carlo Carrera was trying to attach a Claymore mine to the car when it went off prematurely. Carrera survived the blast but never returned to the penthouse apartment where he had been shown all there was to know about Claymore mines.

One previous experiment at the townhouse resulted in a bath being blown up. Although Silbergeld was reputedly behind the assassination attempt there was no proof. About this time, in 1978, Silbergeld and Harris were married and moved to a West Side flat. The penthouse was sub-leased to Jack Tupper. Meanwhile, after five years Melanie Cain was beginning to tire of Buddy Jacobson, especially after setting eyes on the handsome Jack Tupper.

In no time at all, she had dumped Jacobson and was keeping Tupper warm at night. At his trial, authorities postulated that Jacobson and others had killed Tupper because he had run off with his girlfriend. More informed sources believe, as Jacobson claimed, that Tupper was slain by members of his drug gang after double-crossing them in a $250,000 deal.

The Indian Doctor's Scams

Emil Savundra was for much of his professional life a lucky man. He was a lover of Mandy Rice-Davies at the time of the Profumo Affair but was only referred to in court as "the

Indian doctor". He was freed from a five-year jail sentence in Belgium after only two months following the intervention of the Vatican. He described himself as "God's own lounge lizard turned swindler," adding, "I don't like work" – but he did like the good life.

Born as Michael Marion Emil Anacletus Savundranayagam in Ceylon (now Sri Lanka) on 6 July 1923, he had been involved in a number of shady businesses in China, Ghana and Belgium before he arrived in Britain in the 1950s. After discovering that anyone could become an insurance broker if they had £50,000, he founded Fire, Auto and Marine (FAM) on St Valentine's Day 1963. The company offered very attractive deals – premiums were half the cost of other insurance brokers. Brokers tried to match Savundra's deals. He explained, "My methods are the most modern and cost-effective. Traditional insurance companies need to charge exorbitant fees because their out-of-date system loads them with big overheads and costs."

Money began to pour in – some estimates suggest as much as £40,000 per week (today £700,000) – but of course, FAM would only be profitable if no one had accidents or made claims, and that is where it got into trouble. The law dictates that an insurance company must have enough assets to meet claims, but the money that came into FAM quickly left again via Savundra's wallet, buying him luxuries including a speed-boat. It was two years after the formation of the company that money out began to exceed money in.

Initially, Savundra told his staff to limit payouts to £10,000-a-week. The Board of Trade demanded to examine the company's books, but Savundra fooled them by producing a fake document from Liechtenstein stating that FAM had more than £500,000 of government bonds. It only delayed the inevitable.

As FAM collapsed, so did Savundra, taken to hospital with a convenient heart attack. He fled to Switzerland and then, on 9 July 1966, to Ceylon. On 24 July, the company was wound up, leaving 400,000 motorists unprotected.

In January 1967, Savundra unexpectedly returned to England. On Monday, 16 January, he went to the Labour

Exchange on Regent's Park Road to sign on the dole. A week later, he received a writ from the Official Receiver for £386,534 (today £6,859,123.14).

A comedy sketch, which featured on *The Frost Programme* about a thinly disguised Savundra, persuaded him to ring up the show and ask to appear. On Friday, 3 February 1967, Savundra arrived at the Rediffusion studios at Wembley Park. The show began and then Savundra said to the invited studio audience, "I am not going to cross swords with the peasants. I came here to cross swords with England's greatest swordsman." David Frost responded, "Nobody is a peasant. They are people who gave you money", with Savundra riposting, "They have given me nothing at all." He went on to claim that he had no legal or moral responsibility to his former customers, to Frost's evident fury. In fact, for most of the show Savundra was more collected than Frost.

A week later, Savundra was arrested on the orders of the Director of Public Prosecutions. He went on trial at the Old Bailey on 10 January 1968, accused of fraud. At 4.45pm on 6 March 1968, the jury found Savundra guilty. The next day he was sentenced to eight years in prison and a £50,000 fine, with a further two years if he did not pay the fine.

Savundra was released from prison at 7.30am on a wet 4 October 1974, having served six years, seven months and three days of his ten-year sentence. Savundra approached the American government and offered to sell them his wife's land in Ceylon for $200,000,000 on condition she was made Queen of North Ceylon.

Before the Americans could turn down his offer, Savundra suffered a heart attack at his home in Ousely Road, Old Windsor, on 21 December 1976, and was pronounced dead on arrival at King Edward VII Hospital. At the end of 1977, FAM's creditors received a dividend of 30p in the pound.

Sex-Mad Mother Sacrifices Children for Lover

Diane Frederickson married her childhood sweetheart Steve Downs on 13 November 1973, when both were eighteen. He later recalled, "She was attractive with a great body. Her sexual appetite was basically insatiable – she could not get enough with me or anyone else. I'd go to work and I'd be beat. I'd wake up in the middle of the night and she'd be on top of me going at it."

Unsurprisingly, they quickly had two children, Christie (in 1974) and Cheryl (in 1976), but their relationship began to disintegrate. Mr Downs decided that he didn't want any more children so had a vasectomy – but the operation failed and his wife became pregnant again. He demanded that she have an abortion, and he had a second, and this time successful, operation.

Diane Downs wanted another child and seduced nineteen-year-old Russ Phillips at the Chandler Post Office in Arizona where they both worked. She became pregnant by him and bore his son, Steven Daniel, known as Danny, in 1979.

Steve Downs agreed to raise the baby as his own. He later revealed, "I found out that she'd had affairs with scores of men during our marriage. She went through half the mailmen where she worked, especially the married ones."

The couple finally divorced in 1980, when Diane Downs asked Cheryl to lie to her father so she could see a lover. Five-foot-six Downs moved into a caravan and, short of money, offered to become a surrogate mother for $10,000. After an initial rejection, she gave birth to a baby girl on 7 May 1982.

Then she began an affair with married fellow worker Lewis Lewiston. He finished with her when she gave him a sexually transmitted disease. By this time, she had developed a fixation on him and begged him to leave his wife. When he refused, she moved with her children to Springfield, Oregon, 2,200 miles away, in the hope that he would follow her. He didn't.

In her mind, she began to blame her children for losing her the best lover she had ever had. On 19 May 1983, she drove the children to a deserted road and shot all three with a .22 gun. Cheryl died instantly, Danny was shot in the back and was paralysed for life, while Christie suffered a stroke caused by the gunshot wound to her chest.

Downs shot herself in the left arm and then drove to McKenzie-Willamette Hospital in Eugene and told the authorities that a "deranged, shaggy-haired hitch-hiker" had shot her and the children. At the hospital she seemed to show more concern for the car than for her children.

Missing her children, she got pregnant by a friend and was eight months gone when she was finally arrested on 28 February 1984, and charged with shooting her children.

Found guilty on 17 June, she was sentenced to life plus fifty years on 31 August. Her daughter, Amy, was removed immediately after her birth by the state and put up for adoption. Her two other children were adopted in 1984 by Fred Hugi, the lawyer who prosecuted Downs.

Protesting her innocence, Downs escaped from prison on 11 July 1987, but was recaptured less than half a mile from the prison ten days later. Three men were arrested for aiding and abetting a fugitive, including Wayne Seifer, thirty-six, the husband of Downs's cellmate. Unsurprisingly, she had slept with Seifer during her time on the run after he'd fallen in love with her. Having been rejected twice, Downs is not eligible for parole until 2020.

Unloving Husband

Nisha Patel-Nasri, a police special constable, was murdered at 11.45pm on 11 May 2006, because her husband Fadi Nasri, thirty-four, wanted to cash in a £350,000 joint life assurance policy. Some months before his wife's killing, he had begun an affair with Laura Mockiene, a Lithuanian prostitute.

Nasri claimed that the murder was a robbery gone wrong. He played the devoted and grieving husband at a police news conference. He gave them false leads, naming five people who he claimed wanted his 39-year-old wife dead. During this time, he went on holiday with Mockiene. It is thought that she became pregnant with Nasri's baby but had an abortion.

In February 2006, the Nasris took out the joint life assurance policy. Nasri had debts of more than £100,000 and was using his limousine firm as a cover to arrange drug deals. Also unbeknown to his wife, he had been jailed for nine months in 1998 for trying to run over a policeman who had asked him about an out-of-date tax disc on his car.

In prison, Nasri met Rodger Leslie, thirty-eight, a heroin dealer, who in turn arranged for Jason Jones, a nightclub bouncer with burglary and assault convictions, to carry out the killing. Nasri gave his house keys to the killer – hired for £15,000 – and left his wife alone at their home in Wembley, Middlesex. She was stabbed to death as she attempted to flee the knifeman.

Nasri, Leslie and Jones were all found guilty at the Old Bailey of murder by a majority verdict after a three-month trial. Tony Emmanuel, who acted as a driver for Jones, was cleared and walked free. Nisha Patel-Nasri's brother, Katen, said, "They showed her no mercy and have shown absolutely no remorse since. It is not a man but a coward who attacks a vulnerable woman with a knife. Nisha never stood a chance; she was alone and defenceless. The fact that the man she loved was responsible for this makes it all the more surreal and in the beginning I never imagined that he could be the one behind this wicked murder."

In a chilling coincidence, Nasri's divorced father, Farouk, was also accused of killing his lover. In 2000, at Leicester Prison, the 53-year-old used bed sheets to hang himself while on remand, having been charged with murdering Jennifer Elverson, twenty-seven, and her son, Ben, seven.

"Sydney Mutilator"

Gay serial killer William MacDonald murdered Frank Gladstone McLean on 31 March 1962, and then cut off his genitals. MacDonald was born in Liverpool, England, and joined the Lancashire Fusiliers where he was raped by a corporal in an air-raid shelter in 1943. The incident laid bare his latent homosexuality and he began a lifetime of cottaging.

In 1955, he emigrated to Australia where he was soon arrested for chatting up a policeman. In 1960, outside the Roma Street Transit Centre in Brisbane, he met Amos Hurst, fifty-five. The two men went drinking in a local pub before retiring to Hurst's home where MacDonald strangled him. His death was reported as accidental.

On 4 June 1961, police were called to Sydney Domain Baths where the naked corpse of Alfred Reginald Greenfield, forty-one, was found. He had been stabbed thirty times and his genitals cut off and thrown into Sydney Harbour. The press dubbed the killer the "Sydney Mutilator". MacDonald struck again stabbing 55-year-old William Cobbin and removing his genitals. His remains were found in a public lavatory at Moore Park.

When he killed McLean, MacDonald put the genitals in a plastic bag and took them with him. He bought a small shop in Burwood, New South Wales, that came with accommodation.

In November 1962, MacDonald met ex-con James Hackett, a thief and tramp, forty-two, in a wine bar in Pitt Street, Sydney. They returned to MacDonald's home where he stabbed Hackett in a homicidal frenzy – but the knife was too blunt to remove the genitals and MacDonald fell asleep next to his victim and covered in his blood. He put the corpse in the basement and, paranoid he would get caught, fled to Brisbane. The eventual smell led to the police being called, and a badly decomposed body was found. Everyone assumed it was MacDonald.

A memorial service was held and attended by several of his workmates. MacDonald was a free man but his urge to kill made him return to Sydney. On 22 April 1963, he bumped into an old friend, John McCarthy, on Pitt Street who told him what had happened. MacDonald's paranoia returned and he ran away to Melbourne. McCarthy went to the police who did not believe him so he went to the *Daily Mirror* who ran the story under the headline "The case of the walking corpse". MacDonald went on trial in September 1963, was found guilty and jailed for life.

Maniac Kills Doctors

Banner headlines in the newspapers on 27 November 1990 captured the moment when disaster struck a hospital in Wakefield, West Yorkshire. "Madman Murders Top Docs", ran *The Sun*, while the *Daily Mirror* went with "Top Docs Knifed to Death in Hospital". A little detail was provided by a report headed, "Maniac butchers plastic surgeons".

Doctors had completed their morning rounds at Pinderfields Hospital and retired to their offices before seeing the day's outpatients in the Burns Unit. When a secretary went to see Dr Kenneth Paton she found him lying on the floor bleeding badly from knife wounds. She called for help, and while a resuscitation team tried to save his life, staff entered the neighbouring office where they found Dr Michael Masser, also dying from stab wounds. Paton had been stabbed twenty-four times and Masser had received six stab wounds.

The deaths of two leading doctors in the hospital where they worked created a major emergency and police arrived at the scene in considerable numbers, including marksmen armed with shotguns. The hospital buildings and grounds were scoured in a hunt for the murderer. Descriptions were issued of a man who had been seen in the Burns Unit shortly before the murders were discovered.

The hospital was a major facility, employing two thousand staff and caring for over one thousand patients. The tragic deaths of the two doctors highlighted concerns about security at hospitals throughout the country where numerous assaults had been reported. Health unions said that attacks on nurses and doctors were so common they were almost regarded as an occupational hazard. Calls were made for measures to safeguard workers in the health professions.

Late on the day of the double murder a 24-year-old man gave himself up to the police. He was Laith Alani, an Iraqi immigrant, who had been referred to the hospital for the removal of a tattoo. When his appointment was delayed, his frustration evolved into a violent rage and he took the lives of the two doctors.

At his trial, Alani pleaded guilty to manslaughter on the grounds of diminished responsibility. He was committed to a maximum security hospital for an indefinite period. Having been diagnosed as a paranoid schizophrenic, he spent the next nineteen years under psychiatric scrutiny. In February 2010, Alani hanged himself in his cell.

Absolute Cruelty

Delphine Macarty was born around 1775 in New Orleans; her grandfather originally came from Ireland and the Macartys became prominent members of the white creole community in the city. A cousin, Augustin de Macarty, was mayor of the city from 1815 to 1820.

In 1800, Delphine Macarty married Don Ramon de Lopez y Angullo, a Spanish diplomat who by 1804 was consul-general for Spain in Louisiana. The couple went on a trip to Spain in 1804, and on the voyage Lopez died at Havana.

His widow continued on her journey and gave birth to a daughter – Marie Delphine Borgia Lopez y Angulla de la Candelaria – at sea. Mother and daughter remained in Spain for a short time before going back to Louisiana.

In 1808, Delphine married lawyer, banker and businessman Jean Blanque and the family moved to 409 Royal Street, into a house nicknamed Villa Blanque. Their brood increased to five children before Blanque died in 1816, leaving his wife a widow for the second time.

On 25 June 1825, she married for the third time, this time to a much younger man, Dr Leonard Louis Nicolas LaLaurie. She bought a house at 1140 Royal Street in her own name and the building soon rose to three storeys with attached accommodation for slaves.

Delphine LaLaurie was thought of as someone who cared for blacks, although it was noticed that her own slaves were on the thin side. Rumours arose that she chained her cook to the oven and that her daughters were beaten when they gave extra food to the slaves. A lawyer was sent to the house to check on the slaves and remind Delphine LaLaurie of her social responsibility. He came away having seen nothing out of the ordinary.

Then a female slave fell to her death from the roof, supposedly trying to escape a punishment beating. The authorities investigated again and this time found Delphine LaLaurie guilty of malfeasance. She was forced to give up nine of her slaves. She and her husband quickly bought the slaves back and returned them to the LaLaurie household.

On 10 April 1834, a fire broke out in the slave quarters, but when people tried to rescue the slaves from their locked quarters, Delphine LaLaurie refused to hand over the keys. The door was broken down and they found several slaves. They had all been mutilated. Some were hanging by their necks, others had had their eyes gouged out, some had their intestines tied around their waists, others had their fingernails pulled out while a number had been flayed. Two of the men had their tongues sewn together.

One woman had had her arms amputated; another, in a cage, had had her limbs broken and then reset at odd angles. Some had had animal excrement put into their mouths, which were then sewn shut. One girl was wearing an outfit made of the skins of other slaves.

An old man's penis had been segmented into five and each segment was attached to a hook before the body was hoisted to the ceiling. His eye sockets contained candles, making a gruesome chandelier.

When questioned, LaLaurie said that people should mind their own business rather than interfering in other's homes. News quickly spread of what had happened at the Royal Street house and it was quickly besieged and then attacked.

The police arrived to find the house almost destroyed apart from the walls. They took the slaves into custody but, rather than helping, they put them on display. By 12 April, more than four thousand people had been to stare at the slaves.

Delphine LaLaurie fled to Mobile, Alabama, before surfacing in France where she died. In the 1960s, when the house in Royal Street was being redeveloped, seventy-five skeletons were found under the floorboards.

Dangerous and Disturbed

Stephen Akinmurele was a serial killer who targeted elderly people. Born in Nigeria, he came to Britain as a 21-year-old in the 1960s and lived for a while on the Isle of Man. His crimes there would not surface until later.

In 1996, he moved to Blackpool where he worked as a barman. In October 1998, an elderly couple was found dead in their house at Seafield by their daughter. Joan Boardman, aged seventy-four, had been strangled, and her husband Eric, also in his seventies, had been battered to death. Mr Boardman had put up a fight but was overcome by superior force in a vicious attack with a cosh. He had done enough, though, to disconcert his attacker who abandoned the murder weapon at the scene. Fingerprints on it were matched to Akinmurele.

Following his arrest, Akinmurele was charged with three other murders of elderly people, including two killings on the Isle of Man, in 1995 and 1996, that were accompanied by arson attacks. He also confessed to other killings which the police thought might be a tactic to deflect them from the investigations in hand.

While in custody, he assaulted a police surgeon and made an attempt to kill himself. He had written a note expressing regret for what he had done and feared that he would go on to kill again. This was a concern shared by the senior detective involved in the case who considered Akinmurele "one of the most dangerous men I have ever met".

On 28 August 1999, before he could be brought to trial, Akinmurele hanged himself in his prison cell. He was undoubtedly a threat to public safety, and at the time of his death, police were examining the files of ten other suspicious deaths, some of which involved house fires. The Lancashire police described him as "a very dangerous and disturbed young man".

"Have a Friend for Lunch!"

One of the legends of American crime, Alferd Packer (his name is given as both Alferd – the result of a misspelled tattoo – and Alfred) was born in 1842 at Allegheny County, Pennsylvania, and fought on the Union side in the American Civil War.

He later became a prospector, and on 9 February 1874, he and five others – Shannon Wilson Bell, James Humphrey, Frank "Reddy" Miller, George "California" Noon and Israel Swan – set off for Gunnison, Colorado, despite a warning of impending bad weather. Needless to say, they were caught by snow in the Rocky Mountains.

By his own account, Packer went to look for food, and when he returned he claimed that he found Shannon Wilson Bell eating one of the others. When Bell saw Packer he tried to attack him with an axe so Packer shot him.

On 16 April, Packer finally returned to civilization and said that Bell had gone mad and killed all the others. Packer then admitted that the conditions had been so bad that when the oldest traveller, 65-year-old Israel Swan, died, the others ate him. Four or five days later, James Humphrey died and "was also eaten".

Frank Miller died in an accident and also ended up being eaten, as did California Noon. Packer then killed Bell in self-defence. On 5 August 1874, he confessed that he had killed the others and was jailed, but he escaped and went to ground. According to legend, the judge at his trial said, "Damn you, Alferd Packer! There were seven Dimmycrats in Hinsdale County and you've et five of them!"

Contrary to many stories told years later, and even today, Packer was never charged with, tried for, or convicted of cannibalism, or crimes related to cannibalism. On 11 March 1883, he was unmasked as John Schwartze while living in Cheyenne, Wyoming. On 13 April, he was found guilty of manslaughter and sentenced to death "until you are dead, dead, dead, and may God have mercy upon your soul".

The verdict was overturned, but on 8 June 1886, Packer was sentenced to forty years in jail – then the longest custodial sentence in American history. Packer was paroled on 8 February 1901, and died six years later on 23 April 1907.

In 1968 University of Colorado students at Boulder named their new café the Alferd G. Packer Memorial Grill with the legend, "Have a friend for lunch!"

Money for Murder

The trial of a financially aware mass murderer came to an abrupt end when he changed his plea to guilty on 12 January 1982. Clifford Olson was accused of eleven counts of murder in Vancouver, British Columbia, Canada, and had pleaded not guilty when he came to trial. His change of heart was, his defence lawyer said, brought about because he wanted to spare the relatives of his victims the grisly details of how their loved ones met their end.

Olson, forty-two at the time, was a career criminal and had already spent much of his life behind bars. Released from jail in 1980, a number of young people subsequently went missing in the Vancouver area. Three corpses – a girl and two boys – were found in Weaver Lake, about fifty miles to the east of the city.

The police began a manhunt for the perpetrator. Olson was arrested on 12 August 1981, when an eighteen-year-old girl identified him after he had raped her in June. Police searched his home where he lived with his wife, Joan, and baby son, also Clifford, and uncovered a number of items belonging to the Weaver Lake victims.

Olson confessed to the killings and others and offered to show the police where the victims were buried, but only if they gave him $10,000 for each plus another $30,000 for the three they had already found. The police turned the offer down flat, but to their amazement Alan Williams, the Attorney-General, agreed to Olson's demands. He agreed to pay $90,000 to be put in a trust for Olson's son. Once the money had been transferred, Olson took the police to the sites of eight graves.

The victims were aged between nine and eighteen and had been chosen at random; they had been stabbed, beaten or mutilated. When the details of the financial settlement became public knowledge there was widespread revulsion, but Robert Kaplan, the Solicitor-General, defended the deal. A fortnight later, Olson offered a cut-price deal – for another $100,000 he would take the police to twenty more victims. The offer was rejected. On 14 January, the judge sentenced him to life and "you should never be granted parole for the remainder of your days. It would be foolhardy to let you at large."

In 2001, Olson claimed that he should be freed because he had provided the US government with information about the

9/11 attacks. In March 2010, it was revealed that he was in receipt of two state pensions totalling $1,169.47 monthly. He died on 30 September 2011, at the age of seventy-one.

As Seen on TV

A teenager fascinated with murder and sudden death enjoyed watching horror films and crime dramas on television. Watching the soap opera *Coronation Street*, he became absorbed by a storyline that featured Charlotte Hoyle's death at the hands of a hammer-wielding John Stape, who then covered up his crime by leaving the body in the wreckage of a tram crash.

So taken by this episode was fourteen-year-old Daniel Bartlam that he wrote a story on his computer in which he featured as the killer of his mother. On 25 April 2011, fantasy turned into reality when 47-year-old Jacqueline Bartlam was murdered in her home. She had been repeatedly bludgeoned with blows from a hammer, and a fire set to destroy her body. The destruction was such that Mrs Bartlam, Daniel's mother, was identified by means of her dental records.

Daniel's first account was that an intruder had killed his mother in their home. Then he changed his story, claiming he had been provoked in an argument and lost his temper. He struck her seven times with a claw hammer and slopped petrol around her body before setting it on fire.

The teenager's attitude shocked those who spoke to him after the event. Apart from his lies, he dishonoured his mother's memory by claiming she had been a bad mother. The detective investigating the crime spoke about the degree of planning that had gone into it and the level of violence in executing it. Psychiatric reports indicated that Bartlam had experienced voices urging him to hurt people.

Tried at Nottingham Crown Court in February 2012, Daniel Bartlam denied murder and maintained that he had been provoked. The jury announced a unanimous guilty verdict and the judge passed down a sentence of life imprisonment with the recommendation that he serve sixteen years. He lifted reporting restrictions on the case so that the defendant could be named. Describing the killing as "grotesque and senseless", Mr Justice Julian Flaux said that Bartlam had notions of committing the perfect murder.

Those close to Bartlam said that he wrote gruesome stories and fantasies, which he delighted in sharing with his family. But, while this behaviour might have been regarded as bizarre, to all outward appearances he seemed perfectly normal.

The Precious Bird That Flew

John Wilson (aka Charles Sparks; aka Alfred Watson) was a career burglar. He was sent to Borstal at an early age and in the leitmotif that would be the hallmark of his life, he escaped. He was nicknamed Ruby after breaking into the Park Lane home of an Indian maharajah and stealing £40,000 worth of uncut rubies. Ruby was, on this occasion, no bright Sparks – he gave them away, thinking they were not real.

On 27 May 1927, he was sentenced to three years' penal servitude in the tough Strangeways Prison for a smash-and-grab robbery in Birmingham on 20 November 1924, during which a woman died.

A warder told Sparks, "Nobody has ever escaped from here." A fortnight later, Sparks became the first man to escape. He paid £400 in bribes and bought mailbag thread and a knife. Then Sparks made a dummy from a blanket, stool and chamber pot. He was wearing a suit he had had made from a blanket because his clothes had been taken from him and he simply used his knife to saw through the cell bars. He left a signed poem on his bed:

The Cage is Empty
The Bird is Flown
I've gone to a Place
Where I'm better Known

He later said, "I signed it so the screws would know it was me who had escaped and not Shakespeare". It did not deter his criminal ways. In May 1930, he was sentenced to five years for a series of car thefts. On 30 June, he tried unsuccessfully to escape from Wandsworth Prison.

By 1939, he was in Dartmoor Prison. He became the first

successful escapee from the bleak prison, which he absconded from on 10 January 1940, with Alec Marsh and Dick Nolan. Unable to steal the five necessary keys, Sparks mentally photographed them and spent a year making them from metal he had stolen from the machine shop. He became known as "Public Enemy Number One" and spent 170 days on the run. On his retirement Sparks wrote his autobiography *Burglar to the Nobility*.

"What does W. G. stand for?"

A serial burglar targeted the northern boroughs of London in the late 1950s. A combination of murder, rape and theft created a considerable public scare and prompted a massive police manhunt.

In December 1958, a friend reported 31-year-old prostitute Veronica Murray as a missing person. Her body was found a week later on Christmas Eve in her rented room in Charteris Road, Kilburn. She had been battered to death with a six-pound dumb-bell, which she used for exercise purposes. The room had been trashed and there was blood everywhere. Curiously, the killer had inflicted a pattern of minor wounds on the body of his victim. These consisted of small round abrasions in a V-shaped configuration. This led to speculation about witchcraft as a feature of the crime.

Crucially, crime scene detectives found fingerprints in the room and the prints eventually identified the murderer. The same prints were found in fifteen separate locations where burglaries had taken place, but did not appear in police records. The intruder had a pattern of consuming any available alcohol and left evidence of being a chain smoker.

One of the robberies occurred at the Westbury Hotel when the room occupied by George Sanders, the actor, was broken into in his absence. On this occasion, the thief took a fancy to a pair of shoes in the room that he exchanged for his own. The shoes he left behind, when examined, showed that studs had been hammered into the soles, giving the initial letters, W. G. The immediate thought was that these might offer a clue to the identity of the burglar.

On 10 October 1959, a Mrs Hill was attacked in her Fulham home. She was found unconscious in the kitchen with two nylon stockings tied tightly around her neck. Prompt action by her son enabled her to survive the ordeal. She explained later that she had befriended a young man on the train taking her home from celebrating her birthday in the West End and invited him in for a cup of coffee. He became violent when she declined his sexual approaches and, before he made his escape, he inflicted circular wounds on various parts of her body. She described her assailant as a young man called Mick who had a distinctive scar on his nose. Fingerprints left on his coffee cup matched those found in previous crimes.

Reports of the attack prompted lurid headlines referring to the individual who was now a wanted man as a sex fiend, sadist and raving lunatic. In the midst of the panic surrounding the crimes, a public-spirited prostitute reported to the police details of an encounter she'd had with a "scar-faced Mick" who she was convinced was a soldier. In light of this information, detectives began to look at the various military garrisons in and around London. Then the penny dropped; could the initials, W. G., stand for Welsh Guards?

On 24 November 1959, police arrived at the Welsh Guards Regimental barracks at Pirbright in Surrey. An eighteen-year-old drummer with a scar on his nose and known as Mick was quickly identified. He was Michael Douglas Dowdall, regarded by his fellow soldiers as being a loner and a bit odd, believing the world was against him, and addicted to drink. On his birthday, celebrated with his mates, he consumed four half-pint measures of gin served in a beer mug. Under questioning, he readily admitted killing Veronica Murray in 1958. On 3 December, nine days before his nineteenth birthday, he was charged with her murder.

Dowdall was put on trial for murder at the Old Bailey on 20 January 1960. He pleaded not guilty on grounds of diminished responsibility. This was still a relatively new defence, which had been introduced under the Homicide Act of 1957. It enabled a defendant to argue that he was suffering from abnormality of the mind sufficient to impair his responsibility. The medical evidence presented in court confirmed that Dowdall's aggressiveness, sexual perversion and alcoholism made him a psychopathic personality.

He had a troubled background in which he lost both parents before he was nine years old and was brought up by an aunt. He joined the Welsh Guards as a drummer at the age of fifteen when he began to drink heavily. When questioned by police, he said, "When I was drunk, very drunk, I would try anything".

Found guilty of manslaughter, Dowdall was given a life sentence on 22 January 1960. He was released on licence in July 1975, suffering from a fatal illness, and died, aged thirty-six, in November 1976.

"Beyond Belief"

William Wycherley and his wife, Patricia, were a retired couple who kept themselves very much to themselves. On May 4, 1998, they disappeared from their home in Mansfield, and to anyone who asked about them, their married daughter, Susan Edwards, explained that they had gone to live elsewhere. Thus began fifteen years of deception before the truth finally emerged.

During this time, Susan Edwards, a former police worker, and her husband, Christopher, sent Christmas cards to family members reporting on her parents' well-being and activities in retirement. This was all fiction, for Mr and Mrs Wycherley had been killed and their bodies hidden.

While this game was being played out, Edwards and her husband were busily exploiting the dead couple's assets. They drew £800 a month from their benefits entitlements, sold their home and milked their savings to the tune of £240,000. Using this fraudulently acquired wealth, Edwards spent thousands buying celebrity memorabilia. She was particularly obsessed with Hollywood actor Gary Cooper and lived in a fantasy world, writing letters to herself which she liked to think had been sent by French actor Gerard Depardieu.

This bizarre existence came crashing down in 2012, as the late Mr Wycherley approached what would have been his

100th birthday. Prior to receiving a congratulatory message from the Queen, officials needed confirmation that he was still alive. By this time, Susan and Christopher had fled to France where they quickly ran out of money. Christopher asked his stepmother for a loan and, spooked by the letter about Wycherley's centenary, related the sad tale of what had happened to the old man and his wife. It amounted to a confession, and the scale of the Edwards's deception unravelled.

The story was that elderly Mr Wycherley had been killed by his wife, Patricia, with the result that she became embroiled in an argument with Susan. This, in turn, led to Patricia Wycherley's death. There had been a history of festering disagreement between mother and daughter over a disputed inheritance. The bodies were buried in a shallow grave under the kitchen window, while Edwards and her husband embarked on a spending spree and maintained the pretence that the Wycherleys were still alive.

Following Christopher's confession, the bodies were exhumed from the garden grave in October 2013, and it was confirmed that both had been shot. Susan and Christopher Edwards were tried for murder at Nottingham Crown Court where the prosecution maintained that Susan shot and killed her parents, leaving their bodies in the bedroom for a week before enlisting her husband's help to bury them.

Described as "cold and calculating", Susan and Christopher Edwards were sentenced to minimum terms of twenty-five years' imprisonment. Detective Chief Inspector Griffin, who led the criminal investigation, described the idea of burying two people in their garden and keeping it secret as "beyond belief". He added that the convicted murderers had "started to believe in their own lies".

The Cat Gets It!

Although gambling is illegal in China, betting on the results of English Premier League football games online is very popular. Gambling syndicates throughout Asia stand to make big gains if they get their predictions right. Web gambling was a practice picked up by two students in Newcastle who were drawn into a betting scam.

Xi Zhou and Zhen Xing Yang, both aged twenty-five and Chinese nationals, had graduated from Newcastle University with Master's degrees and decided to live and work in Britain. Zhen used his computer skills to visit Chinese-language websites and recruit contributors to report on football matches. As he and his partner, Xi Zhou, became more involved, they attracted abuse and, ultimately, violence.

On 9 August 2008, they were both found dead in their flat in Newcastle, presumed to have been attacked by intruders. When Xi Zhou failed to turn up at the restaurant where she worked, the alarm was raised. She had been beaten and suffocated and Zhen had suffered multiple stab wounds. It also appeared that he might have been tortured. Crime scene evidence suggested that they probably knew their attacker or attackers. A strange feature of the double murder was that the couple's cat had been drowned and left in a bowl of water. No murder weapon was found.

Examination of Zhen's computer confirmed that he had been dealing in fraudulent activities involving online betting. The police theory was that he had been drawn into a criminal syndicate and reneged on his promises. The likelihood was that gang members had paid him a visit to exact revenge for his failure to honour betting payments. It was also believed that Zhen had inadvertently let slip information about the normally closely guarded and highly lucrative scam.

One of the mysteries of the crime scene was the drowning of the cat. It was not believed that this act had any significance rooted in Chinese belief or mythology. It is possible, though, that the cat was sacrificed in an attempt to get the couple to talk. DNA taken from the dead animal's paws produced no clues about the identity of the intruder. The police offered a reward of £5,000 for information leading to a conviction.

A witness came forward to volunteer a description of a man of Chinese appearance, accompanied by two others, seen outside the house where the couple lived. A laptop computer and mobile phones had been taken from the crime scene and were later found dumped in a nearby park. By checking calls made to one of the mobiles, police traced a conversation between Zhen and a man called Guang Hui Cao. He was located in Morpeth and arrested.

Cao was an illegal immigrant working in the restaurant trade. He denied killing Zhou and Zhen, although he admitted being present in the flat. He claimed he had been blackmailed into helping the killers, who had threatened his family in China. Forensic investigators found traces of Zhen's blood on the suspect's spectacles and wristwatch. Put on trial for murder in 2009, Cao was convicted of strangling and battering the two students. He was jailed for thirty-three years. There was no reference to the cat.

Ending Up on a Mortuary Slab

Mary Chatterton met her future husband, Mohammed Khelafati, during a visit to France in 1976. They married soon afterwards and moved to Edinburgh where they set up home and, in due course, had a baby daughter, Louisa. It proved to be an unhappy union, with Khelafati constantly threatening his wife with violence to the extent that she lived in a state of fear.

In 1983, Mary filed divorce proceedings and sought custody of her daughter. She also applied for an exclusion order against Khelafati, which the courts declined to issue. This meant that he had access to the family home and continued to harass his wife on an almost daily basis. On one occasion, he accosted her in the street and threatened to cut her throat.

Khelafati was issued with court orders instructing him not to menace his wife. These were disregarded to the point where Mary confided in her brother, "I'm going to end up on a mortuary slab". This proved to be a tragic prophesy, for, on 8 May 1984, her husband killed her. In the presence of six-year-old Louisa, he hacked her mother to death with a long-bladed knife.

Mohammed Khelafati was tried and convicted of murder for which he was given a life sentence. The background details of the case that emerged during court proceedings provoked bitter arguments about the failures of the police and legal system to protect a vulnerable woman from an abusive husband. Women's groups called for the police to have increased powers of arrest, and greater access to legal advice was called for.

All of this was too late to help Mary Khelafati, and fate had in store an especially poignant sequel. Her daughter, Louisa Ovington, led a troubled life as a young woman, and her actions resulted in a string of convictions for violent behaviour, and worse. Twenty-two years after she had witnessed her mother's murder, Louisa got into a dispute with her much-older boyfriend of six years, Maurice Hilton, forty-six, and, during a drunken rage, stabbed him to death. She admitted manslaughter and was punished with an indefinite jail sentence, the authorities believing that she was a dangerous individual.

Mohammed Khelafati was released from prison after serving fifteen years. His application for political asylum to remain in the UK was denied, and in 2004 he was deported to Algeria, his country of origin. Referring to the killing of his wife, he said he lost his mind when she told him she did not want to see him again.

He might also have given thought to the action of his daughter, so traumatized by her childhood experience that she mirrored her mother's death when she killed her boyfriend.

Cornflakes Clue

In 1980, a sixteen-year-old girl walking near her home in Haslemere, Surrey, was approached by a man driving a van. She thought he wanted directions. The driver got out of his vehicle, grabbed the girl by the throat and attempted to push her into the van at knifepoint. She fought him off and ran away, but she was astute enough to make a mental note of the van registration number. When she got home, the first thing she did was to write it down on a handy packet of cornflakes.

She reported the attack to the police and within one hour they made an arrest. Their enquiries had taken them to the home of 36-year-old Kenneth Kirton at nearby Churt. He was married with two children and worked as a painter and decorator.

Under questioning, Kirton revealed a sordid history of sexual offences that led to an admission that he had murdered fourteen-year-old Claire Hutchison just four days previously. The teenager had gone missing on her way to school and a major search operation was mounted to find her. Kirton agreed to lead police to the lonely wooded spot where he had buried her.

He admitted strangling the teenager after he failed to achieve sexual intercourse. The manner of her burial at Old Frensham Common near Farnham had echoes of a murder that had occurred nearly forty years previously. In 1942, a young woman's body was found buried at Hankley Common. She was known as the "Wigwam Girl" because she was living rough in an improvised shelter made of tree branches. She befriended a Canadian soldier, August Sangret, based at a nearby camp, who was convicted of her murder. Like the "Wigwam Girl", Kirton's victim had been buried face down in a shallow grave covered with bracken.

Enquiries into Kirton's background revealed that he had convictions going back to 1969 when he assaulted a teenager in a churchyard. There were other charges of rape and indecent assault. He told investigators that he suffered mental blackouts and did not remember what he had done. After inflicting violent attacks on women, he regained his calm. Sometimes he played music by Beethoven to settle his nerves. Police investigators said that Kirton's arrest had ended a reign of terror in Surrey.

Tried for murder at the Old Bailey, Kirton pleaded guilty to manslaughter due to diminished responsibility and also to attempted kidnap and assault. He had been subjected to psychiatric examination that concluded he suffered a mental abnormality with the prospect that he might regress to a childlike state. He was sentenced to life imprisonment on 30 January 1981.

The trial judge complimented the young woman who had recorded the registration number of Kirton's van and had exercised a "high degree of common sense". He awarded her £50 "as a little present".

"I May Have Killed Your Mother"

Carmel and Jeremy Lowndes lived in some style in their Spanish villa at Sotogrande on the Costa del Sol. Mr Lowndes, a wealthy 65-year-old man with property in London, moved to Spain with his wife in the early 1980s. Carmel, previously married to the Earl of Kimberley, had been an active participant in the London social scene. She and Jeremy married in 1954. They seemed a devoted couple, with a liking for entertaining their friends.

But the pleasant environment enjoyed by the millionaire set was shattered on 21 July 1992, when Carmel Lowndes was found dead in her home. She had been brutally killed with several savage blows to the head. To compound the tragedy, Jeremy had thrown himself off the villa's terrace, making a hard landing below and breaking his ankles.

What followed was a story of conflicting statements. The prelude to the killing was that Carmel and Jeremy Lowndes had entertained guests to a dinner that lasted until around midnight when they dispersed. The exceptions were Lord Wodehouse, Carmel's son by her former marriage, and his wife who stayed on overnight. In the early hours of the next morning, Lowndes told his stepson "I think I may have killed your mother".

Carmel was found on the landing outside the bedroom, unconscious and lying in a pool of blood. Blood was spattered on the walls and there were bloody footprints on the stairs. Lowndes was reported as saying "I don't know why I did it" before he jumped off the villa terrace and injured himself.

The forensic investigation carried out by the Spanish authorities into the killing left a lot to be desired. Footprints at the crime scene were not examined and bloodstains on clothing were not sampled. While the crime scene evidence showed that a great deal of blood had been shed, some of which must have landed on the killer, no witness reported seeing any blood on Jeremy. And no murder weapon was found.

Lowndes was charged with killing his wife and he spent two years in custody before his case came up for trial in the court at Cadiz. Some details of his personality and background emerged. He had a history of mental problems, which included a suicide attempt when he shot himself in the head. His life was saved in the operating theatre but surgery left him prone to fits. He was also known to be a heavy drinker.

Where he had previously admitted killing his wife, Lowndes protested his innocence in court. He said that after the dinner party on 20 July, he poured himself a nightcap and sat in a chair downstairs and went to sleep. While he was not sure he had not killed her, he thought he knew who the murderer was. No name was given and there was a suggestion that Carmel Lowndes had encountered an intruder. Among the uncertainties was the identification of the weapon used to bludgeon the victim. Jeremy Lowndes claimed that one of the four silver candlesticks, which had graced the dinner table, was missing.

Dr Iain West, a distinguished pathologist, gave expert testimony at the trial. He was intensely critical of the way the crime had been investigated and called into question the competence of those involved. The final outcome was that Jeremy Lowndes, who the prosecution claimed had beaten his wife to death in a drunken rage, was found guilty of manslaughter and sentenced to nine years' imprisonment.

Tramp Takes Revenge for Snub

In December 1852, on his way home to Chadwell Heath, Essex, Thomas Toller was offered a lift by his friend Thomas Smith on Mile End Road. As Mr Toller climbed into the horse and trap, Charles Saunders, a tramp, stopped him and asked for some money. Mr Smith told him in no uncertain terms to find a job.

At 8am on 8 February 1853, Mr Toller left home to walk to Ilford Station. As he reached the junction with Barley Lane, Saunders, who had lain in wait, attacked him. Mr Toller called out, "Murder! Murder!" as he fell to the ground. Two men nearby ran over to help, but before they could reach the scene Saunders took out a knife and stabbed Mr Toller in the neck. Saunders then ran towards Hainault Forest, leaving Mr Toller dead on the ground.

However, Saunders got lost and headed east instead of west and arrived at Little Heath where he bought some tobacco and matches. John Gaywood, a Chadwell Heath butcher, was also in the shops and decided to follow the tramp when his greyhounds took an interest in the man. Saunders then made the mistake of heading back towards the murder scene and at 10.15am arrived back in Barley Lane. PC John Metcalf was at the crime scene and he questioned Saunders and arrested him.

On the way to Ilford Police Station, Saunders confessed, "He once attempted to murder me and now I have murdered him. He once hindered me from getting fourpence and a night's lodging, and something to eat."

A mob gathered around the station and Saunders was taken to Ilford jail for his own safety. His trial began at the Old Bailey on 3 March 1853. The defence barrister asked the jury to find his client not guilty by reason of insanity. Saunders's sister, Charlotte Collyer, thirty-three, testified to his strange behaviour and revealed that their mother had died in a lunatic asylum. The jury ignored the testimony and took twenty minutes to convict. The judge sentenced Saunders to death.

An appeal was made to the Home Secretary, Lord Palmerston, but he refused to commute the sentence. More evidence was produced attesting to Saunders's mental state and Lord Palmerston stayed the execution for a week. However, the execution went ahead above the entrance to Chelmsford Prison on 30 March 1853. Five months later, Ellen Toller gave birth to a daughter, Agnes.

Hit Woman

Graeme Woodhatch, a patient in London's Royal Free Hospital, was making a telephone call when he was approached by a stranger. The figure was in reality a woman disguised as a man. She was wearing a holster over her shoulder from which she drew a gun and fired four dum-dum bullets into his head and body. The hit woman then disappeared.

This murderous attack took place in May 1992, and remained unsolved for several months. Then, out of the blue, 28-year-old Te Rangimaria Ngarimu, a woman of Maori descent, turned up at Scotland Yard. She confessed to killing Woodhatch, after which she had returned to New Zealand, but, having become a born-again Christian, she felt the need to confess her sin.

Her story was that she had been hired by two men in London to carry out a contract killing. They were roofing contractors, Paul Tubbs and Deith Bridges, who offered to pay her £7,000 to kill Graeme Woodhatch whom they accused of swindling them out of £50,000 in a business arrangement.

Ngarimu, or "Sparky", as she was known to her friends, was an unlikely contract killer. She came from a respectable family in South Island, New Zealand, and was well educated. She formed a bond with Deith Bridges who had New Zealand connections and they became like "brother and sister". Her ambition was to buy a mobile home. Bridges supplied her with the gun. Once she reached the hospital, with her target in sight, she had second thoughts about her mission but, then, as she described it later, "something snapped and I did it".

"Sparky" was tried for murder at the Old Bailey in December 1994. Giving evidence, she described the moment she took off the safety catch on the gun she used to kill Graeme Woodhatch, a man she had never met and identified by means of a photograph that she had been given. She remembered seeing him on the floor screaming and holding his hands to his face.

Her co-conspirators, Tubbs and Bridges, against whom she had given evidence, were convicted and sentenced to life imprisonment the week before her trial. After her return to New Zealand she found religion and knew she had to confess to the killing. She said that a weight was lifted from her shoulders. Sentencing her to life imprisonment, Sir Lawrence Verney, the Recorder of London, said she was motivated by money and carried out the act in cold blood.

The mystery remained why a talented young woman committed such a deadly act for a small return. Of the promised reward for making the hit, she only received £1,500. She has the unique distinction of being Britain's only woman contract killer.

Football Is a Matter of Life and Death

At Medellín, Colombia, on 2 July 1994, Andrés Escobar became the only footballer murdered after scoring an own goal in a World Cup match. Prior to the World Cup, Colombia had been a favoured team and it was reported that heavy bets – many by the powerful drug syndicates that run Colombia – had been placed on the team doing well.

Footballing legend Pelé even tipped them to win the trophy. However, the plaudits placed undue pressure on the team and manager Hernan Gomez was reported to have received death threats over matters of team selection. On 22 June 1994, Colombia played the hosts, the USA, at the Pasadena Rose Bowl before 93,689 spectators. It was the fourth match in Group A and the second game for both countries.

The USA had drawn their opening match while Romania had comprehensively beaten Colombia 3–1 in their first game, so it was important for both sides to win. On the thirty-fourth minute America attacked and midfielder John Harkes crossed the ball. Attempting to block the cross, sweeper Andrés Escobar slid forward and, rather than clearing the ball, managed to put it into his own net. Seven minutes after half time Earnie Stewart made it 2–0 to America. Colombia managed a consolation goal through Adolfo Valencia with a minute on the clock, but it was not enough, and despite a win in their final match against Switzerland it meant an early plane home for the team who finished bottom of the group.

Ten days after his own goal, Escobar visited the El Indio bar in a suburb of Medellín. As he left, he was approached by a man who shot him twelve times and reportedly yelled "Goal!" after each bullet. Escobar, a popular figure in Colombia, was given a hero's funeral, which was attended by 120,000 people.

On 30 June 1995, Humberto Castro Muñoz, a local school-master, was found guilty of Escobar's murder and sentenced to forty-three years' imprisonment. The punishment was later reduced to twenty-six years and Castro was released in October 2005.

Going Hunting

Margaret Muller was a prize-winning American artist who came to Britain from the USA in 1989. She set up a workshop and studio in east London. On 3 February 2003, she went for a run in Victoria Park, Hackney, and became the victim of an unsolved murder. Fellow joggers heard her scream and ran to her aid. She had been fatally stabbed in a frenzied knife attack and witnesses saw two men running from the scene.

The Metropolitan Police staged a major reconstruction of the crime, which involved questioning over a hundred witnesses who had been in the park that day. A reward was offered for information leading to an arrest and officers made house-to-house enquiries. Police warned that the killer might have stalked the area looking for a likely victim and believed there might be a link to similar knife attacks during the previous six years. Nine suspects were questioned but no one was charged.

The following year, in August 2004, another knife attack occurred in London, this time in Bethnal Green. Bernard Hegarty, a young architect, was attacked in the street, sustaining serious injuries from which he died a few days later. An arrest followed quickly, when 31-year-old Christopher Olokun was picked up and charged. His DNA was found on a knife retrieved from the crime scene.

While in custody awaiting trial, Olokun told a fellow inmate that he was a crack and cocaine addict who needed £70 a day to buy and sell drugs. On the day he killed Bernard Hegarty he said he had gone out "hunting", planning a mugging that turned violent. At trial, Olokun denied murder, while pleading guilty to charges of robbery. He was convicted of the murder charge and given a life sentence.

In 2009, Olokun was questioned about the unsolved murder

of Margaret Muller six years previously, without any resolution. He was questioned again in 2011, with a similar outcome.

Celebrity Misdemeanours and Malfeasance

One might imagine that with the riches that come with fame, there would be no need for the famous to commit crimes. Far from it – celebrities have been responsible for everything from theft to murder and much in between.

To the tabloid press she was known as the "Countess of Cleavage" thanks to her generous *embonpoint*, which she had few qualms about showing at the numerous film premières she was invited to.

However, Imogen Hassall wanted to be taken seriously as an actress and became increasingly disconsolate when she was offered only dolly-bird roles.

On 22 June 1975, at 1.10am, while living in Hurlingham Road, Fulham, London, she was stopped by police in Daisy Lane, Putney, and charged with being drunk in charge of a bicycle. The next day at West London Magistrates' Court she was fined £10 with £11 doctors' fees.

Five years later, she committed suicide on the day she was due to go on holiday with actress friend Suzanna Leigh. Imogen Hassall was thirty-eight.

Floppy-haired Hugh Grant became world-famous for his role in the comedy *Four Weddings and a Funeral*, although it was then girlfriend Elizabeth Hurley who stole the limelight at the film's London première with a Versace dress held together with large safety pins.

It therefore came as a surprise to many when Grant was arrested on Sunset Boulevard in Hollywood at 1.45am on 27 June 1995, while receiving oral affection from a black prostitute, on a charge of "suspicion of lewd conduct in a public place". He was with the $60 prostitute Divine Brown in a rented white BMW convertible. Brown (née Stella Marie Thompson) told the *News of the World* (who had reportedly paid £100,000 for her story) that Grant had said, "I've always wanted to sleep with a black woman. That's my fantasy." On

11 July, the actor pleaded no contest, was fined $1,180, put on probation for two years and ordered to take an Aids test.

Another Englishman who fell foul of the law in California was the singer George Michael, then a closet homosexual.

On 7 April 1998, Michael was arrested by LA detective Marcelo Rodríguez for lewd behaviour in a public lavatory in Will Rogers Memorial Park, Beverly Hills. Michael said, "I don't feel any shame whatsoever, and neither do I think I should" as was evidenced by his mocking the event in the video for his song *Outside*. Like Grant, Michael pleaded no contest, was fined $810 and sentenced to eighty hours' community service. In September 1999, Rodríguez sued the singer for emotional distress, alleging that the video mocked him and asking for $10 million in damages. The suit was eventually thrown out.

Eight years later, Michael was again in trouble with the police but this time over drugs. He was arrested on 26 February 2006, for possession of Class C drugs.

On 8 May 2007, he pleaded guilty to driving while under the influence of drugs and was banned from driving for two years, and sentenced to community service.

On 19 September 2008, Michael was arrested in a public lavatory on Hampstead Heath for possession of Class A and Class C drugs. He was taken to a police station and received a caution for controlled substance possession.

On 4 July 2010, on the way home from a homosexual rally, he drove his car into the front of Snappy Snaps in Hampstead. On 12 August, the Metropolitan Police said that he had been "charged with possession of cannabis and with driving while unfit through drink or drugs". On 14 September, he was sentenced to eight weeks in jail, a fine and a five-year ban from driving. Michael was released from Highpoint Prison in Suffolk on 11 October 2010, after serving four weeks.

In 1982, the glamorous Italian actress Sophia Loren served an eighteen-day prison sentence in Rome Prison for tax evasion. In 2013, the supreme court of Italy cleared her of the charges.

In 1944, the French actress Arletty was arrested and sent to Drancy concentration camp then to Fresnes Prison (near Paris) where she spent four months, condemned to death by a

Free French Tribunal in Algiers for collaborating with the Germans. After the Liberation, she became the symbol of treason or what was called "horizontal collaboration". She had had an affair with a German officer. In December 1944, she was put under house arrest for another two years and condemned to three years' work suspension. She was not allowed to attend the première of *Les Enfants du Paradis*.

On 6 February 1971, Lionel Bart, the composer, gave an interview to Don Short of the *Daily Mirror* in which he declared, "I'm a communist, homosexual junkie." Ten days later, the police raided Bart's home at 6 Reece Mews, London SW7, and found "under eight grams" of cannabis and arrested him under the Dangerous Drugs Act. Traces of other drugs were found, but the police were happy that he "had no knowledge of these items". He appeared before the beak at Marlborough Magistrates Court on 9 March, and was fined £50 with £10 costs.

John Bindon was an actor who specialized in playing the violent thug in films and on TV, a role that came easy to him since he was a real-life gangster. As a teenager, Bindon was arrested for stealing crates of beer from his local British Legion Club in Parsons Green, London. He claimed it was only a harmless prank, but the magistrates disagreed and sentenced him to three months in Borstal for theft. Inside he sewed mailbags and was proud of his ability to do "the old mailbag stitch".

Bindon was notorious for his violent temper and his habit of provoking fights in pubs for no other reason than to prove what a "hard man" he was. After one such pub fight in 1964, he was arrested and charged with assault, actual bodily harm and wounding. He was sentenced to two years. While inside, he made friends with the feared Frank "Mad Axeman" Mitchell, who later introduced him to the Kray twins for whom Bindon worked "sorting out problems".

The director Ken Loach spotted Bindon in a London pub and cast him in the gritty drama *Poor Cow* (1967), which was about a London villain with a penchant for domestic violence. Bindon ran a protection racket and worked as a drug dealer in Fulham.

On 21 November 1978, a gangster named Johnny Darke, the reputed leader of a south London gang called The Wild Bunch, was hacked to death with a machete at the Ranelagh Yacht Club in Fulham (locally called Bobby's Club). In the fight, Bindon was stabbed five times – one nicked his heart, another punctured a lung and a third slashed his face from nose to temple, just missing his eye. Seriously wounded, he fled to Ireland where a priest administered the last rites.

Recovered, Bindon returned to London where he surrendered to police and was charged with murder. On 13 November 1979, after the jury deliberated for thirty hours, he was acquitted of all charges at the Old Bailey – the actor Bob Hoskins had been a character witness. As Bindon's girlfriend Vicki Hodge left the court, an elderly woman punched her in the face.

Bindon may have been cleared, but the event virtually put paid to his acting career and he drifted into obscurity. He continued to appear in various courts on different petty charges. In November 1982, he was fined £100 for possessing an offensive weapon. The magistrate Eric Crowther said, "I regret I have not yet had the pleasure of seeing you act to my knowledge, except here."

In 1984, he was sentenced to two months for holding a carving knife in the face of a detective constable. Nine years later, and six days after his fiftieth birthday, he died of Aids.

"Evil Gratification"

Jamie Reynolds was obsessed with pornography and driven by sadistic impulses. He wrote a script fantasizing about killing girls by hanging them and watching while they danced at the end of a rope. His technique was to lure young women to his home in Wellington, Shropshire, to participate in photography projects.

In 2008, he attempted to strangle one of his captives but she escaped and he received a visit from the police. He was advised to seek counselling. The course of action he adopted was to seek out images depicting extreme violence to women and to frequent pornographic websites. He downloaded obscene images on which he superimposed the faces of girls featured on social network sites.

Reynolds, twenty-three, met Georgia Williams, the teenage daughter of a policeman, who was head girl at her school. He talked her into participating in one of his so-called photographic projects. She left the family home on 26 May 2013, ostensibly to visit friends, but did not return. Georgia was reported missing and a nationwide search followed. Her body was found on 31 May, in woodland near Wrexham, and the police arrested Reynolds as their chief suspect soon afterwards.

Having lured his seventeen-year-old victim to his home, Reynolds hanged her and took photographs of her dying moments before sexually violating her dead body and taking more pictures. He then sent text messages from Georgia's phone to her family to make them believe she was safe and well. His next move was to put her body in his van and leave it there while he went off to the cinema. Later, he drove to a wooded area fifty miles away where he dumped her.

A search of his home showed the extent of Reynolds's obsession with pornography and scenes depicting violence against women. 16,800 images were recovered, together with dozens of hardcore videos. Some of the pictures of women's faces had been disfigured by having a noose drawn over them.

The case highlighted current concerns about the part that sexual obsessions might play in a progression towards serial killing. Reynolds was not believed to be suffering any mental illness but he was identified as a narcissist with a tendency towards sexual sadism. As such, he was a clear threat to the public. Put on trial in December 2013, he admitted murder and was sentenced to life imprisonment on the basis that he would serve a full-life term.

The trial judge's decision took into account the views of the European Court of Human Rights' ruling that whole-life sentences were inhuman. Mr Justice Wilkie took the view that the full-life term was justified on the grounds that the murder victim, in law, was a child. The victim's father told the court that his daughter had been killed for a "few moments of evil gratification".

Birth of Stockholm Syndrome

The term Stockholm Syndrome (whereby hostages form a bond with their captors) is derived from the taking of four hostages during a robbery at the Sveriges Kreditbank at 10.15am on Thursday, 23 August 1973. Criminologist and psychologist Nils Bejerot coined the term.

Not long after the bank opened for business, 32-year-old Jan Erik Olsson walked in and raked the place with machine-gun fire, announcing, "The party has just begun." The police were rapidly on the scene and two entered the bank. Olsson shot one and the other was forced to sit on a chair and "sing something". He chose *Lonesome Cowboy*.

Olsson then took four bank employees – three women and one man – hostage in the eleven by forty-seven foot vault. Olsson demanded three million kronor and the freeing of prisoner Clark Olofsson who had six more years to serve and who had tried to escape just two weeks previously. He also wanted a fast car, two guns, bulletproof vests and a helmet.

Olofsson was brought to the bank where he took part in the negotiations. Kristin Enmark, one of the hostages, said that she felt safe with the two criminals but feared the situation would worsen if the police attempted to rescue her and the other three clerks. The police negotiators agreed to the demand of a car but refused to allow Olsson and Olofsson to leave in it if they tried to take the hostages.

Olsson rang Prime Minister Olof Palme and threatened to kill the hostages if his demands were not met. The next day, Enmark rang Mr Palme and said that she was upset by his attitude and asked that the robbers be allowed to leave. On the evening of 28 August, the police used tear gas to end the siege after 131 hours.

Jan Erik Olsson was sentenced to ten years in prison for his part in the robbery. Clark Olofsson was returned to jail after also being convicted, but he claimed that he had tried to help the situation and his conviction was quashed. He later became friends with Kristin Enmark. Jan Erik Olsson married one of the women who wrote him fan letters while he was in prison.

Released from prison, Jan Erik Olsson continued to commit crimes. Finally, racked by guilt, on 2 May 2006, he gave himself up, only to be told that the police were no longer interested and were not looking to prosecute his crimes.

The Time Has Come

"If you are watching this message it is because I have been murdered by Alvaro Colom." This terse message was transmitted on video by Rodrigo Rosenberg, a 47-year-old lawyer with a practice in Guatemala City. Alvaro Colom was the president of the country.

Two days later, on 10 May 2009, Rosenberg left home riding his bicycle. A short while later, a car drew up behind him, three shots were fired and the lawyer was left bleeding to death from head wounds as the murderers sped off into the morning traffic. CCTV security cameras captured the whole episode.

Guatemala was a country with an unenviable murder rate; over 90 per cent of murders are never solved. The circumstances of Rosenberg's death made this a killing that reverberated around the country. His video message, relayed on the internet, sparked a political storm which threatened to unseat the government.

Theories about his death abounded. There were allegations of corruption in high places and Rosenberg's message urging the country to get started down a new path included the rallying call, "Guatemalans, the time has come". Opponents of the ruling regime staged public demonstrations calling for the resignation of President Colom. In response, pro-government sources labelled the whole farrago a right-wing plot.

After months of speculation and turmoil, an explanation for Rosenberg's death emerged from a UN investigation, which concluded that the lawyer, in a depressed state of mind, sacrificed his own life in a staged suicide with the hope of provoking a change of government. Copies of the video message he had recorded were handed out at his funeral and soon found a place on YouTube. The response was so enormous that some online sites crashed.

It was known that Rosenberg was personally unhappy and angry over what he saw as a failure of government. Another dimension to this emerged in January 2010, when the reason for planning his suicide came to light. In April 2009, one of his clients, a well-known businessman, and his daughter were driving into the city when they were attacked by two men on a motorcycle who shot and killed them both.

Rosenberg was so distraught at the loss of his friends that he arranged for hired hitmen to kill him in a kind of proxy suicide that would be blamed on government assassins. The final truth emerged when the car containing the lawyer's killers was traced and the pair involved in the shooting told their story. The plot, when it unravelled, was likened to an Agatha Christie mystery. Certainly, it ranked very high on any list of conspiracies.

"I Just Snapped"

Liam Reid grew up in Hamilton on New Zealand's North Island. He was a wayward teenager, an outsider with a taste for violence who served time for robbery, possession of a firearm and assault.

At the age of thirty-five, working occasionally as a forester, he was addicted to drugs and alcohol. He also indulged in extreme sexual practices with his female partners, involving handcuffing, partial asphyxiation and beatings. He explained his aberrant outbursts with the phrase, "I just snapped".

In November 2007, he left hospital in Dunedin in a despondent mood, fearful that his regular girlfriend might ditch him. He confided to a friend in a telephone conversation that if Adrienne left him, he would take his own life. In a black mood, he explained that this would be a better option than hurting someone else.

In the event, Adrienne did not desert him but picked him up and then drove north to Christchurch. They checked in to a backpacker hostel and later drove to Spencer Park, north of the city. They planned to sleep in the car. Rough sex ensued and Reid so abused her that Adrienne decided to call it quits on their relationship.

Two days later, by chance, Reid came across twenty-year-old Emma Agnew who had put her car up for sale. Posing as a possible buyer seeking a test drive, they motored to a nearby forest. There, he raped and killed her and put her body in a shallow grave covered with leaves. It was later found by a man walking his dogs.

Later that day, Reid apologized to Adrienne for his poor behaviour, and then went to Nelson where he attempted to get a passage on a boat to Australia. The fact that he had no travel documents doomed his requests to failure. On 21 November, Adrienne picked him up once more and then drove to a cabin she had booked at Spencer Park. By an extraordinary coincidence, this was located just a few hundred yards from the spot where he had buried Emma Agnew.

As the police search for the missing woman took them to Spencer Park, Reid panicked and fled from the rented cabin. He travelled to Dunedin where he encountered a young woman returning home after an evening out with friends. He attacked and raped her, informing his victim that he had killed someone. She survived the assault and, reduced to a suicidal state, Reid was picked up by the police. He confessed to killing Emma Agnew.

When he was brought to trial and found guilty of murder, the brother of his victim said. "Killing someone just isn't natural; it just isn't fair".

"A Robbery Gone Bad"

Ronni Chasen was a well-known and popular associate of many of Hollywood's celebrities. She worked for stars such as Michael Douglas, the actor, and George Lucas, the film director, in the role of publicist. On 16 November 2010, she was invited to the after-show party at the W Hotel in Beverly Hills to celebrate the première of the film, *Burlesque*.

She left the party in high spirits, drove down Sunset Boulevard in her E350 Mercedes and turned into Whittier Street en route to her Westwood condominium. At about 12.28am, several residents heard the sound of gunshots and Ronni's car crashing into a lamppost. Emergency services were called and she was rushed to Cedars-Sinai Medical Center, but was declared dead on arrival at 1.12am. She had sustained five gunshot wounds to the chest.

Controversy followed the death of the popular 64-year-old, with different interpretations being offered to explain what had happened. Motive was a key issue. Was this a random shooting or was there a more sinister explanation, such as a contract killing? These questions swirled around Hollywood's social circuit as over a thousand mourners gathered at a memorial service to honour Ronni's life.

Despite her popularity, little was known about her private life. She jealously guarded her privacy, although she had confided in a friend that she believed she had been targeted by a stalker. One witness who heard the fatal shots believed they were evenly timed, suggesting, possibly, that the killer was a professional hitman. Set against this was the proposition that Ronni Chasen had been the unfortunate victim of a random killing.

Suspicion focused on Harold Martin Smith, a 43-year-old ex-convict who had boasted to neighbours in the apartment block where he lived that he was the killer. The suggestion was that he had been paid $10,000 to carry out the killing. When police confronted Smith in the apartment lobby on 1 December, he pulled a gun and shot himself in the head.

The final outcome was that Ronni Chasen had indeed been the victim of what was described in official circles as "a robbery gone bad". Smith had been riding a bicycle when he approached her car and fired the fatal shots. It appeared that the gun used was the same weapon he used to kill himself.

The "Bodies in the Car" Killer

Passers-by on Spears Road, Holloway, the street running alongside the north London Polytechnic, noticed a parked gold Toyota Corolla with two women in it. One was slumped in the front passenger seat and the other lay in the back of the car. They were thought to be sleeping. This was late in the evening of 23 July 1990.

The following morning, the car was still there with its occupants apparently still asleep and with the doors locked. The police were alerted, and when the car was accessed it was discovered that both women were dead. They were identified as Elaine Forsyth and Patricia Morrison, who shared a basement flat nearby on Grenville Road. Patricia Morrison was in the back seat in a stiff, awkward position, and Elaine Forsyth was propped up in the front seat. They were last seen alive by neighbours in their garden during the previous afternoon. Patricia Morrison had made plans to meet a friend that evening to attend a Madonna concert, but she failed to turn up.

Scene-of-crime investigators believed the women had been throttled and then placed in the car. The focus of attention shifted to their flat and the people whom they knew. The fact that both women worked as estate agents carried echoes of the disappearance of Suzy Lamplugh, also an estate agent, who was abducted from a London street in July 1986. Her body has never been found.

Police questioned 35-year-old Michael Shorey, a former boyfriend of Elaine Forsyth. The couple had been living together but recently split up. He offered to help detectives but drew suspicion on himself by making contradictory statements. This was heightened when one of his friends mentioned that Shorey had given him a package to look after. On examination, this proved to contain a carpet bearing traces of blood and saliva. Asked to explain, Shorey said the cat made the stains when it killed a bird indoors. He said he planned to have the carpet dry-cleaned.

The police reconstruction of events was that Shorey attacked Forsyth after an argument and then confronted Morrison when she turned up and found her friend beyond help. Neighbours reported hearing screams and people arguing in Forsyth's flat. In the early hours of the morning, bumping noises were also heard. This led to speculation that Shorey was moving the bodies out of the flat and placing them in the car where they were later found.

There were several unsatisfactory elements to the enquiries, which led to Shorey being charged with murder. Forensic investigators were unable to obtain a match between the stains found on the carpet and either of the dead women. Furthermore, Shorey had been provided with an alibi by a girlfriend who claimed he spent the night with her. But against this was the testimony of an unnamed prison inmate who said that, while on remand, Shorey admitted to him that he had killed the women.

At his trial, Michael Shorey was described as having committed "appalling crimes". He was convicted on 3 July, and sentenced to life imprisonment. When the verdict was announced, Shorey, in a state of distress, wept and shouted, "I didn't kill anyone".

"Thrown Away Like Trash"

Murderers usually take care to dispose of their victim's body in a way that ensures they will avoid detection. Peter Wallner's chosen method of disposal simply postponed discovery. Fearing that his wife, Melanie, would be an obstacle to his extra-marital activities, he decided to kill her.

One night in August 2006, while she lay asleep, he took firm hold on a griddle pan and used it to batter her to death. His next move was to put her body in the freezer in the garden shed where it would stay undisturbed for three years.

To cover his tracks, Wallner sent text messages to Melanie and used her credit card. He explained her absence by saying she had died of a brain aneurysm. When Melanie's parents, who lived in South Africa, decided to hold a memorial service for their dead daughter, Wallner flew out to Pretoria to attend the family gathering. He took with him an urn which he said contained Melanie's ashes. In reality, her body still lay in the freezer in his garden shed while the urn contained ash residues from his barbecue.

As time passed, Wallner moved on to a new girlfriend and they decided to live abroad. In preparation, he began to clear his house at Cobham in Surrey which involved disposing of the freezer in the garden shed. The first problem, though, was what to do with Melanie's frozen body. His solution was to dump it in the wheelie bin for the regular refuse collection. When the bin men arrived in June 2009, they found the wheelie too heavy to move and, on inspecting the contents, discovered the body.

Wallner, thirty-five, a chef by occupation, was charged with murder and tried at the Old Bailey in June 2010. He denied murder but pleaded guilty to manslaughter. His explanation of events was that his wife had attacked him when she discovered that he was seeing another woman. He retaliated and killed her and then attempted a cover-up. The depth of his depravity was exemplified by the act he put on in South Africa, when he ostentatiously took off his wedding ring and placed it in the urn, leading his distressed in-laws to believe it carried his wife's ashes when the contents were nothing more than the scrapings from his garden barbecue.

Wallner showed no remorse when the jury returned a guilty verdict, and he was sentenced to life imprisonment. Melanie's father, embittered over her loss, said Wallner had thrown her away like trash.

The Last Witch in Britain

Born in Perthshire, Scotland, in the dying years of the nine-teenth century, Helen MacFarlane was a tomboy who was nicknamed "Hellish Nell" when she was a young girl, and even her mother said that one day she would be burned as a witch. In 1916, Helen married Henry Duncan, an invalided soldier she had "first met in her dreams". They had six children and

Henry spent much of his time helping his wife's spiritualism business rather than concentrating on his own trade as a cabinet maker.

Helen Duncan claimed that she was helped by her spirit guide Albert Stewart, a sarcastic Scotsman who had emigrated to Australia. Peggy – who danced and sang and swung from curtain rails – accompanied him.

Helen became a very popular medium, especially when she manifested ectoplasm from her mouth and nose. Even when this was shown to be a trick (she had swallowed cheesecloth, lavatory paper and albumen), her popularity did not wane among the public, although the authorities did not share their enthusiasm.

On 6 January 1933, at a séance in Edinburgh, she made a little girl called Peggy "appear". An unbeliever grabbed hold of the child whilst another switched the lights on. Peggy was made from an old vest. At her trial at Edinburgh Sheriff Court on 11 May 1933, Helen was fined £10 for fraudulently procuring money from the public, but still her popularity remained.

On 25 November 1941, a German U-boat sank HMS *Barham* in the Mediterranean, killing 868 men. Helen and her husband had moved to Portsmouth, and at one of her séances there a dead sailor materialized for his mother wearing an HMS *Barham* cap. This was a shock for the mother because the Admiralty had kept secret the fate of the ship to confound the Germans and uphold morale. The next day, the mother telephoned the Admiralty for confirmation. Two officers interviewed her and wanted to know the source of her information.

On 19 January 1944, Helen Duncan – by then a twenty-stone, hard-drinking, chain-smoking star who swore like a fishwife – was arrested along with three members of her audience during a séance. She was originally charged under Section 4 of the Vagrancy Act (1824), but when the case came to court on 23 March, she was prosecuted under Section 4 of the 1735 Witchcraft Act – which was not repealed until 1951.

The case caused a sensation and Helen even offered to perform a séance in court to prove her powers. On 3 April

1944, at the Old Bailey, she was found guilty and jailed for nine months. When sentence was passed, she said, "I didn't do anything" and promptly collapsed. When she was released from Holloway Prison on 22 September 1944, she returned to mediumship. She died on 6 December 1956, a few days after police raided another of her séances.

Cross-Dressing Necrophiliac Killer

Murderer Jerome Henry "Jerry" Brudos killed nineteen-year-old Karen Sprinker in a Salem car park on 27 March 1969. Born at Webster, South Dakota, on 31 January 1939, he was the youngest of four sons. His mother, who didn't want a baby boy, dressed him as a girl and constantly belittled him.

From the age of five, he had a fetish for women's shoes. He would become sexually aroused by women in high heels and was arrested when he was seventeen after forcing, at knifepoint, a woman to take her clothes off while he took pictures. He was sentenced to nine months in a mental hospital.

On his release, he joined the army in March 1959, but received a medical discharge on 15 October of the same year. He kept his oddness confined to his home where he insisted his wife walk around naked except for a pair of high heels while he took pictures. He also wore her underwear.

On 26 January 1968, nineteen-year-old Linda Slawson was selling encyclopedias in Portland, Oregon, when she knocked on Brudos's door. He killed her and then cut off her left foot, which he kept in the freezer and took out to model the shoes he collected. He dumped her corpse in a nearby river.

On 26 November 1968, he strangled Jan Whitney, twenty-three, and then had sex with her corpse before cutting off her right breast and making a mould of it. He threw her corpse into the same river as Linda Slawson. On 21 April 1969, he attempted to kidnap Sharon Wood, twenty-four, from a car park in Portland. She fought back and managed to escape.

Two days later, Brudos claimed his last victim, 22-year-old Linda Salee. He kidnapped her from a supermarket by pretending to be a policeman. Brudos was arrested (wearing women's knickers) on 25 May 1969, when he approached girls on the campus of Oregon State University. On 27 June 1969, Brudos pleaded guilty to three counts of first-degree murder and was sentenced to life imprisonment. He was found dead at Oregon State Penitentiary at 5.10am on 28 March 2006.

"Angel of Death"

Three armed men raided the Clydesdale Bank in Linwood, Glasgow, on 30 December 1969. In view of what happened subsequently, it was perhaps significant that, just two weeks before, the use of capital punishment in the UK was abolished.

The bank haul consisted mostly of bagged-up coins which the robbers took to the flat of Howard Wilson. While in the process of sorting out their swag, the police surprised the trio, prompting Wilson to draw a gun killing one officer, mortally wounding another and seriously injuring a third. Wilson had been recognized as a former policeman and was quickly disarmed.

Under Scottish law, all three robbers were regarded as responsible for the killings because they had acted with a common purpose. But the interpretation of the circumstances was that the joint enterprise applied only to the robbery. The shooting at Wilson's flat was considered a separate event for which he alone was responsible.

In February 1970, Wilson pleaded guilty to killing two policemen, the first time in Scottish legal history that a defendant had pleaded guilty to double murder. He was convicted and sentenced to life imprisonment, while his two companions were convicted of robbery. Wilson initially proved a troublesome prisoner and had six months added to his sentence following his participation in a riot at Peterhead Prison.

Thousands of people lined the streets of Glasgow to honour the memory of the two dead policemen when their funerals took place. There was sympathy too, mixed with anger, that the third officer would spend the rest of his life in a wheelchair due to his injuries.

Wilson had been a beat policeman in Glasgow for eight years and had trained as a firearms officer. He left the force to set up his own business and turned to crime when it failed, including bank robbery. Following his incarceration, he became a model prisoner and took up crime writing. In this, he was following the precedent set in the USA in 1982 by Jack Abbott who published *In the Belly of the Beast*.

Abbott, a convicted bank robber and murderer, had been championed by the best-selling writer, Norman Mailer, who helped him become a celebrity criminal. One of the themes Abbott explored in his book was the natural tendency people had towards committing violence. Wilson's novel, *Angels of Death*, a murder thriller, won a literary award.

In 1994, Wilson was made a limited category D prisoner and housed at Saughton Prison in Edinburgh. This enabled him to be released for three days a week to work or study. He had spent twenty-five years in prison. This decision was greeted with anger and indignation by the Scottish Police Federation. In 2002, at the age of sixty-four, and having served thirty-three years, Howard Wilson, crime writer, was released on parole.

"Rookie Gets Her Man"

James Campbell, a wealthy lawyer, and his wife were shot dead while they slept at their home in Houston, Texas, in June 1982. Their deaths left four grieving daughters, one of whom, Cynthia, guarded a deadly secret.

Homicide detectives suspected that Cynthia's boyfriend, 28-year-old David Duval West, a gun enthusiast, might be implicated. He was questioned but there was insufficient evidence to charge him with any criminal activity. However, the investigation took a novel turn when, three years later, the dead couple's daughters (not including Cynthia) decided to hire a private investigator to track down the killer.

They approached a private detective agency which assigned the case to a new employee, 24-year-old Kim Paris. She befriended David West, the chief suspect, and lured him into admissions by means of a charm offensive. He fell for the beguiling young woman, professing his love for her, and he shared details of his past life.

As their relationship evolved, Paris coaxed West to follow the path of truthfulness before they could make plans for the future. What he did not know was that the young detective was secretly tape-recording their conversations via a microphone hidden in her handbag. As her seductive charms began to work, West unburdened himself of some past misdemeanours. He spoke of his relationship with Cynthia Campbell and said to Paris, "I killed both her parents".

West went on to say that the murders were easy to carry out. He spoke about acting in a "soldier mode". Cynthia Campbell who, apparently, hated her parents, had offered him $25,000 to carry out the killings. He believed her motive was to gain access to her dead parents' estate. Having listened to these admissions, secretly recorded over a ten-week period, the police charged West and Cynthia with homicide.

When the media swooped on the story and especially the part played by Kim Paris, the headline writers had a field day along the lines of "the rookie gets her man" and "suspect falls into a tender trap". Paris won many plaudits for the way she had handled her assignment.

The manner in which the murder confession had been obtained provoked fierce legal criticism. Also, under Texas law, Cynthia could not be charged using uncorroborated witness testimony. At the first trial on two counts of murder, there was a hung jury, but at the retrial West's recorded statements were ruled as admissible and he pleaded guilty to the charges. He was sentenced to two life terms of imprisonment, and Cynthia Campbell was also jailed.

"Cold, Callous and Calculated"

In a uniquely bizarre moment during the course of a murder trial, a Ouija board was used by four members of the jury to determine the guilt of the defendant. They shared their findings with other members of the jury and the revelation resulted in a retrial.

On 10 February 1993, there was a fatal shooting incident at the home of newly married Harry and Nichola Fuller. Harry, a reputedly wealthy 45-year-old car dealer, was killed with a single shot to his back, which pierced his heart. His wife, twenty-seven, attempted to call 999 but was gunned down as she lifted the receiver and was fatally wounded with four shots. Due to a misinterpretation of events heard over the telephone, the operator took no action, believing that the call was made by children playing around.

Theft appeared to have been the motive behind the double murder as Fuller had £13,000 in the house, the result of a recent business deal. When the police arrived and made a search, the only money found amounted to around £200.

Suspicion fell on Stephen Young, a 35-year-old insurance broker, who, it turned out, had visited the Fullers' home. A tape recording emerged of a conversation between Young and Harry Fuller made on the night before the killings. The tape recording featured on the BBC *Crimewatch* programme about the murders, and a viewer identified one of the voices as that of Stephen Young.

When questioned, Young admitted visiting the Fullers' house on the night of the murders and discovering their bodies. Fearing his life might be in danger, he fled from the scene. He was known to be a gun enthusiast, although he denied the murders, and it was understood that he was heavily in debt. The killer had sprinkled sugar over the dead bodies in what was believed to be an attempt to make the murders appear to be a drugs-related crime.

Young was put on trial charged with double murder and duly found guilty. But, in an extraordinary development, he was granted a retrial in 1994. This followed the revelation that four members of the original jury had engaged in a drinking session one evening, during which a séance was conducted using a Ouija board. Apparently, they thought it was a bit of fun. The next morning, they told fellow jurors that they had contacted one of Stephen Young's victims from beyond the grave and confirmed that he was the killer.

In consequence, the original trial verdict was quashed and Young was granted a retrial. His conviction was upheld and, to shouts of approval from the public gallery, he was given two life sentences on 16 December 1994. In 2004, he appealed again, but to no avail, and in 2011 he made an application to the Court of Appeal on the grounds that new evidence showed two killers had been present on the night of the shootings.

Commenting on the case, the detective who had led the investigation referred to the events of 13 February 1993 as "cold, callous and calculated murders, and all the evidence is that they were pre-planned".

"The Last Thing in the World"

Seventeen-year-old Jayden Parkinson completed her school exams in summer 2013. She subsequently moved away from her family home in Didcot to live in a hostel in Oxford. On 2 December, she called her ex-boyfriend, Ben Blakeley, to tell him that she was pregnant. The couple met the following day, after which Jayden went missing.

The young woman was last seen late in the afternoon of 8 December, in Oxford, boarding a train which stopped at Didcot. After she was reported missing, police enquiries focused on witness reports of a man seen in the area, struggling with a heavy suitcase in the early hours of 9 December. The same individual was seen later, still carrying a suitcase, in Didcot.

As the police investigation intensified, attention was drawn to the actions of 22-year-old Ben Blakeley, the missing girl's former boyfriend. He was arrested in Reading for questioning, together with a teenager who could not, for legal reasons, be named at the time. The youth was, in fact, Blakeley's brother, Jake.

Blakeley admitted killing Jayden after they had argued about her pregnancy, but he denied murder. His explanation was that he had put his hands around her throat because he believed she had lied to him about being with another man. Meanwhile, more than fifty police officers and forensic investigators searched for possible burial sites in the Didcot area in their endeavours to find the missing girl.

When Blakeley and his brother appeared in Court at a preliminary hearing on 17 December, a picture began to emerge of the tragic encounter which led to Jayden's death and its aftermath. Blakeley said that when he put his hands around her throat, she fell to the ground and he thought she was just fooling around. "When she hit the ground, I laughed," he said. He attempted to resuscitate her, to no avail, and protested that he did not intend to hurt her; her death, he said, was "the last thing in the world" that he wanted.

When he realized she was dead, he moved her lifeless body under a tree and then took a train home to Reading. He returned later with a suitcase in which he placed the dead girl and then hired a taxi to take him to Didcot. Blakeley had devised a plan whereby he would inter the body in his uncle's grave at All Saints' Church cemetery. In this, he was aided by his brother, Jake, who believed the idea was to hide some weapons.

It was Jake who came forward to explain where Jayden's body now lay. Police search teams soon spotted a grave in the cemetery that had recently been disturbed and found the missing girl. Blakeley's reasoning, which was explained later, was that by mixing his victim's remains with those of his late uncle, who had been buried in 2006, the body parts would create a confusing DNA picture.

Put on trial at Oxford in July 2014, it became clear that Blakeley was a control freak who had attempted to rule Jayden's every movement and made her a virtual prisoner in her room at the hostel where she lived. He had a reputation for abusing his girlfriends and intimidating them with petty restrictions on their activities.

He admitted strangling Jayden but denied murder and pleaded guilty to manslaughter. He also owned up to concealing her body in his uncle's grave, an act which the judge later described as "twisted". Angry at the way the case against him was unfolding, Blakeley attempted to disrupt court proceedings by walking out of the dock. On 24 July, he was found guilty of murder and sentenced to life with a recommendation that he serve twenty years' imprisonment. Blakeley showed no emotion as Judge Patrick Eccles QC passed the sentence at Oxford Crown Court.

The case raised issues about violence inflicted on women, and attention was drawn to the fact that every week in England and Wales, two women are killed by a male lover. A call was made for police and other agencies to be more aware of the background to these violent attacks.

A footnote to the case was provided by the police in a statement that they were unaware of any other criminal case in Britain in which an existing grave had been used to hide or bury a murder victim's body. Thus did Ben Blakeley make a contribution to the bizarre history of crime.

Select Bibliography

Books

BLUM, Howard: *Gangland: How the FBI Broke the Mob* (New York: Pocket Books, 1993)

CLARKSON, Wensley: *Hell Hath No Fury* (London: Blake, 1991)

CUMMINGS, John and Ernest Volkman: *Mobster: The Astonishing Rise and Fall of a Mafia Supremo and His Gang* (London: Futura, 1991)

FARRELL, Michael: *Poisons and Poisoners: An Encyclopaedia of Homicidal Killings* (London: Robert Hale, 1992)

LEONARD, Maurice: *Mae West: Empress of Sex* (London: HarperCollins, 1991)

MUSTAIN, Gene and Jerry Capeci: *Mob Star: The Story of John Gotti* (London: Penguin, 1989)

ODELL, Robin: *The Mammoth Book of Bizarre Crimes* (London: Robinson, 2007)

PENROSE, Barrie and Simon Freeman: *Conspiracy of Silence: The Secret Life of Anthony Blunt* (London: Grafton, 1987)

ROOT, Neil: *Gone: The Disappearance of Claudia Lawrence and Her Father's Desperate Search for the Truth* (Edinburgh: Mainstream, 2013)

WATSON, Katherine: *Poisoned Lives: English Poisoners and Their Victims* (London: Hambledon and London, 2004)

WILLIAMS, Andy: *Moon River and Me* (London: Weidenfeld & Nicolson, 2009)

Newspapers & Periodicals

Baltimore Sun, USA
Daily Express, UK
Daily Mail, UK
Era Banner, Canada
Newsweek, USA
Sunday Express, UK
Sunday Sun, Canada
Sunday Telegraph, UK
The Guardian, UK
The Independent, UK
The Independent on Sunday, UK
The Mail on Sunday, UK
The New York Times, USA
The Observer, UK
The Toronto Star, Canada
Weekend Press, New Zealand
Western Daily Mail, UK

Index of Names

The Mammoth Book of

JACK THE RIPPER STORIES

40 dark new tales by M. Christian,
Carol Anne Davis, Martin Edwards,
Peter Guttridge, Barbara Nadel
and many more

Edited by **MAXIM JAKUBOWSKI**

The Mammoth Book of Jack the Ripper Stories

Edited by Maxim Jakubowski

Available to buy in ebook and paperback

Countless theories have been put forward as to the identity of the notorious Victorian serial killer, but in the absence of proof how can we hope ever to unearth his real identity?

In this wonderful collection of newly-commissioned stories, Jakubowski has compiled an extraordinary array of fresh explorations into the identity and activities of Jack the Ripper – this time unabashedly fictional. They propose numerous possible identities, some already suggested by historians, others more speculative, including some famous names from history and fiction – even Sherlock Holmes and Dr Watson are on the case!

THE MAMMOTH BOOK OF

SHERLOCK HOLMES

ABROAD

15 NEW ADVENTURES
AND INTRIGUES

PAUL FINCH, CAROLE JOHNSTONE, ALISON LITTLEWOOD,
DENIS O. SMITH, SAM STONE AND MANY MORE

EDITED BY SIMON CLARK

The Mammoth Book of Sherlock Holmes Abroad

Edited by Simon Clark

Available to buy in ebook and paperback

The spirit of Sherlock Holmes lives on in this treasure trove of 'hitherto lost' overseas mysteries investigated by the great detective himself.

A host of singularly talented writers present a thrilling new dimension to Holmes's career whilst superbly capturing the spirit, style, suspense and atmosphere of Conan Doyle's best work.

THE MAMMOTH BOOK OF

BIZARRE CRIMES

YOU COULDN'T MAKE IT UP

INCREDIBLE REAL-LIFE CRIMINAL CASES

ROBIN ODELL

The Mammoth Book of Bizarre Crimes

Robin Odell

Available to buy in ebook and paperback

This comprehensive and compelling A–Z of murderous crimes spanning the globe and the centuries reveals human criminality at its most extreme and strange.

It's a gripping collection of often unusual, sometimes sensational murder cases, which not only recalls bizarre past crimes but also brings us bang up to date with the most macabre and shocking modern murders. Includes details, too, of how advances in crime detection, law enforcement and forensic science have made a difference over the years.